Directing Beckett

THEATER: Theory/Text/Performance

Enoch Brater, Series Editor
University of Michigan

Directing Beckett

Lois Oppenheim

Ann Arbor
THE UNIVERSITY OF MICHIGAN PRESS

Apr 96

1997   1996   1995   1994   4   3   2   1

*A CIP catalogue record for this book is available from
the British Library.*

Library of Congress Cataloging-in-Publication Data

Directing Beckett / [edited by] Lois Oppenheim.
        p.   cm. — (Theater : text/theory/performance)
    Includes bibliographical references and index.
    ISBN 0-472-10535-3 (alk. paper)
      1. Beckett, Samuel, 1906– —Dramatic production. 2. Theater—
Production and direction.   I. Oppenheim, Lois.   II. Series.
PR6003.E282Z6249   1994
792.9'5—dc20   94-13121
                                                              CIP

For Sarah and Keith

Good. There's our catastrophe. In the bag. Once more and I'm off.

—Director, *Catastrophe*

Acknowledgments

This volume is meant as a tribute to the work of Samuel Beckett, which has been of the greatest significance to me, personally and professionally, for many years.

I wish to express my sincere gratitude to Tom Bishop and Sid Feshbach for their part in the organization of the two-day Festival of Beckett and Joyce held at New York University in the fall of 1991. It was, to some degree, as a result of the success of the panel of Beckett directors at that event that I undertook this work.

Enoch Brater, Ruby Cohn, and Hersh Zeifman deserve a most special word of thanks. All three were invaluable sources and gave liberally of their time.

A word of warm appreciation is also due the many other Beckett specialists and nonspecialists alike who offered suggestions and provided various kinds of assistance. They include Linda Ben-Zvi, Bill Coco, Martha Fehsenfeld, Leon Freidman, Everett Frost and Voices International, Bernard Garniez, Lois Gordon, Jérôme Lindon, Ruth Maleczech and Mabou Mines, Lois Overbeck, Barney Rosset, and Jean Schneider.

Generous financial assistance was provided by the Montclair State University Foundation and the Montclair State University Separately Budgeted Research Program. In addition to the officials of the Program, Irvin Reid, Gregory Waters, and James McGovern are to be thanked for their support.

LeAnn Fields, senior editor at the University of Michigan Press, offered immeasurable aid in the preparation of the book. I thank her for her attentiveness and her expertise.

I thank as well Albert Dichy of the Fonds Beckett (Beckett Archives) and the Fonds Roger Blin (Roger Blin Archives) at the Institut Mémoire de l'Edition Contemporaine (25 rue de Lille, Paris 75007) for giving me access to much needed materials. Chris Hegedus and D. A. Pennebaker (of Pennebaker Associates, Inc.) and Richard H. F. Lindemann (of the University Library, University of California–San Diego) also deserve my sincerest thanks in this regard.

I am indebted to Joan Stevens, Jim Cross, and Florence Sapinart for their painstaking translations and to David Henderson for his tireless transcriptions of the interviews.

Finally, all of the directors represented here deserve my sincerest appreciation for taking time from hectic rehearsal schedules to work on this project and for their willingness to share so much with me. If it were not for their continued efforts on behalf of Beckett's theatrical oeuvre, these plays could not . . . go on.

Grateful acknowledgment is made to the following authors and publishers for permission to reprint either unpublished or previously published materials:

Quotations from essays and speeches by Alan Schneider, including "On *Play* and Other Plays," printed with permission of Eugenie R. Schneider and the Mandeville Department of Special Collections, University of California–San Diego. Alan Schneider Papers (MSS 103), Mandeville Department of Special Collections, University of California–San Diego.

Correspondence by Samuel Beckett printed with permission of Jérôme Lindon, literary executor, Estate of Samuel Beckett; Joseph Chaikin; Noel Blin, Estate of Roger Blin; and L'Institut Mémoire de l'Edition Contemporaine.

Correspondence by Joseph Chaikin printed with permission of Joseph Chaikin.

Extracts from the film *Rockaby* (filmed segments and outtakes), Chris Hegedus and D. A. Pennebaker, filmmakers; Patty Kerr Ross, director, SUNY/Programs in the Arts; Danny Labeille, producer; Alan Schneider, director; copyright 1982. Published with permission of Pennebaker Associates, Inc., and Eugenie R. Schneider.

Extract from Donald McWhinnie's *The Art of the Radio* (London: Faber and Faber, 1959) is reprinted by permission of David Higham Associates.

Contents

Introduction

"Beckett's plays are just play for precise performance. They are play as opposed to unmediated reality, but play is its own mode of reality."[1] Playing on a phrase from Beckett's *Play*, Beckett scholar Ruby Cohn, in a work that pays moving tribute to the *pleasure* of Beckett's theater, points to that existential dichotomy that defines all art. Sartre described it in the following way: "A cry of grief is a sign of the grief which provokes it, but a song of grief is both grief itself and something other than grief."[2] Theater, perhaps more than any other form of art, renders this dichotomy most apparent, for performance, by its very nature, is, as Cohn so aptly demonstrates, a mediated presentation of unmediated experience. And it is the theater of Samuel Beckett that, in its distillation of the tension that is this dichotomy, so succinctly conveys the drama inherent within it.

It is not Beckett's texts, therefore, that in and of themselves expose what is simultaneously a schism between the experiential and the aesthetic and a metamorphosis of the one into the other. Although in both form and content they do continually investigate the structure and meaning of the creative process, it is the rendering of these texts in the theater, the actual staging and performance of these works, that allows for an apprehension of the problem, that posed by the notion of "play for precise performance," *beyond the perimeters of methodological debate,* on the more fundamental level of the relation of author/character/spectator intersubjectivity.

This is to say that it is the process of transforming, of actualizing what otherwise is but frozen on the page, that reveals the play as play. And it is he or she who animates or vivifies the text as theater that uncovers the play as both an experience of life itself and something other than that experience. This, of course, is the director.

The texts of Beckett's plays are profoundly theatrical. More than those of a number of playwrights, they were written with a view to what precisely was to be seen and heard. And yet, if it is truly as "theater experience"[3] (to again cite Cohn) that Beckett's work is to be appreciated, if—for their proper evaluation and the reliable assessment of the significance of their place within the history of modern theater—his plays are to be fully explored not as written texts, but as existing off the printed page and in the theater, the directing of his work must be given its due.

In addition to Cohn's *Just Play,* a small number of books have appeared in recent years that explore technical and practical aspects of the production and performance of Beckett's plays. (Enoch Brater's *Beyond Minimalism,* Dougald McMillan and Martha Fehsenfeld's *Beckett in the Theatre,* and Jonathan Kalb's *Beckett in Performance* are most notable among them.)[4] These are the works of scholars and critics whose efforts and expertise serve to greatly enhance our understanding of the plays in question. The production of Beckett's plays poses a number of unique considerations, however, considerations that no amount of critical exegesis or scholarly textual analysis can address.

Directing Beckett evolved from a panel that was part of a two-day Festival of Beckett and Joyce that I co-organized at New York University in the fall of 1991.[5] The participants, all prominent directors who had mounted noteworthy productions of Beckett's plays, delighted the audience with a discussion of many of these considerations and with anecdotes of their work, and the frustration was palpable when, with many questions left unanswered and many opinions left to be voiced, we were obliged to bring the session to a close. It was immediately apparent that a book *by* directors of Beckett (those present on that occasion and a number of others as well) *on* directing Beckett would bring to a larger public an awareness of some of the issues discussed and highlight the difficulties and rewards of directing the work of one of the foremost playwrights of our century.

Not least among the concerns addressed by the panel was the question of directorial fidelity—not only to the explicit scenic indications of the playwright but also to a more discreet vision to some degree to be intuited or divined. This is a matter of singular importance given, on the one hand, the nonspecific spatial and temporal structure of Beckett's plays and, on the other, the remarkable exactitude of his stage directions and the precisions contained in his production notebooks and drafts of his work. (These are available through a number of library collections, especially that of the extensive Beckett Archive created at the University of Reading in England by James Knowlson. And expert analysis of them is contained in articles by directors Walter Asmus, Pierre Chabert, and others and in McMillan and Fehsenfeld's book, *Beckett in the Theatre.*)

The question of faithfulness is, of course, not limited to Beckett's meticulousness. A multitude of other factors—the silences so prominent in Beckett's plays, for example—contribute to a unique dramatic technique that plays heavily upon the engaging of the spectator on a level other than that of the referentiality that linguistic positivism, and the modes of literary criticism derived therefrom, has declared supreme. "By a technique that clearly owes far more to suggestion and ambiguity than it does to reference," to cite a passage from Knowlson, and hence by the rhythmic pauses so essential to it, "the spectator [measures] what is being seen against what has just been said or [follows], within specific constraints, the multiple associations aroused by preceding statements or patterns of statements."[6] It is precisely the interplay between these "associations" and "constraints" that, in addition to drawing the audience fully into the theatrical experience, poses the question of directorial function as it relates to authorial intent.

The matter of directorial freedom is highly complex, and any temptation to view it merely as generational, reflecting a movement from a pre-*auteur* aesthetic of directorial anonymity to the individualism of *auteur* direction (to borrow a term from film) is misleading. It is true that Roger Blin and Alan Schneider, Beckett's foremost first-generation directors, though strikingly different in their artistry (the one resolutely antirealist, the other pure Stanislavski),[7] did see themselves as invisible orchestrators: Schneider viewed his role of director to be that of "playwright's surrogate,"[8] and Blin thought his directorial contribution should go virtually unnoticed:

> What is a director? Nothing; he shouldn't be talked about; his personality shouldn't exist; he shouldn't seek a style; he should be rigorous about rendering the thought of the author, without adding anything. For that matter, authors should direct their own works; unfortunately, most of them can't do it. In the old days the director was an actor in the company who did the blocking; there was no talk about it. I put my name as director only because I was asked to, but I don't like it. I have no theory, and I try to have no characteristic style.[9]

But their work could hardly be thought to represent some mainstream of Beckett directing against which a younger generation would be collectively reacting. The diversity of viewpoints represented in this volume clearly attests to the fact that the increased number of directors taking liberties with Beckett's plays in recent years is attributable only to the larger number and divergence of directors now working with them.

Several recent productions (in this country and abroad) have raised some interesting and disturbing legal[10] and aesthetic questions. All-female casts have performed *Waiting for Godot, Not I* has been seen with a woman in full view, the ending of *Catastrophe* has been rewritten, and the recorded voice in *Rockaby* has been replaced onstage by speech. In perhaps the most well-known "deviation" from the author's specifications, the American Repertory Theatre's interpretation in Cambridge, Massachusetts, relocated *Endgame* to the tunnel of a subway. The playwright was profoundly distressed by this 1984 production. Despite his efforts to put a stop to it, the show went on,[11] leaving open to debate, among other issues, the transposing of the play's locale for years to come. The legal right of the director, JoAnne Akalaitis, to fundamentally alter the text—or is a radical change in setting not *truly* a textual alteration?—and her aesthetic judgment remain as controverial as ever.

Mike Nichols's staging of *Waiting for Godot* at Lincoln Center four years later "reproduced exactly the aesthetic error of JoAnne Akalaitis's *Endgame*," claims the literary director of the A.R.T., Robert Scanlan. "There was no outcry in that instance, no effort to close the production or demand that it be altered. Was there less harm to *Godot?*" And what of the staging of *Endgame* at the Comédie Française in 1988, another production—with its pink decor, musical score, and numerous mannequins—seemingly at odds with the playwright's intentions? To what extent was this *Endgame,* ultimately mounted with a set covered over with gray canvas and without directorial credit, evidence that the taking of liberties is injurious?

Perhaps now, even more than before Beckett's death in 1989, the meaning of directorial integrity, and the implications of playing with Beckett's plays, is of the essence. In a 1990 *Village Voice* review Dennis Delrogh expressed one side of the controversy:

> Now that Beckett is dead, perhaps there will be more freedom to tamper with his plays. *Waiting for Godot,* despite its trenchant mimicry of conditioned instincts, has become a humanistic chestnut, and it's time someone rattled it up a bit to restore its life. I've always had the urge to put marbles in Gogo's boots during intermission.[12]

Tom Bishop, critic and longtime friend of Beckett, has articulated the other:

While Beckett was alive, a certain restraint, due to world-wide respect for the author, gave relative protection to the work. But now that he is gone, what will preserve the integrity of the plays? Will we have to live through a musical comedy version of *Godot* or perhaps a *Happy Days* with the actress in a wheelchair? At a time when some directors seek to affirm their individuality through new "readings" of major texts no matter how far from the accepted norms—or rather, as far removed as possible—the floodgates may well open up. Will Beckett's plays survive intact?[13]

Again, the answer lies not with the scholars and critics but with the directors. It is with the directors that the ultimate decisions of setting, cross-casting, character gender changing, and the "jumping of genres," to name but a few concerns relative to Beckett productions, remain. It is with the directors that the most determinative choices lie, and hence it is from them that we now need to hear.

❖

In an essay entitled "What Does a Director Do?" the late Alan Schneider, Beckett's best-known U.S. director, relates the following converation:

"Don't all of (pause . . .) Samuel Beckett's plays have very elaborate and detailed stage directions?" one of my friendly neighborhood critics walked up to ask me, the evening my latest Beckett trio of one-acts opened in Washington.

"Yes, they (pause . . .) certainly do."

"And, those three heads stuck in those, uh, marvelous looking urns? [Beckett's entire setting for one of the plays, called PLAY.] That means that you didn't have to think about any actual movements?"

"That's, uh, right."

"Well, excuse my asking, Alan, but what do you *do?*"[14]

It was in the effort to clarify what it is that the director does and, specifically, what it is that the "Beckett director" does that this book was undertaken. Theater-goers have little difficulty generalizing about the quality of acting in a given play. The quality of direction is considerably harder to determine, for a production may be at least partially redeemed by the acting when the directing is mediocre, and, when superior, the director's work may go unrecognized and credit be given elsewhere.

In the same essay Schneider goes on to define the director's function:

"One of my older and wiser colleagues once said somewhere (or should have) that a director has to be a combination traffic cop, tourist guide, choreographer, lion-tamer, trial lawyer, magician, psychiatrist, baby-sitter, and con man. . . . Among other things." Apparently, these words are more true than one might suspect, despite the irony:

> For what a director does, basically, is take the playwright's bare words, together with his stage directions (which may range from Shaw's page-length essays on social conditions through Beckett's well-known array of specific instructions and varied-length pauses to Pinter's even more elliptical dots—and dashes) and try to clothe them in flesh and blood reality.[15]

The question remains, by what process?
Schneider continues:

> The contemporary director in theory decides everything, from the gestures of the leading lady (as well as her jewelry and hairdo) to the color of the wallpaper. In practice, leading ladies (and men) have their own gestures, preferences in jewelry and hairdoes [sic], and wills of their own. And scenic designers, accomplished and not, have been known to go off on their own favorite shades and tones. But then, it is generally the director who has, after all, chosen the designer—and the leading lady. Though not always. More importantly, it is the director whose job it is to give designer and leading lady the confidence to be both cooperative and independently creative.
>
> Most importantly, it is the director who, at the very beginning of the entire adventure, decides on the concept, the idea from which the entire production evolves and flows. It is he who interprets the play as being basically comedic or farcical, tragic or merely melodramatic; the story of a marriage which is doomed but doesn't show it, or the story of a doomed marriage trying to save itself. The first thing I write on the blank pages of my production notebook is not where someone is sitting or moving, but what the play is "about," as well as what its tone or texture should be.[16]

All this seems quite apt for the director of Chekhov or Williams, but what of the director of Beckett—for whom the leading lady may be buried in earth up to her neck (Winnie in *Happy Days*), confined for the duration of the play to a rocking chair (*Rockaby*), or reduced to a single bodily organ (Mouth in *Not I*), and her gestures, if there are any, limited at best? As for the color of the wallpaper, to say nothing of what the Beckett play might be "about" . . .[17]

It is perhaps less apparent in the directing of Beckett than in the directing of any other playwright that the director's taste is the ultimate determination of the play's merit. The director may be intuitive and instinctual or deliberate and cerebral, but the *look* of the play (and theater, after all, is a visual art) results from his or her personal preference. Beckett's instructions being what they are, one wonders where exactly the director's creativity and imagination come into the picture (pun intended). How, when the playwright has given every possible indication for the production of a given play—"If 0 = dark and 10 = bright, light should move from about 3 to 6 and back" (*Breath*) and "Thirty seconds before end of speech lamplight begins to fail" (*A Piece of Monologue*) are typical—does the director distinguish himself?

First, in the casting. (Casting well is in itself a creative enterprise, one that represents "more than half the director's battle," claims Schneider, for it "represents choosing the proper battlefield on which he will win or lose,"[18] a fact to which the debacle of his Miami *Godot* so sorely attested.)[19] Then, in judgment and decision making. (It is in deciding a multitude of only apparently insignificant issues that the director gives shape and style to everything that takes place on stage.) And finally, in uncovering, in the case of a new script, the play's as yet undetermined identity, and in the case of a classic, such as *Waiting for Godot* has certainly now become, "truths and reverberations previously undiscovered or at least not felt by previous generations."[20]

But the answer to how the director of a playwright as meticulous as Beckett distinguishes himself remains far from complete. The example of Schneider with "that urn play of Beckett's" is informative:

> I picked the actors, three who though without star names, Diane Wiest, Donald Davis, and Sloane Shelton, could not be bettered anywhere in the American theatre. I decided on the curve and shape and size and texture and location of the urns in question. I worked out the aesthetics and mechanics (fascinating and difficult) of that omnipresent light beam, which in essence became not only the categorical imperative but the seeing eye of the author. Over our three rehearsal weeks, our ten inadequate days of technical rehearsals, as well as a week of invaluable previews, I was able to arrange and rearrange and select and sample

and change and change again the symphony of tones and volumes and rhythms and sounds and silences which together determined the particular texture and shape of this particular production of Beckett's "Play."[21]

It is, however, but one example—one chosen, in part, because Schneider has left detailed accounts of his experiences directing Beckett and, in part, because of the magnitude of Schneider's work on Beckett's plays. Many other directors, with many other directorial visions, need to be heard from for any real insight to be gained into the complexities of directing Beckett. It is hoped that the voices assembled in this volume will provide a suitable start.

❖

A word about the volume: Beckett's indebtedness to Roger Blin and Alan Schneider is incalculable. His theatrical oeuvre might never have been staged were it not for Blin's steadfastness (simply finding a theater in which to mount the first *Godot* took close to three years), and Schneider's immediate and unwavering dedication to the playwright's work on this side of the Atlantic has been well-documented. Although no longer with us, these two directors continue to play a most vital role in any consideration of the history and continuity of Beckett's theater. (Herbert Berghof's absence from this volume is regrettable. Berghof brought two productions, both in conjunction with Michael Myerberg, to Broadway [one in 1956, the other the following year]. Berghof's method of directing the play was distinctive, and he left copious notes, which, unfortunately, after much negotiating, were withheld by his estate.)

I was indeed fortunate to have access to the soundtrack of Schneider's directing of *Rockaby,* and the quotations from it that open the book reveal much of what Beckett's foremost U.S. director was about. The 1976 essay "On *Play* and Other Plays" that appears at the end has apparently never before appeared in print. It too is most revealing of Schneider's efforts on behalf of Beckett's work, and, as the only essay—as Blin's is the only interview—not undertaken expressly for this volume, it is included with that interview and the letters from Beckett in the appendix.

The interview with Roger Blin is also new to print. Excerpted from a longer conversation that included discussion of Artaud and Genet as well as Beckett, it reveals a loyal but unorthodox interpreter of Beckett's theater: Blin had neither any real method of directing nor any consistent preconceived aesthetic vision. He never prepared for rehearsal but, rather, allowed the play to come together through a series of "successive approximations," and he had little use for notes, auditions, or any of the conventional principles of directing. For Blin directing consisted of executing within the constraints of the real stage what was played out on the limitless horizon of the playwright's imagination, and this while valorizing the text and respecting to the fullest the author's intent. He gave the actors enormous freedom relying on the "physiological imperatives" of the player and the morphology of the very experience of playing in and of itself to reveal to him (most often as spontaneous insights occurring outside of rehearsal) the details necessary to the staging of a particular play.[22]

Blin claimed Beckett to have been disconcerted (his term was *dérouté*)[23] by the director's lack of a working method. Nevertheless, Beckett had a tremendous appreciation for Blin's work (*Endgame* is dedicated to him), and the two also maintained what Cohn has referred to as "a distant friendship," which lasted until Blin's death in 1984.[24] Although he rarely attended rehearsals for the productions of any of his plays, Beckett was eager to share his ideas with Blin,[25] as is evident from the correspondence that Beckett addressed to him, a sampling of which appears in the first appendix.

Mention must also be made of the startling underrepresentation here of women. As Rosette Lamont points out in Linda Ben-Zvi's collection, *Women in Beckett:* "Although Beckett has written some of the juiciest parts for women in twentieth century theater, few women have undertaken to direct him. Part of the answer may lie in the paucity of women directors, but this is hardly the only reason. Perhaps women are intimidated by the austerity and rigor of the Beckett text."[26] *Directing Beckett* attempts to shed light on the question of why Beckett directing is a domain so heavily populated by men as well as on those issues that are probed more directly.

Additionally, the reader will note that in the interviews a small number of questions to the directors were repeated from one interview to another. This was not unintentional, as I was seeking the opinion of several of the directors on certain of the same factious issues.

Finally, listening to the "Beckett director" recount his or her experiences of directing Beckett's work is not without danger. Many of these directors knew the playwright well: some worked closely with him; others met with him regularly to discuss their production; several witnessed his own directing[27] and/or his reactions to the few productions of his work that he saw. As a result, the temptation was to quote him in these contexts. Outside the theater and with the passage of time, how misleading this can be. (Gregory Mosher offers an example very much to the point in my conversation with him.) Hence, in editing the interviews and essays, every effort was made to avoid direct quotation of Beckett when it did not serve the express purpose of this book or it might in any way be misconstrued.

❖

Stories abound about Beckett the man and Beckett's own performance, as playwright and director, in the theater. Some are true; some are myth perpetuated both by prurience and unreliable reporting. What *can* be said, with no fear of distortion, is that Beckett was supportive of directors wanting to serve his work. He never looked for the great notoriety that eventually came to him, nor did he particularly delight in it when it arrived. (He shunned publicity, gave away much of his Nobel Prize money, often anonymously, and the only real change one so close to him as Alan Schneider ever remarked following his success was the acquisition of a telephone!)[28] But he did give generously of his time to those who sought to attend to his intent with honesty and to reveal his vision with integrity. Even so, he said it all when he wrote, or words to this effect: "The text as is, the words as is, that's all I know. The rest is Ibsen."[29]

NOTES

1. Ruby Cohn, *Just Play: Beckett's Theater* (Princeton: Princeton University Press, 1980), 3.

2. Jean-Paul Sartre, *What Is Literature?* trans. Bernard Frechtman (New York: Philosophical Library, 1949), 10.

3. The notion of "theater experience" is fundamental to Cohn's analyses and appreciation of Beckett's work. "It is as theater experience that I cherish these plays—that weary old word *experience*—and if you see the plays as codes of signifiers that conform to a theoretical model, then you and I view the plays from opposite sides of a wall" (Ruby Cohn, "Beckett's Theater Resonance," in *Samuel Beckett: Humanistic Perspectives,* ed. Morris Beja, S. E. Gontarski, and Pierre Astier [Columbus: Ohio State University Press, 1983], 13).

4. Enoch Brater, *Beyond Minimalism* (New York: Oxford University Press, 1987); Dougald McMillan and Martha Fehsenfeld, *Beckett in the Theatre* (London: John Calder, New York: Riverrun, 1988); Jonathan Kalb, *Beckett in Performance* (Cambridge: Cambridge University Press, 1989).

5. Sidney Feshbach and Tom Bishop worked with me on the preparation of this event. Professor Bishop, chair of the French Department at New York University and a former president of the Samuel Beckett Society, chaired the directors panel and did so with his usual eloquence and panache.

6. James Knowlson, "Beckett's 'Bits of Pipe,'" in Beja, Gontarski, and Astier, *Samuel Beckett,* 23.

7. Ruby Cohn, in "Animateurs de Beckett: Roger Blin, Alan Schneider," writes "Blin était résolument antiréaliste et anti-establishment; Schneider ne jurait que par Stanislavski" (in *Samuel Beckett Revue d'Esthétique,* ed. Pierre Chabert [Paris: Jean-Michel Place, 1990], 189). This essay provides an excellent overview of what distinguished the work of two of Beckett's foremost directors and offers particular insight into Blin's nonconventional directing.

8. Alan Schneider, an untitled essay on Beckett, Alan Schneider Papers (MSS 103), Mandeville Department of Special Collections, University of California–San Diego.

9. Roger Blin, interview in *Arts* (24 February 1950); cited in Odette Aslan, *Roger Blin and Twentieth Century Playwrights,* trans. Ruby Cohn (Cambridge: Cambridge University Press, 1988).

10. The dispute that surrounded the A.R.T. production centered on the playwright's right to control the production of his work. As reported by Martin Garbus and Gerald E. Singleton (in "Playwright-Director Conflict: Whose Play Is It Anyway?" [*New York Law Journal,* no. 123 (28 December 1984): 192] and reprinted in *The Beckett Circle* [ed. Lois More Overbeck and Martha Fehsenfeld] 6, no. 2 (Spring 1985): 1–2]), Barney Rosset, former president of Grove Press, wrote to Robert Brustein, artistic director of the A.R.T.: "You have violated the prerogative of Mr. Beckett as an artist—to have his work performed the way he intended." Brustein replied: "A playwright cannot serve as the designer, director and actor of his own play. He has to collaborate." Garbus and Singleton also raise the issues of the public's right as protected by the Federal Lanham Act (one has the right to see a Beckett play if that is what one has purchased a ticket for), the original contract and copyright.

11. The agreement ultimately reached required a statement by Beckett and Rosset and a page from the text of the play to be inserted in the program.

12. Dennis Delrogh, "Still Waiting: Chaikin Directs Beckett's *Godot,"* *Village Voice,* 24 April 1990, 103.

13. Tom Bishop, abstract of an article in progress, currently entitled "Can Beckett's Plays Survive What We Do to Them?"

14. Alan Schneider, "So What Do You Really Do, Mr. Director?" 1; Alan Schneider Papers (MSS 103), Mandeville Department of Special Collections, University of California–San Diego. Published as "What Does a Director Do?" in *New York Theatre Review,* preview issue (Spring–Summer 1977): 16–17.

15. Ibid., 1–2.

16. Ibid., 2.

17. Schneider tells us that, for the purposes of these notebooks, "Winnie's absolute necessity as she sank further and further into the sands of 'Happy Days' was 'to live'" and that "'Play' was 'Last Year at Marienbad in an Urn'" ("So What Do You Really Do," 2).

18. Ibid., 3.

19. *Waiting for Godot* at the Coconut Grove Playhouse in Miami in 1956, produced by Michael Myerberg and directed by Alan Schneider, was wrong from

the start. As Bert Lahr, who played Estragon to Tom Ewell's Vladimir, is quoted by Schneider as saying, "it was exactly like 'bringing *Giselle* to Roseland'" (*Entrances* [1986; reprint, New York: Limelight Editions, 1987], 235). The production was anything but well received. Also in the cast (signed by Myerberg) were Jack Smart as Pozzo and the modern dance choreographer Charles Weidman as Lucky. This cast was certainly not the proper field on which to wage what was a no-win battle before it began.

20. Schneider, "What Do You Really Do," 6.

21. Ibid., 6.

22. Roger Blin, *Roger Blin: Souvenirs et Propos recueillis par Lynda Bellity Peskine* (Paris: Gallimard, 1986), 97–98, 99, 116.

23. Ibid., 97.

24. Cohn, "Animateurs de Beckett," 190.

25. In a letter dated 19 February 1953, for example, Beckett wrote: "J'ai pensé que tu pourrais chantonner l'air de Vladimir en prenant ton élan au 1er. Qu'en penses-tu? Histoire d'ajouter à la confusion" (I thought you could sing Vladimir's air building your momentum in the first act. What do you think? Just to add to the confusion). Reprinted with permission of Jérôme Lindon, Estate of Samuel Beckett; Noel Blin, Estate of Roger Blin; and the Institut Mémoire de l'Edition Contemporaine.

26. Rosette Lamont, interview with Shivaun O'Casey, *Women in Beckett* (Urbana: University of Illinois Press, 1990), 29.

27. For a comprehensive discussion of Beckett as director, the reader is referred to the chapter "Beckett Directing," in Cohn, *Just Play,* 230–79; and Cohn's chronology of Beckett's production in Chabert, *Samuel Beckett. Revue d'Esthétique,* 443–44. Additional essays, well worth the reading, are to be found in the section "Samuel Beckett, metteur en scène," in Chabert.

28. Schneider, *Entrances,* 223.

29. Cited by Alan Schneider, in "Text of Address by Alan Schneider, Carolyn Benton Cockfair Luncheon, University of Missouri–Kansas City, August 13, 1973," 7; Alan Schneider Papers (MSS 103), Mandeville Department of Special Collections, University of California–San Diego. Published as "Waiting for Beckett," *Chelsea Review,* Fall 1958, reprinted in Anon., *Beckett at 60* (London: Calder and Boyars, 1967).

Alan Schneider Directs *Rockaby*

Although he directed the work of a number of playwrights, Alan Schneider's name is most often associated with those of Samuel Beckett, Edward Albee, and Harold Pinter. In addition to free-lance directing, Schneider was on the faculties of the Catholic University of America, Boston University, and the University of California–San Diego. From 1952 to 1954 he was artistic director at the Arena Stage in Washington, D.C., and from 1976 to 1979 director at the Juilliard Theatre Center in New York City.

What follows was taken from the sound tapes (both used and unused portions) for the film *Rockaby* (D. A. Pennebaker Associates, Inc.), in which Schneider directs actress Billie Whitelaw—for the first time—in the 1981 production at the State University of New York (SUNY)–Buffalo. These remarks reveal Schneider's will to remain faithful to the playwright's vision. And they offer insight both into his directing—specifically, his view of his role as director—and Beckett's play.

. . . the voice gets softer, "more" gets softer, the repetition of *"time she stopped"* gets softer, so there is a kind of a diminuendo throughout. . . . To do that, to know where to start and where to end, and the stages in between. . . . You don't have to worry about the lights doing that, presumably we'll do that. But I think the voice, if we can just get that gradual . . .

[Sam] doesn't read it exactly the same way twice. You know that. But he has the right idea. He knows what he wants and then he sort of varies it within that.

. . . I don't know how much he's talked to you. I presume he's told you everything. So I'm really your editor. . . . I'm your eyes and ears outside and I hope to kind of steer you and nurture you and guide you, but I'm really going to edit you. That's all I'm going to do. And I hope you can trust me out there to watch and so on. But I know what Sam wants. And you know what Sam wants. And I'm just going to say, "Yeh, but . . ."

I just want to make you as aware as I can. . . . It isn't a question of their lowering the volume, as we go along, it's a question of your energy being a little bit different . . .

❖

He'd like the eyes to be unblinking. Okay, we try not to blink; but you can close them for periods of time and as the sections go on, you close them more and more.

. . . we are talking about a section always being from "More" to something. Section one: "More" until [the rock] stops. [Section two:] "More" until it stops. There are four of them. They get longer. The last section is the longest.

Halfway through this last section, he'd like to get your eyes closed for good, and she's tuning out more and more. Or maybe tuning out is the wrong word. Maybe she simply concentrates on herself.

❖

. . . I don't know how you work, you could do it any way you like, but it seems to me it should be very clear that her eyes are a little bit closed, a little bit more, a little bit more, fourth section, a little bit more and then halfway through the fourth section, which is pretty long, the blinds come down.

And no movement! That's why we need a headrest. We've got to put you there so you can be comfortable. Because also, we're going to tighten you. It's not going to be as bad as the mouth [in *Not I*]. We don't have to do that . . .

❖

I just want to hear a couple of the lines in terms of the rhythm because that's going to affect how the thing runs.

❖

I always start on the second day of rehearsal. I never start on the first day of rehearsal. . . . So this is the second day.

❖

That's terrific. Notice how you picked up the rock now and then, the rhythm of it. . . . The business of getting softer, if you just gradually do that, it's terrific. It has nothing to do with her drive. It's like a violin string. You know, when that last note hits. It's still playing. It's still vibrating, but it's just getting a little bit . . .

❖

The possibilities for variety within the rhythm, if the rhythm is very strong. . . . Sam talks about lullaby. He said lullaby to me seven times . . .

❖

The same old thing, "No color," but there is color. What he means is, it's not hammed up. . . . When he reads it, he reads it with color. You know damned well. He did exactly what you did with that "whom else." He's searching for that "whom else" all his life. What's outside. That's the big thing of his life. Every work he's ever written is to find the answer to "whom else?" There must be something outside.

Don't be afraid of it, now and then. Sam is going to like whatever you do. . . . But the thing is, the color helps the rhythm, and the monotony. It's a kind of contrapuntal thing there. And the rocking is going to help the rhythm. The rhythm is there. You establish it.

❖

For hours, for days, for years, for centuries. We are catching her in the middle and we don't see the end. My point is that it's not at the end, it's going on toward that parallel line . . .

❖

I don't think she dies so much as she sort of fades away. She just goes to sleep. . . . Maybe there is [a] section five. Each section changes. . . . There are fifty [lines] in the first. It doesn't matter what the number is, but her spurts get longer. Fifty in the first, then fifty-six, then fifty-seven. Then it gets to be eighty-four all of a sudden. She goes a lot longer without stopping. She is getting closer all the time . . .

Nothing in Sam is accidental. Nothing. And it's fascinating to see how his mind. . . . He had that Cartesian coordinate kind of mind. It's all there.

❖

Each line shouldn't know the next one is coming. You don't know. It just comes. Then something else comes. And then the next thing. You don't know how long it's going to go on. In fact you try to hold onto it. That's why, when it stops, you have to say "more" again. Don't know what's coming. Don't know that it's going to be a pattern or a sequence, or a repetition, or a development. It floats in . . .

❖

A—long—time—ago. She is remembering a—long—time—ago when her Mom died. A—long—time—ago.

❖

You say it a bit differently than Mom. Mom said, "I guess it's time I stopped." You're saying, "Fuck life." The same thing in a slightly differ- ent way.

❖

The weakness was there, Billie. The weakness was there. That was the right tone. She's not dragging. . . . It's a sigh. It's a kind of acceptance. It's a coming down to.

❖

"It's time that I stopped trying to reach out. I have been trying to reach out all my life. And now I'm too tired. I cannot do it any more." I think that's what she's saying. "In the end I couldn't do it any more. I can't do it any more. I've got to somehow give up. It's too much . . ."

❖

"I'm not going to go on repeating that. I'm not going to go on echoing that. . . ." It's an echo of that: you're becoming Mom. Her eyes and [your] eyes. Her and she and you. The same. The problem is just simply to find how that incline goes.

❖

Drive. I'm trying to find a better word. Going on. "I can't go on. I'll go on." The only thing that worries me about the word *drive* is that it means determination rather than inevitability. It doesn't stop. It never ends. The first time we did it, it was a little too deliberate. It's not deliberate. It's in spite of. Anyhow. You can't stop yourself. Not because you're willing it, but because it's still going on. Life is not going to stop because you say. . . . It's going to go on anyhow. It goes on without your saying it.

❖

Just get back to it, whatever the aside. The asides tend to hold you back. ["all the years / all in black"] . . . is an aside from the thought. It's an elaboration of the thought. So get back to the thought. . . . [A] feeling of inexorable, inevitable, moving on.

[Billie Whitelaw quoting Beckett: "'The intensity of something coming to its'—he didn't even say her—'end.'"]

But not *at* the end, *coming to* its end. It never gets there. . . . Isn't it amazing how it comes back, always back? There are echoes in each [play], from one to the other.

I said the other day, every line of Beckett's contains the whole of Beckett. Every piece of Beckett's says what every other piece says in a different way. If you were in a uranium mine and you took a microscopic particle, it [would contain] everything that's in the whole mine. I always feel that with Sam, that that's why it is helpful to know the other stuff. He's always choosing a different means. The message is always there. You're saying one thing: *on*.

❖

. . . alone in the universe. There was no one there. That's what happens when you die. She went right down to be her own other. . . . That's a way of saying it that is different from "dying out there." She's alone in the universe.

❖

I think what she's trying to do is come to terms with dying. The closing of the eyes is to remember, to will herself to get to be like Mom. What happened to Mom. I am trying to recapture, reproduce, relive what happened to Mom, to go through what Mom went through. And the eyes make you remember. What did Mom do? How exactly? . . . What did happen? I want to see Mom in her best black sitting in that rocker, like I am now, rocking away.

When you can't remember it closing your eyes, open them again. That's it exactly. And then at a certain moment. . . . It's not that she gets tired and closes her eyes. It's that it's better to see [that way]. Which way is it better to see?

❖

It's not about dying. It's not about coming to die. It's about accepting, accepting—death. We said [it], coming to terms. Okay, so we die. [Sam] did it better for me than anybody else in a completely different context. After two nights we had seen, forgive me, your play, and we had seen another play. It was Saturday night and I said, "Okay, what are we going to see tonight?" And he said, "Oh, Christ, let's not go to the theater." "Okay, so we won't go to the theater. So we'll just have a meal. Or we'll walk around." He is accepting the fact that you don't *have* to go to the theater every night. She is accepting the fact that, okay, so you die.

It's a relief. It's a coming to terms with *Mother.* Mother rocker. Mother earth. Mother death. Whatever you want to say. I'm not sure Sam would put it that way. And it doesn't really matter. I think that's what it's about.

And by the way, he doesn't say a word throughout this text or the instructions about what you do. There's a lot of stuff there. And all that stuff you do in rehearsal with your arms and so on. You've got a lot of things to do with that. You can touch it. You can deal with it. And you're alive. You're not dead by the end of this. You are accepting the inevitability of dying.

Just remember Mother rocker . . .

The eyes should be as wide as you can open them. . . . And I think even when your eyes are closed, you are still trying to see.

❖

What I thought I'd do with you is just sit in a nice relaxed position and arbitrarily see if we can find these proportions that Sam has talked about of eyes closed.

❖

I think you should [close your eyes] on a line and open [them] up on the next line. We have fifty lines in the first section. So I am going to suggest, of the fifty, they will be closed for five, ten percent. I don't want to keep [them] closed for five lines. I want to close [them] and open [them] again. [They're] not going to stay closed for two lines [at a time].

❖

I think we've got a kind of principle going here that is what Sam asked. He wasn't sure where the lines were. He just said it's got to be "more" in each section. And by the time you get halfway through. . . . They'll feel it cumulatively. . . . [T]he light will be diminishing, the voice will be getting softer, and the eyes. . . . To Sam, those eyes are always in contact with the rest of the world. Remember, in *Krapp's Last Tape,* when the guy is in the punt and the girl is sitting there and he says, "Let me in," and all these critics say it's sexual (which it is). What he really is talking about is that he wants her to look at him, so that he can enter through her eyes. The Russians do that: the eyes are the windows of the soul.

❖

The "more" is not just for the voice. [It's] for the rocking as well. You want the "more." The "more" is to get the rocking. I want to be rocked. I want to be lulled, because who is doing the rocking? Your memory. Your Mom.

. . . the "more" is: I want to be rocked, by the voice and by the chair. I want to be rocked to sleep, rocked off to sleep, by this memory. The memory is going to rock me off. So you're asking, the baby is saying, "Do this to me, don't stop." And it is getting a little bit less able, your voice—*you*—are being a little bit less able to do that each time.

❖

I am going to say one word that is different from panic: *need.* Panic is you've been doing it for fifteen minutes. Need is you've been doing it for three hundred hours. It's not an immediate crisis. It's that [you] have been trying to get to her for a long time. And you get a little bit. . . . By the way, you notice that in section four there is no "*time she stopped*"? It means you are getting closer to her.

1. Interviews

The interviews that follow are arranged to reflect only very loosely a chronology of Beckett productions. Some of the directors with whom I spoke worked with Beckett's plays twenty to thirty years ago (one began directing Beckett in the 1950s), and some of these conversations (those with Fred Neumann, Walter Asmus, and Herb Blau) are grouped together to give a sense of the early years of Beckett directing. The majority of those interviewed continue to stage Beckett's work, however (Neumann and Asmus included), and hence chronology could not be a significant determinant of sequence.

In a recent conversation Lee Breuer (who is not included here as he was in India while the material for this volume was being compiled) shed light on those early years as he related to me how the playwright had become, in the late 1950s and early 1960s, a hero of what was essentially the first avant-garde since World War II, the Beat movement. "Beckett fit perfectly," Breuer explained, "as theatrical expression of a certain kind of European nihilism inspired by Sartre and Camus." In recounting the beginnings of his own involvement with Beckett, which dates back to his work with The Actor's Workshop (a resident company headed by Herbert Blau and Jules Irving in the 1960s in San Francisco), Breuer described America's very drastic turning "from an optimistic, believing country, living the image of the '30s musical, to cynicism." "Beckett seemed to be the touchstone of this," he continued, situating initial enthusiasm for Beckett "after a loss of faith and before an influx of spiritual thinking."

Breuer's interest in Beckett culminated in three productions in 1974 at Mabou Mines (an experimental, avant-garde theater company founded in New York in 1970): *Play, Come and Go,* and *The Lost Ones.* His preoccupation was then "poetic theater"—"The company was interested in learning how to perform metaphors as opposed to making psychological statements"—and he considers his staging of *The Lost Ones* close to realizing

Fig. 1. Mabou Mines 1974 production of *Play*, directed by Lee Breuer with JoAnne Akalaitis, David Warrilow, and Ruth Maleczech. Photo credit: Tony Kent.

that ideal. But Breuer's eagerness to mount Beckett waned as the playwright's response to an idea for *Waiting for Godot* was less than encouraging. Breuer was weary of the classic *Godot*s ("one clown after another"), and he proposed staging the play for film on the streets of New York (on the corner of Bowery and Houston), with "winos" and a Christmas tree burning in an ash can. The play was repeatedly done as a "smile through tears comedy," as "neo-Brechtian intellectual irony," Breuer claims, and "I wanted to do it as dead beat tragedy. Dealing with people with drinking problems was the only way I could see doing it with an American accent, but Sam was not thrilled, so I dropped it." And Breuer has not since returned to Beckett's work: "He was afraid of being done wrong, so he became very rigid. If he wanted artists to do his work, he had to let them be artists. I felt very cramped. There was so little room for interpretation when I had a good one. I was discouraged."

Breuer had much to say about Beckett's relation to theater history. "Beckett was beyond brilliant as a writer. He was one of the greater writers of the century and he changed theater completely with his *oeuvre*. I learned an incredible amount about language from Beckett's ability to balance the positive and the negative in every phrase." He was also definitive on the subject of directing: "There is no such thing as directing. You direct as a musician, you direct as a painter. The director as such, in the abstract, doesn't exist. You can direct as a dramaturg, as a sociologist, but you have to have a point of view. A machine can realize the text as written. If you are there to interpret a text, you are interpreting in one of these other spheres." And though he did not particularly admire Beckett's directing, he concluded, "Writers should always direct their own work as they did in Greece."

Fred Neumann, fortunately not in India, was able to tell me a good deal more about Mabou Mines and Paris in the mid–1960s (before the company was established as such). His discussion leads to a lively account of his dealings with Beckett and the genesis of his own aesthetic vision. The interview of Walter Asmus focuses primarily on what distinguishes his directing from that of Beckett (with whom he worked so closely in the 1970s and 1980s as his German assistant) and highlights the evolution of his several *Godot*s from Beckett's Schiller Theater production. And that of Herb Blau takes us from the experimental theaters of San Francisco and the first San Quentin *Godot* to his highly acclaimed *Endgame* and to theater and postmodernist theory.

Pierre Chabert pursues a number of technical questions related to his productions of *Compagnie* and, more recently, *Oh les beaux jours* and offers insightful commentary on inventiveness and fidelity with regard to the execution of Beckett's stage directions. He also provides an invaluable firsthand account of Beckett's thinking on these technical problems and of exchanges with him. As an actor directed by Beckett, he speaks from a dual perspective. Edward Albee also speaks from a unique vantage point in being himself a renowned playwright. His assessment of the director's role and his exploration of the reasons for certain of the decisions made for his stagings of *Ohio Impromptu* and *Krapp's Last Tape* reflect a rapport with the theater distinctive of one who wears both hats.

With Jan Jönson we leave the domain of the theater as such and enter a startingly different locale, one not entirely unfamiliar to Beckett. Jönson has directed *Godot* in two prisons and is currently preparing to direct *Endgame* in a third. (It is interesting to note the number of connections that Beckett had to prison life, from the performance of his work both for and by inmates and the correspondence he had with some of them to his prisonlike existence in hiding from the Nazis in World War II and the Santé Prison, which he directly overlooked from his apartment on the Boulevard St. Jacques in Paris. Life in the cell is, of course, among the most obvious metaphorical and metonymic motifs in Beckett's fiction and plays.) Jönson's reiterating here of his experience of directing *Godot* in Swedish and U.S. prisons celebrates the value of the play for those whose lives are reduced to a microcosm of its meaning.

After contemplating some matters of production, Antoni Libera offers an in-depth analysis of several of Beckett's plays that is at once metaphysical and historical. In identifying metaphors common to the entire Beckett canon, he delineates compelling motives for a unique "philosophical" understanding of this theater while stopping short of linking it directly with any production decisons: "My aim is and always has been to move the viewer, to make him sad, afraid and to cause him to laugh—nothing more."

As founder of the innovative Open Theater, which thrived in the 1960s and 1970s, Joseph Chaikin has long been concerned with the imagistic expression of meaning as recompense for the insufficiences of language. His tendency toward the visual as opposed to the narrative preceded his own difficulties with words (Chaikin is aphasic) and is thus less ironic than the optimistic outlook that he claims replaced an earlier cynicism. In this interview he shares his thinking on a variety of topics, from mood—"I like the worst, like dying and death. . . . I like 'up.' Like the sun. It's good to have open eyes, like the open sun"—to musicality and humor in Beckett.

In the final two interviews a number of issues are explored. Most significant, Gregory Mosher offers observations on Beckett's own directing, while JoAnne Akalaitis looks back on the "brouhaha" that surrounded her *Endgame* at the A.R.T. Common to the remarks of both directors is the effort to articulate what it means to be true to Beckett while not inhibiting one's own artistic purpose.

Frederick Neumann

FREDERICK NEUMANN, an original member of Mabou Mines, directed and performed in the world premieres of *Mercier and Camier* (1979), *Company* (codirected with Honora Fergusson, 1982) and *Worstward Ho* (1986). All three were entrusted to him for adaptation for the stage by Beckett. He also acted in *Cascando* (1976) and the U.S. premieres of *Theatre I* and *Theatre II* (1985). This interview took place at Mabou Mines on 15 June 1992.

LOIS OPPENHEIM: Could you tell me something about how Mabou Mines got started and how you all got started working on Beckett's plays?

FREDERICK NEUMANN: The majority of us, all except maybe one of us, found each other in Paris in the mid-1960s, though some of us were there before that in other careers, or pursuits. David Warrilow was an assistant editor for *Réalités*. The Breuers, Ruth [Maleczech] and Lee, were just passing through. I had been there for a very long time with various theater projects and had lived right at St. Germain des Près, not far from the Deux Magots and what was the Café Royale at the time (which is now the Drugstore). And of course, this area was a hangout for all kinds of people, including Jean-Paul Sartre at the Deux Magots and Beckett occasionally having beer at the Royale, and others.

But I didn't really get to know Beckett then, though I met him at Lawrence Vail's place one time. Lawrence Vail, the famous Dadaist, was one of Peggy Guggenheim's husbands, and that family had become friends, and there were lots of parties and gatherings and people like Preston Sturges and Beckett and a lot of other names, before they were names. Man Ray used to be there.

Lawrence Vail had a huge place, two or three stories, and he had a studio upstairs. There was a little meeting of a sort with Beckett at that time, but I had always been interested in the theater, and somehow when this group of people, and my wife, Honora Fergusson. . . . It all just came together there in Paris.

It so happened that we were doing some plays, and the Breuers showed up, and David Warrilow was part of it. Philip Glass was involved in cooking up the music for us for *Mother Courage*. JoAnne Akalaitis wasn't with us then, but eventually she participated in workshops. She, David Warrilow, Lee Breuer, and Ruth began *Comédie* [*Play*] as a kind of separate project, while in my apartment, on the rue du Bac, with my wife (pregnant some seven months), we (Lee, Ruth, David, and I) worked on Brecht's *Messingkauf Dialogues*.

When we went to the Edinburgh Festival with *Messingkauf Dialogues* Helene Weigel, who was still living, suddenly wouldn't allow us to do that piece because Bertolt Brecht had forbade it in his will, not wishing to have it happen until twenty years after his death. That was in 1966, and he had died in 1956, so we had to wait. Lee Breuer did a lot to inveigle Weigel to let us do part of it. We had spent four months working on this piece. She finally let us do a small part of it.

We worked on Artaud, Stanislavski, and Delsarte (the French theoretician of gesture and so forth). And we presented a piece at the Edinburgh Festival called *Theories*. That was something we worked on—several of us who later came back to this country and started Mabou Mines.

LO: So it wasn't really started as such until you were . . .

FN: No, it wasn't officially named. It was founded here in New York. The problem was whether we could really proceed, starting in the basement of La Mama at fifty dollars a week, and several of us having children.

We decided we had to solve that problem first. We would have to fall back, retrench, so to speak, and live very minimally on the lower East Side, or wherever.

My wife and I chose to stay somewhat near my wife's father, Francis Fergusson, and that meant starting to build our own house in the woods. We called it the Guerilla Headquarters and spent the rest of our lives trying to build that place up.

We continued—almost as if it were a lifetime commitment, which it became—to do theater, original theater, as much as possible.

LO: Could you tell me about the early Mabou Mines vision of how plays should be presented?

FN: We have asserted many a time that we have a different approach to things, and I suppose it was certainly a reaction to the competition that was coming from films. Maybe it was more unconscious than deliberate that we found ourselves creating small pieces, intimate pieces, that could be watched "close-up" by a small group of people, and, in fact, that's what Beckett had done. He had created plays that came off the grand scale and became chamber pieces. He referred to them as that.

In 1976 we all had the chance, except for Lee and Ruth, to meet Beckett as a group, though I had the chance to see him before that. But it was after 1976 that our relationship really spun into something professionally.

It was this aspect of small, intimate pieces where we would invent the different articulations of performed art or performed texts. . . . Often, just narratives. Beckett suited us, and suited me, quite perfectly because one person might be able to deliver an entire text, by himself, inventing or performing the different persons. All of us were able to present Beckett works in the narrative form that they appear. These were pieces not deliberately written for the stage.

I had to sort of persuade Beckett to let me adapt his pieces for the stage. I did not wish to change the texts in any way, so to call them adaptations would only apply to the visual, three-dimensional aspects of the material, the elements on the stage.

LO: What actually happened in 1976?

FN: In 1976 we had gotten permission from Beckett to do *Play* [*Comédie*] again. It had been done here in New York and really sent us off. An adaptation of *The Lost Ones* [*Le Dépeupleur*] was also very successful. JoAnne Akalaitis was then with us. We took those pieces, and *Casando,* along with an original work by Lee Breuer called *The B. Beaver Animation,* all over Europe.

In Berlin we crossed paths with Sam. He was staying down the hall in a hotel. JoAnne Akalaitis slipped a paper under his door, and he met with us, except, as I say, for Lee and Ruth. It was the first wonderful moment.[1]

Then I kept up a correspondence with him. David Warrilow had asked him if, eventually, he would write a piece for him and for Mabou Mines. And he conceded, after four months. He said he would go for long walks and wonder what he would write for such a group. He hadn't quite accepted what we had done with *Cascando,* which is meant to be a radio

---

1. JoAnne Akalaitis offered a somewhat different account of this meeting with Beckett. According to her, Beckett was living in some kind of artist's housing paid for by the government. Akalaitis remembers calling Beckett and meeting him, for the first and only time, at a Berlin museum. Neumann was to meet with Beckett on several other occasions.

play and not a stage play. When it came to *The Lost Ones,* he said, "You have adapted it, haven't you?" He had looked at all the little people that were being used as props and so forth.

LO: What do you mean?

FN: Tiny, plastic dolls were manipulated like grains of sand—thus, the "little people." He meant also the clutter of props on the *Cascando* set. So he wasn't completely satisfied. It was so well received, however, that he had to recognize that, and he knew it was serious and good work.

He took those four months that I was telling you about to return a note to David, as I recall. As David says, it said, "What have you in mind?" And that was all that was on his little card, the kind that he was accustomed to writing on.

So David thought about that a long time and wrote, "The subject of death," and sent his note back to Beckett. I think another four months went by. And Beckett said, "Well, there is no lacking of a plethora on the subject in my extant oeuvre." Nevertheless, when I talked to him later he said he was walking in a field and said to himself, "But why not?" So he wrote a piece called *A Piece of Monologue* for David Warrilow.

In the meantime I had been corresponding with Beckett and I had written him saying that I was interested in doing *More Pricks Than Kicks.* And he said, "Please leave the poor little thing alone." So that was the end of that. Four months later he did give me permission to do *Mercier and Camier,* which is what I really wanted to do anyway. It had a mixed reception. But he seemed to have been satisfied because he gave me permission to do *Company,* both pieces having music composed by Philip Glass expressly for them. I was taking as many trips as I could to Paris, for whatever excuse—dubbing, film work, and so forth—just to talk to him about this work.

LO: Did Beckett work with you at all on the productions?

FN: We would sit in this little café. For a time it was a little café and for a time it was a big hotel where he often went, the P.L.N. He would meet people there, trying to keep his back to the outside windows. When I asked him about *Company,* for example, he said, "What are you going to do to it, Freddy?" (Not *with* it, *to* it!) "It all takes place in the dark." I responded that I would ask the audience to close its eyes. More seriously, I allowed that such was the essence of the theater in the audience space during a play. Said he, "*Touché.*"

So, we would talk about the various things that I was going to do to and/or with his work, about who was going to do what part, and so on.

And that's another thing to know about Mr. Beckett. He was not such a distant person as one would believe from his desire to stay out of the public eye and to be his own man. He could talk on another level too, and not just about his work as a professional and as a hermit, so-called.

I feared asking permission to incorporate music into *Company.* I left it to the last minute. I went to him with great trepidation and asked him if I could, indeed, use *music,* of all things, in a presentation of this wonderful, wonderful text, which is music in itself. And lo and behold, he said, "I think there are the proper interstices." And Philip Glass composed a quartet that fit quite nicely. It wasn't electronic, and it wasn't minimalist in the usual way that people associate with Philip Glass.

About *Company* I told him that I was doing several voices: of his father, his mother, himself as a child, where they seem to be in quotes . . .

LO: How did he feel about that?

FN: He thought it was a huge task—but felt it might work as part of the narration.

LO: Did you see him about *Worstward Ho?*

FN: Yes, he eventually gave me *Worstward Ho,* one of his last major pieces of writing. Ruby Cohn was the person who had encouraged me to do that piece. When I went to see him about it, he said, "No music, for pity's sake, Freddy. It's my last gasp. With all due respect to Philip. . . ." The text itself was music to me, which is one of the main reasons I felt compelled to do it onstage, to do it as a person speaking and to reveal the wonderful intricacies and images. He often spoke of images . . .

LO: Did you go over the texts together?

FN: We would go over the texts, and I have a copy of *Company* where he made corrections. He corrected mistakes in the printing. Obvious mistakes.

LO: But as far as the staging was concerned, he really didn't get too involved?

FN: Well, he would think about it and wonder again whether it should be left on the page. I fought, in my way, without fighting, that is to say. Whenever I spoke of it, I think I let whatever I had to say speak for itself. The theatrical, the presentation of it, for example. I said it was as natural as a tree, that it had to be in three dimensions. It was certainly absolutely necessary to *hear* the text. That's the minimum. I used to say that at least you have to hear it. It can't just be read. Certainly, it had to be thought out and thought out aloud . . . enacted. There has to be time and space for that. Thus, three dimensions.

In fact, in all of those writings there are pauses. There are breaks in the paragraph, not necessarily in the subject matter, but there are breaks. And he would often ask about that and how I treated those.

LO: Did you ever violently disagree?

FN: Only when I said to him, for example, that there was a woman in *Worstward Ho.* He said, very surprised, "A woman?" I said, "Oh, yes, on page such and such." And he said, "Show me." And so I hauled out the book, and then he complained about his memory and things like that. Then he said, "Read it to me." And of course, it's clear that there's an old woman kneeling, and so forth, in the text. To me that was a major character, silent though she be, as she often is in Beckett, but he made up for it in the theater pieces, where I think the parts of women are major.

I would talk about my visualization of things. And that he would study and talk again. For example, Jennifer Tipton did the lighting. And when we talked about it at the beginning, I said: "You see, the main character in this piece, as far as the stage is concerned, is light. Or the lack of it: dimness." And in fact, she saw it that way too. So I said, "This is the star of the piece," even though there is a narrator, which I, once again, performed as a grave digger. Then I said that Jennifer had thought that, maybe, instead of all the darkness, which is what I saw, and which is what Beckett saw, the dimness was because of the surrounding darkness; there was some light that appeared in darkness. I told him that Jennifer had this notion of a set dominated by whiteness. He thought about that a long time, and he said, "I don't think so, Freddy, I don't think so." I said, "But I'm sure that whiteness is a peculiar quality of the play. It must be next to darkness." He said: "Of course, then yes, off-white, off-white. That would be all right. That would be appropriate."

There was always something humorous and watchful. . . . It would go into the mind, so to speak, and we would sit there, both with various visions of things.

LO: But he never actually saw . . .

FN: He never did. I asked him about coming to New York. He only came once.

LO: For *Film.*

FN: For *Film,* right. And he said: "There's too much exhaustion, Freddy. Too much exhaustion." Not "exhaust" or "too exhausting" but *spent* energy. He had the right term. I said, "But what about hearing it? You must peek at it." He said, "What would I do, Freddy, sit in the back row?" He meant that, you know. He had directed *Endgame* in Paris with Pat Magee and Jack MacGowran. He refused to do it in London.

LO: Why?

FN: Because he didn't want to go to London. He said, "If you bring the same actors to me in Paris, I'll do it," and they did that. That was the first time he actually directed.[2]

LO: Did any of his directing work influence any of your directing work?

FN: I don't know how much he directed *Waiting for Godot,* but I saw that, the "Roger Blin version," in 1953. I happened to be there on 3 January 1953, and I must say that I saw that particular production five times. It certainly influenced me a lot.

LO: How so?

FN: It made me believe that a lot of very difficult things could be expressed by way of the theater and in a new way, and in a free way, a much freer way than I had thought looking at a lot of theater in Europe and in this country, thinking about whether this was what I really wanted to do. Did I want to knock on stage doors and go to casting directors? . . . This was in the 1950s, when there were a lot of Arthur Miller and Tennessee Williams plays. This theater didn't quite attract me.

I had a chance to work with Orson Welles briefly when he came out west. He was invited along with Paul Robeson to do the Scottish play [*Macbeth*]. And Paul Robeson did *Othello.* It was *so* theatrical, in a traditional way, although Welles was also very nontraditional. I was really attracted to the fact that he took a saw and cut off the legs of tables and did a lot of hands-on things himself to get his vision of things that were opposed to realism or naturalism, which infused everything in those days of method acting, or seemed to . . .

LO: In those three productions—*Mercier and Camier, Company,* and *Worstward Ho*—you directed yourself. Could you talk about directing the same production in which you appeared?

FN: It was hard! In fact, with *Company* my wife, Honora Fergusson, was an outside eye for me, but it was Mabou Mines theory to work in collaboration. Very often we served as outside eyes to each other and got used to directing ourselves. We considered ourselves as directors. All actors

---

2. According to Dougald McMillan and Martha Fehsenfeld, the rehearsals of this production were not in Paris: "The first *Endgame* strongly marked by Beckett's direction was the 'English Theatre in Paris' production which was rehearsed in London, and opened at the Studio du Théâtre des Champs-Elysées, Paris, February 20, 1964, and ran later at the Aldwych Theatre, London." And Michael Blake, not Beckett, was credited with the direction. As McMillan and Fehsenfeld note, however, "According to Jack MacGowran, . . . Beckett himself asked MacGowran to play Clov, approved of his suggestion that Patrick Magee play Hamm and in fact directed the play. According to Patrick Magee, Beckett directed the whole production for six weeks in London" (*Beckett in the Theatre* [London: John Calder, New York: Riverrun, 1988], 169).

were directors and are directors still. They are all thinking components of
the theater, even though there may be someone who does decide aesthetically in the end. You have to give into that in the end. Everybody who
participated in the theater would serve as director. It was almost natural,
if I may say so, to direct myself in these monologues.

The vision, the images that Beckett had drawn—I seemed to be able
to see at least something of what he was seeing. He spoke of images and
his working on images, and, in fact, toward the end of his life he was
complaining of a lack of images, of the empty cranium.

LO: How did the three satellite dishes in your production of *Company*
evolve?

FN: It took a long time to come up with this image, this physicalization
of something that is interior to the cranium. And if you like, that's exactly
where this idea of these white shells came from. They represented, in some
way, the parts of the interior of the skull depending on the configuration
onstage.

LO: In other words, the three twelve-foot-in-diameter dishes turned
in on themselves formed the cutaway of a skull?

FN: Yes, and these dishes were used as reflectors of light as well as of
sound. It began for me right in the text because one of the main considerations in that text was sound. That's why the music and so forth is . . .

LO: I was going to ask you how you came to the idea of having Philip
Glass do something for it.

FN: I can answer that right away and try to get back . . .

LO: Sorry.

FN: No, no, it's all related. With Philip Glass, I often found, as one
does find in reading Beckett, that not only does the mind keep churning
but that there is some kind of music, not quite words. Beckett had a piano
in part of his house by the Marne where he lived with Suzanne, his wife,
which he played in one end of the house. He had in mind music to
accompany various pieces that he wrote. That, in fact, is what he said
when Joe Chaikin asked permission, later on, to do *Texts for Nothing*. Beckett
said that he had encouraged Joe to not do the particular rendering that
he understood Joe was up to, to not try to cover the whole gamut of the
texts that are in *Texts for Nothing* but, rather, to take the first text and make
it as a film. Beckett said it should be filmed and that it should have music.
He had a Beethoven trio that he thought should accompany it. I don't
know whether he told me that before Joe started working on that piece or
whether it was in some earlier discussion that he talked about this trio,

which he was very fond of, and said that music should be a centerpiece. I think Joe chose not to do it that way.

That also led to the notion that music was appropriate to accompany *Company.* Sound, you know, is such an important matter throughout, even though there are these different persons, these pronouns, the "you," "he," and the "I" voices that he used. It was often about the difficulty of just barely perceiving aurally the voice. In fact, that's how it starts: "A voice comes to one in the dark. Imagine. To one on his back in the dark." It's a wonderful text. It's about hearing things.

To transcribe that to the stage, I said, "Here we are, lying on our backs on the face of this earth, peering up into the darkness, and perhaps expecting a voice, and a voice did come from the darkness." So, I use these satellite dishes, without that center antenna part, but nevertheless as captors of a possible voice, of possible company, coming from some place in the universe, from the darkness.

And of course, no voice comes from those places. The voice is produced in one's own skull. And little by little, these three dishes that were listening would turn in on themselves, all three. We had human beings turning these things, so that it could be as quiet as possible, and the three dishes then became the interior of a skull, chalk white, because of a special kind of phosphorescent paint and the lighting, which would cause this dry bone look.

In the middle of the skull was this little man in a rocking chair. Well, it was a big man—it was myself—but he appeared little, because the dishes are twelve feet in diameter. But those dishes were not only to reflect light or to create a set that would remind one of an enormous cutaway of the skull in which everything transpires. They were also like seashells held up to a child's ear. They were receptors of sound, which is the whole idea of radar-type things, so that, if I turned my head ever so slightly to say anything, the sound would bounce off one dish, ricochet off another, and go off to one side of the audience, so that the audience might think it was enhanced by Mabou Mines's technological innovations, but I wanted to leave that technological help out of the picture.

In fact, eventually, when the props—the little rocking chair and the little home, the little study, the little living room, where this character was recalling his past on his back in the dark—disappeared from the stage there was just a bare stage. Then I was left to light a bare stage and these three dishes on which one could project brilliant light and, by shutting off the light quickly and turning off all lights, leave them glowing, blue and green and hazy as if they were portholes that looked out on the universe.

It was so strange because they would change size. Some kind of optical illusion would happen. If you sat at one side, they seemed to be moving, coming closer, and much larger. It was as though you were going through space in a way.

LO: And Beckett knew about all of this?

FN: Oh, yes.

LO: And he liked it?

FN: He said, "Well it's simple enough, but elaborate nevertheless." I said, "I hope it is somehow an evocation of the images in the text."

LO: It must have been a very faithful rendering of the text while being very innovative at the same time.

FN: I could contribute some original and imaginative parts to the text, which is so rich in its own way and so simple, so wonderfully simple.

There was a wooden milk crate brought into the show after a while, and there was a cane and a hat, and the sound of the sea, which is called for. Again, it's sound, the ebb and the flow, the ebb and the flow, and the coming and the going of things that sets up a sense of time.

One of the wonderful things you could do, again with a blast of light (that the paint would "hold" for a while), was to create a shadow by standing in the way of the bright light. You could step away, and the shadow would remain in place. In fact, I would project three shadows and find company from these projections. They would fade, and, just as the sound of the sea would ebb, so would the images. I would get in fights. I got in a fight or two with myself and left the configurations on the bright surfaces. It was quite a wonderful thing to do, very hard for people to take at the time, because it was a one-man thing, long, eighty pages. The first part almost went to two hours. It ended up being one hour and forty minutes.

I did it first as a dramatized reading at A.R.T. on Monday night. And Beckett said, "How long did it take, Freddy?" [I said,] "It was very strange because, not only did it take fifty-nine minutes when I did it onstage as a dramatized reading, but, if I sat home and did it, it was fifty-nine minutes." Long pause. [Beckett said,] "I think it can go to sixty."

So, we talked about these things, and he acquiesced, if you like, more with silence, a tacit approval of things, as if saying, "Well, we'll see," meaning, "Wait until it's happened." *Worstward Ho* was extremely difficult to try to imagine as a dramatic piece onstage, or as a piece of drama, only because of the play of light and of the set that John Arnone designed, a wonderful set.

Fig. 2. Fred Neumann (director/actor) in *Worstword Ho* at CSC Repertory, New York City, 1986. Photo credit: Tom Victor.

LO: How involved did you get in all the lighting and set decisions?

FN: Well, I told you about Jennifer Tipton's notions about the light and what Beckett said about "off-white." I told him I was using the idea in *Hamlet* of the grave digger. Just as sound was important for *Company,* light, or the lack of it, was important for *Worstward Ho.* And that was the major image. The language moved in and around this element of light. That's why, in *Worstward Ho,* the "star" was really the lighting designer.

The set consisted of a pyramidal shape that lay on its back pointing toward the upstage and disappeared across the horizon almost, as though one were standing on a road in Texas. It seemed like an endless road, wide, beginning with the audience and then disappearing at the point, several points, pieces of points. Jennifer sliced them so that she could play with the illusion of distance even more.

LO: This was your image?

FN: Originally, I had a more realistic thing. I was going to do it in the South Bronx with fifty-gallon drums on fire, in the no-man's-land of "the zone," as it's called sometimes. Where all that destruction was, and still is.

I wanted to bring audiences, in Mabou Mines style, to such a place, but it became an impossible notion. The city started asking questions about the safety of people and the transportation of people, and all of the problems became too difficult. I had wanted to light up the facades of all those half-demolished or hollow buildings and use that as the backdrop and have somebody, with a microphone hidden somewhere, who would talk about *Worstward Ho,* like land-ho. That's what amused Beckett, the "ho" part of it, because it alluded to the novel *Westward Ho,* by Charles Kingsley. That was a story written in the nineteenth century about something that happened in the sixteenth century, when the explorers were heading west across the Atlantic Ocean and there was the land of milk and honey, the land of the "setting" sun, if you like, not the "rising" sun. That's why, I think, Beckett chose that image. He said he liked the élan of the title, that one was springing toward the setting of the sun, or death. The end beyond the end of things.

LO: Since we are talking about locale, the changing of sets, and so on, I can't help but bring up Akalaitis's *Endgame.*

FN: I didn't see it. I was on my way to Europe when it opened. It so happened that I was flying right over Cambridge, on my way to Paris. As you know, the plane leaves about seven o'clock from Kennedy, and the show began at eight o'clock, so I was just flying over it, and I looked down, and the turmoil had already spread across the continent, across the ocean, and I was on my way to see Beckett. The first thing he said when I arrived was, "Freddy, let's not talk about the. . . ." He said, "It's a piece of chamber music played by a brass band. Let's not mention it again, Freddy."

LO: I've heard both that it was entirely preposterous and that it was really rather true to the text.

FN: Well, I know that JoAnne swore by her intention to keep it faithful to the text and that Bob Brustein [artistic director of the A.R.T.] did also.

LO: It has been said that the scandal was all out of proportion to what really took place.

FN: This is what I hoped to report when I got back. Beckett said, "You can tell them all, Freddy, that I am not a racist," as was reported in the *Herald Tribune* while I was there. [The production had an interracial cast.]

Somehow we had this agreement—Brustein, JoAnne, myself, and even Beckett—that, although I was going to see Beckett, I would not act as some kind of person who could help clarify the situation. But it turned out that phone calls were exchanged, and we did talk a little bit about it. I was, of course, defending Beckett to the extent that I understood his request to have them say that it was *based on* or *adapted from* a play by Samuel Beckett. He would have accepted that. The A.R.T. and JoAnne did not go along with that. JoAnne felt she was being faithful to the text. Beckett said, "It was meant for a small, tightly confined space." That was the biggest thing he objected to, this enormous space. You never had the sense of Clov's enslavement or confinement. Beckett was not going to deny this claustrophobic tightness of space.

His point was (like my interior of the skull in *Company*)—and everybody has said this, of course—that that was what he was talking about in *Endgame,* that that was what the room designed with two windows and so on was meant to be. He just talked about it being a room, a small place where everybody was confined.

LO: So, you accepted his point of view?

FN: He said that with JoAnne's set there was no confinement. There was no use having a set if it was such a universe. Clov, instead of taking ladders, could take the shuttle somewhere! I think he felt that, dramatically, you could not sense this terrible confinement, or Ptolemaic universe, or his notion that it's all in our heads, with something that was grandiose and perhaps being stretched for political allusions as well. But I didn't see it, so I can't . . .

LO: But your notion of the responsibility of the director to the playwright is not such that you would object on principle to the departure from Beckett's indications as published?

FN: I could hardly be one to object, though Beckett considered adaptations of texts separately from his dramatic pieces. One could be freer.

I saw the very first thing that he directed, which was *Endgame,* in Paris, as I told you, and, just as with *Waiting for Godot,* I again felt that I was seeing really new theater. I guess now we wouldn't think that so much, but that was the mid-1960s. I just thought it was an extraordinary piece of work.

LO: One last question—your relationship to critics and reviews. Have you ever found yourself changing anything because of critical response?

FN: Well, yes, but I don't think it was necessarily because of a particular critical response. I know that the first time I did *Company* there was some complaint that my voice was not mellifluous enough. Of course, I had worked for years, radio stuff, bringing out pear-shaped tones. Nevertheless, I certainly resisted this pleasant kind of reader radiophonic voice quality. On the contrary, I wanted to use something that reminded me of Beckett and something damned cantankerous, as this character is referred to in the text, even cankerous. *Cantankerous* and *cankerous* often seem interchangeable.

I certainly wanted to use an old man who was extremely embittered and ironic at all times—sarcastic, downright cynical. Cynicism never really took hold, but I wanted to use voice qualities that were negative.

And then I just thought about trying to not go so fast. Fifty-nine or sixty minutes. . . . Mel Gussow talked about that. I thought that surely I should make it accessible enough, because it is so much about the language, and I had every reason to believe that different people would hear this differently, and I wouldn't wish the language to be lost. So, I slowed down, and I did it often in a vaudevillian way, like a stand-up comic, back in the old days of one-man shows, talking to himself, stumbling and falling all over himself in his little tight universe. Then it became anecdotal with more shape, clearer.

So, while it seemed that it was extremely metaphysical because of those portholes on the universe that I told you about, and the business of trying to create some kind of god, if only for company. . . . All of that seems heavy and Beckettian in the way that some people see Beckett, that is, almost autumnal, and as if he really belonged in a church. I saw it as much more outside, open, and human. He loved sports. He loved watching soccer. When I was with him and we talked about the work, he would always point out that everything in his texts was quite real, that nothing was made up. That's why he preferred that most of his writing not be called fiction. Maybe that first piece of writing was fictional, since some of the ideas were taken from Dante, and certainly there are fictional aspects to the portrayal of certain minds in the writing and characters.

He would often point out that academics would come to him and speak of metaphysical this and metaphysical that. He would resist this. I couldn't quite leave out the metaphysical aspect. I always felt that Beckett took us by the hand, in a way, led us to the edge of the universe, to the brink, so that we could have a good look-see.

Walter Asmus

WALTER ASMUS assisted Beckett on several productions. These included, at the Schiller Theater in Berlin, *Waiting for Godot* (1974–75), *That Time* and *Footfalls* (1976), and *Play* (1978). He assisted Beckett in directing *Godot* at the Riverside Studios in London in 1984 and worked with him on several television productions in Germany. Asmus has also directed Beckett's work for the stage and television independently of the playwright, both throughout Europe and in the United States. His most recent production was *Godot*, which he directed for the Dublin Theatre Festival in October 1991.

This interview took place in The Hague, at the Second International Beckett Conference, in April 1992.

LOIS OPPENHEIM: Was the production of *Godot* that you did for the Dublin Theatre Festival an entirely new production, or was it in some way a recreation of the Schiller Theater production of 1975, when you worked as assistant director to Beckett?

WALTER ASMUS: Of course, I start off with the Schiller production every time, and I've done *Godot* seven or eight times. I always start with a blank script, but I have the Berlin production very much in my mind. The basic choreography, I would say, goes back to the Schiller production, but many details have changed.

Also, I don't just recreate. The set and costumes are different. The actors are different. That means the overall atmosphere and mood of a production will be different. It's always a new creation, a new and exciting experience. You never really know where you are going. You put a different emphasis on different aspects of the play, or you discover entirely new aspects. Your own experience of life has increased, and that flows into the new production. When Beckett directed the San Quentin Drama Workshop production of *Godot* in 1984, which I had prepared, it was very different in its entire mood. The second act alone, for example, was some fourteen minutes longer than in the Berlin production. Beckett himself had become ten years older. He was seventy-eight then, and his own rhythm of life had changed.

LO: Does the audience in any way affect your work? Are you at all aware of directing for a particular audience, an Irish audience, for example, as opposed to a German audience?

WA: No. It doesn't affect it at all. At least not during rehearsals. But yes, certainly during performance. What does affect it is when different actors come together. You get new ideas.

I did *Godot* in Copenhagen and had the idea of Pozzo being someone coming into the wrong party, coming into a party where the terms of the party are different. He is not suited for it. He wants very much to join the party—which is played, in a way, by Vladimir and Estragon—but he does it in the wrong way, and he fails the whole time.

This image is very much a theater thing since theater people are a very close society. If theater people are together, for example, and someone comes in from the outside, he had better watch what he says because theater people have their own code, their own language, and so on—like many other groups. If someone says something about a particular per-formance at the theater, it can be very, very out of place, very ridiculous. Theater people throw words and lines at one another, and the outsider remains outside. He doesn't know what is going on. He's mystified, and yet he tries to play the same game, but the rules are closed.

This really struck me very much in Copenhagen a couple of years ago. Through this image we came to a very realistic, down-beat approach to Pozzo: he was not the bombastic, loud landowner, but a very, very normal person—just a lonely man who wanted to join some other people at a party or in a conversation, and he didn't speak the same code. He failed, and he realized he failed, and he tried hard to get into it again, and he failed, and so on. That has a lot to do with Pozzo's situation, I think.

LO: The director is traditionally thought of as someone who "knows." *How* do you "fill in" the play with all of this extra information that comes to you? Do you transmit these images, this "knowledge," to the actors?

WA: I learned the hard way. I had to learn it myself. The very first *Godot* that I directed was in 1979 in New York. Samuel Beckett was asked to do it himself, and he didn't want to go to New York, so he recommended me. The Berlin production was the Bible, and I was supposed to be someone who knew everything, but it was very difficult to commit it to the actors without being too far ahead of them. They were somehow over-awed because they expected me to know everything, but I was not prepared for that. Or I couldn't really convey the meaning of what Beckett did. I knew the choreography. I knew the shape. I had everything in my mind, but to explain to them the situation, to start from scratch, to talk to them as actors who didn't know anything about it . . .

LO: Do you feel they *should* know the meaning? When they ask you, do you try to explain it to them, or do you want them to arrive at it intuitively?

WA: I try to explain. Normally, I do. I like to talk about life and observations they have had themselves and ask about situations and the experiences they have had, and so on. I try to find a realistic approach to situations in the plays.

LO: You would say, then, that in this respect your approach to directing is actually quite different from what Beckett's was? He wasn't interested in psychological explanation. And from what you've said, it seems you are.

WA: I am not particularly interested in psychological explanations, but they belong to my way of communicating with the actors. They have to forget all about it when they perform anyway. I am interested in the artistic result. The way may be different, but the result I am heading for is the same, I dare say.

LO: What other similarities and differences between the way you direct Beckett's work and his own direction of it could you point out? Do you do line readings as he did, for example?

WA: As a shortcut to avoid long discussions or because I don't have an explanation at hand, I give line readings sometimes, but you very rarely get away with them, because actors need to know why they are supposed to say a line in a certain way.

It was different with Beckett. For most actors who worked with him he was the absolute authority. They took the pains to find out themselves what the line reading meant for the character they played. Or they under-stood intuitively. Billie Whitelaw, for example, did. She claims to have been his medium, and I believe she was.

No, my way of directing is very different. As I said, I tried Beckett's way the very first time, but I failed, and I had to find my own. When we rehearsed *Play* and *Come and Go*—he directed *Play,* and I assisted him, and I directed *Come and Go,* and he watched rehearsals now and again—

he used to rehearse from ten to twelve or perhaps one o'clock, and I started with *Come and Go* after that. I went to see him once in the late afternoon, and he asked what I had been doing. I said rehearsing, and he couldn't believe it. "It's five o'clock now. It's only a ten-minute play!" Those are the blessings of talking "psychology."

Once he came to a rehearsal. The actresses and the costume designer and I had talked a lot about what background these women in the play might have and so on. We had looked at photos of elderly ladies in Atlantic City, for example, with their bluish dyed hair and their colorful flowery dresses. We tried to find a sort of social context for these ladies in the play. That day we had decided to let them meet after shopping. That meant they were sitting there on the bench in the sun with plastic bags at their feet. Beckett was standing in the dark auditorium. There was a glaring spot on the scene. Tense silence. The actresses started to speak. Furtively, I watched Sam. Again and again, his eyes wandered down to the plastic bags. After the run, tense silence. "Sam, the plastic bags will disappear, it's only a rehearsal process. . . ." And with a sigh of relief, he would say, "They are not necessary. . . ."

No, they weren't, but we kept the airy flowery dresses, which were more realistic and at the same time more poetic than the stylized ones as described in the text. And I believe he liked them in the end.

This tiny dramaticule has all the complexity and ambiguity of real poetry. We worked hard to fill it with a lot of realistic details, to find the reality in its poetry and open its secret for the audience to read within it and perhaps find some truth.

When I talked with Beckett about realistic connotations he would always say, "It's all poetic." Beckett started off with the poetic side. I have to make my detours to arrive, hopefully, at the same point.

LO: Of all that you must have gained as an independent director from working as Beckett's assistant, what would you say remains most significant for you today? What did you learn most from working with him?

WA: To strive for precision. To strive for simplicity. In both you find a lot of truth. To encourage actors to be simple with their means, to trust simplicity, to dare not to act. To act concrete and functional. Art is reduction. Most of all, I think I learned to fail better . . .

LO: In an interview with Everett Frost [for Voices International] done some years ago in Scotland, in answer to a question concerning Beckett's effort to strip everything down to its simplest form, you responded that it had to do with his being both an author and a director. You said that, as an author, Beckett tries to be extremely precise in his use of language, that he is striving for an identity between form and meaning that would prevent, ultimately, their being differentiated one from the other. "The *way* it is written or said," you claimed, "*is* the meaning. There is no meaning beyond that."

You went on to explain that, as a director, Beckett tried to match the form/meaning problem with regard to the dialogue and movements on the stage. You said that "the choreography, the movements serve the identity of the meaning of the text on stage and [that] that's why, . . . as far as the physical movements are concerned, he tries to be as exact as he is in his writing, and as reduced at the same time." Does this explain your frequent use of the word *choreography* with regard to Beckett's plays? And is this a word that you associate more readily with Beckett's theater than with that of any other playwright because of the precision, the exactitude, on the one hand, and, on the other, the evolution toward "lessness" of which you and Everett spoke in that interview?

WA: The reason I came to use the word *choreography* is because Beckett himself, when directing *Godot* in Berlin, used the word *balletic* in the context of the actors' movements. But I think the words *balletic* and *choreography* shouldn't be overvalued. It was not that Beckett wanted them to move like ballet dancers. It was simply to express the exactitude and that there was a design in the blocking that had a meaning. Movements step by step on a line or a word, or a crossing in silence, had to do with the reunification or separation of Estragon and Vladimir, for example, who belong inseparably together. The design of the movement structure tells the story of the relationship of the characters to one another, to a certain extent.

The "lessness" of Beckett's later plays caused him to shape the earlier ones more strictly, especially *Godot,* which he regarded as disorderly. But *Endgame* and *Krapp* also. His development as an artist is certainly to be seen in the way he treated his own earlier plays while directing them. He got rid of a lot of redundancies.

LO: What was it like directing *Godot* in Dublin this last time?

WA: The Dublin *Godot* is the ultimate result, as far as the shape is concerned. It has changed, but in Dublin they have a very good command of language. Irish people talk a lot, and Beckett's plays are very talkative. The early plays, all the plays, are all about language. They go toward monologue more and more—*Not I,* for example.

To have an actor who can talk very fast and is very quick in his mind helps you to find a different timing for the play. Many actors say that, if you talk very fast, you stop thinking, that it's just gibbering. It's not. Now for me in Dublin, where I expected the audience, to a certain extent, to know the play, the problem was to find a pace, a very fast pace. Audiences today know something about the plays when they come into the theater. They know enough about the play to follow it in a very fast way, and today they are used to a fast pace. Everything is faster. We speeded up tremendously in Dublin, and that worked because the two main characters, ultimately there are four of them, worked together very well. The chemistry was just right.

LO: I know directors don't generally like to talk about other directors' work, but did you see the Dutch *Wachten op Godot* here in The Hague? It seemed to me that one of the problems with that production was precisely that the pace, the timing, the rhythm, was too slow.

WA: No, I didn't see it. But let me say that lately I have seen quite a few productions of Beckett plays in Germany that I have hated, though I am not orthodox when I see something that I like.

The German *Endgame* here in The Hague from Bochum was two hours and ten minutes, and the normal *Endgame* is ninety minutes. That was forty minutes longer, and I didn't mind. I like that production. I like what this director does. Jürgen Gosch is very conscientious about language. I listened to the dialogue in a new way.

Hamm, for example, wants Clov to look at the earth and asks him, "All is what?" and Clov answers, "What all is? In a word? . . . Corpsed." In German it is "*kaputt,*" an everyday word used, for example, when your car has broken down. But the actor said it in such a way that it gave you the shivers. It was open to all sorts of associations. In its slow pacing the production succeeded in giving the audience freedom for fantasies about the closed world of the play as well as the real one.

LO: Is there any danger that these fantasies will deform the play in some way?

WA: Not in that case. In any production, if it's good, people want to "read" it. It's not something imposed on them. They sit there, they relax, and they breathe with what is going on on the stage. The breathing can be slow, it can be fast, but you have to force them to breathe what is on the stage. Music can be charged in different ways. The same piece can be played slower, faster, more rationally or emotionally, and so on.

LO: Have you worked with other than a proscenium stage? Can you envision doing Beckett in some nontraditional space?

WA: I could. I haven't.

LO: You wouldn't be adverse to that?

WA: No, not at all, especially with the later plays. I haven't done it with Beckett, but I like very much to work in other places than the commercial theater. I have worked a lot in factory halls and places like that. But I wouldn't change the work very much.

LO: It wouldn't affect the staging?

WA: Not really. If I did *Godot* in a factory, I think it would be the same choreography somehow, but it would be different. It's like putting a grand piano in a factory and playing Beethoven or Mozart. It feels different. You don't change the piano, and you don't change the music either, but the atmosphere is different. That's very intriguing for me. I have these fantasies of putting Winnie in a heap on a faraway farm and Krapp sitting with his lamp above his table in his loneliness in the void . . .

LO: You did *Godot* on video. Was that a theatrical performance, or did you change it for video?

WA: It was a theatrical performance. We did the French in 1988. And we did the San Quentin Drama Workshop production that year also. I directed the French cast in the same way as the American cast. And I did *Krapp's Last Tape, Rockaby* with Billie Whitelaw, and *Footfalls* and *Eh Joe*. The smaller plays were very rewarding, especially because of Billie.

LO: When you first started out you worked very closely with Beckett, did you not? What kind of working situation was that?

WA: I was simply his assistant on a *Godot* production. There was a professional working atmosphere and a mutual respect in the beginning, and by and by we became sort of friends.

LO: I was particularly struck when Jim Knowlson said in his talk here at The Hague that many productions of Beckett's work are not grotesque enough. That was actually how I responded to the Dutch *Godot* the other night. The set was too "pretty." There was a pretty blue backdrop. And the lighting was pretty. I felt the lighting was well done, but the blue was wrong. It was disturbing because it was too pleasing.

WA: It kills the play. It superimposes on the play. I had this experience in Dublin. Louis Lebrocquy had made a beautiful set with flats on the side and scribbles on it and colors and a road going into the distance, painted on the horizon. Last year in Dublin, when we did it again, he agreed to do away with all of that. It became very simple, just black flats and a very simple screen, grayish, a bit hazy, and a tree. It worked much better. The stage had just been too busy the first time. It really had been beautiful but too busy. One must be very careful and very diligent with one's means . . .

LO: Did you ever violently disagree with Beckett?

WA: No. I saw his vision. That's why we got along so well. He wasn't with someone who had fancy ideas himself. I myself hate having an assistant who has fabulous ideas all the time. You have your own vision. Once or twice I did get a sneering remark. He was trying to get rid of something redundant on the screen when we did *What Where* for television. When he got rid of it I said, "I thought it was quite nice before." And he said, "Quite nice!!!" That was his way of dealing wth these matters at times.

LO: Now that Beckett is no longer with us to correct what directors impose upon his texts, are you more opposed to the various kinds of liberties that might be taken with his plays?

WA: I was never opposed.

LO: An *Endgame* in a subway tunnel doesn't bother you?

WA: Not really. If it works, it doesn't bother me. I can't judge whether that production worked or not. I haven't seen it. But on the other hand, I am very skeptical about its chances of working. I saw in Berlin recently *Godot* in a parking lot. I hated it. I thought it was horrible. Of course, critics will say you can hear the cars, the noise of the city, there was atmosphere, and so on. But there was nothing of the play. The audience didn't know what the play was about. It did damage to Beckett. People who didn't know the play didn't get into it. They were not involved at all. The Beckett plays are all very delicate. They can become very banal. Beckett knew that.

LO: You're not tempted to change the locale or play with settings of his plays in that way?

WA: No, not in that way. I could do it, as I said, in a factory hall, and I wouldn't mind. But his plays require concentration from the audience, not trains passing by. They are written as images, and there is a lifetime's work in exploring these images by putting them onstage. There is no desire on my part to superimpose anything on them.

Herbert Blau

HERBERT BLAU was cofounder, with Jules Irving, of the Actor's Workshop of San Francisco (1952–65), codirector of the Repertory Theater of Lincoln Center (1965–67), founding provost and dean of the School of Theater at the California Institute of the Arts (1968–71), and artistic director of KRAKEN (1971–81). He directed *Waiting for Godot* (1957) and *Endgame* (1959) at the Actor's Workshop, which did other Beckett productions as well. Currently, he is Distinguished Professor of English and Comparative Literature at the University of Wisconsin–Milwaukee.

What follows was extrapolated from a conversation that took place in Professor Blau's Paris apartment in July 1992.

The San Francisco Actor's Workshop

How did it start? There were a lot of little theaters in those days. The little theater tradition had come out of the 1920s. The Bay area was polka-dotted with them—not much, however, that was very memorable in the quality of performance. Actually, there *was* some adventurous or experimental work (e.g., the Hillbarn Theater in San Mateo or the Interplayers in San Francisco), but, overall, the actors were not very good. Jules Irving and I—Jules, my former partner, now dead—knew a group of actors in San Francisco, some with professional experience (including our wives), who were restive working in the local theaters, because of the acting level. They became the nucleus of the Actor's Workshop.

There was no great ethic in our beginning, except to provide good roles in a studio setting for each of the actors. Nothing like Beckett was on our agenda then. We started in a shabby loft above a judo academy on Divisadero Street, and in due time the Workshop became the major theater in San Francisco. We had at times three or more theaters playing simultaneously—at one dizzy moment there were five productions going on at various sites around the city.

The Workshop became known for several things over the years. First of all, its durability, if always on the edge of bankruptcy. It was one of the early, exemplary "regional theaters"—exemplary in its insistence on survival. A few such theaters were spread over the continent but without much contact at first and without being acknowledged as a movement until the pump-priming advent of the Ford Foundation, which showed up in a period when there were no such things as grants or subsidies of any kind. At the outset Ford sponsored four theaters as its "backfield": the Seattle Repertory Theater, the Arena in Washington, the Alley in Houston, and the Workshop. There was the old legacy of decentralization from the days of "Tributary Theater" (i.e., paying tribute to New York), but it's unlikely that the newer mode of regional theater would have been authenticated— nor the work that these theaters had been doing for some years—if Sir Tyrone Guthrie had not come to Stratford and then to Minneapolis. Just when American painting, say, was starting to dominate the world, taking over from Paris, the theater's inferiority complex had to be given a boost by English knighthood.

The Workshop was, from the perspective of the Ford program, the most bizarre or anomalous of these theaters, because, for one thing, Jules and I were still teaching at San Francisco State College, and we were by then doing avant-garde plays. We were more outspoken on social issues than the other theaters, gravitating toward questions of style, certainly more innovative in our play selection. We became known, too, for developing the concept of a company, with an emphasis on continuity. That was spurred on by my first experience in Europe, where I was very impressed with the state theaters in Germany, where the actors had a certain dignity in the guarantee of longevity—a guarantee that can, of course, wear out its benefits when the actors age into predictability. At the time, however, given the humiliating circumstances of the American actor, the continuity of European theaters seemed like a utopian blessing. Then there was also the prevailing notion—to which even famous actors, like Gérard Philipe, were committed—of *théâtre populaire*. This was the period of Jean Vilar and the exhilarating years of the Festival at Avignon.

The man who was sort of my patron when I first came to France was one of the legendary figures behind this tradition: Michel Saint-Denis, Copeau's nephew, and founder of the Compagnie de Quinze. During the occupation he was head of the Old Vic Theater School in England. Michel had come to the United States when he was consultant to the prospective theater program at Juilliard. He visited San Francisco and saw our work just about the time we were doing *Waiting for Godot*. It was through him that I came to know most of the major theater people in France—particularly those involved in the popular theater movement—ranging from Vilar to Roger Planchon and Jean Dasté, and including Roland Barthes, who was writing then for *Théâtre Populaire,* the journal titled after the movement.

Actually, I had been put on to Barthes by Eric Bentley before I left the United States. I had directed the first production of Brecht's *Mother Courage* in America, and Eric—who was the source of most of what we knew about Brecht then—told me to look up this young, bright critic in Paris, who, he said, was also Brechtian. This was the earlier semiological Barthes, who was dazzled by the appearance of the Berliner Ensemble in Paris. It was then that he wrote those short but still insightful essays on Brecht. I met Barthes the same week I met Beckett, who knew by then of the production of *Godot* we'd taken to San Quentin, and (in 1958) to the Brussels World's Fair. I had also corresponded with him when we were doing *Endgame*.

But back to the Workshop: first there was the company concept, which was infused when I returned from Europe with the ideas developed from seeing the work of Vilar and Planchon, Littlewood in England, and Strehler at the Piccolo Teatro in Milano, as well as the Berliner Ensemble. I'd been invited to East Berlin by Helene Weigel, Brecht's wife, because of the production of *Mother Courage*, which was done at a time when Brecht was still pretty much on the canonical margins in America, relatively unknown, except perhaps as the lyricist for "Mack the Knife." The utopian ideal of popular theater was to be doing plays of high intelligence, from the modern and classical repertoires, for an audience of workers, students, intellectuals: in short, the great dream of the century, with a desire at its extremity for a fusion of socialism and surrealism—a notion revived in May 1968 at the barricades in Paris.

This had nothing to do, quite obviously, with what passed for psychological drama in the mainstream of the American theater. After a series of plays from Brecht, Arthur Miller, and Sean O'Casey we had developed something of a leftist following in San Francisco, some of whom felt betrayed when we turned toward the Absurd. About Beckett there was scorn and ambivalence. I had no real interest in what were the dominant American plays of that period. Our gestures in that direction—partly to keep the riskier work afloat—consisted of Miller and Williams. They paid the bills. What we became known for, however, was our devotion to what are now the classical avant-garde plays of the time, including some of the earliest productions of Beckett; aside from *Godot* and *Endgame,* we did *Happy Days, Krapp's Last Tape,* and various workshops of other pieces. We did the first production of Pinter in America (*The Birthday Party*), along with Genet, Duerrenmatt, Frisch, Ionesco, etc., and a precursor to Pinter, the remarkable playwright, John Whiting. Jules and I were the principal directors, then Bob Symonds from the older generation of actors. But as the Workshop developed, it attracted various younger people from around the country, who have since established reputations for their own seminal work.

Among my assistant directors were Lee Breuer, Ronnie Davis (the San Francisco Mime Troupe was founded by Ronnie on the perimeter of the Workshop), Andre Gregory, Ken Dewey (who became known later on for his action events or happenings, in one of which he died in a plane crash). Ronnie was my assistant on *Endgame,* but since he was very much on the Brechtian side of the dialectic, with mixed feelings about Beckett, there was to him something suspicious in the obscurantism. Andre later did a production of *Endgame* when he was for a while head of a theater in Philadelphia, and, of course, the repertoire of the Mabou Mines (aside from Lee, Ruth Maleczech, Bill Raymond, and JoAnne Akalaitis were also with the Workshop) pivoted around Beckett. The Workshop was for such younger people—in the late 1950s and early 1960s, before things took an experimental turn off-Broadway—a kind of beacon or last outpost. They came there instead of dropping out of the theater entirely, since there was not much else around that they could believe in.

Some were not to begin with theater people but were drawn over from the other arts, as the other arts were theatricalized during the 1960s and 1970s. The performances of Beckett at the Workshop not only attracted artists—painters, sculptors, filmmakers, the new developing hybrid types— who had no previous interest in the theater but also served as models for the alternative modes of theatricality eventually known, through the era of happenings and multimedia events, as performance art. Along with these developments, we were doing productions that involved direct collaboration with visual artists and musicians, with a scale pretty much unprecedented in the American theater and not much like it even today. Beckett was also determinative in some of this, not only in an altered sense of dramaturgy but visual style as well. If you had seen our production of *King Lear* in the early 1960s you would have sensed, whatever you thought of it, that it couldn't have existed without our production of *Endgame,* if you'd seen that at the end of the 1950s. There was a conceptual and stylistic continuity between the two, evolved on our own premises, though the connection between Beckett and Skakespeare was, it seemed, part of the *zeitgeist,* crossing continents. There was, you recall, the Beckettianism of Jan Kott's book and its impact on the *Lear* of Peter Brook.

Approaching Beckett

I knew of Beckett's work shortly after the war—that is, World War II—but we couldn't get the rights to it until after the Michael Myerberg production of *Godot* in New York, following upon the disaster in, was it? Coral Gables. By the time we came to *Godot* we had already done some reasonably way-out work in our theater. But *Waiting for Godot* was something else again, though it may seem now like second nature.

We gathered to read the play for the first time in my house just above Haight-Ashbury in San Francisco, after which two of the older, more experienced people dropped out of the cast. They simply refused to be in it. They had always been suspicious of my experimental tendencies (naturally "gratuitous"), but with *Godot* they thought I was crazier than usual. When they read through the play they simply didn't know what was going on, which didn't seem to be much, and much of that they didn't like. And these were quite intelligent people. There was a lot of skepticism about the play around the Workshop even when we replaced the actors and started rehearsals. When we finally decided to present the play Jules and others were wary of doing it as a full-scale production at our theater downtown, so we compromised and played it, at first, only on Thursday nights. Suddenly, unpredictably, it became a kind of cult phenomenon. There was something in the air, it received a lot of attention, the audiences grew, and we multiplied the number of performances.

I think the hardest thing to reconstruct, now that Beckett has been deified among American theater people, particularly academics, is just how startling those plays were.

How did we work on the play? First of all, it was really a matter of *explication de texte.* Beyond that we talked about it in diverse ways, from the psychopathology of its dubious "characters" to its elegiac tone, a sort of drama of lamentations on civilization and its discontents. I tried to situate it historically. "On this soil of Europe, yes or no," Beckett had asked, "is man dead?" That seemed pretty un-American. So, we talked out the transition, from a European context to our own. Then there were the formalistic aspects of the play—its repertoire of subverted conventions. This was before the ubiquitous postmodern consciousness of self-reflexive forms, but it was soon apparent that the play within the play was a kind of discourse on the theater itself. You could take almost any theatrical convention and point to ways in which the play, in some sense, reflected on the convention. We were conscious of these reflections, deviations, inversions, during the course of rehearsal. Eventually, you have to do it, sure, but the talking here was a precondition for insuring that the actors would *want* to do it as it could be done. I mentioned the resistance in our cast, but once *Godot* came to be a sensation, and even the newspapers approved, every actor in the company was ready, when we came to it, to jump into the ash cans of *Endgame*.

As regards the acting—and I have always felt this about Beckett's drama—the substance of it is realism in extremis. Which is to say that the realistic vision, its methodology, is taken about as far inside as it can go, interiorized so intensely that it seems to occur at the nerve ends. In the late 1950s actors were, reflexively, still inclined to think of themselves as interior actors. If they had any training, it was in that tradition. But there was something about the surface tension of Beckett's dramaturgy that seemed, paradoxically, to double up on interiority. At the same time there was a movement of thought through the phenomenology of the play— its things to be done, beginning with the opening "nothing"—around the dubiousness of the distinction between inside and outside.

San Quentin

We were invited to San Quentin through a series of circumstances, though I can't quite remember exactly how the invitation came. A lot of work has been done over the last generation in prisons, factories, Indian res- ervations, wherever, but there was no such active tradition at the time, and the production of *Godot* at San Quentin became a prototype. In any case, when the contact was first made we proposed a play that I had written. But that didn't go because there were women in the cast, a taboo at the prison (which, by the way, had never had a theater performance, unless—if rumor is correct—Sarah Bernhardt did appear there on her tour of America at the turn of the century). Our presentation of *Godot* was, so far as we knew, the first in a maximum-security prison in this country. When we proposed to substitute *Godot* for my play, however, there was trouble: an argument at the prison, with the prison psychiatrist. He was put off by the "depressing" material of *Godot,* felt it would be too obscure, even traumatic, for the inmates. There was a confrontation before Warden Duffy—who looked like a southern redneck—and we weren't counting on his approval. But he heard us out, seemed to like me, and said simply: "That's it, let them do it."

We had a sensational response. It had such an impact on the prison that the language of the play, the names of the characters—a Gogo, a Didi, a Pozzo—became part of the therapeutic vocabulary at San Quentin. It may be so to this day. Afterward we helped the inmates set up a drama group of their own. That performance had a major impact on the lives of some who were there, most notably Rick Cluchey, who was in for armed robbery and attempted murder. As a result of his work in the drama group, Rick was paroled, was introduced to Beckett (by which of us, I forget— maybe Ruby Cohn?), named a child after him, and was directed by him in Berlin, to top it all off. But that story is now pretty well-known.

On Beckett as Director and Other Productions

Was I interested in Beckett as a director? I would have been interested in almost anything Beckett did, because I cared about him personally. But no, I was absolutely not influenced by his productions. First, for the obvious reason that he hadn't directed yet when I was doing his plays. When he did start to direct I didn't see any of the productions for some time; when I did, the couple I saw were quite ordinary, pedestrian.

Of other productions I've seen the most remarkable was Lee Breuer's *The Lost Ones,* with the fastidious focus of its funneled specularity in that claustrophobic arena of foam rubber. (I've written about that, briefly, in *The Audience.*) I saw a production of *Waiting for Godot* here in Paris last year (at the Théâtre des Amandiers in Nanterre) that was, scenically, very evocative—a vast blitzed space, below a viaduct perhaps, the action receding into it occasionally but mostly confined laterally to the forestage. David Warrilow was in it (his French is very good), but the acting was nothing special and, in any case, outdone by the magnitude of visual image. But I found that image, its bleak audacious scale, more interesting in itself than many more dutiful transcriptions, literalizing every stage direction. I think the directions are, at their most minimal, vastly suggestive, like those of *Imagination Dead Imagine.* It's the quality of the imagining out of the datum of nothingness that compels me in performance.

I'm not particularly interested in versions of the plays that you can see without half-trying by merely reading the texts.

From time to time, then, you may see something really unusual, but, as you know, that turned out to be a problem with Beckett himself, though he never went to see productions. I happened to be in Paris a few days after he had tried to stop JoAnne Akalaitis's *Endgame* at Brustein's theater in Cambridge. I was meeting with Beckett and, though I hadn't seen the production either, questioned his having tried to stop it. I reminded him that I'd known JoAnne since she was very young: "She grew up on your plays. People with the Mabou Mines were all deeply influenced by your work [as he knew], and they probably know it a good deal better, are engaged at deeper levels, than many who appear to be faithful to it." I ventured that, even if she did something strange, it was with no less respect for the text, perhaps more. But whoever had gotten to him before this had done a good job: he was very upset, wouldn't listen. That had never happened between us before. Things were getting intense, so I made what I thought was a pretty good joke, something he'd have laughed at another time, about here we are in Paris, all that stuff about the death of the author . . . he was furious.

Nothing to be done. So, I said, "Maybe, after all, Alan [Schneider] was your best director." Alan was always very dutiful. He'd fly over to Paris to check out difficulties in the text and did, so to speak, what Beckett wanted. And he would do that, of course, with considerable skill. I never felt, however, that I had to see such a production. As I said, I'm simply not taken with productions of what, when you read a text, seems pretty much the way you'd do it if you did it straight. But I feel that about all productions, not only of Beckett. It's like in the teaching of dramatic literature, you hear people say the students have to go and see the plays; otherwise, they won't understand the drama. Maybe so. Maybe better they don't go to see the play, because they have to constitute it then in their own minds, see it there, finding their own image, no ready-made standing between.

Particularly if it's a good production with famous actors. That gets in the way. If that's the only image they have of it, they're very likely to think that's what it's supposed to be. Oh, I'm not saying they won't gain something from seeing a performance, but there has always been an alternative tradition in dramatic theory that thinks of the casting and staging of a play of any stature as necessarily reductive, canceling out the prospects of one's own imagining. Of course, that tradition also intersected the antitheatrical prejudice, the notion that representation itself was bound to be *mis*representation.

Beckett understood this, I think, from the beginning and shared the antitheatrical prejudice as well: years ago, when I asked him why he'd turned to the theater, he said it provided some relief from the novel, because the theater is a contained space. But if it is in some way manageable, it is also a violation. As for the audience, what audience? He always knew that he was "writing into a void" or, worse, as with the tramps in *Godot,* gaping over the forestage: "a charnel house, a charnel house." Where does the play really take place? "There's something dripping in my head," as Hamm says. It's the dripping in the head from whence the drama comes, its deep structure. So, in a very real sense what's happening up here, the dripping at the temple, the throb in the fontanels, is a lot more important than what's happening out there.

We weren't talking on that level when we argued that day. Which is why I said that maybe Alan, after all, was the most appropriate director. As for myself, Beckett had more than once wondered, other times, why I had stopped directing. But if I were, I could simply never have assured him that I'd do what he wanted or strictly follow the manifest text. As for his knowing what he wanted, well, that's up in the air these days, if there's any truth to French theory and psychoanalytical thought—the degree to which the author's authority or the authority of the text has been, if not legitimately, provocatively questioned, as it has been with the canonical drama in revisionist performance. Despite all theory, a lot of people still have this incredible investment in the Master's voice. This Master has given us, however, the conceptual ground for doing precisely what he didn't want us to do. I put the emphasis on the precision, which, as I've written before, is next to godliness in Beckett.

There was, by the way, a development at San Quentin many years before that reflects on this issue and any claim of infallibility for the Beckettian text. Some years after we did *Waiting for Godot* at San Quentin the drama group there did its own version. We were all invited from the Workshop, but I couldn't go myself because I was rehearsing that night. But others from the company went, including Robert Symonds, who had been in the production we'd brought there years before. He described to me afterward what appeared to be one radical change in the course of things onstage: as I recall it, when Pozzo and Lucky came on, they stayed for about a minute then went off for a while and then came on again. Or something like that. Bob watched this somewhere between astonishment and bemusement, and at the end of the performance he questioned the actors about the sequence and somehow came to ask about the text. What happened was that when *Godot* was first published in the United States it was done by *Theater Arts,* not the old yellow-covered journal but the later glossier one that published Broadway plays (Meyerberg's production having qualified *Godot*). When the play appeared it was with ten or more pages out of place! The inmates had used that text, and it seemed perfectly suitable. They hadn't remembered what had happened exactly in our production. And so far as the "true text" is concerned, they apparently didn't know the difference. I assure you that's not because those inmates were uneducated or naive.

That characterizes the theoretical problem itself. Beckett, after all, gave us the paratactical model of postmodern thought. Dramaturgy as combinatory sets, repetitive, additive, recursive with permutations. With no old-fashioned causality at work you could switch this here, put that there. The connectivity is musical. That's not wholly true, I know, but true enough.

I don't have any problem with people adapting Beckett's prose texts for the stage. Nor did Beckett eventually, though he objected to that at first. But he finally gave up, resigned himself. He couldn't keep up with it, though he remained vigilant, once he started to direct, about other productions. Or others were vigilant for him, to his detriment, I think. The vehemence of his objections, given his usual grace—didn't become him. And in a way it made no sense, for he had given us, as I said, the intellectual, theoretical, and ideological grounds on which any text becomes liable to dispersion, with the disarming authority of an open field. If you really understand what is going on in his texts, you don't need deconstruction, for that's the work in progress. I realize some would say that's the point: Why do it when it's already done? It's not a matter of licensing any capricious reinvention, but who's to award the license in any case? As with Brecht, there's no law against turning his methods back upon Beckett, rethinking some aspect of the drama, or shifting the site of its occurrence. At any rate, Beckett taught us before theory that paratextuality is built into the language, and, as with the gospels derided by Didi and Gogo, no text is sacred. That people are inclined to do odd things with Beckett's own texts is, one might say, a matter of poetic justice.

A Beckett Sensibility

Did Bert Lahr have a Beckett sensibility? In some ways, yes. Did Buster Keaton have a Beckett sensibility? He and Beckett did not entirely get on together, and yet we know that Beckett was interested in these vaudeville types, though I do have some objections to what passes for comedy, the kidding around that I've seen in some productions. The substance of it wears pretty thin. The Beckettian theme—it's funny, then it's no longer funny—is okay, so long as you know that the datum, the bleak landscape of Beckettian thought, wasn't all that funny to begin with, as Didi said, funnily, "APPALLED!" What's funny, as they say, is to *have* thought—that is, not only in the past tense but also in the sense of possession. To really think about it is to die laughing. Take it or leave it, that's an appalling thought, almost worse than Hamlet's there's nothing either good or bad but thinking makes it so.

There is, sure, a peculiar sort of optimism in Beckett (*On!*), but it's as stringently minimalist, as parsimonious, as the form. People try to make something positive of Beckett but somewhat more than the drama concedes. "They give birth astride of a grave, the light gleams an instant. . . ." There is something indefatigable, tragic, with an elegaic heroism that seems to be transcendent . . . well, okay, it's there, but minimally there, the light gleams an instant only, then it's gone, the large massive doses of bleakness also there. And the pain, the pain, it must be finished, nearly finished, because so painful, something dripping in the head . . .

An aspect of Beckett that seems to me of major consequence has to do with the pain of birth. Some time ago I was asked to write an essay on Beckett and deconstruction. It turned out to be about Beckett, Derrida, and the birth of my daughter. It's a very theoretical essay but also very performative, "The Bloody Show and the Eye of Prey." As it turned out, the morning I was about to start writing the essay, my wife—who was very pregnant—came down and said she was bleeding: the bloody show had begun. I couldn't help thinking about the subject of the essay as I watched my daughter being born. As I eventually wrote, "It's a little strange to watch a birth with Beckett on your mind. As a fetal monitor he leaves something to be desired." You can look up the rest if you want to, but the gist of it is the *pensum*, curled up worm in slime, at first suck the fiasco, and the monstrosity of it all—a little hard to take when your wife is having a baby, who should be a sign, a portent, rather than the first cruelly extorted deposit of a minimal quantity of being. This all has to do, if you want to be linguistic about it, with being born into the symbolic, the long interminable sentence of *The Unnamable*, the sentence of language, the sentence of punishment, language *as* punishment, the price of being born. If you don't have that right in performance, you can look for all the hope you want, but, sad to say, you don't have Beckett at all.

Theory and Theater

Theory has always been an issue with me in the theater, and all the more so after first encountering Beckett, who seemed to raise about the theater, in the deepest theoretical sense, all the most elemental questions. My own thinking went through a lot of changes before the formation, in the 1970s, of the KRAKEN group, where from my point of view it was like starting all over again—after more than twenty years in the theater—with those elemental questions. If Beckett had any sustained influence on me, it had to do with a certain obsessiveness about the theater in its most rudimentary form: What is it, ontologically, when you try to separate it out from whatever it is it is *not?* I've written a great deal since about that fine distinction, in a series of books starting with *Take Up the Bodies: Theater at the Vanishing Point,* to which disappearing point the work of KRAKEN was, in a sense, always directed. Those who saw that work know that it was physically adept and demanding, but it was also, to be sure, very heady stuff: something dripping in the head.

There may be a disarming playfulness in the distresssing thought of Beckett, and he can even make a vaudeville turn of the excesses of lapsed consciousness—when the tramps put on their thinking hats, to "Think! Think! Think!" I find it all profoundly moving, but all the more so when push comes to shove, as at the bitterest end of *Endgame,* in which, if you're going to insist upon living at all, it's a desperate matter of thought: "Use your head, can't you! use your head! you're on earth, there's no cure for that." What I was always moved by in Beckett, through the woeful antics of the music hall routines, the slapstick comedy in the dying fall, was a certain manic fitfulness of mind, as in the iterations of *Footfalls:* "It all, it all." Where you could virtually bite your tongue over the painful indeterminacy of that (w)hole in *it.* It all, it all. What's the referent? I certainly didn't think of it, when I was first doing Beckett, in those theoretical terms, but he did: read his little book on Proust, which sounds—and in its interlocutory, dense, elliptical prose—like poststructuralism *avant la lettre.*

So far as my own work with KRAKEN was concerned, what appealed to me in poststructuralist thought was that it seemed to be theorizing what we were doing, which was in the process theorizing itself. Which is why I say somewhere at the start of *Take Up the Bodies* that if the productions of KRAKEN that I describe in the book never existed, that if I were simply making them up on the page as I went along, the theory derived from them would be no less true.

On *Endgame*

I knew Beckett for about thirty years. I was not in touch with him when we did those early productions. I wrote to him afterward, commenting on what we did. Was he curious about them? Certainly. I don't believe I sent him pictures of the productions of *Godot* (we actually did two of them, quite different), but he did see pictures of our *Endgame* and seemed to admire them. Given, however, what he later came to feel about allegiance to his texts and stage directions, I'm surprised that he didn't take amiss some aspects of the design and costumes quite palpable in the pictures. I also described to him what we'd done with the opening sequence of *Endgame,* in which there were twelve to fifteen minutes of silent mime before the dialogue began. He didn't, as I recall, raise an eyebrow.

As I recall, I even described to him the lengths we went to in rehearsal to let the resonances of the play sink in, before we extruded the dilatory excess, which was itself a reflection on the indeterminacy of the finish that must be but is never finished (*in*terminable in the Freudian sense). That was compacted in performance into the recursive enumeration of its almost diabolic resources of hilarious pain, so exquisitely painful that the laughter can't bear itself. (That's what Beckett called the *risus purus,* the laugh laughing at the laugh.) Sometimes this protracted endurance would take almost four hours in rehearsal, though the actual performance lasted about an hour and a half. That's not much more than par for the course ("something is taking its course"), though I've never seen a production that was as excruciating to begin with, in the almost paralytic lyricism of its opening moments, distended to the uncountable silent minutes of an eternity onstage. I don't think I've seen anything like it since.

If you'll forgive a further immodesty, I think the production of *Endgame,* entrusted to memory now, was probably one of the most richly conceived in the American theater. It was simply unusually seen; the seeing of it was unusual. In the simpler sense of sight, it was scenically extraordinary. Beckett calls for gray walls. What does that mean? Do you paint the walls gray? Or what? What we did was to give him grayness, an abstraction of gray. The designer was Robert La Vigne, whose prodigious gifts included a capacity for mutilations and the grotesque in art that were nevertheless a function of exquisite taste. "First of all," I said to Bob, "let's think of those gray walls in this way: there's a structural relationship to the other gray objects as first perceived onstage." What materializes there, so far as the perceiver can tell at first, are inanimate objects: gray. You see a mass in the foreground (the ash cans), you see another mass center stage (Hamm enthroned), another form in the background, not yet perceptible as a human figure (Clov), and all of these gray, enclosed by gray. You see these things, and what you have, with nothing clearly discernible, is a kind of lumpish materiality of nonobjective forms: gray. Maybe Clov, depending on how he is lit, might be seen as incipiently human, but he too, ideally, would seem no more than a phenomenological object.

Then, later, they take this trip, the journey around the room. This, by the way, I did confirm later with Beckett, that is, the itinerary of it. "Shouldn't we go backward, counterclockwise?" I said. When Hamm makes that trip, wheeled by Clov, you have a decision to make as a director. Does he move erratically, or in a clockwise or counterclockwise direction? Since it seems to me that the play has a certain recessive aspect to it, it should be something like the uroboric snake—the one that eats its own tail—turned back upon itself temporally. At any rate, we went to the wall, the hollow, counterclockwise, and in the process there was the subliminal appearance of a reversal of time.

It was gray, as you saw it, when the lights came dimly up. So far as one could tell, it was absolute gray. But I also suggested to Bob that there be inherent in the grayness a sort of history of Western culture moving backward, inscribed on the gray walls, so Hamm would have something to see on his journey; it wouldn't be totally boring: there in the ground zero of grayness the reversed processions of time. What Bob did over the weeks of rehearsal was to accumulate a mound of junk, tin, broken porcelain, rusty and fresh nails in front of the stage, and various fabrics, gauze, brocade, velour, lace. Out of all this he composed, as we rehearsed, an assemblage of gray that was precisely what I'd asked for, a cultural history in reverse, by no means literalized, but shadowy, suggestive, articulated by dispersion in the matrix of gray, mere hints and intimations of various historical periods in the abstract figurations of metal and fabrics, clusters of nails. The walls were in a sense encrusted with history but, unless you were alert to their visual nuances, nothing more than gray.

Those walls were just great. They were so beautiful people ripped them off. We couldn't keep them, which was usually the case with whatever Bob designed; they were art objects. They were gorgeous walls. But they looked bleak.

Everything in sight was similarly designed. Hamm's hands, for instance (Robert Symonds played the role), were painted and furred; the sheet that covered Hamm was embroidered with a soiled elegance. As for the costumes, same thing, La Vigne had another pile of material around the stage, some of it onstage. I had spoken to him about Clov's rage for order, the anal intensity of it. So, as we rehearsed, he would be there, too, as in a dance, lay leather on him and then, wielding a razor blade, cut. Over a series of rehearsals, cut by cut, Clov (Tom Rosqui) was totally sewn into his costume, with a tight cowl of leather around his face, as if he had wanted nothing more than to be totally sealed in. This was also reflected in the acting, the spastic movement of Clov as well.

The relation between the materiality of the scenic elements and the acting was something Beckett's work encouraged as a matter of consciousness. I directed, after this work on *Endgame,* a second production of *Godot.* In the first production—the one we took to San Quentin—there was a large backdrop with faint streaks of white (painted) cloud and, like a fence or circus ring around the tree, an equally faint configuration of barbed wire on posts (which Beckett certainly didn't call for either). Yet there was a sense, nevertheless, of a very bare stage (which he did call for). The movement was, over a fairly large surface, more or less athletic or balletic, even in its incapacities. (The setting was by Robin Wagner, the first production he ever designed.) The second production was very different. It had a sort of see-through curtain that couldn't get (it) up. It would struggle to go up then plaintively fall down. The mound was made from an old rusted automobile radiator. It was quite drearily elegant too, didn't look like a radiator exactly but, rather, a mound or maybe a large toadstool. The floor of the stage was entirely foam rubber, so that throughout the entire action—in a more intimate theater than the other—you couldn't hear a step. The actors would also sort of sink into the ground as they walked.

We did it in San Francisco at what was then (the theater still exists) called the Encore Theater. It was a long, narrow space with soffits and a specially rigged curtain; and, to navigate the soffits, a somewhat baroque scalloped curtain. When we did *Endgame* we didn't use the curtain. Now that presents an interesting acting problem, because it meant that Hamm had to be in his seat before the audience came in, and he was actually there for something like thirty minutes or so before the start of the unveiling within the play. Since he has a sheet and a handkerchief over the black specs, that can be suffocating, claustrophobic. It would make him psychotic at times, which was exactly the condition in which we wanted him. Under the double veil he'd be hyperventilating. That was all conceived, to his silent sorrow.

When we were rehearsing, as I suggested, a run-through would sometimes take as much as four hours. If it took fifteen minutes to unveil him, as played, it sometimes took in rehearsal something like forty-five minutes for Clov to open the window curtain. This was to get some sense into the metabolism of the actor of what it is to *not-want* to do it. It was excruciating to see him open that curtain millimeter by enduring millimeter, every ounce of resistance to the doing at every impossible moment. Why do it at all? What's out there, anyway? Zero. When Tom Rosqui opened it in the production he went like this: *whoom!* The slide of the curtain rings on a brass rod would make the audience jump. But that instantaneous movement had congealed in it each tormented instance of the hours of rehearsal, where he experienced the ignominy of having to do it at all. What made him do it? Well, what keeps them there? As the text says: the dialogue. The opening of that curtain was chilling in its compressed materiality.

One of the things that determined what we did with *Endgame* involved a structural contrast with *Godot,* not often talked about, if at all. Only Beckett is Beckett, but not all Beckett is the same, within the dramaturgical spectrum of universal grayness. There are improvisational appearances in all his texts, but not all improvisation is alike either, being a function of the psychic mechanisms at work. Let me put it in terms of the problem of memory: in *Waiting for Godot* not only can Didi and Gogo not remember what happened a million years ago, in the 1990s they can't even remember at times what happened a minute ago. Gogo, in particular ("I'm not a historian"), seems to be wanting in historical memory. They fall down with Pozzo, and, because they can't quite remember why, they just get up. Child's play! Without historical memory you can, like a child, be open and improvisational; there are no impediments in that regard to starting all over again, to enter again unthinkingly into the vicissitudes of play. In *Endgame,* however, the play is deadlier, if anything, more unendurable. And then there is this conceptual difference as regards the uses and abuses or liabilities of memory: let's suppose I take an object that can be turned on or off. In the moment that I am poised to shut it off I can think of every conceivable reason in the two thousand–year history of Western culture why I shouldn't, and every reason why I should. Stalemate. That's exactly Clov. He functions like a kind of extension or exacerbation of the "ratiocinative meditativeness" that Coleridge attributed to Hamlet, an impacted figure (as a tooth is impacted) of the Hamletic condition. As when Hamlet finally kills the king, he does so out of maximum indecisiveness, as a reflex against the near-crippling inability to act. No wonder Clov lurches when he walks, as if he were impelled only by stasis itself.

That was a question raised by the actor in rehearsal: Why does Clov walk as he does? You might say, like Bert Lahr about picking up the pot, "It says pick up the pot, so you pick it up." I could have said to Tom Rosqui, "Don't ask. He justs walks like that." It would never have passed muster with Tom. In any case, I think he walks against a resistance to walking at all. In other words, he'd rather not move at all. It is like some kind of competing reflex is built into his body, if not genetically programmed, as a function of history. Now, would Beckett have confirmed that? I wouldn't have cared if he confirmed it or not. The point is that it seemed to me inherent in what is going on. If something is taking its course, it is utterly anal. Clov is absolutely constipated. And when he moves he moves in such a way as to reflect that, the anality being almost metaphysical as well. There is also the immense pain in the body. That is also why he was sewn in, to seal him off as much as possible from the air, the world, the presence of others, who are the source of pain.

Things make sense, if you want to make sense, but they also have to have a performative sense. What does this mean in the way it looks? What does this mean in what he wears? What does this mean in the way he walks? That I had a good visual idea? I don't offhand think, despite my defense of possible relocations of the plays, that it's a particularly impressive idea to set *Endgame* in a subway. It depends, however, aside from the desire for relevance or updating, on the substance of the subway, what could be revealed there and not otherwise. That it is updated doesn't mean anything. But to think through the sense of metaphysical stalemate at the logical impasse of late capitalism, that is a different matter. This is not a question of delivering a message but, rather, of the thinking through itself, with precision about the complexities of the idea.

It's like when, in *King Lear*, Edgar leads Gloucester out to the edge of the cliffs of Dover, and the blinded father says to the disguised son, as Edgar is about to recreate the landscape, to give his father eyes: "Set me where you stand." I don't think he means that vaguely or approximately.

Precision is next to godliness, or the fairies and gods that are conjured up by Edgar for his father, after the leap into nothingness. Set me where you stand. Not here or there, but exactly where the other stands: the father in the son's footsteps. It is just like when Clov pushes Hamm back from the hollow in the wall after their vast journey around the room. "Am I right in the center?" Hamm asks. More or less, a push here, a push there. Am I in the center? An indifferent push. *In the center!* But we well know there is no center. We are talking deconstruction, no? There is no center, no origin. So, where do you put him? If you care about these things, if you care about thought . . . and if you don't, no matter, it's just a laugh. But that ain't Beckett. There may not be a center, but the desire for it—the source of his unerring poignancy amid the facile parody of the postmodern—determines the way the thing looks, and sounds, its *soundings,* the way the body moves, the way one thinks. Think!

Beckett has the virtue, it seems to me, of consolidating issues that way. That's the part of his idea of directing I admire, the intention of it, as he has spoken of it himself: the insistence in the soundings out upon an absolute music. Whether he saw what its absolute nature should be in material terms and could realize *it* onstage, that's another matter—it all, it all . . .

Pierre Chabert

PIERRE CHABERT played in *L'hypothèse* by Robert Pinget (Théâtre de l'Odéon) and *La dernière bande* (Théâtre d'Orsay, 1975) under the direction of Samuel Beckett, with whom he maintained a close friendship for more than twenty years. Beckett also advised him in the role of Hamm in *Fin de partie* (directed by Sandra Solov) and *Voix de Samuel Beckett* (an ensemble of narrative texts that he conceived, staged, and interpreted at the Théâtre du Rond-Point in 1987).

Chabert directed *Berceuse, L'impromptu d'Ohio,* and *Catastrophe* in 1983 at the Théâtre du Rond-Point and again, with the addition of *Quoi où,* in 1986. These plays were filmed for French television (by Helen Gary Bishop) and aired in 1991. He also adapted and directed *Compagnie,* with Pierre Dux (Théâtre du Rond-Point, 1986), and *Mercier et Camier* (1988). All of these productions have played abroad, in English and Spanish, and Chabert continues to perform, throughout the world, in *La dernière bande*. In 1992 Chabert directed *Oh les beaux jours* at the Théâtre National de la Colline (with Denise Gence and sets by Yannis Kokkos).

This interview took place in Paris in July 1992.

LOIS OPPENHEIM: You adapted *Compagnie* for the theater.

PIERRE CHABERT: It was a great French actor, Pierre Dux, who was for a long time the administrator of the Comédie Française (and who is now dead), who asked me to direct it. He wanted to act in this work and had spoken to Beckett about it, and Beckett had agreed. But he didn't really know how to go about it. He had seen my productions of *Dramaticules,* and, on the strength of that, he asked me if I would take on this production.

Translated by Jim Cross and Lois Oppenheim.

I thought about it long and hard because I respected Beckett's desire to not stage those of his works that were not written for the theater.

LO: But it would not have been the first adaptation of *Compagnie*. It had already been done before.

PC: Perhaps, but I respected and shared Beckett's opinion: one should not "adapt" texts not written for the theater.

LO: Didn't Beckett's thinking on that evolve somewhat toward the end of his life?

PC: It is believed that it did because, at a certain point, he didn't do anything about the adaptations. But most often that was due either to friendship or to weariness.

Personally, I led him to collaborate on the "adaptations" that I was undertaking. And indeed, at times they really interested him, like the idea of the machine in *Compagnie* or that of the narrative voice in *Mercier et Camier* that he asked me to represent on the set by a light, a "distant star." But there was a contradiction, for, in fact, he rejected the very idea of an adaptation. So, one could say that his thinking on this issue didn't evolve, contrary to what is generally thought. I am emphatic about that. He made it very clear to me, since he asked me at the end to give up, from then on, "my" adaptations. (He also wanted to remind me that he had written for the theater.) The theater plays were written for the theater, the radio plays were written for radio, the television plays for television, and the "novels" for voice, "written in the dark." And that's that. To one who doesn't understand that, an essential dimension of Beckett and his genius is lost.

At that time I already had the *Mercier et Camier* project to do. But *Mercier et Camier* is different in that it's a dialogue. In a way it's already theater. I myself wouldn't have thought to bring *Compagnie* to the theater. It was because of Pierre Dux's request that I began to think about how to transpose it, and I worked hard on it.

LO: And Beckett was in agreement?

PC: Beckett agreed, and he was very pleased that I would be the one to direct it. But he conceived of this production a little like a reading or something very simple. So, I put a great deal of thought into it, and I explored many different ideas.

At first my ideas were far too complicated and stemmed, essentially, from an explication of the text: from the sort of doubling of the "I," this "character" who reveals himself as several selves and whose different facets would be shown onstage. Through a play of mirrors, through reflections and, perhaps, even a double of the leading actor, there was to be a sort of concrete visualization of the dramaturgy implicit in *Compagnie*. But, I found this all much too complicated, and I arrived finally at an idea for the production at once simple and striking, which consisted in having the character, of whom there would be only one, move in the dark, without the audience seeing him moving, which is to say, without there being any movement.

LO: When you say in the dark . . .

PC: It was a question of conciliating movement and immobility. The actor had to be totally immobile but moved, moved in the dark. When I spoke to Beckett about this idea he understood immediately, and he summarized it in this wonderful formula: "In sum, an invisible machine." It was an invisible machine, which meant that we would build a machine in which the actor would sit. It only remained for us to decide on a method of moving it. There were many possibilities: it could be a motor or a system of remote control or something much more simple and more human. I immediately leaned toward this solution, namely someone invisible, as the machine would be, who would push and guide the machine in the dark, but, even though this idea was very simple, it was exceedingly difficult to stage. It meant integrating the entire lighting system into the machine so that it wouldn't be seen.

Beckett was fascinated by this idea of a machine. And in thinking about it, I saw that I had been "doing Beckett" without realizing it. I had extended the very idea of Beckett's dramaturgy, in which there is a sort of synthesis, of osmosis between movement and immobility, in which characters become the objects that are moved, like in *Berceuse,* which I had already directed.

The important point in *Berceuse* is the fact that it is not the woman who rocks herself but, rather, that she is rocked. And that completely changes one's perspective on the play and on the production of it as well. I have seen many productions of *Berceuse,* and often it is the actresses who rock themselves, and that is contradictory. This approach doesn't respect the fundamental idea of the play. The woman is rocked by the voice, by her own voice.

When I directed *Berceuse* Beckett said to me: "Be careful. You know, Alan Schneider, in the United States, had a great deal of trouble inventing the process for the rocking." I worked with my stage designers, and they quickly devised a marvelous system with a simple cord and pulley. It was a system of great sensitivity and finesse. It was like a fine musical instrument. A whole range of movement, strong and delicate alike, was possible.

Getting back to *Compagnie,* this idea of a machine ran in the same vein as Beckett's own ideas, and it didn't surprise me at all that he was fascinated by it because it was truly pure Beckett. So, we started with this idea, and he made some stipulations: the movement was to be reserved for the sections using "He," that is to say, the moments in which the man invents the story of his doubling, the scenario with the man lying on his back, in the dark, with the voice that speaks to him. And in those moments when "You" is used, in the moments of recollection, of memory (Beckett's autobiographical recollections), Beckett envisioned total immobility, the immobilized machine, with a change in the lighting. He also asked me— we discussed this at great length—to reduce the movement, to make smaller movements. That would be magnificent because one would see a head that moved in space in a totally mysterious manner, magically.

I began to work with the actor, Pierre Dux, and it became evident that the machine was going to be very unwieldy. The more we tried, the worse it got. It was quite an affair with the whole lighting system inside it. We couldn't use exterior lights without having it be obvious that it was a machine that was moving in space. We wanted the audience to see only a face moving mysteriously in the dark: the machine became a kind of monster. It became too important, and the stage designers fell behind schedule.

It also turned out that when I began *Compagnie* Pierre Dux rehearsed on the stage of the Théâtre du Rond-Point in an armchair, without moving at all. I said to myself: "After all, why look for complications? It's fine like that. The man is immobile in an armchair, and all that's necessary to pass from 'He' to 'You' and 'You' to 'He' would be a change in lighting. That would work very well." I told this to Beckett. Evidently, it didn't fall on deaf ears. Beckett liked anything simple; that was the mainstay of all his work.

Then the machine arrived, and it was extraordinary. It had a chain drive system to produce an entire series of movements: to advance toward the audience, to retreat upstage, to move across the stage on an angle. It was very complicated, very delicate to manipulate. It also had a steering wheel for different kinds of maneuvers and for shifting from one type of movement to another.

So, we began to rehearse, and Beckett was supposed to be there for the first rehearsal onstage. The first rehearsal with the machine was a catastrophe! It's always like that in the theater when one begins to introduce material elements, when the set, props, and costumes are brought in. But this was even worse because the machine had never been used before. It was a new invention. And furthermore, as the machine was very heavy, it made a terrible noise. The stage creaked and groaned.

There were some extraordinarily beautiful movements—for example, when the machine traveled toward the public. But otherwise it was "crap." We started wondering how we were going to cope with it. In fact, I let things run, and we ran the play through to the end. I said to myself: "We can't show this to Beckett. It's really not fair. It's the first time that we're rehearsing." And then I said to myself: "So what! We'll run it through to the end. Drain the cup of bitterness, even to the dregs." Amid the absurd bungling of the machine and the lighting I had the whole text recited through, and at the end of the rehearsal I accompanied Beckett to the exit, which I always did, because at the Théâtre du Rond-Point we always worked in the little room in the basement. I went up the stairs with him, and at a certain point he turned toward me and said, "Do you want me to speak frankly?" I said yes. So he said: "You should throw the damn thing away."

After a rehearsal like that, and with my own misgivings, I wasn't surprised but, rather, relieved. I expected Beckett to say to me: "Give it all up." So, I replied almost instantly: "You're right, of course, but, on the other hand, we can't use tape recordings for the 'You.' The voice must be live, with a microphone." In short, consciously or not, I was trading the machine for the microphone. I could well see that the idea of the machine was impossible to actualize in so little time. We would have had to change the entire floor of the stage.

I had seen very quickly, though, that Beckett's idea (a taped voice, as in *Solo* or *Berceuse*) wasn't at all acceptable to the actor. He didn't like it. He couldn't agree to being the "listener," to listening to the voice. That didn't work. And besides, Pierre Dux had wanted to do this text because he liked it immensely. So, for him the idea of recording was horrifying. He wanted to speak the lines, especially the "You," the memories, the stories.

I traded Beckett my idea of the machine for another idea, the microphone. He no doubt accepted it in order to avoid any further chaos. For me it was evident that we had to give up the machine, though it was quite useful, because, when we had to look for a place for the actor's armchair, we found the ideal place inside the machine. And it was great, because the machine had its own integrated lighting system. It was a miniature stage onstage, and the audience couldn't see where the lighting came from. Everything was hidden, and that made for a strange lighting. In fact, all the work we had done for the machine was not for naught, far from it.

LO: You really didn't agree, then, with Beckett about the voice in *Compagnie?*

PC: Beckett had explained to me that for him the voice had to be recorded. I had tried to do it with Pierre Dux, and it really didn't work. But I saw from the beginning that there were two very different hypotheses: either the recorded voice or the voice over a microphone. I preferred the invisible microphone. And that was the solution that I finally adopted.

Once this decision was made, without consulting each other, Beckett and I came up with exactly the same idea: namely, that for the "You" passages we would, using lighting, cut the face just above the mouth. The spectators wouldn't be able to see that it was the man who was speaking. I thought that the idea and the realization of it was magnificent, because the spectator was forced to wonder who was really speaking. One couldn't really know if it was the actor who was speaking or if he were simply lip-synching like singers do on television. The audience wouldn't be able to figure it out because the voice would move in space (so there were multiple sources of sound). I found that this worked perfectly with the play, as the voice has an exteriority—because the character hears the voice, it's a voice that speaks to him—but it's also a voice that comes from within him. Thus, for me it fit perfectly the ambiguity of the text.

I thought that Beckett, who hadn't seen the play with an audience, would have gone along with this idea of a microphone. But that was by no means so. Sometime not long before his death he reproached me vigorously for it, and that threw me. To see a man, so close to death, reproach me so vehemently for an idea of staging not in keeping with his directions. . . . I find it very moving that he spoke to me so frankly, and it still affects me profoundly. I think that there is a lesson to be learned from this, because I thought that I had been faithful, unbelievably faithful, to his text. But in his reproach he was saying something very important, namely: the "voice" that I speak of so tenaciously in my work is a truly exterior voice. That voice is outside of me. I believe that that's a very important point for understanding his work, the process of creation, and his particular genius.

LO: And the next time?

PC: The next time, as a matter of fact, I had spoken with Beckett about it. We had gotten into a discussion of *Compagnie* because I said to him, "You know, I'm leaving soon for Spain to do *Compagnie,*" and it was at this moment that he said to me, "Fine, but this time you will do it with the recorded voice."

LO: And you did?

PC: No, not at all. Beckett had died since our conversation, and I determined that the microphone idea was what needed to be done. I talked it over with the actor, who was himself a great enthusiast of Beckett and who had seen my production in Paris. For him, too, it was obvious. It was not at all interesting for the actor to use a recorded voice. I chose to use a microphone because I thought that it was the best solution. I believe that a director also has the right to have ideas insofar as he remains absolutely faithful to the essence of the text, which I do. Even if Beckett didn't agree. And so I decided, along with the actor, to use a mike, because we saw that the other solution didn't work, didn't satisfy us.

LO: I must admit that I have never met a director who claimed not to have been faithful to the essence of a text. Even those who move very far from Beckett maintain that they, too, are . . .

PC: They are insincere.

LO: Were there other disagreements?

PC: That was the only real disagreement that I had with Beckett.

LO: And when you acted in plays that Beckett directed were there any "clashes"?

PC: Perhaps at certain moments I wasn't able to realize his every direction, but when I am acting I try to stick as close as possible to the directions. And once again, *Compagnie* is something very special; it's a text that was not written for the theater . . .

LO: You wouldn't make such changes in a text written for the theater?

PC: No. For *Berceuse* the actress who did the play in French didn't want her lines to be recorded. Actors don't like having the text taped. They miss out on the enjoyment of speaking their lines. But in this case I was uncompromising. I said to her: "That's not possible! The play was written that way." And the matter was settled in two seconds. For me there was no question of changing anything whatsoever.

But with *Compagnie* it is different insofar as the text was not written for the stage. Naturally, I had Beckett's stage direction, but, in my estimation, what I did was profoundly in keeping with what Beckett was all about.

LO: Could you elaborate on what you have learned about directing from Beckett?

PC: I learned everything from Sam Beckett. He gave me everything. He taught me artistic *necessity* and the necessity of the text to its staging. He taught me respect, respect for the text, as for any other living form. He taught me exigency. He taught me love. Not by words but by example. What does it mean to "make theater" if all that isn't there? He taught me that fundamental thing of the absolute connection between aesthetics and ethics: the passionate search for truth, the refusal of all facile effect and vulgar gratuity, insulting to oneself and to others. I learned everything from him, or, rather, I have everything to learn from him, constantly. I won't say any more about it, but that will be understood.

On a more practical level Beckett taught me precision and simplicity, the most unequivocal simplicity. And I learned to play a lot on the music and not on the superficial meaning. But I must also say that you have to be very careful with Beckett's own stagings.

LO: In what sense?

PC: Beckett had genius, and he had it also as a director. But one must not try to imitate it. That's important to realize. I think that it's very dangerous to imitate Beckett because one risks only imitating the surface, catching only the mannerisms. It's also dangerous to fail to bring into play one's own sensibility and that of the actors with whom one is working. For example, I know that there are little things that bother me in Beckett's productions. So, I do something different. But again, I find him brilliant. Though I believe that he could demand certain things of the actors.

LO: For instance?

PC: He could demand anything of the actors because he was Samuel Beckett. He was the playwright and the director. He could require that the actors conform entirely to what he wanted and to the way in which he understood his text. But we can't do that. We have neither the authority nor the right.

I felt this very strongly when I saw the production of *Godot,* which is absolutely remarkable, brilliant, and also when Beckett directed me in *La dernière bande.* And I saw it very clearly when I watched the video of *Oh les beaux jours* with Billie Whitelaw while I was preparing my produciton of that piece.

Naturally, Beckett's productions are always a point of departure for my own. That is to say that, having known Beckett as I knew him, knowing the value of his work as a director, which is somthing extremely precious, extremely rich, if I didn't consult his directions, his notes or the videos of his work, I would be a Philistine, an ass. I believe that to be an enrichment that I don't have the right not to make use of, and I even believe that one must go farther.

Everything that Beckett wrote in his notes is a part of the text of the play; it integrates itself into the text. So, I make use of it. But I separate from him a little, because I find that through his desire to always be extremely musical he has a tendency to "mechanize" the actors somewhat.

My aesthetic, or my poetic, is the following: there must be respect for the form, thus for the music, but at the same time something very human, something a little more natural. Now in Beckett's productions, due to his desire for musicality, its preeminence, there is something that runs counter to the natural and that sometimes evokes something artificial.

I felt this in *Godot* and in *Oh les beaux jours* with Billie Whitelaw, which is an absolutely fantastic production. At certain moments, however, I find that Billie Whitelaw (who is an actress whom I like and profoundly admire) is a little affected, not natural. She appears somewhat like a mechanical puppet whose strings, one knows, are being pulled by Beckett himself. But there is also something very moving in that. To see that woman who is basically a sort of doll, that also has its beauty, and that brings us back to what I was saying earlier. Like the woman being rocked, she is a little like Beckett's doll, she is being rocked by Beckett. That's wonderful, isn't it? And most of the time it is sublime. And yet, personally, I am inclined to find a certain balance between this form, this musicality, and something more natural, something closer to life.

So, Beckett leaned toward music, and music basically goes against what is "natural" in the theatrical interpretation of a text. Personally, I think that one must find an equilibrium that tends toward something more human, something that has a more spontaneous feel to it.

LO: But isn't this mechanical quality related to Beckett's direction of Billie as an individual? In other words, doesn't it derive from the rapport between the director and the actor? Wouldn't it have been different with another actress?

PC: Certainly. But this conception is customary for Beckett. He had this extremely musical vision of an actor's work. Of course, Billie Whitelaw is a person who had sufficient experience with Beckett and who had enough modesty, admiration, and savoir faire to be able to achieve exactly what he wanted. Few actors have gone so far toward attaining what he was after, toward achieving his theatrical vision. But I also saw this mechanization in *Godot.*

For me it has to do with oiling the machine, with not adhering too strictly to an overly brutal and somewhat mechanizing form. For the actor it is a matter of discovering within himself the truth of everything that he does, and that includes the musicality. The musicality must never be merely a veneer but, rather, the expression of this inner discovery. This balance is very difficult to achieve. The actor must find the inner necessity for the music.

LO: Does the mechanical quality come in part from the fact that Beckett had everything blocked before rehearsals began?

PC: Yes, it comes from several things. Beckett heard, very precisely, the words, the sentences, that he had created. Having worked on them, he heard them in a certain very precise manner. He knew exactly how they had to be said. So, it came from his work with the word itself and from the fact that he demanded that the actors say the lines just as he did. He could allow himself to do this, as I said, but no one other than Beckett can, except for the plays that are entirely musical and rhythmic, like *Berceuse.* But there are plays that are more "realistic": *Godot, Fin de partie, Oh les beaux jours.* And there are degrees of musicality. The Beckett director cannot simply apply Beckett's ideas as though they were a mathematical formula. We absolutely must avoid doing to Beckett what was done to Brecht. A sort of Brechtian convention developed, which gave rise to productions of disgusting conformity after his death. They were nothing but copies, and there was, basically, only one schema, which was hollow, because what Brecht did only Brecht could do. People took piles of photos and tried to reproduce Brecht's productions. That doesn't work. With Beckett it's just the same. That must never be done.

LO: So, you see a difference between yourself and Beckett with regard to how natural a production should be. Could you indicate some other differences?

PC: That's the main difference. But I know that the notion of "natural" is completely relative. So, I put the word in quotes.

It's linked to another fundamental aspect: a director must always be open to all the nuances of new interpreters. A good or exceptional interpretation is always a surprise. It allows the work to be seen or heard in a new manner. Think of some great interpreters of music, Glenn Gould, for example. . . . The interpretation transforms a work; it transmits something that was hidden, something enigmatic, something that Wilhelm Klempff, the interpreter of Beethoven, called "hidden forces," and which he compared to radium. Perhaps it must be said that I am against anything arbitrary, against everything that does not emanate, organically, from within the interpreter. I would argue, therefore, for more invention, for an "evolution" that would create itself from itself and that I am incapable of predicting. For every creation is a surprise. In fact, nothing, absolutely nothing, opposes me to Beckett. On the contrary. I simply reveal the interpreter's point of view, or "voice."

Who can play Winnie? A great actress. And this great actress must be able to give—of course, within very precise limits—all her feelings as a human being, the whole range of her talent, the whole measure of her humanity, of her living being, and of her inner self. And for this the director must be very aware of what she is doing, of what she can do, and must have a dialogue with her while directing her. He must let her act while guiding her and while drawing on the things that she has invented. There must be more inventions. It must evolve; it's obligatory.

I believe that to reproduce exactly what Beckett wanted is impossible. But I make a distinction with regard to the principal stage directions, which are fundamental and inviolable. For example, in *Oh les beaux jours* there is Winnie buried to the waist and then Winnie buried to the neck. That must not be changed. There are certainly many ways in which it can be done, but the image must be maintained.

Beckett's direction in French is *"étendue d'herbe brûlée"* ["expanse of scorched grass," Beckett's trans.—LO]. There are a thousand ways to visualize, to concretize, this *étendue d'herbe brûlée*. Should it suggest blackness, because the *herbe brûlée* is black? Or red? Or something sandy like in the magnificent set by Matias, which was all in ocher tones? That remains part of the interpretation.

LO: What did you choose?

PC: I was obsessed by the whole question of the set and the stage design for that piece. Fundamentally, it's all linked to a question of lighting. The lighting is fundamental in Beckett's theater and, in particular, in *Oh les beaux jours,* since it is the light, in addition to the bell, that forces Winnie to wake up, to speak, to continue. Personally, therefore, I found that the lighting had to be of primary importance, and, to that end, it had to be concentrated in space. I put a great deal of effort into this idea, and all of my productions of Beckett have been based on the lighting. Of course, there is the text, with all its musicality. But as far as the visual is concerned, the lighting is, for me, fundamental. I've worked a great deal on this, and I've gained inspiration from certain painters.

I believe that Beckett was sensitive to this vision. It has to do with a lighting that is very tightly delineated in space, that is gathered together, concentrated. For example, I saw Alan Schneider's production of *L'impromptu d'Ohio,* which was done in Paris in 1981, in which he used very bright lighting, which illuminated the whole stage, the whole table. When I read the text afterward I said to myself, "That's odd." And I asked Beckett what he thought about it, because in Alan Schneider's production there was a kind of strong, very raw, very violent lighting. He said to me, "He did that?" He was very surprised. And I told him that I saw something very different, something very nocturnal, corresponding to the atmosphere of the play. And when I directed *L'impromptu d'Ohio* I condensed the lighting with my lighting designer, my set designer, and we broke up the table a little. We didn't really break it up, but in order to concentrate the focus on the two characters we were led to pool all the light upon them and to slightly obscure the other half of the table. That was quite a job— very, very elaborate.

So, the work that I did on *Oh lex beaux jours* is a continuation of that work, a very condensed lighting. It was also the lighting for *Compagnie,* thanks to that machine, a lighting focused very much on the faces, in which we broke up even the faces of the "Listener."

I was haunted by the idea of the primacy of the lighting, and I awoke one night with a vision that the set for *Oh les beaux jours* should be black, grayish black, because it's thanks to the black that the light can be focused. If one were to do as it was done earlier in France by Matias (and, once again, it was magnificent, ocher, the color of sand, the desert), then the lighting invades the entire space.

"*Lumière aveuglante*" ["blazing light," Beckett's trans.—LO], Beckett indicated. But *aveuglante* for whom? For Winnie, not for the set and what surrounds her. That's very different. I found that a lighting that was very concentrated on the characters fit much better with Beckett's notion of lighting, which is both a physical and metaphysical "principle." That's what pushes Winnie to speak, and there, already, is the idea that will be exploited subsequently in *Comédie,* in which "light provokes speech."

I was therefore led to distinguish between the principal stage direction, which must be respected to the letter (Winnie buried to the waist then to the neck) and the secondary directions—for example, the direction concerning the "*toile de fond très pompier*" ["very pompier backcloth," Beckett's trans.—LO], which is so extremely difficult to create. Naturally, that's a very interesting direction, because it introduces the whole dimension of artificiality, of art, of theatrical representation. This is exactly the kind of stage direction that must be interpreted in order to find a subtle equivalent.

In our version, with Yannis Kokkos, this equivalent is a frame set on the stage, or inside the frame of the stage, if there is one. The aim of this frame is, first, to concentrate the audience's attention on Winnie. Also, it gives a certain mystery to the mound that emerges from the frame, its lower part, while not letting the audience see that it rests on the ground. The mound appears suspended. But this frame also combines several ideas or images: that of a theater stage, that of a theater "box," that of a painting or a film screen.

In sum, the frame, in addition to its beauty and the advantages just described, suggests to the audience: you don't have reality before you but, instead, a representation. So, it is an "interpretation," but, in my opinion, it is very close to the stage direction of the text.

LO: You are very well-known as a director of Beckett's works, but you have never done either *En attendant Godot* or *Fin de partie*. This seems to me to be somewhat paradoxical. Would you like to direct them?

PC: It is, in fact, very paradoxical, but at the same time this paradox pleases me greatly. You must take into account how extraordinary, but also terribly difficult, it was to do Beckett here in Paris, first because of the prestige of Paris and then because of the many presences—that of Beckett himself, who came to my last rehearsals (though Beckett's presence was always a fantastic help to me), that of Roger Blin, the first director of Beckett, and so on.

I think that it was out of a kind of discretion that I was slightly intimidated. Beckett was undoubtedly waiting for me to attempt these "great plays." But I kept delaying. It was only a few months before his death that I spoke with him about a production of *Oh les beaux jours* (and there again there was the presence of Madeleine Renaud, who had played the part for almost thirty years).

To answer your question: of course, I would like to direct these other plays. But that is not really the issue. Would my direction of a play of Beckett's bring something of value to Beckett's works? We'll see this autumn when my production of *Oh les beaux jours* opens. Can I bring something new, something interesting, something useful, something inventive, to his work? Can I help his work evolve while remaining completely true to it? If I can, then, of course, I would love to direct these plays. It's quite normal—the interpretation of a work and its reception evolve with time. One must not interfere with that. That would be contrary to the very spirit of Beckett. And I want always to act in Beckett's interest. Always, and, if possible, more and more.

Edward Albee

EDWARD ALBEE is the author of some twenty-two plays, winner of three Pulitzer Prizes (For *A Delicate Balance, Seascape,* and *Three Tall Women*) and numerous other awards, including the Drama Critics Award for Best Play for *Who's Afraid of Virginia Woolf?* and a member of the faculty of the University of Houston–Texas. He has directed many of his own plays and three of Samuel Beckett's, *Krapp's Last Tape* and *Ohio Impromptu,* at the Alley Theatre in Houston in 1991, and *Happy Days,* which opened in Houston in January 1993. This interview was compiled from conversations in New York in June and September of 1992.

LOIS OPPENHEIM: What was your first Beckett experience?

EDWARD ALBEE: I don't know when I first became aware of Beckett's work. I probably started reading him as soon as he was published in English. My first Beckett play may well have been *Krapp's Last Tape* in Berlin, where my play *The Zoo Story* was done with it in 1959. Or I may have seen *Endgame* in New York before then.

I certainly became aware of him fairly early, and he was, along with Chekhov and Pirandello, the most profound influence on my own dramatic aesthetic. Not that I think I write particularly like any one of them, but certainly what Beckett taught me about comedy and precision, clarity and humor, was terribly important to me as a playwright.

LO: Why did you wait so long to direct Beckett?

EA: Respecting Beckett as much as I do, knowing how precise he is as a playwright with language and with stage directions, and knowing what a stickler he is for nondistortion, as a director I wanted to be able to approach his work with all of my equipment, and that's why I moved slowly, to make sure I was ready. I started off directing in 1962, and it took me a while. I guess by the time I directed *Seascape* on Broadway in 1975 I felt I was a good director.

I never direct plays that I don't respect or like. But directing someone else's work is a different matter from directing my own work, especially the first performance, when quite often I am making changes, doing a final polishing, because something that works on the page doesn't necessarily work on the stage. While I make fewer changes in production in plays of mine than most other playwrights do—it is mostly cutting with me—it's a different matter to direct somebody else's work.

LO: Why did you choose to direct *Krapp's Last Tape* and *Ohio Impromptu* first?

EA: When it came time to direct Beckett at the Alley Theatre in Houston, I was going to be using the small theater-in-the-round downstairs, which in certain ways limits what you can do. I wanted to do *Happy Days,* but you can't do *Happy Days* in-the-round unless you revolve Winnie, and that would look sort of silly.

Maybe I also had the thought that the Houston audience, not necessarily being as sophisticated as some others, might be happier with two short plays than one long one. And I thought it would be fun to do two of Beckett's plays that I admired greatly. It was a sort of reunion with *Krapp's Last Tape,* and *Ohio Impromptu* was such an extraordinary experience when I saw Alan Schneider's production in New York. They seemed to be plays that were so different and yet so much the same—one a voluble play and the other down to silence and essence—and I thought they were an interesting contrast.

LO: You stopped a production of *Who's Afraid of Virginia Woolf?* in Texas when the director wanted to cast four men and a production of *The Zoo Story* because two actresses wanted to do it. And yet in your productions of Beckett's plays you took a number of liberties.

EA: You're mistaken; I didn't take "liberties." I've stopped many productions of my own plays for various reasons. I don't believe that distorting the playwright's intentions is permissible. I find it reckless and destructive. It is reckless to change a play. It is reckless to rewrite it. It is reckless to cut it or to change the sex of the characters. There is a fine line between interpretation and distortion. When people are adventuresome within the bounds of reason I am happy. When they do damage to the play or distort it to show off what clever directors they are I get very annoyed.

We have to remember that the playwright is the creative artist. The

Fig. 3. Edward Albee's production of *Ohio Impromptu* with Charles
Sanders (Listener) and Lou Ferguson (Reader) at the Alley Theatre,
Houston, 1991. Photo credit: Jim Caldwell.

director and the actors are the interpretive artists. Interpretation does not
permit distortion. Would anybody tolerate a pianist getting on a stage to
perform a Beethoven piano sonata and rewriting it or playing it on a
saxophone? Nobody would tolerate that. Why should anybody tolerate it
in a play? These things are intolerable because they are destructive.

In *Krapp's Last Tape* the only adjustments—and I won't say changes,
because I didn't make any changes, aside from one, which I will tell you
about—the only adjustments I made were to alter certain stage directions
because it was for theater-in-the-round. The audience had to be involved
on all sides. I translated Beckett's stage directions from proscenium theater
to theater-in-the-round and made what was valid for one valid for the
other. I did not alter the play.

The one change I did make turned out to be something that Beckett
had done in a production that he had directed of the play. The last time
that Krapp goes to get a drink he goes off stage and then comes back and
puts a new tape on and starts recording. The more I looked at that in
rehearsal, the more it came clear to me that he shouldn't go offstage that
last time. It breaks the intellectual and emotional continuity of what Krapp

is thinking about. He should start to go offstage, stop, turn, look at the tape recorder, and then come back and record. I said, "This is the way it should be." So, that is what I did. I crossed my fingers. Was I taking a chance here? Was I doing something that would make Sam very unhappy?

At a symposium a couple of weeks into the run of the play I believe it was Bob Scanlan who told me that Beckett himself had done this when he directed it somewhere. I felt rather pleased that what I had done was exactly what Beckett did. I don't think even any purist to the point of absurdity would have objected to anything I did in *Krapp's Last Tape.*

With *Ohio Impromptu,* I don't think I made any changes. Everything was exactly as Sam wrote it. Only in my production the text was repeated twice. It was done three times—in other words, with two repetitions.

LO: Why? What made you decide that doing it once was not enough?

EA: Whether we like it or not, it does take a trained theater listener to absorb, especially in the late Beckett plays, everything that is happening. I've seen more than one short Beckett play that has been performed twice in succession, and once I even saw one performed three times in succession, so that people would have the experience not only once.

With *Ohio Impromptu* it occurred to me that it would be an interesting thing to do. But I didn't want to do just a literal repetition. I tried to find some way to make the repetition involving and interesting and persuasive, without doing any damage to Beckett's intention and without distorting. What I did was realize that there is a speaker, who comes many, many times, and a listener, and Beckett says toward the end of the play that "they grew to be as one." He does not say that they became the same person.

LO: Does it not say at the beginning of the play, however, that their appearance is as alike as possible?

EA: Yes, it does, indeed. And that's why I made them as alike as possible.

LO: With an interracial cast?

EA: Yes, what I had was black and white. These are not colors. They are opposites, and they are, therefore, the same. I had one white actor and one black actor, black and white being the totality of color and the absence of color.

LO: How did the repetitions differ?

EA: The three times that the play was performed I had the actors alternate position and identity. There was a slightly different light on the table each time, and the actors didn't reverse their positions, but they changed position. Also, the white actor was the speaker first, while the black actor was the listener. The second time the black actor was the speaker and the white actor was the listener. The third time they alternated lines.

LO: So there was no special significance to your doing it three times as opposed to any other number of times?

EA: No, except for the sake of clarity. The play suggests that what is happening keeps on happening. We see three of the occurrences. I tried it once. That was not enough. I tried it again. And I realized we had to do it a third time. I wanted the audience to have the intensity of the Beckett experience. The Houston audience is not so familiar with the avant-garde, and I don't think that any theater should be only for the cognoscenti, only for the intellectual, or for the professional. With a play that strict and that spare it takes people a little while to get used to what is going on. It runs only seven minutes, so it would have been over before the audience had even begun to relax into the nature of it.

But I certainly didn't alter the text. I wanted perhaps to amplify it. I'd like to think that, if Beckett had seen the production, he would have liked it. A number of people who respect Beckett tell me they think he would have. All of this comes up, I suppose, because Beckett was so strict about what was done with his work, even though he did make changes when he was directing and supervising other people's directing. If you read some of his instructions to actors from one production to another, you see that they are almost diametrically opposed.

There has been some fuss over the past few years about people who have done productions of Beckett's plays in which they changed the environment. There was the one in Cambridge, in which *Endgame* was done down in the subway, deep, deep under the earth, when it is meant to be not outdoors but certainly up on the surface. That brings in all sorts of strange sociological connotations, and, though I didn't see it, it strikes me as changing the work in a way that I would never change Beckett. It would seem to alter the kind of no-man's-land that Beckett was after.

LO: I suppose you are particularly sensitive to this issue being a playwright yourself.

EA: Yes. You take the trouble to write the words in a specific way . . .

Now, on the other hand, I plan to do a production of Shakespeare's *Macbeth,* and I'm going to set it in East Hampton [New York], because

I've decided that the whole thing works very nicely with upwardly mobile yuppies who get involved in the drug racket.

LO: But doesn't this contradict all that you have just said?

EA: No, it doesn't. I'm not going to change the essence of Shakespeare, nor will I change a word.

LO: But JoAnne Akalaitis would say the same thing of her *Endgame*, that she didn't "change the essence" of Beckett's play.

EA: She moved the set underground.

LO: And you're moving the set to East Hampton.

EA: I don't see that as a distortion. I'm not making any sociological comment the way going underground does. Akalaitis went further than just setting the play underground. These are homeless people. That is a distortion.

LO: In other words, the underground set implies a social context that distorts the play's intention?

EA: Yes. What I plan will not distort what Shapespeare intended.

LO: If *Macbeth* were a Beckett play, would you take the same kind of liberty?

EA: No, I certainly would not.

LO: Why does it work for Shakespeare and not for Beckett?

EA: One has to make a Shakespeare play as clear, as persuasive, and as moving to a contemporary audience as one possibly can. I am not William Ball, who felt the need to rewrite Shakespeare's plays when he directed them in San Francisco. I wouldn't dream of rewriting Shakespeare. I wouldn't dream of rewriting Beckett. Sometimes I wouldn't even think about rewriting myself!

The Shakespeare plays were written four hundred years ago. Everybody knows them terribly well. I thing there is a way of refracting them slightly differently, seeing them from a slightly different point of view. I happen to believe that *Macbeth* is a play about upwardly mobile yuppies. And I think it is very interesting to do that.

I went to see Peter Brook's production of *The Tempest* a year ago in Vienna. To me that production was the essence of *The Tempest*. Not a word was changed. It certainly all seemed to be there. But I don't imagine that Shakespeare envisioned *The Tempest* taking place in a huge rectangle filled with sand, with the formality of Asian theater. I don't think he imagined Asian musicians to one side. I don't think he imagined that Miranda was from India, that the king was Japanese, that Prospero himself was North

African, that Ariel was from the deepest Africa, and that Caliban was German. I don't think that Shakespeare imagined any of that, but there was *The Tempest* seen and thought afresh. That distinction seems valid to me. Maybe it is the four hundred years.

LO: Well, four hundred years from now would you resituate a Beckett play? From what you have said I don't think you would.

EA: Since I have found nowhere that Shakespeare gives very specific instructions on anything—minimal stage directions, no line readings that have come down to us—I think that one is allowed a certain, not leeway, not distortion, but finding of other ways into the core of the text. But Beckett is so precise and so specific. You conduct the work. It is like music. The rhythms, the sounds, the durations of the silences, the pauses, are all so specific. If we had that in Shakespeare, if it were there, if we had a rehearsal text, then I imagine the whole world of Shakespeare would be different; the Shakespeare performance would be quite different.

LO: How did you work with the actors when you were directing *Krapp's Last Tape* and *Ohio Impromptu?* Did you have actors experienced with Beckett's work, or were they mystified by the scripts?

EA: I worked very differently with each play.

LO: In what way?

EA: In *Krapp's Last Tape* I counted every mote of dust on the set, put everything where it should be, and spent time talking about how much dust should rise from the ledger when it closed, for example. I was concerned with everything about the reality of the man, the subtext of the man. It was completely an Actors Studio approach.

With *Ohio Impromptu* it was exactly the opposite. I said: "You are a reader. You are a listener. This has been happening over and over again." I talked about nothing but the rhythms. Interesting that you can direct two plays so differently. I was an Actors Studio director for one, and I was a conductor for the other.

LO: Are there any particular attributes that might make one director more successful in working with Beckett's plays than another?

EA: I think it would be difficult for some people to direct Beckett. It would be difficult for anybody who thinks the text is there as a starting point, who thinks that the text is there to mess with. That person is going to have a lot of problems.

A profound knowledge of classical music would help because there is so much music in Beckett, and he knew music so well. He heard as well as saw so precisely. He heard duration. He heard lilt. It is interesting that my two favorite twentieth-century playwrights, Chekhov and Beckett, are highly musical. Any director who does not understand the music of Beckett, who can't hear in that way, who doesn't have the training and ability to think musically, would be incapable of directing Beckett properly.

A playwright needs the ability to write, the ability to be a composer, and the ability to be a visual artist. And the director needs, requires, the ability to *see* the playwright's vision as the playwright saw it, not to translate it into the director's vision. This doesn't lead to identical productions, necessarily.

LO: Did you appreciate Alan Schneider's directing of Beckett's work as much as his directing of your own?

EA: I think Alan did a very, very good job with Beckett's work. He stood to one side. He guided the work and let it happen. Alan did not impose.

LO: He is occasionally faulted for that.

EA: Yes, but Beckett doesn't need any help. Beckett doesn't need any improvement. He doesn't need that new point of view that the director's ego imposes. The director's responsibility with Beckett is to put what is on the page on the stage with absolute clarity. Beckett can stand on his own feet. I've seen Beckett productions that I thought were trying to help too much.

LO: Did Alan work with Beckett's plays differently than he worked with yours?

EA: I never sat in on a rehearsal of one of Sam's plays that Alan directed. I would imagine that he asked Sam a number of questions, a whole long list of questions, as he did with me. He wanted to be sure that he was directing the play that the author wrote.

Alan would come to me before rehearsals, before we even started rehearsing, with hundreds of questions. It startled me the first time he did it. I didn't know I was supposed to know all these things. I realized pretty soon that I had all the answers but that I just hadn't been thinking about them. I became aware of what I hadn't known that I knew. I had all the answers, but I hadn't translated them into something I consciously knew. I knew the nature of the characters, but I hadn't had to put it down, except in the lines that I gave the characters. When Alan started asking me questions about subtext and the backgrounds of the characters, I didn't have to invent. All of a sudden I instantly knew it. And Alan made me aware of a good deal about the creative procedure.

LO: As a director, he prepared everything in advance. Do you do that?

EA: No, I don't. I know the way it should go. I have some visual pictures and some sense of where people are going to be.

LO: As a playwright, do you find yourself directing as you write?

EA: When I'm writing a play, I see it, and I hear it being performed on the stage. I'm sure Beckett did also.

LO: Are you aware of your audience?

EA: No, I don't think about the audience. I just think about the experience of the play being done onstage. The audience is implied, of course. I see the play as a performed piece, obviously before an audience, certainly before the audience of me. I have discovered, to my amazement, that when some playwrights are writing a play, while they're writing it, they don't see it being performed on the stage.

LO: How can they not?

EA: They see it as some kind of amorphous reality. They don't see the necessary artifice of the stage at work.

LO: And you do and Beckett did?

EA: Yes, very specifically onstage. That distancing, that removal.

LO: For those who don't there isn't much difference between writing for the stage and writing fiction.

EA: They are writing something theoretically for the stage. But it has to go that extra jump and be translated by the director.

LO: Then what you are saying is that you feel an affinity with Beckett in writing something inherently theatrical from the start, something already directed, in a sense, from the beginning?

EA: Yes, and it doesn't need anything but to be put on its feet as written.

LO: You have mentioned the musical element and the theatricality. Any other affinities with Beckett?

EA: An interest in painting. Beckett was very interested in it, and this shows up in his work. I think that's important for a playwright, since a play is music and painting, sculpture, and words as well. I think it's important for a playwright to have that.

LO: How do you feel about Beckett's prose works being done in the theater? Or the radio plays?

EA: I don't find that much difference between the so-called prose and the so-called plays. It's all one large prose work. It's all one large theater piece. It's all one piece.

LO: So, it doesn't bother you to see them transposed to the theater?

EA: Oh, no. Listen to the radio plays, the sound plays. Certainly

Beckett heard what he wrote more clearly than most writers, and it's the same ear, the same voice in the prose pieces, as it is in the plays. It's all the same person.

LO: What do you see as the future of Beckett's theater? Do you think it will become outrageously distorted and that directors will do ever more terrible things now that he is no longer here?

EA: What I worry about is that he will become a prisoner of the academics. It's a parallel, though certainly not an exact parallel, to my play *Tiny Alice* done on Broadway. We did two weeks of previews. I wouldn't necessarily say that everybody in the audience liked the play, but nobody seemed particularly confused. The critics came and told them it was a very confusing play. Then they started going into the theater confused. If Beckett ever becomes the prisoner of humorless academics, then a lot of people are going to be turned off before they have had the joy of the experience. There is a Beckett industry. There is a Joyce industry and all sorts of other industries, of course.

LO: In a sense he probably already has fallen to the academics.

EA: I think it is happening.

LO: Why?

EA: Because the plays are not the kind of plays that the American audience theoretically wants: the synthetic happy ending experience, the ones that don't take you out of yourself and put you into the play. And that bothers a lot of people.

LO: Do you therefore think that Beckett's plays will not continue to reach any kind of real public in the next few years?

EA: I never know about the next few years. I'm more concerned about the next couple of hundred years. Beckett is going to be one of the few twentieth-century playwrights anybody will be paying any attention to two or three hundred years from now. I grew up, intellectually, on Ionesco, Beckett, and Genet. That's a far cry from any theater you can find anywhere now. It is too bad, but I don't notice that Mozart's string quartets are selling or that Satyajit Ray's or Akira Kurosawa's early films are constantly being performed. And a lot of us grew up on that being the standard.

LO: You will be doing *Happy Days* next year. Are there any particular difficulties you envision in directing that play?

EA: If I get the right actress—I'm honing in on one or two who I think would be wonderful, who have the peasant humor that I think is so important for that role—I think the play will take care of itself. It's context again. If people who come to the theater are used to seeing living rooms, they are going to be a little surprised seeing a lady buried up to her waist in the earth, up to her neck in the second act. But if they're willing to relax into that reality—it is not a convention; it is absolute reality—and say, "Yes, this is really happening to a real person," then there should be absolutely no problem. The play is completely clear.

LO: You won't be changing the locale? You won't be repeating it three times?

EA: No, it's a full evening. It's not a seven-minute play. It is not as compact as some of the other plays. And also there are a lot of repetitions in that play. Beckett repeats phrases and images throughout the play continually, which he does not do in a play like *Ohio Impromptu,* for example.

LO: And the set? I'm sure that poses a certain number of problems. Will you get involved?

EA: Yes, I'll try to make the set that I understand that Beckett was after. I was annoyed by a production I saw a while ago in Los Angeles, where the mound that Winnie sat in looked like a huge hoop skirt with vines coming down like lace. That is a distortion. It's a mound of earth, not a hoop skirt. I certainly don't think that that was what Beckett had in mind. It is a gradual mound of earth, and this was a hoop skirt that the actress could have gotten up and walked off with.

LO: You have said that the only Beckett play that you don't like a lot is *Godot.* Why?

EA: I think it's a fairly clumsy play. I think it's too "plotty." I think it hits its points over the head. It's repetitive without augmentation. I just don't find it as rich as some of the other plays. Mind you, I would rather see *Waiting for Godot* than almost anything that I get to see in New York these days. But it doesn't happen to be my favorite Beckett play.

LO: How do you feel about the two Beckett productions you have done? Did you achieve what you set out to achieve? If you were to direct *Krapp's Last Tape* and *Ohio Impromptu* again, would you do them in the same way?

EA: I'm pretty happy with them. If I had a different actor playing Krapp, I would not do it differently, but the actor must become the character, and no two actors become the character in exactly the same way. I wouldn't try to duplicate one performace with another.

LO: So, you would be obliged to make some changes with a different actor?

EA: No, not changes. We would arrive at the same destination, maybe a second and a half slower here and maybe a little bit differently over there. But the character would not change, nor would the text, of course, nor would the intention.

LO: Any other comments you would like to add with regard to your experience of directing Beckett?

EA: I'm having a lot of fun with it and learning, which is important.

Jan Jönson

JAN JÖNSON directed *Waiting for Godot* at the Swedish prison Kumla
(1985–86) and at California's San Quentin Prison (1987–88). The
San Quentin production was filmed as part of the Beckett Project
series produced and directed by John Reilly and Global Village,
and Jönson is completing a book about his work at both prisons,
to be published in the United States and Europe. What follows
is derived from his participation in the New York University
"Festival of Beckett and Joyce" and a series of conversations I
had with Jönson in Paris in July 1992.

Jan Jönson began his contribution to the directors' panel at New York
University by looking back over the beginnings of his career as an actor
in Sweden.

"I came to *Waiting for Godot* for the first time when I was fourteen
years old. I played the boy in a small theater in Gothenburg, Sweden.
The first time I went up on the stage I immediately fell deeply in love
with the characters, Vladimir and Estragon. Every performance I stood
in the wings and listened to them. Then, after about an hour, I went
onstage and gave them the message, 'Mr. Godot told me to tell you he
won't come this evening but surely to-morrow' and went off again to wait
until the end of the second act. I did that for one year.

"When I was nineteen I auditioned for the drama school at the
National Theater in Sweden. Of the ten texts we had to do for the jury
one was the end monologue of Vladimir: 'Was I sleeping, while the others
suffered?' I was accepted and was a student there for three years. The
whole last year we did *Waiting for Godot,* and I played Estragon. So, in a
way I grew up with Sam Beckett's *Waiting for Godot.*"

Jönson went on to explain that after school he became an actor at
the Royal Dramatic Theater, where one of the producers gave him a script,

The Man Himself, by Allen Drury. Following the final performance of a three-year run of Drury's play, the warden at Kumla prison came to Jönson's dressing room to invite him to perform the monologue for his inmates, "because they need to see something like this." Jönson obliged, and his performance at the prison was the beginning of a new career: "After that performance the inmates didn't applaud. It was totally quiet. They cried. One big man from Honduras asked me to please come back and teach them drama." Having never before directed or taught, Jönson offered simply to come back to read a play, *Waiting for Godot,* with the prisoners.

When I met with Jönson in Paris several months following the New York University panel, I asked about his casting of the reading, which soon grew into a full production of the play. He related the story of his return to Kumla some six months later—copies of the script, books about Beckett and Peter Brook's *The Empty Space* in hand. With twenty inmates eager to read, Jönson had them alternate characters after every scene.

"Then I saw this guy from Spain," Jönson said. "With his dialect, his way of looking at people, his way of listening to people, his way of sitting and looking out through the cell window, he was Vladimir for me. I don't know why. It was just a feeling."

"And at San Quentin was your casting equally intuitive?"

"Exactly, the same." At San Quentin, however, there were considerably more inmates enthusiastic about participating. It seems that when Jönson told the prisoners that he had taken the inmate-actors from Kumla on the road with *Godot* and that, despite an advance sale of sixteen-thousand tickets, the show never went on, as four of the five men escaped a few hours before the opening, twenty-five San Quentin prisoners poured into the room where Jönson was casting his new production.

With a knack for storytelling, Jönson related other of his more (in retrospect) amusing prison experiences, such as his first meeting with one of the officers at San Quentin. "What is the name of the play you are doing?" the officer wanted to know.

"The name of the play is *Waiting for Godot.*"

"Waiting for what?"

"Godot."

Perplexed, the officer turned to two big guards standing nearby. "Do I know him?" he inquired of them. And turning back toward Jönson: "Is Godot coming? Is he in the play?"

"No, he's not coming."

"Then who in the hell are you waiting for? Should everybody wait here?"

Returning to the Kumla production, the director talked about the international flavor of the cast. Few of the one hundred or so inmates at the Swedish facility were from Sweden, he explained, which means that the members of the cast of Beckett's play, reading in English, were from China, Spain, Honduras, Portugal, and Russia. Vladimir's line—"But at this place, at this moment of time, all mankind is us, whether we like it or not"—came immediately to mind.

I wondered about the influence of the directors Jönson had worked with at the Royal Dramatic Theater in Sweden, Ingmar Bergman and Alf Sjoberg, for example. Had they helped prepare him for his role as prison director? Not really, Jönson claimed. What helped him learn to direct was his ability to be a good listener.

"I told the guys, 'I don't know how to direct, but I can tell you why I love this play. I can tell you how much I love the characters and the silence of this play.' That's one way of directing. And then I sat there for about twelve months listening to these men talk to each other. It was very hard work for them, because it really opened them up. Hundreds and hundreds of different things happened every day! Strange, heavy, very heavy reactions! And they cried. One of the inmates said, 'Do you know what is happening here? You are giving me my life. This play is my diary. What Vladimir is thinking about and talking about, screaming about and crying and laughing about is me.' For him, the play was a kind of primal scream."

I asked if the prisoners had any difficulty taking direction from Jönson. He indicated that there was a difference in directing the inmates at Kumla, where the men knew that, eventually (usually after fifteen years), they would be set free, and directing at San Quentin, where for most there is no light ahead. At both prisons, however, the inmates changed radically over the course of their work with Jönson.

"In the beginning the prisoners were very shy, very scared, and they talked very softly, nearly so softly that I couldn't hear them. They were very nervous. Then they became stronger because they could express themselves."

"Did you try to make the inmates look like actors even though they didn't have the theater as their common focus the way professional actors do, even though they were not there to do *Godot* for the same reasons actors do it and had no previous acting experience?"

To answer Jönson contrasted the inmates' experience of playing *Godot* with his own as a young actor of fourteen. He described what it felt like to wait in the wings, listening to two friends speaking the parts of Vladimir and Estragon, enchanted with the poetry of Beckett's lines and the thrill of the stage.

And then: "When I came to these inmates, I said, 'You are not actors. I am not a director. The only thing you should think about when you are reading this play is not to answer the other man if you don't believe what he is saying. It is as simple as that. So many actors appear onstage talking at the same time they are thinking about other things. Don't talk to each other if you don't have the tennis ball over the net. It's impossible to send the ball back if the ball is going into the net.'"

"So, you were striving most of all for authenticity."

"Certainly, reality. I told them that we would begin like that and that we had years. We could work for years. I told them just to take it easy, to read the play and to make comments about it if they wanted to."

Jönson met with Beckett several times in Paris to discuss his work with the inmates. It was Beckett who encouraged Jönson to accept the invitation to San Quentin, and he was eager to know what was happening with particular parts of the play at different stages of rehearsal.

On one occasion he inquired about "the sound" of his play in the prison environment. He wanted to know what "the silence" of the play was like behind prison walls. Jönson describes the sound of the play as Spoon Jackson reciting, as Pozzo—"They give birth astride of a grave . . ."—in front of an audience that included his mother, whom he had not been permitted to see for many years.

The sound and silence of the play had additional meaning for Jackson: for several years he had protected himself against the reality of his life in the cell by not speaking a word. He wrote poetry but spoke to no one. When the play was in its early stages of casting and Jönson was unable to find a satisfactory Pozzo, he noticed "a big black guy standing in the door watching me very carefully like the Indian in *One Flew over the Cuckoo's Nest*." He was told he couldn't use Spoon Jackson because the man never spoke. Jönson was determined.

"I started to read Pozzo very loudly because I wanted to see his reaction. He started to listen. He stayed the whole day. When the day was over he disappeared. The next morning he was there again. Then he disappeared once more. The following morning he stood a little closer. By the end of that week he was coming in with a chair. He took his chair and put it back to back with mine. When I got to the place where I read, 'They gave birth astride of a grave, the light gleams an instant, then it's night once more,' he stood up, removed the chair with his feet, and stood in front of me face to face. He finished his cigarette, took off his dark glasses, gave me his hand, and said, 'My name is Spoon Jackson. Are you coming back here? Can you come back and give me the part of Pozzo and help me to express myself?' I said, 'Yes,' and then after a long silence he said, 'Can I trust you?' I told him I wanted him as Pozzo, and he said, 'Thank you. I'll see you tomorrow.'"

I asked Jönson about the differences between the Kumla and San Quentin productions.

"The Kumla was a kind of warm-up for the very big one, the San Quentin one, because at San Quentin I was in the bottom, in the 'roots of the play,' as Sam said."

He continued. "When Beckett saw [in photographs] these guys talking to each other with the scripts of his play, when he saw the set, he was sitting very quietly, and I saw his face, how it changed, how he was listening." After asking Jönson about his reasons for undertaking the prison production, Beckett offered his only comment: "I saw the roots of my play."

The most significant difference between the two productions as Jönson described them was the kind of talk that took place between the men as they acted. In San Quentin the inmates "really talked to each other," Jönson explained. "They didn't play theater. They were not acting. It was 100 percent reality. They were standing in the gym at San Quentin with their families sitting in front of them for the first time in years, and the warden and the director of the Department of Corrections were there. Behind the audience five gunmen were standing, pointing guns at these guys. If these actors treated the gunmen badly, the gunmen were allowed to kill them. If the gunmen felt scared of the inmates, they could shoot them. And then it would be over. That was how the rules were. There are signs at San Quentin that say, 'No warning shots.'

"When I was reading the line, 'To-morrow, when I wake, or think I do, what shall I say of to-day?,' Donald 'Twin' James (Vladimir) asked me, 'Who should I say this line to?' I told him: 'Your mother. She will be sitting in front of you. And beside her will be the warden and his boss, the director. The people in front of you are the people who are keeping you in prison and your family, the people you love, but will never see again. The audience hates you, and the audience loves you. And behind these people are the gunmen pointing at you with machine guns. Look at a gunman and look into his rifle.' That was how I directed.

"I told him: 'Look into the eyes of that man. For as long as you want. Let it take two minutes. Just wait out the silence, listening to it. Talk to him as a human being and ask him, 'What shall I say of today?' The beginning of the monologue is asking something. Ask him that question. Then you will be doing Samuel Beckett's play, *Waiting for Godot.*'"

"Were there ever any conflicts between you and any of the inmate-actors or problems between them that you had to resolve?"

"There was a problem with one man, a beautiful guy with a big beard who played Estragon. He was an amateur actor when he came into the prison, so he thought that he knew exactly how to do this play. He was white, and Twin was black. Sometimes he talked to Twin in the wrong way. I wanted to use Twin as he was. I didn't want him to be an actor. He was bluesy, and I didn't want to tell him he should play jazz. We had an argument. I met him two years later, and he took the script, signed for him by Sam, and gave it back to me through the bars. Then we had Happy Wilson instead."

Jönson never asked any of the inmates why they were in prison. Feeling very close to them, "like brothers," he avoided any discussion of their incarceration until one day they asked, "Aren't you interested in why your best friends on this planet are sitting in prison for the rest of their lives?"

Jönson answered that this was not at all important to him, that which deepened all the more his friendships with the men. Some weeks later, however, they determined that they must reveal to him, one by one, why they were at San Quentin. Jönson's reaction to the stories that they unfolded simply pointed to the "absurdity" of their situation: "I could be one of you. Or I could be in your cell, and you could be outside. It just happens that this is how life is."

Jönson was quick to articulate for me the connection between the situation of one of the inmates—J. B. Wells (Lucky), a Vietnam veteran who received life imprisonment, upon his return from the war, for causing one more death—and Beckett's play. "This is what the play is about," Jönson offered incredulously. Jönson's next project will be *Endgame,* to be undertaken at Beckett's suggestion. A film will be made of his work on this play with the inmates of the Folsom Prison in California by Pennebaker Associates, Inc. Asked whether the playwright had made any corrections in any of his texts to adapt them for the prison productions, Jönson explained how Beckett had changed some lines in *Endgame* so that it could be done with two males in the ash bins. He anticipates casting Twin as Hamm. Jönson also expressed a desire to direct Spoon Johnson in *Krapp's Last Tape*, which Beckett asked him to do as well.

The conversation then turned to other productions of *Godot*. Jönson was somewhat incensed as he spoke of the Mike Nichols's production at Lincoln Center in 1988. He took issue with the ad libbing: "That was not playing Beckett!" and with the set: "The stage was a desert with dead animals. There were bushes and trees and three or four stones."

What kind of set did you have at San Quentin?"

"We had a black carpet and black sets, a stone and a tree. I took the stone from the old prison wall. I especially wanted that stone because this meant sitting on a piece of something that locked these men up. I wanted them to sit on something they had a connection with."

"And the tree?"

"It was a real tree. Inside the prison there was a garden, which was dead. They gave it up because no one took care of it. So, I took one dead tree. It looked like a Giacometti. It was important to have that tree instead of a normal tree. I took five fresh leaves from a tree that was full of life. I didn't want leaves from Golden Gate Park, because that represents life. I had to have them from a tree growing inside San Quentin."

"What did you do about costumes?"

"They couldn't do the play in their prison clothes because they wear jeans, T-shirts, blue or white, and sneakers. I went to the ACT [American Conservatory Theatre] and took coats, bowler hats. . . . And the day when I came into the prison with the costumes and props was a historic day at San Quentin! I put all the clothes in the rehearsal room. There were hats, coats, trousers, boots. Spoon, Twin, and everyone else came in, and, for the first time in years, they changed their clothes."

"And you were able to bring in all the props?"

"I had a list of props I had to give to the security captain for him to sign. Three weeks before the opening I asked, 'Can I bring in a bottle of wine?' He said, 'Is it empty?' 'Yes.' 'Five or six hats?' 'All right.' 'Boots?' 'Okay.' And so on. 'A rope?' 'No, no, no.' 'I can't do the play without a rope.' I had been rehearsing there for a year and a half. And three weeks before opening night he asked me, 'Do you know that down in San Francisco there are twenty-eight different theaters?' 'Yes, I know.' 'Then I want to ask you something: Why the hell are you doing this play here? This is a prison, and a gym for inmates!'

"I couldn't answer him, because it would have taken me two days. So I said, 'What should I do?' 'Well, use something else.' 'Something else? What do you mean? Should I use a chair? A rope is a rope. I can't use something else.' So he said, 'So do another play, a play without a rope.'"

"Did you finally get permission?" I asked, amused.

"Yes! I took the rope inside, and I actually have a picture of Spoon carrying it on his shoulder, walking from the rehearsal room to the gym, an inmate walking inside the prison with a big rope around his shoulder!

"After the last performance at San Quentin I went back into the gym. The pictures were there and the carpet, the tree, and the stone. I went up to the top of the bleachers and sat for two hours thinking about the time I had been working in the prisons, 1985 to 1988. And I thought, 'What am I going to do now?' And I saw from the bleacher on the carpet, the dead tree, and the stone with one red rose lying there dead. You can see on the video the audience standing up after the performance and screaming with the guys onstage. And you see one of the mothers running up onstage and hugging her son after so many years."

"They were never allowed family visits?"

"Very few. The visiting room had to be free, and sometimes the families didn't have the money to go to San Francisco."

"How could you stand that?"

"Sometimes I couldn't. Beckett saw that on video and reacted very strongly. I remember opening night at San Quentin when, at the end of the play, Twin and Happy were standing before that tree. Happy asks Twin, 'Why don't we hang ourselves?' And Twin replies, 'With what?' Happy says, 'You haven't got a piece of rope?' He is standing there asking his best friend if they should hang themselves. [The inmates are childhood friends from Watts, the Los Angeles ghetto.] I told them to talk to each other as though they were standing on the street in Watts. Then Happy says to his best friend, 'And if he [Godot] comes?' What he is saying is, 'What shall we do if the Department of Corrections opens the gates and we're saved?' So he faces the director of the Department of Corrections, and he smiles and says, 'Then we are saved.' That was my present to Sam Beckett. I gave him that. The production was for him and for us and the audience. And then I walked up onstage and gave each of the actors one red rose.

"After the performance, I was cleaning up, and the guards came and put the men up against the wall and made them strip. I saw these guys standing there totally naked, and it was a shock. I started to scream, 'What are you doing?'

"I saw this squad come with plastic gloves and start looking all over their bodies for drugs. And on top of each of the men's clothes was the red rose. Spoon was standing there, and when the guy came up behind him he said, 'You have my body, but not my soul.'"

Antoni Libera

ANTONI LIBERA has directed a number of Beckett's plays in his native Poland and in England and Ireland. His productions have been televised in Warsaw and Krakow. Libera has translated most of Beckett's work into Polish, and he has written extensively on Beckett's work as well.

This interview was conducted both in person, in April 1992 in The Hague, and in writing over a period of several months in the same year.

LOIS OPPENHEIM: In 1989 you directed *Krapp's Last Tape* at the Haymarket Theatre in Leicester [United Kingdom]. Would you talk about that production?

ANTONI LIBERA: It was a double bill. *Krapp* was played together with *Catastrophe*. David Warrilow played Krapp (for the first time in his life) and Protagonist (for the second time, after the New York world premiere).

We prepared the spectacle in three weeks. At the first rehearsal David asked me the meaning of the opening sentence of the play, "A late evening in the future." I explained that this was a reference to a point in time that was future with respect to the time the play was written, the late 1950s. The amateur tape recorder used by Krapp had been available for no more than ten years (since about 1950) and had been invented as a technical device merely twenty-five years earlier (in Germany in 1936). The text clearly implies that Krapp had been recording his tapes for at least forty-two years. On a tape recorded thirty years earlier he states at a certain point: "Just been listening to an old year, . . . it must be at least ten or twelve years ago," and it doesn't seem this was the first tape he ever recorded. (Otherwise, he would have mentioned it. It would have been marked in some way.) Moreover, one has to assume that Krapp didn't acquire a tape recorder the moment it became possible (when the device was still an expensive novelty) but only when it had become relatively popular in the West, which was in the mid-1950s. Therefore, the time of the play would be 1992 at the earliest or, more probably, somewhat later, in the second half of the 1990s. Only then, realistically speaking, does everything make sense. Krapp, who is sixty-nine years old, could have been born at best in 1930, bought a tape recorder in 1954, and recorded his tapes ever since. The tape on which he mentions Bianca from Kedar Street would have been recorded, let's say, in 1957, and the tape to which he listens on the stage in 1969. Therefore, the play we are watching would be set in 1999—a very appropriate number for Beckett and a very meaningful date: the twentieth-century's last year.

Please excuse me for dwelling on this issue in such detail, but it is not as insignificant as it might seem. Choosing the type of recorder that is to be used in the play depends on determining these dates. In many respects (visual, technical, etc.) a model from the mid-1950s is the best choice: on the one hand, it is not as huge as the prototypes; on the other, it still remains old-fashioned in a way. The tape recorders that appeared in the 1960s, despite the fact that they give an impression of being outdated, are not as "picturesque" as their predecessors.

This brings us to the question of how *Krapp* is to be staged in the twenty-first century, let's say, forty years from now. An "old-fashioned tape recorder" will then stand for our contemporary miniature devices. Can you imagine a performance in which Krapp listens to his own voice, recorded thirty years earlier, on a tiny machine? How would he hold it? In one hand, close to his ear? That might not even be too bad, but what would you do about the indispensable "spools"? What could he possibly call his cassettes? And what about the very spectacular activities connected with working the machine? A recorded cassette eliminates them. You simply insert the cassette, snap, and that is all there is to it. What I am saying is that the future referred to in the opening sentence is not, in fact, undefined or infinite. The time is the turn of the twentieth to the twenty-first century. And in the distant future, if the play is still staged in one or two hundred years, its time will have to be set very specifically, namely: "A late evening at the end of the twentieth century," because this is the only time that justifies the type of recorder that Beckett had in mind and is best suited for the stage.

LO: In your production of *Krapp* the tape is wound forward and backward manually, not automatically. Why?

AL: For three reasons. First of all, to stress the fact that the recorder is already very old and hardly works anymore. It is characteristic of old recorders that they do not operate properly and that they even fail to wind the tapes. Moreover, it implies that the machine is as dilapidated as its owner. How was it put in *Happy Days?* "Old things. Old eyes." Second, it allows Krapp to be more active, creating a counterbalance for the lengthy static fragments. And finally, manual winding allows for a deformation of the voice. (With automatic winding, for technical reasons, this type of effect is rather impossible.)

LO: How did you achieve this effect technically?

AL: By the same method I applied to the rest of the tape. I recorded all the forward and backward windings in fast motion and inserted them into the edited tape, which was operated by the stage manager. There were about seven such insertions. I tried to retain probability, that is, a conformism between the activities of the hero and what was heard. When Krapp winds the tape forward (with his right hand), a fast-forward rewind effect may be heard; when he winds it backward (with his left hand) a backward rewind effect is heard. The basis for recording these effects was the prerecorded text, which was already in the proper place on the tape—whenever possible, of course. In the instance when the tape is wound forward between three consecutive "jetty passages,"[1] unseparated by any text, I had to use an already existing one. Therefore, I restored the very text that is heard at regular speed because it had a similar intonation pattern.

We achieved the most amusing effect where Krapp first starts listening to the tapes. I suggested to David that Krapp, who clears his throat before recording in the present, used to clear his throat also in the past. So, the first sound is a clearing of the throat and then come the words: "Thirty-nine today, sound as a ———." At that very moment Krapp accidentally knocks a ledger off the table, which causes him to stop the machine and

---

1. When I asked him about this later Libera replied, "By three 'jetty passages' I mean these fragments of the text:

1. from 'Spiritually a year of profound gloom and indigence . . . ' to 'that the belief I had been going on all my life, namely—'
2. from '—great granite rocks . . . ' to 'is in reality my most—'
3. from '—unshatterable association . . . ' to 'and the fire—'

The text between these three passages does not exist. So, as a base for recording the fast-forward effect at these points, I used passage 1 between 1 and 2, passage 2 between 2 and 3, and passage 3 (plus the fragment of the text just before 'my face in her breasts') between 3 and the words 'my face in her breasts.'" See "Krapp's Last Tape" in *The Collected Shorter Plays of Samuel Beckett* (NY: Grove Press, 1984), 60.

rewind the tape to the beginning. Because he has only a small fragment
to rewind, he turns the reel carefully and slowly. As a result, this short
passage, although it is heard backward, remains comprehensible, especially
the clearing of the throat, which is a pure sound, devoid of any linguistic
meaning. Krapp, hearing it and assuming once more a listening position,
instinctively repeats it, as if he were going to record, not listen. He then
switches on the recorder, which immediately repeats exactly the same
sound. Therefore, we had somewhat of a multiple echo effect: first, the
clearing of the throat from the tape (before ledger's fall); then the same
again, recorded backward and at a somewhat slower pace; then the sound
of Krapp clearing his throat on the stage; and finally, the clearing of the
throat coming from the tape again, the same as the first.

LO: That's wonderful!

AL: Yes, it's really effective and . . . funny. The audience likes it very
much.

As far as the effect of a deformed voice (due to the fast-forward and
fast-backward winding) is concerned, I would like to add that this idea,
apart from being purely theatrical, carries a deeper meaning. It is a form
of irony. For Krapp words, especially those he spoke in his own voice, are
the dearest keepsake: they are what is left of him. Presenting them in the
form of unintelligible "duck clangor," like in a Walt Disney film, is a way
of sneering at and ridiculing them, depriving them of their seriousness
and value. It suggests that everything he has ever said in his life (what
we all say throughout our lifetimes!) is not even "a tale told by an idiot,
full of sound and fury" any longer but simply childlike gibberish disturbing
the silence. A similar idea or motive may be found in *Not I*, where human
speaking is compared to "buzzing" and even straightforwardly referred
to as such.

LO: Did you direct *Krapp's Last Tape* in Poland?

AL: Yes, twice. The first time in 1982, at the Warsaw Drama School,
and the second time in 1985, at the Warsaw Studio Theatre, as part of
the Beckett festival prepared for his eightieth birthday. That was when I
also did *Play, Not I, Footfalls, Rockaby, Endgame,* and *Catastrophe.*

LO: Were these two productions of *Krapp* the same as the English one?

AL: Not exactly, although many things were very similar.

LO: What were some of the differences?

AL: The major difference was that the Polish productions did not have
the manual rewinding of the tape and, therefore, did not have the noise
of the voice being rewound. Another difference was that Krapp, in the

Polish productions, slipped on a banana skin and nearly fell, whereas in the British production he only trod on it and withdrew his foot from the ground in disgust. There was one more difference of another kind. In the British production the song was cut, and in the Polish one it was not. What's more, Krapp did not sing the same song, "Now the day is over."

LO: What did he sing?

AL: Poland being a Catholic country, nobody would have understood that Krapp had sung "Now the day is over" in church at Vespers, because it is a Protestant hymn. So, I had to change the song and choose an appropriate one from the evening service in the Catholic church in Poland.

LO: And Beckett allowed you to adapt whatever you wanted?

AL: He agreed with me that I should choose something else, but he did not indicate what it should be. He said, "It is your decision," so I chose a very popular Polish Catholic song that people sing in church in the evening and everybody knows from childhood. Its words go like this:

> Good God, please, accept all our daily things.
> And when we go to sleep,
> Let even our dreams glorify you!

The song obviously lacks the Manichaean oppositions of day and night or darkness and light, which Beckett was so fond of, but it does contain the concept of dreams in which God is glorified and which, to the best of my knowledge, was equally appealing to Beckett.

LO: Did Beckett work with you on your British *Krapp?*

AL: No, only by mail. This production of *Krapp's Last Tape* with Warrilow was the last production that Beckett—not in prison, but from afar—supervised. He gave me much advice and even made corrections in the text. For example, in the passage "Fanny came in a couple of times. Bony old ghost of a whore. Couldn't do much, but I suppose better than a kick in the crutch," he changed the expression "a kick in the crutch" to "a finger and thumb." Probably, he concluded that it was, on the one hand, too vulgar and, on the other, not clear enough because "kick in the crutch" is an idiom not often understood even in England and America. So, it's like female masturbation, you know. It's better for her, not better for him. Another interesting modification, or rather addition, is that Krapp, in the process of looking up *viduity* in the dictionary, murmurs: "vide ante . . . vide infra . . . vide supra. . . ."

LO: I would be curious to know how much you allow the movements, the gestures, to evolve from the actors you are working with and how much you limit input from them. In your London production of *Krapp*, for example, David Warrilow laughs, or rather chuckles, several times I believe, into his right shoulder. Then there is a moment when he again turns rather abruptly into his left shoulder, and the movement echoes the previous ones. It's very effective. I don't remember this being a part of Beckett's scripts. Did this come from you or from Warrilow?

AL: You are talking about two things. One is the abrupt turn Krapp makes backward over his left shoulder, as if he were convinced someone was standing behind him. Krapp makes this movement twice, before he switches on the recorder for the first and last times. Beckett must have arrived at this solution during his first production of the play at the Schiller Theatre in 1969, because I can't recall Patrick Magee ever doing anything similar. Beckett gave this gesture the cryptonym "Hain" and explained that out there, lurching in the darkness behind Krapp's back, was death.[2]

The motions of the head while laughing were my idea. As you may remember, Krapp laughs five times while listening to the tape: after "... aspirations!" after "... resolutions!" after "To drink less, in particular," after "... yelp to Providence," and after "... on her virtue." Each burst is a continuation of his laughter from many years back, which is heard from the recorder (except the third one). When editing the tape, I inserted pauses of silence, several seconds each, after each burst of laughter, to give David time to laugh onstage without drowning out the recorded text. I wanted to create an echo effect: first, the clear, youthful laughter of thirty-nine-year-old Krapp, followed by the croaking, senile laughter of Krapp at sixty-nine, kept in the same rhythm.

But this is not all. The first three follow each other in succession, as if in a series, forming a triple crescendo, which is not topically contrasted: after the third outburst of laughter there follows the word *Statistics* and an enumeration of hours spent on "licensed premises." The other two separate outbursts, on the other hand, are very strongly contrasted with the text

---

2. As Dougald McMillan and Martha Fehsenfeld note in *Beckett in the Theatre*, for an explanation of "Hain," Beckett's name for the gesture described by Libera, the playwright referred James Knowlson to Mattheus Claudius's poem "Death and the Maiden": "The figure of death as both a protector friend and a threatening presence in *Krapp*, however, is much closer to the description of 'Hain' presented in the dedication to Claudius' collected works where the author explains the opening engraving of death and then goes on to dedicate his work to him" (*Beckett in the Theatre* [London: John Calder; New York: Riverrun, 1988], 281).

that immediately follows. In the first instance there follows a bitter, doleful question: "What remains of all that misery?" and in the second a lyrical exclamation: "The face she had!" Given this, I decided that, in the first three cases David should laugh tilting his head toward his right shoulder and, in the remaining two, toward his left. In the first three cases I made the pauses for laughter shorter (two seconds), and in the remaining three they were longer (three, maybe even four, seconds each). I wanted David to turn his head away from the tape recorder as far and for as long as possible while he was laughing. The longer he was laughing and the farther away his ear was from the loudspeaker, the more abruptly—and thus the more visibly—he was able to return to the listening position. This created a sharper contrast between cheerfulness and sadness (or serenity). What's more, the fact that Krapp so suddenly put his ear to the loudspeaker made it clear that his hearing was poor.

LO: And when Krapp's voice on tape says, "I lay across her with my face in her breasts and my hand on her," Warrilow lays his head down on the tape recorder in a manner more suggestive of a kind of gentleness than I can associate with any other productions I have seen of this play. Again, did that movement, and others like it, come from you or from the actor?

AL: From both of us, but most of all from Beckett himself, because similarly to "Hain," he also included this in his subsequent productions. I simply showed David how I thought it should be; the rest was up to him. He did exactly what I showed him, but it was to his credit that it is so suggestive and moving. My rendering of the gesture would not be interesting, despite the fact that I created it—I am not an actor. David has charisma. He knows how to make very simple gestures or words seem beautiful.

Apart from showing David how to put his head on the tape recorder and his right hand on the dictionary, I remember giving him one other suggestion: "There can't be anything sensual about this; he touches her, even lies across her, but this is really Platonic."

LO: Did Beckett see the production?

AL: No, but Edward Beckett came to see it in Leicester, and he gave Beckett a long report. For the premiere, which was 5 October 1989, about two months before his death, Beckett sent a telegram for me, the actors, and the whole ensemble. It was a beautiful text: "With you all heart and all." You have an expression in English: "heart and soul," right?

LO: Right.

AL: So he wrote, "With you all heart and all," not soul. Such a little poem.

LO: Did you ever work with Beckett?

AL: Unfortunately, no. I regret it very much. I can't really say that I am a disciple of Beckett-as-director, as, for example, Pierre Chabert and Walter Asmus, in particular, are. But I feel like I was a student of Beckett, an extramural student at least. Anyway, my aim is to continue his way of directing . . .

LO: To remain loyal to his . . .

AL: To what Beckett suggested, to the Beckett canon of directing. It's my main point of reference.

LO: Could you be more specific? What do you mean by "the Beckett canon of directing"? And to what exactly in Beckett's way of directing do you aim to remain faithful?

AL: By "the Beckett canon of directing" I mean all his own productions. Some plays were staged by him many times. For example, *Krapp's Last Tape*, four times, and *Waiting for Godot, Happy Days, Eh Joe, Footfalls*, and others, twice. There are always some differences between consecutive productions of the same play. All these differences belong to the canon. You can prefer one version to the other, but the version you like less is also valid.

Becket's way of directing consists of the following elements:

1. Approaching a play (both the text and stage activities) as if it were a musical score. Perceiving everything in formal categories. Establishing how many times a given theme, word, or gesture reoccurs. Insuring that all types of repetitions are like echoes, refrains—that is, seeing to it that they are performed in exactly the same or a very similar manner.

2. Attempts at bringing out the melody and rhythm of the text. Treating each text as if it were poetry. Proper placing of logical accents.

3. A very precise designing of the stage movements, as if in a ballet. Measuring the number of steps taken, establishing such details as over which shoulder the actor turns around, with which foot he begins to walk, how long (in seconds) the pause is between one movement and the next.

4. The pace of the acting and speaking. The majority of the plays were intended to be acted or played quickly (allegro, presto). Play-

ing Beckett's plays too slowly kills them. Pauses marking a falling silence should be distinctively different from pauses that mark a change of tone (or topic).

5. Bringing out comic elements, which are a mixture of Irish humor and classics of the silent movies (Chaplin, Keaton).

6. Bringing out sadness and lyricism, with all their delicate shades. No black gloom.

7. The spirit of German romanticism: paintings by Caspar David Friedrich, the music of Franz Schubert, German romantic poetry (as a source of inspiration, not simply to use).

LO: You have directed the plays of a number of other playwrights as well, have you not?

AL: Rather incidentally. I worked on Slawomir Mrozek, Harold Pinter, Václav Havel. But I am focused on Beckett.

Those who dispute the question of faithfulness toward Beckett can be divided into two groups. The first group includes those who unquestionably consider him to be an eminent representative of contemporary drama but don't see him as exceptional. That doesn't include me. I think of other writers in this way. Pinter, Albee, Miller, Williams, for example, are very eminent modern playwrights. But Beckett is unique. He is of a special kind. The second group consists of directors who see Beckett as a unique playwright and believe that his plays should be staged as faithfully as possible. This does not mean that they should totally discard their own creative individualities. They should use all their talent and abilities to fulfill the task set by Beckett. I can assure you, this is not as easy as it might seem. Who knows if it isn't even more difficult than producing one's own variations on the subject. I think I belong to the second group, to the group of directors who are "conductors" who don't happen to be "composers." I myself am a composer when I write my own plays or direct plays by other writers.

LO: I'd like to talk now about some of your other productions. You directed *Not I* more than once in Poland, did you not?

AL: Yes, three times. In 1980 (at the Poznan Theatre Nowy), in 1981 (at the Warsaw Drama School), and in 1985 (at the Warsaw Theatre Studio).

LO: Could you describe some of the major directorial differences between the three productions?

AL: There were no major differences. There were only some of a technical nature, due to improvements in the lighting.

In all three productions I used a small cabin of sorts, which I designed myself, the most important elements of which were a narrow armrest, a small ledge for resting the forehead, and a screen, made of black material, with an opening cut out for the mouth. The actress sat in this cabin on a stool, with both arms on the rest (one upon the other), her forehead pressed against the ledge, and her face within the screen, so that her mouth was exactly in the center of the opening. It was as if she fitted her face into a mask that was built into the stage set.

It was crucial where and how to place the spotlight, so that the mouth could be lit properly, in other words evenly, with a small oval spot, approximately 8 × 6 cm (which was the shape and size of the opening in the screen). It soon became clear that this effect is best achieved when the beam of light is perpendicular to the lips. This required placing the spotlight behind the audience and concealing it. Otherwise—in any other position at this level—it would either be visible to the audience, or it would cover the mouth. I had to abandon this solution immediately, however, as I did not have at my disposal a light strong or sharp enough to give an adequate spot, 8 × 6 cm, from a distance of 30 m (the length of the audience). Besides, I realized that, even if I had had such a light, this solution wouldn't have been satisfying because the audience could see the beam of light over their heads, and for me this was inadmissible. It was obvious that the source of light had to be hidden for this play. It wasn't to be known where the light came from or that it came from anywhere at all. I had to achieve the effect of the lips shining on their own, as though they were not illuminated.

Do you remember the sentence from *Company* "By the voice a faint light is shed"? I had it in mind when directing *Not I*. The mouth is visible; it emerges from darkness as it begins to speak. The viewer should have the impression that *the very act of speaking is the source of light*. (To stress this even further, throughout the whole monologue I controlled the intensity of light, so that when the voice waned or became a whisper the light dimmed, and, as the voice became louder, it became brighter. This was impressive, particularly at two abrupt shouts: for a second the mouth flashed with very strong light, which, together with the sudden increase of decibels, caused the audience to shudder.)

Finally, the spotlight for illuminating the mouth was placed in a light-proof box, only open on one side and only across the diameter of the lens, set on a stand right in front of the lips, just slightly beneath them. The mouth was lit at an angle of about forty-five degrees.

I think the ideal solution to the problem of lighting would be a laser beam, which could be concentrated into the smallest spots from any distance and the force of which could be freely adjusted.

The second lighting problem in *Not I* relates to the figure of Auditor. The difficulty here is that, no matter how delicately and discreetly he is lit, the light he reflects creates a certain glimmer around him and thus disperses the darkness onstage and in the audience. Even if it doesn't, the constantly visible figure of Auditor would distract the viewers' attention from the speaking mouth. After a series of rehearsals without Auditor's presence, I realized that the visual force of the play is the function of a certain inherent feature of human perception—namely, that it does not stand emptiness and is always focused on something. Hearing heeds sound; vision craves light. In complete darkness people feel ill at ease; their eyes search for something to "rest" on. The object of attention can be very small and insignificant, as long as it's there. In *Not I* it is the small spot of the mouth that should be the remedial "food" for the eyes.

I understood this after having spent a lot of time in darkness at rehearsals. After barely several minutes the shining spot of Mouth becomes a "lifeline"; it becomes soothing. After another five or eight minutes the viewer experiences fascinating optical illusions. The glimmering mouth, like a phosphorescent butterfly fluttering its wings, begins to move in space—upwards, downwards, sideways; it seems to move in circles, stop for a while, and then move again. This occurs only under one condition: that apart from the shining mouth there is no other point of reference. I don't mean only Auditor but, most of all, any source of light in the audience: lamps under the steps and lighted "exit" signs. The play should be performed in complete darkness; otherwise, the effect is only partial. Oh, I know very well that security rules do not allow for turning off the step and exit lights during a performance. But if you have the good of the play at heart (or if you are an artist as uncompromising as Beckett himself was), you must persuade the theater officials to grant you exclusive permission to put out all emergency lights on the stage and in the audience for about fifteen minutes.

LO: What did you finally do with Auditor? You didn't eliminate him altogether, did you?

AL: No. I decided that he should be visible only when he performs his mysterious gesture. Therefore, the spotlight directed at him lit him only five times throughout the play and only for as long as the scene of vehement refusal to speak in the first-person singular—so crucial to the play—took place ("what? ... who? ... no! ... she!"). This is exactly what it looked like: Auditor appeared in barely visible light upon hearing the word *what;* at the very moment his right hand began to move upward, as if in warning; then, as the hand continued to rise, the light became slightly brighter, reaching the maximum peak of intensity at *no!* As "no!" was shouted, the hand became immobile in its highest position. Finally, after *she!* the hand slowly, helplessly, came down, as the light gradually faded. The whole sequence lasted about five seconds.

This solution had two advantages. First of all, the sudden and fleeting appearance of Auditor rendered him unreal and ghostlike. His first appearance made a particularly strong impression on the audience, because it was so unexpected: abruptly, with no prior warning, a thin and tall figure, as if of a hooded monk performing a strange and mysterious gesture, loomed out of the murky darkness right in front—out of nothingness—and just as suddenly disappeared. Second, the fact that Auditor always reappeared for a very short moment when Mouth refused to relinquish the third person attributed more meaning to his reaction.

LO: Could you describe some of the nontechnical aspects of your directing of *Not I?* Did the actress with whom you worked expect your assistance in understanding the text, for example?

AL: Of course, the technicalities were the main problem, but only in the final phase of rehearsals, when the actress had already learned the monologue by heart. Until then we worked only on the text and its interpretation. My role consisted in three basic activities: (1) dividing the text into separate segments, which made it easier to memorize; (2) instructing as to intonation and placing logical accents, that is to say, presenting the text as it should be spoken; (3) explaining biblical and autobiographical allusions ("God is love," "tender mercies ... new every morning," "Croker's Acres").

Once the actress had learned the text by heart, together with the proper accents and intonations, I set her the following task: I told her to say it as if she were telling her own story and using the third person only for disguise. And we did an exercise: when she approached the five moments at which Mouth is just about to refuse relinquishing the third person, I—as if in accusation—shouted out the last sentence she had uttered in the second person back at her from the audience:

ACTRESS ONSTAGE: ... and she found herself in the—
ME FROM AUDIENCE: You found yourself!

ACTRESS ONSTAGE:	What?
ME FROM AUDIENCE:	YOU found yourself!
ACTRESS ONSTAGE:	Who?
ME FROM AUDIENCE:	YOU!
ACTRESS ONSTAGE:	No! She!

We applied the same technique to those fragments in which Mouth omits a word. For example:

ACTRESS:	. . . whether standing . . . or sitting . . . but the brain—
ME:	or kneeling!
ACTRESS:	what?
ME:	OR KNEELING!
ACTRESS:	yes . . . whether standing . . . or sitting . . . or kneeling . . . but the brain—
ME:	or lying!
ACTRESS:	what?
ME:	OR LYING!
ACTRESS:	yes . . . whether standing . . . or sitting . . . or kneeling . . . or lying . . . but the brain still . . .

For someone who didn't know what this was all about it looked as if I were actually correcting the actress who omitted words from the text because she had forgotten them. My aim, however, was to make her feel that everything she said was controlled by somebody, that an invisible someone interrupted the flow of her monologue, and that with some inner ear she heard these corrections and included them all except for one: that she speak in her own name, that she begin to use the pronoun *I*.

"Notice," I told the actress, "that in this specific case she not only does not want to but is simply not up to uttering it. She does not say: 'what? . . . I (or: me) . . . no! she!' but 'what? . . . who? . . . no! . . . she!' She is capable of changing only the question from 'what?' to 'who?' which implies that she understands that it is about a person, not a thing. But she is not able to say it even in the negative. The words of the title, *Not I*, come from the author and not from the protagonist, Mouth. It would not have been able to say them."

LO: The exercises you are talking about resemble the situation we deal with in *Play*.

AL: That's right! My aim was to make the monologue sound like a confession, in which certain things are left unsaid, or like the testimony of a suspect who does not want to admit he is guilty. I think this is where the dramatic tension of the play lies. The woman speaks to obtain absolution or acquittal, which would allow for her release from the prison of darkness—where she is tortured by the light forcing her to speak—and would let her roam "back in the field . . . April morning." The precondition for release is telling the truth, which in this particular case does not mean certain facts but, instead, the person they refer to. The mouth, however, refuses to tell the truth—not because it wishes to conceal or distort anything but because it does not speak in the name of the woman it belongs to.

"If you say it is you—" an invisible and inaudible interrogator seems to be telling the Woman-Mouth, "If you admit this is about *you,* I will set you free. Otherwise I will keep interrogating you indefinitely. Well, is it you?"

"No, she!"

And so the testimony/confession goes on.

LO: What is *Not I* all about for you? Who is this woman?

AL: I see *Not I* as a play about the need for purgation, about speech as its means and about the infinity of this process. The woman personifies mankind, which by means of language—the only true invention of Man—strives to deserve redemption. The situation—complete darkness with the spot on a human mouth gleaming and speaking fervently—is a metaphor for the night between Good Friday and Holy Sunday (the day of Resurrection, "early April morning"). In other words, it is the metaphor of a time without God and Light, with no hope for His return, when Man has only himself to depend on, when his condition, as defined by a *dialogue* with some Divine Being, has undergone a drastic change, to become the condition defined by the *monologue.*

LO: Do you generally see Beckett's work in this context, or is this thinking characteristic only of your interpretation of *Not I?*

AL: I think it is typical of all Beckett's work. The writer considers the principal metaphysical, historical, and philosophical problems of mankind. To express them he employs, for example, signs and symbols of Christian mythology. One such sign is specifically the night between the day of Crucifixion and the day of Resurrection, which represents a time without God. I think this is a sign Beckett was particularly fond of. I might even risk the statement that Beckett not only made it one of the predominant motifs of his writing but that it also became the most important sign of his own life. He was born on Good Friday, "at the close of the day when in darkness Christ at the ninth hour cried and died" (*Company*), and died on Friday, this time two days before Christmas, "one dirty winter night" (*Eh Joe*). A life lived within such brackets is a sign in itself. It symbolizes failing to meet God. "I was born when God died," his soul seems to say. "I died when God was not yet born. I lived when God was not on earth." This could be the motto of all Beckett's works, while parabolically diagnosing the condition of contemporary man.

"The bastard! He doesn't exist!" says Hamm of God.

"Not yet," Clov adds or corrects him.

Contrary to what is frequently claimed by critics, Beckett is not only a eulogist of religious despair. Although he does seem deeply rooted in the Cartesian tradition, he also questions what might be called a "rationalistic mythology," such as was expressed in the form of a precursory, optimistic philosophical theory formulated in the Enlightenment by Giambattista Vico [1668–1744]. (Beckett became interested in Vico in his youth, under the influence of Joyce, who referred to this theory when writing *Finnegans Wake*.) Without going into further detail, I would just like to add that Beckett adopted only the primary notions of Judeo-Christian mythology and the above concept, rejecting the "happy ending."

If, from Christianity, Beckett takes only the original sin, poverty, destitution (in a word, Job's experience), and most of all the Crucifixion, while rejecting the Resurrection and Redemption (that is to say, the Gospel), then from Vico's rationalistic theory (which represents the attitude not only of this particular philosopher but also of the whole rationalistic and optimistic thinking that developed from the Enlightenment), he takes the ingenious concept of language as the chief tool for man's self-transformation and the concept that the evolution of mankind proceeds along a spiral. At the same time he questions the overall message of this theory, that is, the belief that, after having passed through three consecutive epochs, or stages of development—the Theocratic Age (symbolized by Birth and Religion), the Heroic Age (symbolized by Maturity and Marriage), and the Human Age (symbolized by Corruption and Burial)—mankind shall enter what Vico called the Age of Divine Providence (symbolized by Reawakening and Generation), when people will become gods, beginning the whole cycle anew.

At this point Beckett creates an image in which contemporary times are interpreted as an "endless winter" (*That Time*), as the third age of development (the Human Age), which does not, however, give way to the

joyous fourth age (Divine Providence) but, instead, goes on and on, becoming more wearisome and gloomy: "year after year as if [winter] couldn't
end the old year never end like time could go no further."

LO: How did this interpretation impact on your directing of Beckett's
plays? Are there any specifically directorial decisions that you made based
on these ideas?

AL: My "philosophical" understanding of Beckett's plays has very little
impact on my directing, if it has any at all. These are two very separate
things. When I work on a production I never submerge into these deep
meanings. Of course, I give my actors interpreting lessons when they ask
me to. But in such cases I always stress that by no means do I want to
express any ideas or concepts. *My aim is and always has been to move the
viewer, to make him sad, afraid, and to cause him to laugh—nothing more.* What
these feelings evoke in him, where they lead him—well, that's his business.
If he arrives at the same conclusions I have, that's all right. If his conclusions are different, even completely different, that is just as well. The
most important thing during a performance is to make him shudder—
with anxiety, wonder, revelation. Intellectual speculation may follow, but
it is not necessary.

Therefore, in the process of directing I concentrate only on what is
concrete and measurable. I aim at gaining maximum credibility: to simply
render what is done onstage as real.

LO: You have shown me copies of sections of your director's notebooks
for *Krapp's Last Tape* and for *Endgame*. Could you tell me something about
the way you worked with them? How much of the notebooks, for example,
were prepared in advance? How much did you stage in preparation of the
first rehearsals? And how much of any preblocking you may have done
did you find you needed to change while you were in rehearsal?

AL: As I already mentioned, the two productions—the British *Krapp*
and the Irish *Endgame*—were not my first productions of these plays. I had
directed *Krapp* twice and *Endgame* once before. So, the preparations for
these productions were much easier for me. When I began to elaborate
the director's notebook I knew virtually everything about the plays. That's
why the plans could be so detailed. When I staged the plays for the first
time in Poland I did not have such plans. Back then I was still searching,
checking various possibilities, gaining experience.

As you probably noticed, the director's notebook consists of several
parts. The first is the script: the full text of the play together with staging
instructions (the author's and mine). The second part, "Refrains and

ECHOS

„I have things to do" (CLOV)

    (1) I can't be getting you up... I have things to do p.4
    (2) I'll leave you, I have things to do p.10
    (3) I'll leave you, I have things to do p.14
    (4) I'll leave you, I have things to do p.45

„I'll leave you..." (CLOV)

    (1) I'll leave you, I have things to do p. 10
    (2) I'll leave you, I have things to do p. 14
    (3) I'll leave you, I have things to do p. 45
    (4) I'll leave you p. 46
    (5) I'll leave you p. 46
    (6) I'll leave you p. 50
    (7) I'll leave you p. 57
    (8) I'll leave you p. 69
    (9) Then I'll leave you p. 81
    (10) I'll leave you p. 93

„Go and get/see..." (HAMM)

    (1) Go and get the sheet p. 6
    (2) Go and get two bicyclewheels p. 10
    (3) Go and get him [the dog] (twice) p. 47
    (4) Go and get the gaff p. 51
    (5) Go and get the oilcan p. 52
    (6) Go and see, is she dead p. 73
    (7) Go and see did he hear me p. 79
    (8) Go and get it [the glass] p. 89

„I'll go and get/see..." (CLOV)

    (1) I'll go and get the sheet p. 7
    (2) I'll go and get the catheter p.30
    (3) I'll go and get the tape p. 33
    (4) I'll go and get the glass p. 34
    (5) I'll go and get the powder p. 40
    (6) I'll go and see [the alarm, is it working?] p. 56
    (7) I'll go and see [a small boy] p. 92

„I'm back again..." (CLOV)

    (1) I'm back again, with the biscuit p. 12
    (2) I'm back again, with the glass p. 34
    (3) I'm back again, with the steps p. 35
    (4) I'm back again, with the insecticide p. 40

Fig. 4. From Antoni Libera's Director's Notebook.

Repetitions in the Action," is a kind of list of recurring actions and situations. The third part, "Refrains and Echoes in the Text," is an analogous "concordance" referring to the spoken text. In the case of *Krapp* there is also the text recorded on tape (separately written, as it was spoken by Krapp, without the repetitions) and a description of editing the tape. In the case of *Endgame* there are "Notes to the Text," with explanations of biblical and literary allusions.

All the parts, excluding the basic script, have an auxiliary function. Their purpose is to make the actors and me aware of the play's structure and facilitate control over the whole thing.

As for changes introduced during rehearsals, I can give you several examples.

Krapp's Last Tape

The scene in which Krapp remembers when the "farewell to love" took place is described in my director's notebook as follows:

> he remembers at last ("it was thirty years ago!")
> turns away (rightabout) quickly towards the closet
> becomes still at the sight of unfinished banana in his right hand (his
>   right profile to the audience)
> hesitates: finish it or reject it in order to be able to go quicker to the
>   closet for tapes and tape-recorder
> finally tosses the rest of banana away backstage left ... etc.

In the performance the scene is shortened and simplified to:

> he remembers at last: suddenly raises his left hand to the level of his
>   face and opens wide his mouth, as if he were thinking "ah yes, it
>   was thirty years ago!"
> turns away (leftabout) to 180 degrees and goes with all the speed he
>   can muster backstage right into darkness
> in the last moment before he draws curtain and gets in to closet he
>   tosses the rest of banana away backstage left

In the director's noetbook, Krapp murmurs to himself: "ah stupid young bastard" after the second "jetty passage," i.e., after the words: "is in reality my most—," while in the performance utterance appears only after the third passage, i.e., after the words: "and the fire—."

Endgame

In the director's notebook Clov carefully folds both sheets in the first scene:

he goes to ash bins, stops behind them, removes sheet covering them, folds it carefully and hangs it over his left arm [. . .]
he goes to Hamm, stops at his right, trailing sheet, removes sheet covering him, folds it carefully and hangs it over his left arm

In the performance he folds only the first one and doesn't fold the second at all:

he goes to Hamm, stops behind him, takes a sheet covering him by the two topmost corners (with two hands), removes sheet with one quick gesture towards his right, takes the corner in his left hand into his right hand, goes towards Hamm's left with the first sheet folded and hanged over his left hand and with the second kept by two corners in his right hand, trailing behind him on the ground

This image was much better for Clov's first monologue.

Now I would like to give you an example of a change in rhythm. In the second to last scene Clov makes funny mistakes. First, he asks Hamm if he had seen the steps, although he knows perfectly well that Hamm is blind. Then he confuses the windows: he forgets he is at the window overlooking the ocean and thinks that the earth has been flooded. After each of these errors he makes an amusing excuse:

1. "Sometimes I wonder if I'm in my right mind. Then it passes over and I'm as lucid as before."
2. "Sometimes I wonder if I'm in my right senses. Then it passes off and I'm as intelligent as ever."

Clov says the first line when he approaches the steps underneath the window overlooking the ocean and the second one when he carries the steps to the window overlooking the earth. Each time he has the same number of footsteps to make. Both lines, each consisting of two sentences, have almost identical rhythm. In my director's notebook Clov says them while walking from one window to the other. In the performance, however, he says only the first sentence as he walks: "Sometimes I wonder if I'm in my right mind." / "Sometimes I wonder if I'm in my right senses"; stands still (or stands still and puts away the steps), and only then— straightening his back—says the second sentence: "Then it passes over and I'm as lucid as before" / "Then it passes off and I'm as intelligent as ever." This is much better. It has a better rhythm and is funnier.

Both changes were suggested by Barry McGovern, who played Clov in the performance, and I accepted them without hesitation.

I also introduced another modification during rehearsals: when near the end of the play Clov hands Hamm the gaff Hamm doesn't put it on his lap, as it was in the director's notebook, but takes it more or less in the middle into his left hand and rests it on its end on the floor (the hook pointing upward). In this position he looks like a king. On his lap sits a dog, which he holds with his right hand, and in his left hand he holds the gaff, which now looks like a scepter or a halberd. Alan Stafford, who played Hamm, quipped: "It's Neptune standing on guard."

LO: Do you think your future productions of *Not I, Endgame, Krapp's Last Tape,* and any other of Beckett's plays you may do again will vary significantly from your previous productions? Do you have the sense that in any of your Beckett productions you have achieved all you can or would like to? Is there any particular play that you feel you need to redirect to more fully realize your vision of it?

AL: I don't think that any future production of *Krapp's Last Tape, Endgame,* or *Catastrophe* that I might do would be much different from those I did in England and Ireland, because in terms of the acting, the set, and the final effect they were exactly as I had intended them to be, and they fully satisfied me. Of course, a lot in the theater depends on the actors. If I ever stage these plays with different actors, they will differ somewhat from what I did already. But I suppose the only differences would be due to the personalities of the actors.

I am not satisfied with my productions of such plays as *Waiting for Godot, Eh Joe, Footfalls,* and *That Time,* and I will definitely attempt to perfect them in the future. I haven't said my "final word" on these plays yet.

LO: Can you specify any ways in which your directing has both resembled and differed from Beckett's own directing of any of his plays?

AL: I have already mentioned some of the similarities. As for the differences, I would list the following:

1. My productions have a faster pace than Beckett's. This is because most of all I fear slowness in the theater, particularly in his plays. I realize the hazards of quickening the pace, but I prefer if something is played too fast rather than too slow.
2. There is more "color" in my productions than in Beckett's, which are more "monochromatic." I employ more variations of voice, mimicry, and motion.

In *Krapp,* for instance, I let David react more vividly while listening to the tape than was the case with the actors Martin Held or Rick Cluchey. I even encouraged him.

In *Catastrophe* I treated the situation more realistically than Beckett. I told the actors: "This is only a rehearsal, nothing more. Play it as if this were only a rehearsal."

The main innovation I introduced was the type of armchair the director sits in, and particularly the direction it faces. In Beckett's production and, for that matter, in all the other productions I've seen, the director sat in a huge, thronelike armchair facing the audience, so that every time he wanted to look at the Protagonist he had to turn his head and look sideways. (Sometimes he didn't even look at him.) This struck me as unnatural. It did not resemble even the most bizarre rehearsal. I suggested we use a folding wood-and-canvas chair, the same type film directors use, and placed it—in accordance with Beckett's instructions—"*downstage audience left,*" only it faced not the audience but the Protagonist. Besides, as the director leaves at a certain point, I let him come to the rehearsal. In my production (we played without a curtain) the performance began with a tableau of the Protagonist standing on a black block, and his assistant, also immobile, standing with her gaze fixed on him. The director's armchair stood empty. The director entered when the lights in the audience faded.

LO: How do you perceive the role of the director of those plays by Beckett in which the staging, lighting, timing directions, are so very precise that one must wonder how the director can be at all creative? When you directed *Ghost Trio* and *Nacht und Träume,* for example, where did you feel you could be creative? Where was there room for your interpretation as a director, given that literally everything is spelled out for the actor by the playwright?

AL: Let's begin with what it means for a director to be "creative" and what is implied by his "interpretation."

I would like to return to my comparison of a director to a conductor. Why is it that when, say, Fritz Reiner conducts, the music he gets out of his orchestra is rich, full, and overwhelming, and when X conducts, the music does not sound the same? It's the same notes, the same notations for defining the tempo, force, and tone of the sounds.

I believe that "being creative" in the theater, especially in the case of Beckett's theater, does not consist in "being inventive" or in "inventing something," but in the proper understanding of the author's intentions and in the ability to render them. I wish to stress that this is by no means an easy task; on the contrary, it's terribly difficult. It requires humility and patience.

In such plays as *Ghost Trio,* . . . *but the clouds . . .,* or *Nacht und Träume* there is no need for the director to give his "own interpretation." These are not plays for any type of interpretation, like Shakespeare's or Racine's tragedies, nor are they "perfectly polished," like Dürenmatt's tragicomedies. These television plays are detailed plans for moving pictures inlaid with words and music, and the director's task is to put these mosaics together, like a jigsaw puzzle. I do not mean that these plays are explicit, that they have only one true meaning. Nothing could be farther from the truth. I simply mean that their ambiguity lies in the *effect* Beckett intended and not in the *substance,* out of which the effect is to be created.

The director's "creative role" in these plays is, therefore, a "servile" one. The director should be a diligent engineer, attempting to reconstruct the architect's idea from the plans.

Is there any room for freedom? Yes—in the realization of details. In *Ghost Trio,* for example: What should the cassette look like? Should it be small and real or a bit bigger and artificial? How do we make the rain outside the window? How do we shoot the image of the pallet seen from above (through the eyes of F)? How should the Boy knock at the door (one knock or several)? How is the Boy to shake his head faintly?

In . . . *but the clouds . . .:* How should M be presented? I was inspired by Rodin's *The Thinker.* I filmed him in profile rather than from the back (head bent, forehead resting on the hand, the one visible eye closed, so that the fading image of M1 would appear exactly underneath the face). In which direction should the woman "with those unseeing eyes" be looking? Should her face be turned to the right, to the left, or should it look straight ahead? Against what background should it be shown, dark or light? How is M1 to walk, casually or in some specific way? a laborious walk? slightly limping?

In *Nacht und Träume:* How is the left hand to rest gently on B's head if he is to awaken? What are the wine cup and cloth to look like? In his production Beckett used a wine glass and a studiously folded napkin, which evoked associations of objects used during mass. I used a "poor-looking" cup and a "poor-looking" wrinkled cloth. This was to intensify the impression of the poverty of the Dreamer: even in his most extravagant dream he sees objects that he probably uses everyday; only the fact of who uses them and for what is remarkable.

LO: Are there any particular attributes that you think a director must have to direct Beckett's work well, as opposed to directing the plays of any other kind of playwright?

AL: Do you remember the basic rule of medicine laid down by Hippocrates? "First of all, do not harm." This is the formula I would give to directors working with Beckett.

Seriously speaking, any director who wishes to stage Beckett's plays should *trust* the author. This is true of Beckett more than any other author. He should be devoid of or get rid of any ambition to be "wiser" or "more inventive" than Beckett and any feeling that he will be the first to turn his plays into "the real art of the theater." He should be humble and have the will to understand. If he meets these conditions, he is halfway to success. The rest is, as I have already said, patience, precision, a formal and not psychological treatment of the characters, and, most of all, an inner ear. An ear for the language and its beauty, rhythm, tempo, and subtleness of intonation. It would be good if the director had at least a vague knowledge of music.

LO: I would like to conclude by asking you how you see your role as the primary director, critic, and translator of Beckett in Poland.

AL: My chief aim has always been to acquaint the Polish viewer as well as the Polish actors and people of the theater with Beckett as he really is, as he understood and interpreted himself—mainly through his own productions. I wanted to put an end to the long period of misunderstanding that had developed around his art. If I were to define my role, I would say that I launched the process of normalizing Beckett in Poland.

LO: And of all this what has been the most satisfying?

AL: Being, as Beckett called me, his "deputy in Eastern Europe."

Joseph Chaikin

JOSEPH CHAIKIN, actor, director, and playwright, and founder of off-Broadway's renowned Open Theatre, performed Hamm in *Endgame* at the Open Theatre in 1969. This production was taken to Paris and was also performed in several American prisons. He later directed the play at Princeton University (1977) and again at the Manhattan Theatre Club (1979), with Daniel Seltzer as Hamm. He directed *Waiting for Godot* in 1990 at the Taper, Too Theatre, the small theater at the Mark Taper Forum in Los Angeles, and in 1992 at Atlanta's Seven Stages. In 1981, with Steven Kent, formerly of the Provisional Theatre in Los Angeles, he adapted *Texts for Nothing,* performing in it (under Kent's direction) in New York, at the Public Theatre, and in London, Paris, and Toronto. In the fall of 1992 Chaikin directed Bill Irwin in a new production of *Texts for Nothing* at the Joseph Papp Public Theatre in New York.

On 10 June 1992 I interviewed Joseph Chaikin in his New York apartment. Since 1984, when he suffered a stroke while undergoing open-heart surgery, Chaikin has been aphasic. His diminished use and understanding of language causes him to fragment both words and sentences and is responsible for a distorted syntax that is often astonishingly poetic. In preparing such an interview for publication, one is faced with two alternatives: either it can be rendered in narrative form to relate in the third person the interviewer's interpretation of what was said, as is usually done with interviews of Chaikin, or it can be left relatively untouched. With Chaikin's approval I chose to edit his often truncated but rich and meaningful phrases, un-

My sincerest thanks to Bill Coco for his assistance in the final preparation of this interview.

Chaikin's letters to and from Beckett will appear in *The Correspondence of Samuel Beckett,* to be edited and annotated by Martha Fehsenfeld and Lois Overbeck.

canny in their similarity to those of many a Beckettian voice, only to facilitate the reader's understanding.

Bill Coco, dramaturge for a number of Chaikin's productions, was present at the interview. A few comments by him are included here.

LOIS OPPENHEIM: You are going to be directing Beckett's prose piece *Texts for Nothing* this fall at the Joseph Papp Public Theatre here in New York. Did you have Beckett's permission to adapt this work when you originally performed it at the Public in 1981?

JOSEPH CHAIKIN: Yes.

LO: Did he work with you at all on the adaptation?

JC: Not really. I had been corresponding with Beckett, and eventually we met on two occasions in Paris. In the early 1980s I wanted to do another Beckett work, after *Endgame,* and I wrote to him about this. Beckett originally suggested a scene from *Watt.*

Steven Kent, who was directing, and I gave more thought to the project, and we read a number of Beckett's works and decided upon doing *Texts for Nothing.* We adapted the work together. Then toward the end of the rehearsals we experimented with including a short section from the end of *How It Is.* We felt that the production needed a stronger ending, so we asked Beckett if we could use the last page of this work, and he gave us permission. [In a letter to Chaikin dated 19 January 1981 Beckett wrote, "I give you *carte blanche* to use the *Texts* as you please + end of *How it is*—P&P." Later, in a letter dated 17 March 1981 Beckett asked: "How stage that bodilessness? That groping *vox inanis.* Your effort moves me greatly."—LO]

I ... I loved him, I loved Sam Beckett, but I really. . . . I loved him and I hated him. Because he was a pessimist.

LO: You loved him and hated him at the same time?

JC: Because he was a pessimist. . . . I appreciated his pessimism because it is one of my moods, too. I like the worst. Like dying and death, which we explored in the Open Theatre. I really like the theme of dying and death. But sometimes I change my mood. I like "up." Like the sun. It's good to have open eyes, like the open sun. So, I like changing moods, but Beckett is mostly a pessimist. I used to be very much a pessimist. And after my heart surgeries I was better, better, better. Now I like *Waiting for Godot.* It was very good for me to direct *Waiting for Godot.* It's most upbeat, funny. . . . And that's fun for me.

LO: Would you talk a little bit about your relationship to the text? Did you choose this particular text because you are aphasic?

JC: No, no, we did this several years before my stroke.

LO: Yes, that's right. The stroke was later, but you have lived the experience, in a sense, that this character or these voices describe . . .

JC: I was not aiming to express a personal experience. I simply love the book. [Chaikin mentioned his profound "love" for Beckett's *Texts for Nothing* several times. His letters to Beckett dated 18–24 June 1983 reveal how meaningful it was to him to perform this work. In a note, drafted before the final performance Chaikin wrote: "What an honor, pleasure, and opportunity for theatrical intimacy this 'Texts' has been for me. . . ." And following the performance he added: "It's over. A terrible, eventful, loss. A kind of crisis."—LO]

LO: But perhaps more than in any other Beckett work, there is in *Texts for Nothing* an intense discussion of language, of the meaning of words, of the relation of stories to life, and, particularly, of words failing the character; you seem to have some kind of real affinity for all this?

JC: Yes, yes. . . . These are themes that we were always dealing with in the Open Theatre, in the Winter Project at La Mama (during the mid-1970s), and in other aspects of my work. I sometimes got lost exploring these themes, and Beckett provided a language.

LO: Could you talk a little about how you direct and, particularly, how you will direct Bill Irwin in this production? Do you work with images? How do you work?

JC: I really don't "know" how to work. I prefer to surprise myself when I work. Bill and I simply agreed to work on the script. We are only at the very beginning of rehearsals. We don't know about the technical detail of production until we go through rehearsals. I like to surprise myself and the actors.

LO: In a letter to Beckett dated 23 June 1983 you wrote: "I feel I am carrying your voices. I don't think the production is continuous with your own directing of plays, but I think it is fine; and I feel invigorated from the music of it." The title *Texts for Nothing* is obviously reminiscent of *mesure pour rien,* a musical term in French meaning a "measure of rest." Does *Texts for Nothing* have a musical element for you? Does it seem more musical that Beckett's other works? And if so, can you explain how you have dealt with the musical dimension in your directing of it?

JC: The musical dimension is always important for me—the characters expressing rhythms for the audience.

LO: Were there any major differences between the L.A. production of *Godot* and the Atlanta production?

jc: In both cases I cast the roles six months ahead of the start of rehearsals, so the actors could explore the play more deeply. In Los Angeles, where there are many fine Beckett actors, I was able to cast the play interracially with a black man [Shabaka, known also as Barry Henley] as Didi.

lo: How much rehearsal time do you usually . . .

jc: One month.

lo: And you'll have one month here in New York before you open at the Public?

jc: Yes, that's right. But we are also doing preliminary work this summer, because the text is very difficult, and we need to experiment.

lo: Were there any other ways in which the L.A. production differed from the Atlanta production?

[BILL COCO: The occasional acknowledgment of the audience in the Atlanta production is one different element. From time to time the actors on stage acknowledge the audience with their questions. That's a big difference.]

lo: You have acted in Beckett's work as well as directed it. Can you tell how your experience as an actor of Beckett has affected your work as a director of Beckett?

jc: I don't know. I don't work in a technical way. We explore things together. For example, Bill Irwin's work as a clown—we can use that element in the performance, but nothing is set.

lo: How close is your staging of *Godot* to Beckett's directing of *Godot?*

jc: I am not able to evaluate his directing because I have not seen a live performance under his direction. I did, however, see two videotapes: the German and American versions of *Godot*. Beckett's directing is not of interest to me. As a writer, he is wonderful, a genius. But the directing, though it is very clear, is only average and not inspired.

lo: So Beckett's directing didn't really influence you in any way as a director?

jc: No.

lo: Is there anything else you would like to talk about?

jc: I am concentrating on *Texts* now; it will be very different from what it was eleven years ago.

lo: In what way will this production be different?

jc: I am always thinking about plays I have already done, along with those I want to do. It is a complex process. When Ruby Cohn and Bill Coco came up with the idea of doing *Texts* again, this time with me

Fig. 5. Bill Irwin in *Texts for Nothing,* directed by Joseph Chaikin. The Joseph Papp Public/Susan Stein Shiva Theater, New York City, 1992. Photo credit: Martha Swope.

directing and with Bill Irwin performing, I took to the idea immediately. Although I had met Bill only recently, I had admired his work for a long time. I liked the physicality of his presence, and now that we've begun to work together I find we really enjoy collaborating together. He is excellent for *Texts*.

LO: Do you consider yourself relatively faithful to Beckett, as a director?

JC: Sure.

LO: Very?

JC: I'm not *so* orthodox. We have compressed *Texts* to a running time of about an hour, for example, but we haven't changed the words.

LO: You wouldn't change a word?

JC: Certainly not.

LO: And you follow the stage directions very carefully?

JC: With *Texts*, of course, there are no stage directions, but when I stage a Beckett play I am very faithful. I believe that is the way to do the plays.

LO: And you wouldn't go along with changing the setting of any Beckett play?

JC: No, I wouldn't. No. But that is not the only way to be true to Beckett.

LO: How does directing Beckett differ from directing other playwrights for you?

JC: I prefer to be faithful to a script, by Beckett or anyone else. Next spring I shall be directing *The War in Heaven* for the first time. I wrote it together with Sam Shepard, and I acted in it a number of times. When we did it last year at the American Place Theatre we sat down and changed the play, which was originally written in 1985. Since Sam and I wrote it together, I felt freer to make changes. In the future I hope to direct Pirandello's *Enrico IV* and then Adrienne Kennedy's *A Movie Star Has to Star in Black and White*. I like plays, and I like to be faithful to the writer.

[BC: When Joe is working on a classical text, an established text— Beckett, Pirandello, whatever—he is very true to the work. It is not an experimental production. However, when he is working with Sam Shepard on a new play, such as *The War in Heaven*, they collaborate together. For example, last spring, when we produced *The War in Heaven*, Sam came back, and together we all reworked the text; we added a few new lines, shifted things around, compressed it a little bit. It was about ten minutes shorter than the original, and so forth. The original was for radio. This was for the stage. So Joe is much freer when he is generating his own text.]

LO: Obviously, since you have adapted *Texts for Nothing,* you have no objection to transforming one genre to another. Doing the radio plays in the theater is okay with you? And you would be in agreement with all the prose texts being staged for the theater?

JC: Yes.

Gregory Mosher

In 1974 GREGORY MOSHER went to the Goodman Theatre in Chicago as assistant to the artistic director and the inaugural director of Stage 2, Goodman's experimental series. In 1977 he was named director of the Goodman. Former Mayor John V. Lindsay, then chairman of the Lincoln Center Theatre, appointed Mosher to head the fifth administration of that theater in 1985. After thirty-seven productions he resigned from that position in January 1992. In addition to producing many of Beckett's works at the Goodman and Lincoln Center theaters, Mosher was responsible for the Lincoln Center Theater's memorialization of Beckett, entitled "Beckett's Words: A Celebration of Samuel Beckett" (which featured Billie Whitelaw, Barry McGovern, Chris O'Neill, Ruth Maleczech, and Alvin Epstein). What follows is an abridged version of a conversation that took place in New York in the summer of 1992.

GREGORY MOSHER: My run with Beckett began in high school, in 1966, when a fellow student suggested that our English class read *Waiting for Godot*. I had never heard of it or Beckett. I remember being haunted by that beautiful black-and-white photo on the cover. And I remember thinking that *Godot* was *exactly* like life. I had no interest in the theater then, so this was really the beginning of something new for me.

In college I tried to be in *Godot*, but I wasn't cast. I tried to direct it, but another student got that assignment. I ended up at Juilliard, where a faculty member directed it, so I started to prepare a production of *Endgame*. This effort led me to Alan Schneider, first his notes and correspondence with Beckett and then a few days of conversations. Alan was remarkably generous; I was, after all, only a student. I remember his insistence that everything be specific. He asked why I thought Clov couldn't sit down and cut off my thematic answer with an impatient: "He's got hemorrhoids, for Chrissake! Keep it simple!" But then a few students quit school, and a few more were thrown out, and suddenly I had no cast to go with my research, and I left school, too.

In Chicago, where I had gone to assist Bill Woodman and run a second stage at the Goodman Theatre, I got a call from Rick Cluchey. This was 1975, and Rick had just returned from Germany, where he had been assisting Beckett with *Waiting for Godot.* He came over that afternoon and showed me rehearsal photos, along with Rick's young son, Louis, in Sam's arms. The proud godfather.

Beckett had directed Rick in *Krapp's Last Tape,* and Rick wanted to know if we would present it at the Goodman. We did, of course, and that was the first of the "Beckett Directs Beckett" projects that we were to do over the years.

A year or so later, after a Chicago run and extended tour of *Krapp,* Rick and Sam came up with a plan to do *Endgame.* We would rehearse in London, open in Ireland, and then come to Chicago.

So, off we went to London. We were doing this on a shoestring, of course. For a day or so work went quietly, almost anonymously. Inevitably, though, word got out, first in the theater community and then through the general academic world, that the great man was in town rehearsing one of his masterpieces. So, two parallel events progressed—the production of *Endgame* and the tracking of the reclusive maestro. We arranged to have seats set up in the rather large rehearsal room for visitors. They were at some remove, perhaps even cordoned off. *Everyone* had a pad and pencil. But Beckett spoke rarely, and when he did it was a whisper, so I don't know what, if anything, they heard.

So far as the process of directing the play went, it was very straight-forward. He heard the play clearly in his head, and he had planned all the moves. He proceeded with great patience, of course, and with enormous attention to detail. He had memorized the text, down to the punctuation, and he was very strict about rhythm.

I think that this approach was sometimes counterproductive to his wishes, which were, so far as I could tell, that the play sound as lifelike as possible. When he himself did Nagg's ash can speech, for instance, it sounded for all the world like any story you'd hear in a pub. It was in no way stylized. The text itself is, of course, not naturalistic, but it comes alive when delivered in a simple, truthful way, with no attempt to create a Beckett style.

There is a danger in quoting writers about how their work should be performed, and it is the most obvious one, which is removing the comments from the context in which they were spoken. Good directors don't theorize a lot; they respond to what the actors are doing. Therefore, their directing is often corrective.

Here's an example. I happened to be in London when Beckett's great actress, Billie Whitelaw, was rehearsing *Rockaby*. Alan was directing, and Sam was at the rehearsal, in the Cottesloe. Of course, the actress has only one line, which is spoken live, in accompaniment to her taped voice. It is the word *More*, and it is spoken at several intervals to get the remembered voice to continue. They ran it through once, and, while Alan was off dealing with lights or something, Billie asked Sam what he thought. And he said, "Well, Billie, I think it's very important that there be no emotion at all." What she had been doing was to say the line almost as a cry, and he simply wanted less voice, less stress. She said the line for him more simply, and he was pleased, as well he should have been, for the emotional power of the moment was strengthened immeasurably. Now, that's all fine, until somebody somewhere says, "Well I heard that Beckett told Billie Whitelaw that the lines should have no emotion." And you can imagine what kind of production that would lead to. So, I am suspicious of these anecdotes, including mine, of course.

LOIS OPPENHEIM: Do you need specific skills to direct Beckett?

GM: No, that's my point, you see. Beckett was a great playwright. You can't do a slapdash production, because, if you haven't thought it through and cast it well and so forth, it's going to show. It's not the director's job to be interesting or original or provocative. You just have to be true to the play, which you will inevitably do after your own fashion.

I'm leery of the notion of received wisdom, as if there were some special, secret code. A story has come down that Beckett saw the first English production of *Godot* and turned to Alan and said, "It's all wrong." My problem with this is the implication that Beckett's confidant would always be *right*, that there is a right and a wrong way to do a play. I don't believe that there is the drama and then there is a separate thing, Beckett.

LO: What about the critical response to Beckett?

GM: If you are referring to the daily press, as opposed to serious scholars, I have to say that they are pathetic. They sit in the most pompous and ludicrous kind of judgment on their betters, and what they have to say is, I'm afraid, utterly worthless.

LO: Do you explain much when you direct?

GM: I don't think that the meaning of the play is of much use to the actors, if that's what you mean. It may or may not be interesting to them, but they can't act the meaning. They can only act the action, the story. It's their job, in Stanislavski's phrase, "to live truthfully under the imaginary circumstances of the play." And I will do what I can to help that process. What it comes down to is telling a story.

Plays that were generally classified as part of the Theater of the Absurd generally fell into two categories. First was the extended metaphor, such as Ionesco's *The Chairs*. The other was a very simple story, stripped of all the naturalistic goo that had accumulated since the 1880s. Pinter once said about one of his plays that it was about "a guy who wants to get somebody, and he gets him." *That's* what you direct, not "Pinter Pauses." You *direct* a story about two guys who are waiting for a guy who doesn't show up.

What makes Beckett so powerful is precisely this ability to condense the experience of an apocalyptic century into a simple story, rendered with the absolute simplest of dialogue. He is not a miniaturist. He compresses the universe into an atom, which then explodes in our imagination.

JoAnne Akalaitis

JOANNE AKALAITIS was a founding member of Mabou Mines. She directed Beckett's radio play *Cascando* (adapted by Lee Breuer) for the stage in 1976 and, in 1984, directed *Endgame* at the American Repertory Theatre (A.R.T.) in Cambridge, Massachusetts. From 1991 to 1993 JoAnne Akalaitis was artistic director of the New York Shakespeare Festival at the Joseph Papp Public and Delacorte theaters. In addition to directing, she has acted in the Mabou Mines productions of *Play, Come and Go,* and *The Lost Ones.*

LOIS OPPENHEIM: There were several other productions before your *Endgame* at the A.R.T. that could well have provoked as much of a negative reaction on Beckett's part but didn't. Why yours, when others got by?

JOANNE AKALAITIS: I think it was a fluke. I think that someone got Beckett riled up, got him upset, and it just captured his imagination. You're right. There were productions set in water, and so on.

LO: And then there was Andre Gregory's . . . [1]

JA: . . . even my production of *Cascando,* which was an adaptation for the stage of a radio play. Beckett knew about that, and he was upset. I

---

1. As Jonathan Kalb explains:

The "Bare interior" specified in the script [of *Endgame*] has been rendered variously as a skull, a womb, a fallout shelter, and, in a particularly unrestrained production by Andre Gregory, a cage. In his 1973 version with the Manhattan Project, Gregory seated the spectators in cubicles of four (the number of characters in the play) separated from each other and from the hexagonal arena stage by chicken wire. One saw the playing area only blurrily through this wire and a covering scrim, which was flooded with bright light reflected off a shiny metal floor. Certain details nevertheless did appear clearly, e.g., the location of Nell in a refrigerator box and Nagg in a laundry hamper, inside which he later hangs himself. And many liberties were also taken with Beckett's language, seemingly in the interests of humor. (*Beckett in Performance* [Cambridge: Cambridge University Press, 1989], 78) don't think he particularly liked the set. I think [the *Endgame* scandal] was a very strange event in the history of theater.

LO: Barney Rosset came out strongly against your staging of the play, though he hadn't seen it. [Jack] Garfein was sent to see it, but he was in the midst of his own production of *Endgame,* not the most propitious time for an objective evaluation. Beckett hadn't seen it. Regardless of who was "right" or "wrong" in the whole affair, wasn't there something fundamentally unjust in all that?

JA: I tend not to think in these political ways about exterior motives. I was more perplexed by it. I thought it was clearly wrongheaded.

LO: Were you ever tempted to back down at all?

JA: No. We did the play. That's what we did; *we did the play.*

LO: Would you like to take this opportunity to comment on any of the remarks about the production that have been made by other directors in their contributions to this book?

JA: For every production that one does there are people who adore it, and there are people who don't like it. Some people loved *The Balcony;* other people hated it. In that way *Endgame* is no different from any part of a director's work.

LO: How do you feel about all that happened now that several years have passed?

JA: I loved the production. I look back on it with tremendous fondness. I had an intensely rich time working on it. I'm very, very proud of the work we did. I feel toward it the way I feel toward practically everything I do. I feel that it was good work. Sometimes one has a very difficult time. Sometimes one has an easy time. To work on it was intense and thrilling.

LO: Has your thinking about it evolved in any way since 1984?

JA: I don't think much about old productions. I think about what I'm doing in the present. That seems quite a long time ago. Nothing has changed. I think it was a fabulous production.

LO: Do you think you will ever direct Beckett again?

JA: Sure.

LO: Does the fact that he is no longer with us have any bearing on that?

JA: It will probably be easier for me. I doubt that when Beckett was alive I would have gotten permission to direct another play.

LO: Is there anything about Beckett's work that requires any particular skills on the part of those who direct it?

JA: I think the language is very rigorous, so you really have to pay attention to it. But any good director does that anyway with any play. With Beckett the rhythms are really in high relief. Dramatically, their music is so particular, so brilliant, that you have to go very deep into that, into the rhythms. And there is also the great humor. And the form is clear, rigorous, outstanding.

I'm directing *Woyzeck* right now. [Georg] Büchner's unfinished play is so open, so all over the place there is hardly any language in it. In a Beckett play there seem to be seven words for every one word of a normal play. It's like Ben Jonson, like *Volpone* in a way, although that's totally different.

LO: Why did you take it underground?

JA: It was a subway. It was not necessarily underground. I wanted a kind of ruined contemporary place, an urban contemporary place. The subway seemed . . .

LO: But Beckett didn't want an "urban contemporary place," and he wrote the play.

JA: He obviously didn't want that because he tried to bring an injunction against the performance.

LO: Then what made you feel that you could situate it there?

JA: I think that when a playwright licenses a work, especially if it's not the premiere of the play, it is licensed to a director, and in a sense it is given over. It's gone. You buy the Samuel French edition of some play in which Noel Coward says, for example, "A blond woman walks in and sits in a purple chair." Are you violating Noel Coward's play by casting a brunette who sits in a maroon chair? So, Beckett says, "Gray room, two windows." It simply never occurred to me that one would actually *do* *it* in a gray room with two windows. I mean, what do we do as directors and designers? We don't just buy the Samuel French edition and say, "Here's the prop list; here's what the set should look like."

LO: What *do* you do as a director?

JA: You create the play. The script is the starting point. The script is dramatic literature. The script is not the play. The play is an event.

LO: So, you do more than interpret the play. You create the play.

JA: I don't think about interpreting or creating. I think that one does it. One *does* the play. There is this very silly reaction toward directors as *auteurs*—that, if you have a visual idea, if you do more than put a tree on a stage, you have violated the author's intentions. Are directors ruining plays? It's really a very false, a misguided, notion about what theater is, because theater is what happens on the stage. It's about design and actors and director and audience.

LO: Lee [Breuer] told me that "there is no such thing as directing," that "the director, as such, in the abstract, doesn't exist." And he has compared directing as a "skill" to that of a typist? Would you agree?

JA: I don't believe that at all. I think the director is like a sculptor, a shaper, a former, an idea person, a visionary, an artist. I don't think typists are artists. I think directors are artists.

LO: He feels that every great director was either a poet who happened to have another skill—that of directing—or a painter who happened to have another skill or an artist of some other kind who happened also to be able to direct. You wouldn't agree with that?

JA: No, I don't think so.

LO: Why are there so few women directing Beckett?

JA: Why are there so few women directors?

LO: There really is an incredible paucity of women directors, but I don't know if that's the only answer. Do you think there is anything endemic to Beckett's work that keeps the few women directors there are from taking on his plays?

JA: I think his work is very male in a sort of unsexed way. *Waiting for Godot* is basically a buddy story. Beckett's own strangeness about women in his own life. . . . It's not a question of reading his biography and saying, "He didn't talk to his wife for thirty years, so why should I direct his plays?" I never thought about it that way. Certainly, *Happy Days* is just a great, great play and just a wonderful role for a woman.

LO: There are many great women's roles in Beckett, but there are so few women directing them.

JA: I don't think it has much to do with anything. How many women direct *Henry IV*? I did. Some women might be inclined to cast Beckett's work with women. I did see a scene at the Women's Project of *Waiting for Godot* with women, and seeing that scene performed by women made me realize how much that play is about male psychology.

Endgame is about male relationships. And then, of course, there's Nagg and Nell. Nell is very beautifully written. So, Beckett really does know how to write for women, and in the radio plays there are great roles for women. I think that Beckett understood the female soul in an old-fashioned literary way, in a way that is very moving, especially as it manifests itself in *Happy Days*.

LO: Do you think that as a female director you bring anything to Beckett's work that a male director might not?

JA: I bring to all my work the fact that I am a woman, and it is apparent in varying degrees. I don't know how it's apparent in Beckett.

LO: How has it been apparent elsewhere?

JA: It varies from show to show. Sometimes it's about choice. The fact that a woman who is a feminist decides to direct *'Tis Pity She's a Whore* exposes something about that play. I come at it as a feminist; it's not that you see it.

LO: Were there any particular influences on your production of *Endgame?* Were you at all interested in Beckett's own directing of it?

JA: I'm not interested in Beckett's direction. I don't know it. I was very influenced by the book *Awakenings* by Oliver Sacks, which is about being stuck and then being released. I've used it in *Woyzeck*. I've used it a lot. I'm very influenced by that book.

LO: How do you use it?

JA: Just descriptions of behavior. I gave it to the actors in *Woyzeck*. I think the way Sacks writes about psychology is very interesting. To write about these psychological or neurological states in which one is either spinning through space or absolutely rigid is very hooked into the Beckett psychology, the Beckett rhythms.

LO: How did you direct *Endgame?*

JA: We worked rhythmically a lot. I didn't spend a lot of time talking about the play. I spent a lot of time talking about rhythm, music, and a lot of time just doing it—doing it and doing it. Oddly enough, for a play that people said violated Beckett it was very rigid, kind of fascist in its rehearsal process. We had a stage manager count out the beats of the pauses to determine which pauses were three beats, which pauses were two beats. I'm very interested in the physicalness of it. I had an actor who played Clov, John Bottoms, who I think was the ultimate physicalization of that character. And I was very interested in the environment that had water in it, in this basically hostile actors' environment. That was a lot of work for them, a lot of work for me, and fascinating and rich.

LO: How did it compare with your experience of doing *Cascando?*

JA: With *Cascando* I loved the idea of doing a play in a room, in a corner of a room, in which the people are sort of trapped. I'm setting *Woyzeck* in a room now. Since *Cascando* my work has become very big and scenically rich, with a lot of moving scenery. This *Cascando* was about a company of actors around a table and a kind of shared psychology, a shared

voice. We rehearsed it for months and months. It was complicated, and
it had very beautiful music. I loved that the actors didn't get up until the
end of the play. I thought it was a formidable challenge.

LO: Any final remarks you would like to make?

JA: I think the whole *Endgame* brouhaha came out of an unnatural
reverence for Beckett that I think is strange. I feel it's academic. Bill Coco
said to me, "The Beckett people like *Woyzeck.*" I said, "*Who are 'the Beckett
people?'*" It's like "*The Rocky Horror Show* people.*" I mean, *who are these
"Beckett people"?* There is this sort of Becketty cult. I don't get it. Indeed,
for me Beckett and Genet are the two greatest dramatists of the twentieth
century, complete opposites, and at this point in my life I feel more
emotionally attuned to Genet in every way.

LO: Edward Albee expressed a fear of Beckett's falling to the academics and what might be the consequences of that, and Lee Breuer just
made a remark very similar to yours about being much more connected
to Genet now.

JA: I don't think there's a Genet group. The Genet people would
probably be drag queens from the lower East Side, or S&M brothel people.
It's a kind of mystery to me that these Beckett people rose from the ranks
of academia to be the conscience of the Beckett aesthetic. I don't know
where that comes from. It's like a postwar European idea about theater.

LO: That's where your *Endgame* affair originated?

JA: Yes. Absolutely. I think it was grounded in protectiveness toward
Beckett, protectiveness toward the austere. His stage directions are no
more important than any other writer's stage directions—those of Ibsen,
Shakespeare, anybody. I pay a lot of attention to stage directions, a lot
more attention to Beckett's than to any other modern writer's, because of
the obvious rigor of his work, of his internal plan about the work. So, I
don't know what that's all about, who the Beckett people are. It must be
some strange club that meets in a gray room with no windows or
something . . .

LO: But Barney [Rosset] is not an academic. And Garfein is not an
academic. They are the ones who initially objected . . .

JA: That's right, but I think the ranks of the academic world lined
up for or against it.

LO: Some found it a very faithful production despite the urban context
you gave it.

JA: I think it was very, very faithful.

2. Essays

In an essay on Beckett Alan Schneider relates an "apocryphal story about Sam's next play": "Untitled, of course. In two acts, the usual pause between. In the first act, the curtain rises on a bare stage. No actors, of either sex. Runs about half an hour. In the second act, the curtain doesn't rise at all; but it's a very short act."[1] One wonders how it might be staged (the question of fidelity notwithstanding)! The essays that follow reflect such originality of practice in the directing of Beckett that one might indeed speculate on the possibilities.

"Performing Voices: Notes from Stagings of Beckett's Work" pleads for a better understanding of the distinction between "artistic freedom" and "aesthetic license." In an effort to elucidate what exactly is violated when a director transposes the site of a Beckett work (either by the moving of locale or the jumping of genres), Robert Scanlan is led to comment on a number of productions including JoAnne Akalaitis's *Endgame* and Gildas Bourdet's staging of the same work at the Comédie Française. Articulating the boundaries that Beckett's voices in and of themselves delineate, this essay examines the reduction imposed on Beckett's texts by what he considers to be erroneous directorial conceptions.

Bourdet, as though in direct response to the questions Scanlan raises, defends his vision and justifies his choices for the production that provoked the Paris outburst. Considering directing as much a matter of ethics as aesthetics, he defines the kind of rapport a director must have with a play to legitimate its staging and argues that, in principle, whatever it takes to ensure that rapport is theatrically valid. In a letter to Beckett dated 5 October 1988 Bourdet explained his position and gave further evidence of his deeply felt conviction that his production conformed to the spirit of Beckett's work:

> The author's rights justify the decision you are making; the moral

rights of the director are as legitimate insofar as, repudiated by you, he must move aside, sick at heart, to give way to emptiness and, as far as I am concerned, sadness and pain; for sadness and pain represent for me the true "consequences" of this affair—as, from now on, I will have to give up this fervent, passionate, and fraternal rapport which, for three months, I have maintained with your work and through it, who knows, with you yourself, although you were never aware of it. The rest is insignificant compared with the violence of this personal catastrophe that resembles only too much those described in your play.[2]

Bourdet was ultimately refused the right to stage the play as he had conceived of it. *Fin de partie* was played at the Comédie Française "in a version free of any production element imagined by him or by any of his collaborators."[3] As expressed in the official statement issued by the theater, Bourdet acknowledged Beckett's right "to not allow the staging of one of his plays if he thinks the production might displease him." But he "profoundly and sadly deplores the way Mr. Beckett disposes of his right," for the playwright had not seen Bourdet's work before deciding to prevent it and based his decision on a description written by the director at the request of Jérôme Lindon, Beckett's publisher at the Editions de Minuit. This, of course, raised the question for Bourdet of a confusion of author's rights with censorship: he feared that, should such practice "become widespread among living dramatists, French theater would again run the risk of being 'museified,' something from which Samuel Beckett himself suffered in his time."[4]

None of the four essays that follow deals with particularly controversial issues. Rather, each focuses on the power of Beckett's plays and the specificity of the directorial point of view that concretizes it. Carey Perloff brought to her production of *Happy Days* the experience of having recently directed a play of Harold Pinter ("a startling homage to Pinter's mentor, Beckett") and that of being the mother of a year-old child ("who exhibited so many of Winnie's behavioral traits"). Both serve as points of departure for her exploration of the rehearsal process that preceded the play's run, first in Los Angeles and then in New York. Xerxes Mehta is concerned with the "hauntings" that define Beckett's later short plays. His seemingly phenomenological view of Beckett's images as referential only to themselves pays moving testimony to the kind of intersubjective experience of performer and spectator that determines the success of Beckett's utterly humanistic theater.

Everett Frost has encountered logistical problems of a nature limited to work in radio, and in the essay included here he outlines those dealt with in his directing of *All That Fall* and their resolution. The comparison of some of his efforts to those of Donald McWhinnie (who had previously produced the play for the British Broadcasting Corporation [BBC]) serves to distinguish an approach exquisitely sensitive to the insufficiencies of methodology in the accurate projection of concept. Directing Beckett "down under"—which is to say, in a milieu not attuned to the likes of this playwright—has posed a rather unique set of problems for Colin Duckworth, who introduced Beckett to his audience in ways only a detailed examination of the rehearsal process can account for. This he provides in the context of both textual interpretation and the transcription of rehearsal dialogue.

The next two essays do have controversy of one sort or another as a focal point. At the center of Ilan Ronen's discussion of his staging of *Waiting for Godot* is not only the aesthetic debate over the validity of contextualizing the play spatiotemporally but his integration into the play of the political conflict between the Arab and Israeli populations of the Middle East. Transforming Vladimir and Estragon into Palestinian laborers "waiting for a Godot to deliver them from their misery" and having the dialogue spoken partially in Hebrew and partially in Arabic resulted in a production enormously challenging to director and audience alike. Gerry McCarthy's rethinking of the process of directing Beckett unveils conflict of another kind: that between the actors' habitual quest for coherence in interpretation and the kind of disintegration the performance of these plays, at first, requires. The reintegration or synthesis of a Beckettian role, McCarthy argues, implies an initial fragmentation that expresses the self on an implicitly dramatic horizon.

Eve Adamson and Robert McNamara close this section by discussions of the Beckett play in larger contexts: Adamson explores the staging of Beckett in repertory, in which each production is nourished by those that precede or follow it, and McNamara, within the framework of directing Beckett in the playwright's native Ireland, writes of the effectiveness of juxtaposing his dramatic works to the work of another on the same program or to his own narrative voices.

NOTES

1. The manuscript of this untitled essay is with the Alan Schneider Papers (MSS 103), Mandeville Department of Special Collections, University of California–San Diego.

2. This letter, along with a number of other documents relating to the production in question, was provided to me by Bourdet. All quotations from the letter and the statement issued by the Comédie Française were translated by Florence Sapinart.

3. Official statement of the Comédie Française.

4. Ibid.

Performing Voices: Notes from Stagings of Beckett's Work

Robert Scanlan

The purest possible performance version of the "voice" of Beckett's prose works—those which were not written for the stage—is probably recorded sound emanating from the dark. The plays written for the stage present a different problem, and this concerns visualization, or the *setting* of these plays in actual theaters. The points of reference for "proper" staging of the dramatic works, and the acceptable limits of formal "genre jumping" for the prose compositions, can and should be set. These things are not just matters of opinion. Accessible criteria can be readily mapped out, primarily by *locating* the voice in the formal structure of each piece and next by realizing that the location of voice is central to the formal and aesthetic integrity of almost all of Beckett's work. There are two basic principles that summarize all I have to say: (1) it is possible to do Beckett wrong, and (2) it matters.

Beckett himself has said to me (and to others) that certain texts come from "things heard" and others come from "things seen." Some texts are generated by a visible figure, and others are heard only by an invisible auditor. These distinctions, in fact, define the difference between the dramatic and the nondramatic texts. The internal *action* (in the Aristotelian sense of that word) is our surest path to locating voices. If a voice cannot be located, then its text cannot be "staged" by a live actor without disrupting the action (and thereby the intrinsic nature) of the piece. Since all the Beckett works are fundamentally structured around the voice, any handling of the text that fails to locate the voice accurately will disrupt the formal coherence of the work.

Several notorious stagings of Beckett's plays and prose have brought up the issue of acceptable interpretation in performance and the "proper handling" of Beckett's works. The question of "author's intent"—an inaccurate catchphrase for a real issue—will not go away, and the permissible range of Auteur/Director tamperings with finished works of art comes up too frequently to be ignored. The pluralist approach of broad tolerance for any and all experiments and failures is unacceptable, for it hides timidity in the face of disintegrating standards, and it is predicated on a demoralizing assumption that these controversies are of no real consequence: that works of art (and especially performances) are as ephemeral as leaves, that no single production carries a burden of lasting cultural consequence.

In 1988 the Comédie Française got into an altercation with Beckett over a production of *Fin de partie* that it had invited to the Palais Royal. The production, conceived and directed by Gildas Bourdet, of the Théâtre de la Salamandre, took enormous scenic liberties with Beckett's text, and it led Beckett and his publisher, Jérôme Lindon, to intervene. They asked that the production be withdrawn. This imbroglio was similar, in the way it unfolded, to the notorious *Endgame* affair four years earlier at the American Repertory Theatre (A.R.T.) in Cambridge, Massachusetts. In the Paris incident the offending production "concept" was signaled earlier to Beckett's attention, and his objections to directorial liberties prevailed before the production opened. His *"droit moral"* was recognized, and the production was modified to acknowledge his objections, but the settlement was awkward, and the resulting production of *Fin de partie* hobbled along rather grudgingly, displaying its sense of injury. The offending set was conspicuously draped in unbleached muslin, and props and costumes were allowed to clash rather obviously (in ways it would have cost nothing to modify) with the lamely corrected setting.

The Comédie Française managed to look sulky and petulant in its compliance with the *droit moral* it conceded while begging the larger questions of outright *legal* rights and aesthetic integrity. The entire incident lacked grace. It was saved only by the superb performances of Roland Bertin and Michel Aumont, who seemed unperturbed by the disgraced remnants of an interdicted "concept" of production. By leaving traces of what they had been forbidden to present visible everywhere, the Comédie Française complied with the letter only and not the spirit of their settlement with Beckett. Gildas Bourdet removed his name from the programs. The production as it finally appeared had clearly managed to reserve its own *droit moral* willfully to depart from the authority of the text and author, even if the full realization of these intentions would have to await another occasion.

Beckett seemed to find it self-evident that the young director in question did not know what he was doing with *Fin de partie*. The decision,
among others, to crowd the stage with a dozen or more wax dummies in
various attitudes convinced Beckett that he was dealing with nothing more
than a young director's struggle to get noticed and advance his career. In
the year before his death Beckett expressed a weary resignation in the face
of the decreasing likelihood that such revisions and tamperings with his
work might effectively be controlled. He was not happy, quite obviously,
about this state of affairs. He clearly felt at the last as he had always felt
about this matter: that there was something significant at stake.

Is it possible to define what it is that is at stake? I believe that it is.
Recognition of formal accomplishments and respect for them as values in
their own right are defining acts of a culture. With Beckett we seem to
be confronted over and over again with the recognition that he has somehow
achieved fame, but we see far less frequently the evidence of any deeper
understanding of his accomplishment as an artist. This is an issue in our
time, precisely because we see the pursuit of fame, notoriety, and fortune
displacing the values contained and expressed by formal mastery such as
Beckett's. In addition, there is the question of the meaning of the plays.
Have we conceded that these meanings are nonessential? Is the willful
marring of the forms—through addition of visual material or bold new
concepts of performance—not a disregard for the *meaning* of the plays?
Both theater artists and the critical profession seem to be increasingly
intimidated by current trends of postmodernism and a few ill-digested
caveats derived from "deconstructive" criticism. We are afraid of the idea
of right and wrong in artistic procedures and equally timid about a mission
as teachers: that there are criteria of excellence to be learned from the
example of masters, to be practiced, and to be eventually mastered, if that
is within our power. Also there are significant acts of witness to be experienced in major works of art, and there is a duty to attend to these.

One objection to the *Endgame* presented in Cambridge at the American
Repertory Theatre in 1984 was the transposition of the play into a real
location: an abandoned subway tunnel under a New York City devastated
by nuclear war. This central aesthetic error was the governing "concept"
of JoAnne Akalaitis's directorial take on the play. It has been debated ever
since Beckett sought to have the production stopped, but very little discourse has centered on the grounds for objecting to the staging. *Endgame*
is hopelessly confused when presented as a horrible thing that happened
to two homeless bums in Manhattan. The text no longer made any sense

in its transposed setting. The careful ballet of words and actions in the
stark, bare space of the original became a driveling patter and capricious
antics. The play was trashed for "effects," and Beckett was quick to strike
back. "Anybody who cares for the work," he wrote in a program insert,
"couldn't fail to be disgusted by this." It was to be Beckett's most intem-
perate public outburst.

But four years later Mike Nichols staged *Waiting for Godot* at Lincoln
Center in a setting that reproduced exactly the aesthetic error of JoAnne
Akalaitis's *Endgame*. There was no outcry in that instance, no effort to
close the production or demand that it be altered. Was there less harm
done to *Godot*? Beckett was not so sure. He certainly monitored the production as closely as he had any production outside of Paris. He expressed
early reservations about the casting of the play, met with Nichols and the
Lincoln Center's producing director Greg Mosher in Paris, sent his trusted
German collaborator Walter Asmus to New York to look in on the evolving
production, and corresponded with American friends and colleagues who
either knew the actors or had seen the play. The same Beckett "network"
that had told him about the Akalaitis *Endgame* appeased his growing apprehension about what was happening to *Godot*. In the end he concluded
that what had been done to *Godot* was acceptable, whereas what had been
done to *Endgame* was not.

These two cases illustrate the boundary I am talking about. The
slightly larger latitude Beckett could allow for *Godot* results, I think, from
the fact that it was less fully "visualized" at the time of its composition.
As a result, *Godot* is less formally dependent on the question of place. Yet
the play was still diminished by being set, in Tony Walton's design, on
an old state highway in Nevada, midway between the Nevada nuclear test
flats and Death Valley. The association of ideas was apparent but conceived
on a disappointing level of literal free association: the royal road to full-
blown postmodernism. It could be argued that Nichols's entire production
of *Waiting for Godot* was a game of substitutions: Native American equiv-
alencies were dreamed up for every aspect of the original, including Famous
American Clown substitutes for Didi and Gogo in the form of Robin
Williams and Steve Martin.

Postmodernism, as a style, does have a case to be made for it. It is
not in itself the responsible culprit for damage done to Beckett's work in
recent stagings. There is a profoundly legitimate impulse behind a wildly
eclectic style that borrows freely from popular culture, from high and low
references, mixing new visual effects and advanced sound engineering with

the more traditional theater arts: lighting, sets, costumes, props. There is a grim desperation being expressed by the artists of excess, who reach as readily for advertising jingles or neon advertising signs as they do for the resources of so-called high culture. The flotsam and the jetsam of a culture out of control, fragments shored against a sense of ruin—these are the medium of postmodernism. Its pop incongruity and quirky transpositions to the unexpectedly familiar are its idiom.

The plays of Shakespeare have been given provocative new stagings by innovative directors intent on deconstructing old conventions and a received "language" in the theater that has traditionally signaled that one is doing Shakespeare. The results have often been spectacular and illuminating. I have found myself in the odd position of defending a production of *Twelfth Night* staged by Andrei Serban, again at the American Repertory Theatre, to a high school teacher who wanted to cancel tickets for 120 students because she thought this staging was a poor way to introduce students to Shakespeare. I strenuously disagreed. How does Beckett's work differ? Why should these new styles and free reinterpretations not be used for new explorations of Beckett's work?

The answer is that Shakespeare's plays cannot survive manipulations that disrupt their formal principle of coherence any better than can Beckett's—but Shakespeare's plays have a different form, which is not automatically jeopardized by certain transpositions of style and setting. The plays are made of traditional scenic interplays of character and story, and their internal actions can remain intact in a wide range of languages and settings. Beckett's plays, and especially his late work for the stage, cannot survive analogous formal manipulations, because these disrupt the central action of the play, which is often a quest for the origin of voices. In the case of the prose works written for the page the transposition seems outright impossible, for purely formal reasons.

The extreme case of the prose in performance illuminates best what I mean by formal constraints that lie beyond questions of opinion and mere preference or loyalty to the author's expressed wishes. In prose works (or writings not intended for the stage) the action is often the location of a voice, or "placing the voice." One of the best methods of analysis I have found for Beckett's works, whether they are for the theater or not, is the identification of each "locus of being" as it is revealed by the presence or absence of a voice.

Company is one of the clearest texts for illustrating the notion of locus of being in Beckett's work, because the text makes consistent use of grammatical "persons" to clarify the locus of being, or the source of provenance of the voice recorded in the text. The clarity of this rigorous bookkeeping has attracted an unusual number of theater artists to this work. I have written elsewhere about Frederick Neumann's 1982 version of this text and John Russell Brown's staging of it in 1981 at the National Theatre.[1] *Company* has subsequently been staged by Pierre Chabert in Paris and by Stan Gontarski in a well-documented version in San Francisco, and Katharine Worth directed Julian Curry in a London version that was meticulously musical and astute in its choice of images. But the prominent visible figures in all these versions, I still contend, falsify the situation of the text, especially if "he" speaks. And the situation of the text is its entire meaning. The problem of *Company* is one of heard voices. In Gontarski's version, which seems the best conceived of the many I have heard of or seen, the audience was allowed to see Alan Mandell *listening to* rather than producing text—but who was he meant to be, and when did he speak? What was *he* meant to mean?

Another example of the unusual degree to which Beckett pieces depend on the *exact* concomitants of the forms he has devised for them is *Not I,* which I staged in Cambridge, Massachusetts, with Kristin Linklater in the fall of 1987. We identified four distinct loci of being operative in the text:

1. the mouth, which spews the written text;
2. "she," whose story is told in the text;
3. the figure, whose gestures express helpless compassion while hearing or "witnessing" the text; and
4. an elusive interrogator, who interrupts Mouth's text, prompts her to say "I," forces her to revise some details, questions her.

Not a single one of these is properly "I." But all four coexist in complex relationships that are perfectly rendered by the image Beckett devised for performance. Any tampering with text or image disrupts the problem of the four loci and the agony of finding a coherent being among them.

After performing this difficult text, Kristin Linklater found strange dislocations and discharges of speech triggered in her own psyche, obviously induced by her absorption in Beckett's *matière,* the strain of memorizing it and performing it over and over again. She fashioned a performance of her own, which made use of Beckett's text but which "broke out" at unpredictable points into a *text* of her own. Much of the new text was

Shakespeare, as it turns out, reflecting Linklater's many years as a vocal coach and director with Shakespeare and Company, Tina Packer's theater ensemble in the Berkshires. But *Not I* would not leave Kristin Linklater alone, and she also developed a full, outdoor, "liberated" version of *Not I*, a sort of antidote performance to all the strains and tensions and repressions of the piece as conceived by Beckett. In this version the actress portrayed "she" as a demented bag lady, dressed in rubber boots and a trench coat, and she led a cluster of mesmerized spectators through the woods, into gullies, and over fields as she hurled herself about, gesticulating wildly, and ranted and raved her text—most of it what was written for the mouth in *Not I*.

I found Kristin Linklater's an unusually passionate and honest personal response to the power of the original Beckett work. Her work also testified to the strain Beckett performance puts on serious actors. But I would not call her two derivative performances acceptable versions or interpretations of Beckett's play. Kristin asked Beckett for permission to perform the "wild" version of *Not I,* the one that is intercut with spontaneous regurgitations from her own psyche (these eventually took on a fixed form), but he respectfully declined to be associated with the project. He did not, however, hamper her in any other way, and it should be pointed out that, in the case of the Akalaitis *Endgame,* his request had been to have his own name removed from the production or some clear indication given that it was a derivative work. It seems a fair request, if the essence of the original has been dissipated.

Several years ago I formulated the following progression in an attempt to define the boundary crossed in genre-jumping experiments with Beckett's work. Consider the three following situations:

1. Reading (as we say, "to yourself")
2. Reading aloud
3. Performing

These three situations create differing relations between *voice* and *text.* When we read we are in effect listening to an *implied voice,* in the ear of the mind. This is the condition of prose fictions. It is the condition assumed by Beckett as his formal medium when he writes for the page. He makes use of this voice in a constitutive way: it is part of his meaning.

Reading aloud creates a new relationship—one in which the voice is quoted. The reader who is understood to be reading is quoting aloud the voice that is implied when we "hear" ourselves read. The third situation, that of performing the voice, incorporates the source of the voice: it manifests the provenance of the voice. It "solves" any problems inherent in a purely "heard" voice and initiates all the different problems associated with the presence of a being. The formal situation in performance differs entirely from the formal situation in prose fiction. Because Beckett made the formal constraints the sources of the actions, these do not survive genre jumping.

We can look at a work like *Ohio Impromptu* for Beckett's own exploration of the three situations of Reading, Reading Aloud, and Performing. And I would like to report on a reading of *Ohio Impromptu,* which I prepared with David Warrilow in Boston in the spring of 1989, as another instance of mishandling Beckett in performance. The reading situation in *Ohio Impromptu* pits text against reader and text against listener. We see what is said to be happening also happening, as consoler and consoled read and listen to the tale in the book, which is their own story. The magic of the stage performance of this piece comes from the gradual recognition of these various relations. But as a mere reading, without the stage image of the two identical characters, without the listener's raps for pauses and repetitions, the consoling action is absent, and we have only the cadences of the written text—pleasurable, to be sure—but a tiny fragment of the whole work conceived by Beckett. It is a compelling text *about* grief but no longer a ritual of consolation. Clearly, much is lost.

Warrilow and I also presented *A Piece of Monologue* in the same manner, with the speaker (Warrilow) merely quoting the text rather than, were he fully performing it, being the source of the text, the incorporation of the voice. Obviously, on a superficial level, the "performance" and the reading may seem almost identical, for the beauty of Warrilow's sounding the text in a reading is homologous to his performance of it fully staged, but the meaning of the unstaged version is almost obliterated by the loss of the *originator* of the voice, and this is the inverse of the violence to form done in "staging," usually with extraneous images, one of the nondramatic texts.

Warrilow and I had our greatest success that last April of Beckett's life, with a public reading of *Stirrings Still* we prepared for the Poets' Theatre. We preceded David's onstage reading of Beckett's farewell text by a screening of the video composition *Nacht und Träume*. The immediate juxtaposition of the image of the figure leaning head on hands on the table with the same textual image in the first part of *Stirrings Still* made it clear we were in a soundscape of "things seen" rather than the more usual and more problematic soundscape of "things heard." After the performance Beckett wanted to know exactly where David had been seated—how, in what kind of chair, illumined by what sort of lamp placed where, . . . and what sort of prop had we used for the text? It was clear he could not gauge what we had done without a clear visualization of the stage as we had dressed it.

Beckett's work is notoriously harder than the average fare in a contemporary theater, and many audience members experience Beckett's work—even in its "pure," or accurately realized, form—as an opaque nonsense. But this opaque experience should not be used as a rationale for "expressing obscurity" or larding Beckett's work with extraneous images of alienation and confusion derived from the experience of having difficulty understanding Beckett. Nor should his difficulty induce anyone to add explanatory and reductive images. Both Akalaitis and Nichols, with their characteristically American instincts for what amounts to all-out Naturalism, "placed" and greatly reduced the Beckett plays they staged. Akalaitis compounded this reductivism by missing the mark on all other relations in the play as well. Her production was a bad one, and it was erroneously conceived.

Theater artists animated by inadequate ideas create disappointing work. But the merely disappointing becomes reprehensible in any single instance when it misleads the audience and seriously misrepresents the achievements of the author. Furthermore, in our transactions with audiences, we have only single instances to bank on. No production, no performance, should be considered inconsequential.

A few years ago Denis Donoghue caught my attention when he wrote, "There is a certain weightlessness in postmodernism that makes it possible for an artist to do anything he chooses, but [that] doesn't suggest that he should try for anything in particular: like a game without rules."[2] It is revealing, in the light of this comment, to note that it is always Beckett or Shakespeare or some other major figure who is chosen for the postmodern staging. Why does it never occur to a young director to stage a postmodern rereading of *Come Blow Your Horn?*

Artistic freedom should not be invoked to justify aesthetic license. And stage directors and their critics should practice the difficult craft of telling one from the other. We should, as Beckett did, *stand* for something.

Notes

1. Robert Scanlan, "A Voice Comes to One in the Dark," *Romance Studies,* no. II (Winter 1987): 23–29.

2. Denis Donoghue, "The Promiscuous Cool of Postmodernism," *New York Times,* 22 June 1986, sec. 7, 1.

Fizzle

Gildas Bourdet

Beckett does not specify the color to be used for the set of *Fin de partie;* at the very most he indicates that the light is gray. It is Beckettian tradition that imposes the use of this color, not the text itself. When one stages a text from the past with the intention of restoring something of the original emotion it inspired at the time of its creation, one is legitimately inclined to guard against the conventions or commonplaces surrounding it. To respect, a priori, these conventions or commonplaces is conveniently to express a superficial faithfulness to a work. It is to refuse to direct, in other words, to take a position, to interpret, if one considers that a production is nothing other than an interpretation. There is no other way for a director to respect a classical text, contemporary or not, than to produce a critical interrogation into the connection he is able to weave with a work necessarily shrouded by time. We have, indeed, recordings of Stravinsky directing his own works. This does not mean that any new interpretation is impossible other than to fix them, once and for all, and to forbid their further interpretation in concert. What is true of music is no less true of the theater, which is also an art of live representation.

The use of gray in the first stagings of Beckett's plays, as well as those of Brecht during the first years of the Berliner Ensemble, contributed to producing in the spectator of the time an overwhelming feeling of anguish and grief. Since then it has been superabundantly used in all European productions, so much so that it has become the mark of a certain cultural propriety. Aesthetically, the absence of color, or monochromy, is no longer disturbing. On the contrary, it comforts the spectator with the notion that the performance he is attending is really charged with a cultural bonus that he hopes to find there. It solicits his approval from the start. Color,

Translated by Florence Sapinart.

on the other hand, is suspected of being the mark of a contemptible kind of entertainment, vulgar and bourgeois at the same time. Thus, after many years and our many theatrical uses of it the Beckettian gray has lost its dissident virtue to become merely a convenient convention. If I felt the need to question this convention, it was in no way for self-advancement or self-validation; I would hope that not to be necessary. Rather, it was an effort to give back to the play something of the contestational force it initially had. A lot was at stake, especially since the play was entering this temple of sacred culture that is the Comédie Française. And it was really against my wishes that I contributed, in part, to turning it into an object of display.

If I chose for the set of *Fin de partie* a "squashed raspberry"–like pink and a "bloody" red, it was perhaps because of the correspondence I saw between Beckett's universe and that of the painter Francis Bacon, who makes abundant use of pink and red in the background of his canvases, where certain beings, like Beckett's characters, melt away. It is also because I did not find any hues that seemed to translate better the absence of green—that of young shoots, of leaves on the trees in springtime, or of English lawns in a solar and bucolic universe, whose definitive loss, which leaves us inconsolable, the text seems to herald. "But beyond the hills? Eh? Perhaps it's still green. Eh?" But outside—if an outside exists—there is nothing by "grray," or so Clov, who knows that his seeds will never sprout, maintains. Thus, in *Fin de partie* the chlorophyllian function is forever suspended, outside as well as inside. Since I chose not to transpose the gray from outside to inside, I had to find colors to coat the derisive inferno, where the four characters are walled in. I carefully copied them from the backstage and dressing room halls of an old Parisian theater, where, at the time, another of my productions was playing. Undoubtedly, one had painted the walls over in order to brighten them—but the attempt was in vain. The impression of sadness and of the ends of the earth, born of the monstrous coupling of these two colors, was such that I wanted the set of *Fin de partie* to be pink and red to the point of nausea. Basically, in this sad affair, which set a dying Beckett and his praetorian guard against me, it was only a question of the colors of hell. Who will ever say who was right?

The sole purpose of the music, or what served as such—conceived like the confused echoes of a forever fading life, of a henceforth inaccessible place—was to reinforce the feeling of solitude of the four human beings trapped there, like the shreds of an uncertain and stammering memory.

I had no idea whatsoever of turning *Fin de partie* into a musical. The bet was that, after the performance, no one would be able to say that he had heard the slightest musical note—a bet lost before ever having been waged.

The characters in *Fin de partie* are alone in the world, or in what seems to be left of it. They were rightly imagined as the survivors of a nuclear war. The date the work was written allowed for such an assumption. But today this kind of worldwide catastrophe seems less imminent, and the postatomical parable of the play has lost some of its relevance. So much the better for the world, and so much the better for the play, which gains in strength and radicality. It is no longer History that it questions but, instead, the soul. The solitude of the characters is no longer a consequence but their ontological condition. Their soul is the place of all the confinements; social bonds are quasi-nonexistent. The suffering is all the stronger for coming from within. Hell, here, is not "other people," contrary to what Sartre asserted in the same era; it is oneself, radically. If I filled the stage space with human figures directly inspired by those of the American sculptor Kierholz—adults, old people, child, all frozen in a snapshot of life as though in front of a photographer's lens—it was less to conjure up the petrified corpses of Pompeii than to try to translate the hopeless inner isolation to which Beckett condemns his characters by setting it against these silent and paradoxical figures. The point of this scenic artifice was to materialize the feeling the play induced in me, the feeling that what is dead sometimes seems more alive than what is still alive and that what is alive also seems sometimes about to be frozen in death. Nothing to me was more Beckettian than the effect thus produced.

Thus, this production of *Fin de partie,* as I conceived it, was meant to be a paraphrase of the *Perhaps* that controls the entire play, in which nothing is certain since God himself—this *"salaud"*—does not yet exist. The set was really neither filled with people nor completely empty, neither here nor exactly there, neither gay nor sad, simply hopeless and uninhabitable yet inhabited, I had dreamed the set as the place of an almost voluptuous nightmare, so morbidly was it pink and red, the enemies of green. Curiously, this set and this production did exist, since I saw them; yet they did not exist, since I was the only one to see them. Nothing is more Beckettian.

To me directing is a question of ethics as much as aesthetics. Any individual who directs must, in his work, constantly define himself in relation to the one as to the other. It would be useless, even for an author, to set rules in this manner. As an author myself, I realized, seeing some of my plays produced abroad, that some productions faithful to the letter were not true to the spirit of my plays, and others, freer and more personal, made me discover things I had not seen in my own texts. Yet I would not make a rule out of that, though I do believe that a director's sincerity and personal involvement in a work are always preferable to an absence of opinion or of imagination that wears the mask of an apparent faithfulness. I would therefore say that, if, for JoAnne Akalaitis, whose work I have not seen, the change of site in *Endgame* to a subway tunnel was the condition that made it possible for her to maintain and make heard a real rapport with Beckett's play, I approve of its principle. If, on the contrary, it was nothing but a gimmick, I disapprove of it as much as of a conventional and flat staging with the set such as Beckett describes it. I would say the same of the idea of having the parts of *En Attendant Godot* played by women. The necessity of it does not seem obvious to me, but I would not refuse a priori to let myself be convinced.

I decided to have the set I had imagined for *Endgame* at the Comédie Française covered over to show the public that something that remained present, though invisible, had been taken from it. I did not interfere in anything else. Out of friendship for the actors and at their request I worked with them until the day of the dress rehearsal, trying to overcome a weariness and a disgust one can easily imagine. I was not at the opening, of couse, as I thought I had no more official responsibility in the performing of the play as given, and I had withdrawn my name and those of my collaborators from the credits. It was naturally impossible for me to erase two months of work from the actors' memory. And even if it had been possible, I would not have done it. They therefore played as well as they could, scrupulously respectful of the directions that had been mine. The play was performed under the same conditions in the theater I used to run in Lille and in Paris at the Comédie Française.

I persist in liking Beckett's theater. Yet burned by this experience, which was perhaps the most painful in my professional life, I will be careful not to dare stage any other of his plays. As a matter of fact, the same causes producing the same effects, I think Mr. Jérôme Lindon, Beckett's executor, would not allow me to do so. A theatrical text, if it has some value, always more or less escapes its author's intentions. It is not the author who speaks in his text but, rather, something within him of which he is not necessarily aware. When one writes for the stage one takes the risk of being misstaged, as one does of being misread. There are stupid directors just as there are stupid readers. He who does not want to take this risk condemns his work to die with him. But I admit that one may prefer death and embalming to imagination and life. This was the case with Beckett in the affair that set us against each other, and it was his right. I regret that this right is also that of the guardians of his grave for another sixty years.

❖

[What follows is a statement distributed to the audiences of the Théâtre National de la Région du Nord (in Lille, France) at the time of *Fin de partie*'s run in 1988. —LO]

As has been the case since 15 October at the Comédie Française, *Fin de partie* will be presented in Lille without the mise-en-scène that I conceived and staged with my collaborators for this play. Such is the sad result of the disagreement between myself and Samuel Beckett represented by his publisher Jérôme Lindon. Hence, the author's copyright legally triumphed, in accordance with a very Beckettian logic, as neither the author nor his representative accepted to see a rehearsal in order to judge in full knowledge of the case, and they have neither seen nor heard the elements of the production that have been the subjects of the dispute. The opposition was a matter of principle, and the principle, which asserted that nothing was preferable to anything, prevailed. We have thus personally experienced, like a painfully ridiculous lesson, one of the essential themes of Beckett's very dramaturgy. Nevertheless, I am still convinced that to stage a work of the past, even a relatively recent one, consists in measuring the time that separates us from it and in finding the means to make it heard again in the present, which is ours. This is what I tried to do with *Fin de partie,* as I had done in the past with *Britannicus* and *Le pain dur,* for example. More than once, in the course of the rehearsals, I happened to believe that we were on the verge of success. But of this will I never be sure. True respect for the theatrical text one brings to the stage necessitates, from the actors, the use of a creative freedom without which the worst can be expected, by which I mean platitude and convention. It is this freedom that was finally forbidden us, obliging us to retreat with, at heart, the certainty of a waste and, like one who has been judged without evidence, a feeling of sadness and injustice.

Yet if we decided, after much hesitation, to keep this mutilated production in this season's program, it is because we thought that the work we had accomplished on the text with the actors could justify it and that it was not a ridiculous idea to allow our public to see and hear it, as the

public at the Comédie Française saw and heard it. The performance of
this play certainly does not conform to my wishes, but it seems that it
might suit Samuel Beckett and his representative—which does not in any
way prove that an author cannot be wrong. Having seen abroad the
production of some of my plays, staged in a way not very true to what I
had thought they should be, I became convinced that a play conceals
several truths of which the author is not necessarily aware. This conviction
Samuel Beckett does not share. He undoubtedly has less confidence in his
works than I have myself, that which, as an author, I can understand,
though I infinitely deplore it.

But, for the time being, "Since that's the way we're playing it . . .
let's play it that way . . . and speak no more about it . . . " (Samuel Beckett,
Fin de partie).

Three Women and a Mound: Directing *Happy Days*

Carey Perloff

I recently had the pleasure of directing Charlotte Rae as Winnie in *Happy Days,* first in Los Angeles at the Mark Taper Forum and then in New York at CSC Repertory. The experience was a fascinating one and quite different from what I had expected; it led me to think about the directing process, in general, and the unique nature of directing Beckett, in particular.

I came to Beckett via Pinter, with whom I had recently worked on the American premiere of Pinter's new twenty-minute work, *Mountain Language,* part of a double bill we presented with Pinter's first full-length play, *The Birthday Party. Mountain Language* has been analyzed by many critics, including Martin Esslin, as Pinter's closest work to Brecht, yet, despite its overt political themes, the play is also a startling homage to Pinter's mentor, Beckett. There is a sequence in *Mountain Language* in which a political prisoner and his wife are facing each other in a corridor; the prisoner's head has been covered with a burlap sack, and he has clearly been tortured. In the silence between them (as the prison guards look on) their voices are heard over the speakers, communicating almost telepathically:

MAN'S VOICE:	I watch you sleep. And then your eyes open. You look up at me above you and smile.
WOMAN'S VOICE:	You smile. When my eyes open I see you above me and smile.
MAN'S VOICE:	We are out on a lake.
WOMAN'S VOICE:	It is spring.
MAN'S VOICE:	I hold you. I warm you.

Fig. 6. Charlotte Rae in Carey Perloff's *Happy Days,* CSC Repertory, New York City, 1990. Photo credit: Jay Thompson.

WOMAN'S VOICE: When my eyes open I see you above me
                 and smile.

Out of the brutality of the prison comes this brief shred of extraordinary lyricism. The echoes of cynical old Krapp suddenly hearing his earlier description of romance are clear:

KRAPP: I asked her to look at me and after a few moments—
(*pause*)—after a few moments she did, but the eyes
just slits, because of the glare. I bent over her to get
them in the shadow and they opened. (*Pause. Low.*)
Let me in. (*Pause.*) We drifted in among the flags and
stuck. The way they went down, sighing, before the
stem! . . .

I cite this connection between Beckett and Pinter because, as I began
rehearsing *Happy Days,* much of what Pinter had told me about how to
approach his own work came back to me in useful ways. It consistently
infuriates Pinter to hear his work labeled "abstract," and he fails to understand the tenor of most of the critical writing on Beckett, which describes
the plays as "absurdist," "imagistic," "oblique," "symbolic." Pinter will
repeatedly assure you that he has known people exactly like the characters
in his plays and has heard these seemingly bizarre conversations in real
life. Clearly, what we see in Pinter's work is "real life" put through the
unique filter of his own artistic psyche, but Pinter's refusal to abstract or
intellectualize his work is an important warning for any director. No
symbols where none intended. For example, in *The Birthday Party* Meg
repeatedly begs Petey to read to her from his newspaper. We wondered if
this was an important clue about Meg and Petey's inability to commu-
nicate, about Meg's unfulfilled needs vis-à-vis her marriage. "No," said
Pinter. "I think she's forgotten how to read."

Pinter's extraordinary pragmatism and respect for the characters he
had created stayed with me closely as I began to work on Beckett. Winnie
is in many ways a cousin of Meg: she has retained a childlike pleasure
about the world that is both hilarious and deeply moving, and she has a
resolute faith in the power of conversation (even if one-sided) to keep
herself alive. Having been away from ordinary human discourse for many
years, Winnie's words are "found objects" just as her props are; they are
all that she has left in the world and are thus treated with veneration and
deep respect. I had learned from Pinter to be religious about the rhythm
and structure of writing that was this meticulous; after watching a run-
through, Pinter would remember (without ever referring to the script) that
an actor had forgotten to take a particular pause or would inform us that
a series of "dot dot dots" was being ignored. This is not because, as some
would have it, Pinter is a fanatic, but because he knows that the meaning
of his work lies in the interstices. For Pinter's (and Beckett's) characters

words are often just a complex web designed to cover the terrifying possibility of silence. If one constructs the web carefully enough, the shape of what is being covered will also emerge.

Thus, I told Charlotte Rae that, above all else, it was crucial for us to listen as closely as possible to the rhythm of the text when we began rehearsing *Happy Days*. Whereas usually in rehearsal for a "classical" play I give the actors a great deal of material about the historical and literary context of the work—its levels of meaning, some relevant production history, and so on—it became clear that this approach would be useless in trying to unlock the mysteries of *Happy Days*. We began, instead, with the extreme specificity of the language, both verbal and gestural.

I should point out here that one of the reasons I had cast Charlotte Rae in the role of Winnie was that Charlotte was trained as a singer and has an acute musical ear. She was thus totally comfortable with learning the play by rote, as she would learn a piece of music before beginning to analyze it psychologically. Charlotte also has the endlessly changeable "rubber" face of a clown and has rightly been acclaimed over the years as a superb comic actress. As such, she knows that the essence of comedy lies in rhythm and timing. So, between her musical and her comic training Charlotte seemed right at home in the mad world of Beckett's prose. Though trained as a "method actress," she was never tempted to refuse to pick up the toothbrush on a given line because she didn't "feel" like brushing her teeth at that moment. She knew that, if she picked it up exactly where and how Beckett had specified, she would eventually understand why she was doing it.

Language and gesture are inextricably related in Beckett, so the choreography must be learned in conjunction with the text. Repeated physical behavior is particularly important to a character like Winnie, for *Happy Days* does not just *describe* a woman trying to survive a slow death, it *reveals* that slow death in almost real time and in painstaking detail. For Winnie each word and each physical object are lifelines to be treasured and clung to. Charlotte said kiddingly to me on the first day of rehearsal that she was not a "prop actress." But *Happy Days* is all about props, for in a metatheatrical sense *Happy Days* is a play about making theater, a play about creating a theatrical world from as few physical givens as possible. Like the actress playing Winnie, Winnie herself is kept going by her beloved props when all else fails; each item, no matter how mundane, takes on a quasi-religious significance when it is all one has left in the world. So, we spent the first few weeks of rehearsal doing exercises and rituals to invest each item in Winnie's bag with its own particular meaning. We would repeatedly load up the famous black bag and then, very slowly, pull the contents out, one thing at a time, caress that particular object, and place it in its own sacred place on the mound. Charlotte's arrangement of the props on the mound was akin to flower arranging: everything had to be within reach but combine to form the perfect whole.

At the time of rehearsals my daughter Alexandra was just a year old, that age when the favorite game is pulling everything out of Mommy's purse. Often during the *Happy Days* rehearsal process Lexie would sit in the corner of the theater, stealthily opening my purse and removing the contents, arranging everything carefully in a circle around her. She knew the contents of the bag by heart; it was not the surprise factor that kept her returning to the "empty-the-purse" game but, instead, the sheer joy of recognition in seeing those familiar objects reappear every time the game was played. She exhibited so many of Winnie's behavioral traits that Charlotte and I would stop rehearsals sometimes and watch Lexie perform her illicit game. The lipstick was always first; she would very carefully remove the top and place it beside her and then slowly, with great anticipation, twist the stick until the color began to appear. She would then place it very carefully beside her so that it would stand up like a flag. ("Ensign crimson. Pale flag.") Her favorite object was the mirror, which was reserved for last. Some days she would circle around the purse, obviously dying to play with it, making herself wait until she had exhausted all of her other toys first. ("Do not overdo the bag.") The pleasure of her delayed gratification was almost palpable, and it certainly made clear to us that Winnie's seemingly bizarre behavior was rooted in precisely observed human behavior. We thus worked hard to make Winnie's pleasure of recognition at seeing the landmarks of her life as concentrated and sensual as Lexie's.

In doing so, we followed every detail of Beckett's instructions with regard to Winnie's treatment of her props: how to unfurl the parasol, how to squeeze the toothpaste, how to wear the hat, and so on. Through relentless repetition the rituals emerged. Each day before rehearsal Charlotte did two hours of "drilling." It was exactly like working on a dance piece: two hours of technical work for every hour of new exploration. Slowly, the prescribed movement became her own, and the props themselves kept her continuously grounded.

We approached Winnie's habitat in much the same way as we approached the props. It is traditional in the American theater for the actors to rehearse in a studio for three weeks or so before that magical moment when the scenery is loaded into the theater and the actors can finally explore the play upon the actual set. However, I insisted from the beginning that since the mound in *Happy Days* was truly Winnie's costume, and since she wore it as much as it wore her, we had to have it ready to work on for the first day of rehearsals. Having accomplished this, we then wasted a great deal of time trying to make the mound comfortable for Charlotte to sit in, incorporating foot rests, back supports, and so on. Eventually, we realized that, no matter what we did, Beckett was always going to have the last laugh. He had created this hostile environment so that the actress playing Winnie didn't have to *act* being suffocated and constricted; she actually *lived through* these emotions every time she rehearsed or performed the play.

It is hard to describe what it does to someone to be locked inside an unmovable wedge of dirt for hours and hours every day. Eventually, your mind snaps. It becomes unendurable. And then the play begins. There were days when Charlotte would sit in the mound and weep because she felt so completely impotent. But what we quickly learned was what a gift that set was to an actor. If you are given the impossible acting task of communicating your life's experience with no one to talk to, no physical movement, nothing but (in act 2) your facial muscles and your voice available as tools, you begin to treasure every tremble of the lips, every turn of the eyes, every quiver of the nose, because that is all that is left. Charlotte said afterward that she couldn't imagine doing a play again in which she sat around on regular furniture talking to other actors; it would all seem so excessive and imprecise!

Because of our feelings about the constricted nature of Winnie's environment, our production employed a black volcanic landscape upon which nothing could ever grow, rather than the more customary sandy slope. Under Frances Aronson's relentless white light the effect was terrifying. (The intensity was unintentionally increased by the fact that we performed *Happy Days* in a theater with no air conditioning during the hottest October in record in New York City. There were days when I truly believed Charlotte would melt into the mound. The sequence "It is no hotter today than yesterday, it will be no hotter tomorrow than today, how could it, and so on back into the far past, forward into the far future" brought down the house every night.)

It is one thing to accomplish Beckett's choreography and another to own his language. Beckett's language is among the hardest of any playwright's to memorize because it doubles back upon itself with maddening regularity. *Happy Days* is structured like a long song in which one keeps returning to the refrain "that is what I find so wonderful, that not a day goes by, to speak in the old style . . ." and then the appropriate tag. We learned the piece in sections, each punctuated by the refrain. What we discovered was that beneath the seemingly random stream of consciousness of the language lay a clearly associative pattern of thought, and I found that the best way to help Charlotte trace that pattern was to provide her with a series of hooks that linked one thought with the next and told the overall story of the piece.

Often the hooks were benchmarks or landmarks in Winnie's own experience that she couldn't help returning to. The most critical seemed, not surprisingly, to have to do with love and sex. When you have had a limited number of key experiences in your life, each must get revisited over and over again to extract its full savor. Similarly, the terrifying experiences must get buried. Clearly, the memory of "Millie" and the "mouse" is a deeply traumatic one for Winnie, which she buries ("Gently, Winnie") until she simply can't stand it anymore and begins screaming, as if remembering a rape: "Suddenly a mouse ran up her little thigh and Mildred, dropping Dolly in her fright, began to scream (WINNIE gives a sudden piercing scream)—and screamed and screamed. . . ." This moment of sexual terror, which Winnie tries desperately to avoid, stands in stark contrast to the moments of romance that she repeatedly evokes ("The sunshade you gave me . . . that day . . . (*pause*) . . . that day . . . the lake . . . the reeds").

In act 1 the romantic memories are sought out and savored; in act 2 Winnie runs from them because she is so far gone that she fears they are signs that she is losing her mind and that such events never happened at all: "What day? (*Pause.*) What reeds?" It is this counterpoint that we found so rich in and among Winnie's endless babble; the tension between the deliberate evocation of certain memories and the equally deliberate avoidance of others provided the conflict that carried Charlotte through the play.

Underlying all our work on *Happy Days* lay our firm belief in Winnie's utter ordinariness. I had seen both Irene Worth's and Madeline Renaud's famous interpretations of the role, each thrilling in very different ways. But what struck me about the play, particularly after having read a great deal about Beckett's own life and his relatives, was that he had not created in Winnie a heroic or highly theatrical character; he had created a real woman whom he recognized and knew in great depth. American women of Winnie's class may have a still more uneven smattering of education than Winnie, and some of her expressions sound flowery to us because they are Irish, but at her heart Winnie is a woman you could see on a bus in New Jersey any day of the week, counting her pennies and trying to get through the day. That to me is what is moving about the play. And indeed, the most moving experience we had while performing the play came one evening when a cab driver whom Carlotte had invited to the play joined us at the bar after the show. I asked him what he'd thought of it, bearing in mind that Beckett has the reputation for only appealing to intellectuals and others with a morbid slant on life. He informed me without hesitation that this play was about his life since he had retired. When I asked him to elaborate he replied: "The day I left work, my friends said to me, 'Just remember one thing—don't ever get a shave and a shine on the same day.'" Life's treats have to be carefully rationed if there is to be anything left to keep one going later on.

Many people found our production of *Happy Days* a more emotional one than they had remembered seeing, and perhaps this is true. Charlotte and I found ourselves in the rare position of being two women working on this play, and Winnie became the third woman in our circle; we felt that we knew her intimately. In her recent book *You Just Don't Understand: Women and Men in Conversation,* linguist Deborah Tannen talks about the differences between male and female conversation. She calls male conversation "report-talk," while female language is "rapport-talk." In other words, for most men "talk is primarily a means to preserve independence and negotiate and maintain status in a hierarchical social order," while for women conversation is "a way of establishing connections and negotiating relationships."[1] Along these lines Tannen points out that for men, since talking is about power, silence is the greatest form of intimacy. But for women silence can be deeply insulting. Tannen describes in hilarious detail a scene we all know well, in which after a passionate night of lovemaking a man will sit at breakfast happily reading the paper, while the woman is burning up inside because she feels that, since the man is not speaking to her, the intimacy of the night before is being rejected.

Happy Days is filled with these kinds of fabulously missed moments between a man and a woman. Winnie makes Willie furious by insisting he play word games with her: "Fear no more the heat o' the sun. Did you hear that?" Willie on the other hand just wants to be left in peace, to remain near Winnie in silence. Winnie is deeply wounded by this, since she needs constant proof of his presence and love in order to go on. There is no possible way Willie can give her that. Yet he is clearly bound symbiotically to her and uses superhuman effort at the end of the play to come to her side of the mound. The tragic and hilarious thing is that even then the connection is missed. He reaches out his hand, and we have no idea whether his gesture is toward Winnie or the gun. "Is it me you're after, Willie . . . or is it something else?" Even between people bound together in this absurd way communication is never really possible. And Beckett mined this vein of linguistic confusion for all it was worth. It is fascinating how perfectly he understood the peculiarities of marital conflicts, and what an acute observer of the intricate details of male-female behavior Beckett was.

Perhaps this is why *Happy Days* is, ironically, one of Beckett's funniest works. In describing the play to my board of directors when I selected it for the season, it was difficult to convince them that a play about a woman buried up to her waist in sand could be anything other than horrific. And of course, it is horrific. But it is also hilarious. For in Winnie's desperate attempt to connect to Willie and in Willie's astonishing inability to give her the small crumbs she needs lies an anatomy of modern marriage that no one could fail to laugh at in both despair and recognition. It is a universal situation precisely because it is so ridiculously particular. It is a tiny play that is epic in its proportions. And we could have rehearsed it forever.

NOTE

1. Deborah Tannen, *You Just Don't Understand: Women and Men in Conversation* (William Morrow and Company, 1990), 79, 77.

Ghosts

Xerxes Mehta

The prescriptiveness of Beckett's stage directions, especially in the short plays he wrote toward the end of his life, appears to leave the director with little to do. This is, in fact, an illusion. The deeper the director, designers, and performers venture into these works, the more they realize that almost everything is unknown, and perhaps unknowable. What follows, therefore, is offered tentatively, and with humility, as one director's experience of an art whose power and intractability, grandeur and mystery, are inseparable.

Eye

In my view, Beckett's stage works since *Play* are ghost-plays, hauntings, their spectral quality lying at the heart of their power. What the spectator sees appears to come swimming out of blackness, near yet far, floating yet fixed, obsessively present in the manner of visions and nightmares. To achieve this quality requires control of darkness and light. Darkness in these late, short works is, I suggest, of a different order than the normal theatrical blackout. Darkness here is part of the weave of the work, the most important single element of the image. It should be as absolute as can be managed. Darkness at this level becomes a form of sense deprivation. Its effect is to cancel the group existence of theater; to cancel the awareness of surrounding space, to throw the spectator into a physical void, and thus to create in the spectator a psychological dependency on the image that finally appears. If that image, then, is itself disturbing, unbalancing, assaultive, or recessive, the spectator topples into a world of nightmares, will-less to resist, on the edge of sanity.

The image that finally appears is spectral, wraithlike—from the floating heads and funeral urns in *Play,* to the floating mouth in *Not I,* to the lower-body apparition in *Footfalls,* to the white heads and hands in *Ohio Impromptu,* to the residual skull in *Rockaby.* These images immediately reinforce the assault on reason: the heads in *Play* appear and disappear with bewildering speed and randomness; the mouth in *Not I,* eight feet off the ground and thus decisively dematerialized from any possible connection to a human form, seems to move around in a kind of optical illusion, although it is in fact quite fixed; the rocker in *Rockaby* starts to rock on its own, silently, without apparent human agency. All of these images float. All are white or gray, except for the red of the mouth in *Not I.* Finally, all are fixed, with a fixedness that goes far beyond their fixedness onstage. They have the force of the unchanging, the eternal, there before the light finds them, there after the light departs, there as in nightmares, with no beginning and no end.

In the effort to summon such dreadful ministers—in rehearsals, in design sessions, in private communings—the production team begins to intuit their sources of power. Our quotidian nightmares attack us when we are most vulnerable—in sleep, in exhaustion, depression, or weakness. Therefore, to successfully subvert an alert and normally sanguine theater audience Beckett's ghosts must first create states of susceptibility. As already suggested, the ghost's first great weapon is its inky domain, a blackness that, if held long enough, will destroy time, place, and community and

Fig. 7. Robert Poln in *Act Without Words II,* directed by Xerxes Mehta, Terrace Theater, Kennedy Center for the Performing Arts, Washington, D.C., 1979. Photo credit: Thomas Arnsten.

force each spectator into herself. Abetting inwardness and further loosening her grip on reality is her inability to ground the image. Her eye cannot find its source or complete its outline. Even such apparently solid objects as the rocker or the white table and chairs fade into the night, their lower parts invisible, they and their occupants suspended in dim and fitful light. Light, in turn, intensifies destabilization by offering the viewer little comfort or guidance. Beckett light does not shape action, define space, cue mood change, or focus meaning; nor does it collaboratively lead the viewer through the work's ebb and flow, beginnings and endings. Not only does it not help the viewer to receive, respond to, or understand the image; it seems to have no source outside the image. It seems, in fact, to emanate from the image toward the viewer, rather than the reverse. The result is that Beckett's ghosts glow in the dark, dimly or blindingly, and when they cease to glow one is left with the near certainty that they are still there, near us, always with us, capable of reappearing at any moment, as in *Play* and *Footfalls* they do.

Brought low by radically original and ruthlessly assaultive treatments of darkness and light, the viewer now drifts into timeless realms. The burning image begins to be felt as unshakable. Time stops. Pressed in by a seemingly endless and hellish present, the viewer is without control, without rescue, desperate for rest but unable to wake up. This experience, of course, exactly mirrors the experience of the performer, of the anonymous (and usually partial) being ghosting the performer, of the "he" or "she" ghosting that being, of the whispers, rustles, and murmurs ghosting the "he" or "she," and so on across "all the dead voices" to the beginning of time. I shall return to some of the implications of this extraordinary equation. For now perhaps it is enough to dwell briefly on one other aspect of the image, as I see it.

It is intellectually nonconvertible. By this I mean that it cannot be understood, and thereby denatured, with reference to something else. The image does not enter, exit, move, change, interact with other images, or partake of larger symbolic visual patterns. It does not draw from our image bank or our well of cultural memory and so cannot be assimilated to visual habit or tamed through visual association. By forcing confrontation with itself and nothing else, it defeats meaning. It is just there. It *is*.

Ear

So far I have spoken only of the visual image in Beckett's later short plays. The sonic image is, if anything, even more problematic and terrifying than the visual, grounded in silence as the visual is in darkness—the silence both a threatening presence and a palpable absence, again destroying communion, concentrating being, yawning like a pit, creating extreme anxiety, and giving the sound that finally breaks it a mythological force. These sounds tend to be one of two kinds. Like the visual image, the sonic image is either assaultive or recessive. Sound is either used in furious and relentless attack, as a kind of racing, dazzling, shrieking, laughing, mesmerizing logorrhea, or it is used as a receding presence, an evanescence, a slow, quiet, even, toneless murmur, like the wraiths that twist through grief-stricken dreams, leaving traces on the heart but not on the memory.

Sound coalesces into language, and the language is of the simplest kind—unliterary, stripped of rhetoric, without metaphysics, with barely a nod to the great tradition, uninterested in ideas or ideals. In concrete words of one or two syllables the plays speak of love lost, love never gained, abandonment, death, the search for self, the torment of consciousness, childhood memories, the yearning for rest. But Beckett asks his performers to speak of these things without expressed feeling, and I would now like to offer a few thoughts on his request.

"Voices toneless. . . . Rapid tempo." This direction, for *Play,* also sets the pattern for the works that follow it. Beckett's wishes are not always made clear on the page; sometimes they have to be discovered from the production history. In every case, however, it becomes apparent that the voice the audience hears, whether live or taped, is to speak faster than normal or slower than normal and is to remain—brief, specified moments excepted— "toneless" or "expressionless." I think the success of the plays depends on these directions being respected. Whether one agrees with this view or not, it is undeniable that such drastic limitations evoke anxiety in performers, shock in audiences, and confusion in critics, perhaps because they fly in the face of the central performance tradition of Western theater, the expressive actor.

The first comment I would make about imperatives such as "expressionless" and "toneless" is that they are less absolute and less lucid than they seem. Just as no person can rest a perfectly neutral gaze on another's face, no speech can be perfectly toneless, if only because there are two subjectivities involved. Similarly, *rapid* and *slow* are elastic terms. In order not to lose itself in a maze of seemingly equally valid rehearsal choices, the production team must therefore ask itself what these rather clumsy directions are trying to achieve.

As more productions have emerged and our experience with these

plays has grown, the answer to this question becomes clearer. I think that
Beckett is moving toward a treatment of *sound-as-image* that will exactly
parallel and complement the visual image that each play sets before us.
Sound-as-image should be distinguished from the notion of text-as-music,
commonly used to describe Beckett's language. The latter carries with it
overtones of cost-free eroticism, and, while eros is amply present in these
works, it is not cost free, nor does it stem from a direct response to the
performer's voice but, rather, from the sense of surrender that the ines-
capability of the work, as a whole, compels in the spectator. In my view
the core purpose of Beckett's use of sound is to strike ear and brain with
a sonic image as hard, fixed, and relentless as the visual image that
accompanies it. Sound becomes an icon.

To realize the icon the performer's verbal delivery must acquire three
characteristics: it must become an abstration; it must be felt as possessing
enormous magnitude; and it must cancel the audience's sentimental response to individual suffering. Sonic abstraction is achieved in one of two
ways: through delivery so constantly rapid that it is initially unintelligible
(*Not I, Play*) or through an even, unchanging rhythm slightly slower than
normal (*Footfalls, Ohio Impromptu, Rockaby*). Magnitude is achieved more
variously: the assaultive amplification in *Not I;* the unlocalized voice from
the dark that becomes a racial memory of loss and desire; the instantaneous,
puppetlike response to the demonic light in *Play;* and, in several works,
the stillness and catastrophic silences that make us cling to sound as to a
lifeline. Finally, even as the spectator begins to understand and react to
the ghastly human story bleeding through each work's formal brilliance,
the icon's relentless rhythms and underinflected voice enforce distance,
reject sympathy for the speaker's plight (strictly, for the plight of the
creature the speaker is describing), and so turn grief that is flowing toward
the stage back upon the sender. In the process, sound-as-image/sound-as-
icon desentimentalizes, universalizes, and focuses suffering, and therefore
the awareness of suffering, away from a particular and perhaps dismissible
life onto the life that each of us holds most precious, that each of us is
condemned to live.

Once these essential structural dynamics are intuited in rehearsal it
is not difficult for director and performer to arrive at decisions about
intonation and tempo. A key to such decision making is the gradual
awareness, more instinctive than deductive, that the scripts are misleading
us by asking for a negativity in the performer—absence of expression/

tone—whereas what Beckett is after is a positive and active creation, a mask of diamondlike hardness, brilliance, depth, and mystery.

The type of alienation achieved by this mask is, in my view, entirely original in the history of our medium. Unlike Brecht's distancing devices, which gather strength in proportion to the clarity and breadth of social vision and judgment they solicit from the viewer, Beckett's masks lead us inexorably inward and downward into darkness and personal chaos. How this sense of chaos is achieved I will speculate on in a moment. For now it is enough to see that, by first using image and narrative to invite sympathy for human distress and then, by formal means, blocking the release of that emotion, Beckett locks the spectator to his own consciousness. The spectator falls into a kind of horrified trance, trapped in a world not of his making but one in which he is absolutely implicated.

Chaos

Nightmares, by nature, are ambiguous, mysterious, threatening, obsessive—personifications of our desires and repositories of our deepest fears. What they are not are discursive, linear, explicit, and moralistic. Crowning his lifelong pursuit of a form that "admits the chaos," Beckett finally arrives at works that successfully join the intense subjectivity of personal experience to a shape that "accommodates the mess" and yet survives the demands of a gross and public medium.

How gather a ghost? How harness a haunting? Based only on my own experience with these plays, and offered most tentatively, I suggest a response along the following lines. Chaos is achieved in two interwoven and mutually reinforcing ways, which for argument's sake I will separate out. First, eye and ear subvert each other. Second, the art object self-destructs, forcing performer and spectator to confront each other personally in their unaccommodated nakedness.

Eye versus Ear

Extended darkness and silence break the communal bond and, by turning the spectator inward, isolate her. When the ghost finally appears it does so with such force that the spectator, condemned to deal with it alone, immediately admits it into her inner sanctum. As time passes, the apparition—itself unchanging, fixed, and monomaniacal but increasingly saturated with the play's tonal values of terror, grief, and loss—acquires the quality of an icon, starkly emblematic of one view of the human condition. I suggest it is at this stage, roughly two or three minutes into the performance, when the emblem is at the height of its power, that, paradoxically, the play is also in greatest peril of failure. For the spectator's conscious mind, having absorbed the shock, having noted with relief that sight and sound show no sign of changing, moves to defang the haunting—either by retreating into reductiveness and intellectualizing the emblem down to "a point of view" or by rejecting the feelings it evokes and so denying the validity of the emblem altogether. But it is also at this moment, I suggest, that Beckett's ghosts show just how malign they can be. The spectator becomes uneasily aware that sight and sound seem to be diverging, and that ground he had assumed to be stable is in fact shifting under his feet. In *Not I*, for example, the brilliance of MOUTH burns the audience's eye from start to finish. First moment to last, all vision in the theater is focused on that twelve square inches of palpitating redness. At first the accompanying sound is heard as babble, drone, buzz, clamor—sound and sight all of a piece. But gradually, as the ear adjusts to the furious pace, individual words detach themselves; patterns of repetition begin to register; screams, laughs, increasing panic, increasing vehemence begin to be subliminally absorbed, "faster and faster" becomes clearer and clearer, until, miraculously, *both* the unitary impression of sound-as-image, words-as-babble, *and* the ghastly human story bleeding through are somehow suspended together in the spectator's shrinking soul.

The early stages of comprehension yield something like this: abandoned old woman, wretched life, lost her mind, poor thing, delusional, obsessive, that's life, poor thing. Very quickly, however, and in no particular order, Beckett's telegraphic spirals of repetition throw up clouds of questions. Who is "she"? Who is the interlocutor whom "she" can hear but we cannot, who knows all about "she," and who corrects, prompts, and asks "she" unanswerable questions? This interlocutor is not "she's" thoughts, for "she" refers to and recounts her thoughts. Who is the one who laughs? Certainly not "she," for "she's" attitude to "a merciful . . . God," here and throughout, is far from humorous or scornful. Who is the one who screams? Certainly not "she," for "she" makes it clear that her attempts at screams resulted in "no sound of any kind . . . all silent as the grave." If not "she," then, is MOUTH the laugher/screamer? If MOUTH knows all about "she," including the content of the unheard interlocutor's innermost promptings, how does MOUTH achieve the distance necessary to mock "she's" illusions and general ineptitude, and why is MOUTH unable to de-mystify the "buzzing," the "dull roar" that torment "she"? "She's" "stream of words" and "beam . . . ferreting around" obviously echo what we hear and see. So is the visual/sonic stage image the inside of "she's" mind?

Who, then, are we in the audience, we who also are "straining to hear . . . make something of it," we who also have "something begging in the brain . . . begging the mouth to stop," we who also make a "quick grab and on . . . nothing there . . . on to the next," we who also keep "trying to make sense of it . . . or make it stop," we who also have no idea, finally, "what to try"? The gigantic and barely visible figure on stage who listens to MOUTH and reacts first with anger and later despair to MOUTH's failure to say, presumably, "I," seems telepathically to be soliciting a different answer. Is this listener transmitting to MOUTH or to "she"? Is this listener a ghost of "she's" interlocutor? Since we respond to MOUTH's failures as the listener does, does the listener also embody us? Is MOUTH "she's" mouth as well as the performer's mouth? Is the expressionless performer, then, to be supposed to be personifying "she," presenting MOUTH, rep-resenting "she," acting MOUTH, being "she," or none of the above? These are only a few of the questions that beat at us as we race to keep up with the ghosts before us. The pressure of the questions' accumulation, coupled with our intuition that they are unanswerable and the work unknowable, lead to fresh spirals of terror, terror now stemming less from the wretched simplicities of the life on view and more from the inescapable equation de-veloping between "she" and "we." The sonic image horrifies through its unrelenting fixity, even as it horrifies through its simultaneous self-destruc-tion. Words spew out ceaselessly as a hedge against the dark, a lifeline to sanity, a bridge over chaos, even as they lead us inexorably into darkness, insanity, and chaos.

This example from *Not I* shows only one of the ways in which Beckett plays with the tension between the fixed and the dynamic. It is possible, in fact, that every one of these works uses it differently. In *Ohio Impromptu,* for example, I suggest that it is the sonic image that takes on the emblem's stony cast. Although a narrative, and therefore dynamic by definition, the slow, even telling of the inner story of deprivation and grief is so inexorable in its progress and so ineluctable in its outcome, that it acquires the force of a parable, the exemplary permanence of one of those bedtime stories that sum up the human condition. The visual image at first seems to parallel the sonic one—a still life of two identical old men at a table, in the heart of darkness, one reading out, the other listening to, the story being told. Both images, the visual and the sonic, appear emblematic of a single vision, a black but nonetheless coherent and intelligible view of life. At the very end of the work, however, after all sound has ceased, the two ashen ghosts before us lift their heads from their hands and look directly at each other. It is on this tableau that darkness finally descends.

This mirror move, which is quite shocking in performance, acts like the opening of a dam, releasing in the spectators all the half-formed ambivalences and insecurities that they have suppressed under the melancholy spell of the narrative and the formal spell of an almost motionless *pas-de-deux*. Among the thoughts that flood the mind are: Are there two present at all? Is there not, rather, one? Is the reader an invention of the listener, called up to make fictional what would otherwise be an unendurable torment? Is the listener the suffering "he" of the tale? Does the listener stand in the same relation to Beckett as the "he" stands in relation to the listener? Is the work, then, about art rather than life, about the creative process itself, in keeping with the tradition of the Impromptu? If so, "where are all these corpses from," whence these feelings of intense personal melancholy expressed by many members of the audience, why do we still see "the dear face" and hear "the unspoken words"? I suggest, in short, that the visual image at the end of *Ohio Impromptu,* one of the most powerful in the Beckett canon, subverts the play's emblematic dimension by once again dropping us into that floating world in which all we can cling to is the intuition that the less these works clarify the more nakedly and profoundly we respond to them.

Staying with this contradiction for a moment, I think it is precisely the tension between sight and sound, between the fixed and the dynamic, between emblem and chaos, that lifts Beckett out of the company of didacts into the realm of the greatest artists. But the trick succeeds by only a hair's breadth. Were both what one hears and what one sees to feel static (as they do, for example, when the plays are done at the wrong speed), were the emblem to hold firm, the works would not only feel too long, despite their brevity, but they could also be written off as hectoring moralisms, much in the manner of those medieval sermons with their cautionary death's-heads and pseudoprofound abstractions used to beat away life's complexities.

Being Perceived

The treachery between eye and ear is, in my view, one of the ways in which Beckett "accommodates the mess" by finding a form for chaos.

Another way, bound to the first, is through fictions that consume themselves and so bring performer and spectator into a unique and unbearable confrontation. Since this issue is of overriding concern to the performer, I will discuss it here from the performer's perspective.

The central performace dilemma of these plays, as I understand it, is the necessity for the performer to face an audience without any stable identity to rest upon. The performer does not know whether he or she is an actor, a character, or some form of transparency for an unknowable other. All that can be known with certainty is that a being in front of the stage is looking at and listening to a being on the stage. Nothing else can be asserted unequivocally, least of all the identity or function of the being on the stage, the being perceived.

The performer has no character to represent. The performer is asked only to look a certain way, sound a certain way, and, in that created and anonymous persona, tell a story about another being who is not present. Sometimes this absent being hears a voice, which, the story tells us, is the voice of still another, who in turn is absent even to the absent one, although the voice is heard by all—the absent one, the anonymous stage being, the performer, and the audience. After a few days at these altitudes performer and director feel the strongest urge to reclaim their sanity by assuming that there is a character there after all, a character without a name but playable all the same, that this character is none other than the "he" or "she" of the story, that the anonymous persona with "the look" and "the voice" is merely a disguise, and that the character's recourse to the third person is no more than a transparent effort to avoid implication in the pain of his or her own life. Unfortunately, these assumptions cannot be made. Even as one admits the suspicion that such an obvious psychologism as the last is far removed from the level of invention on display elsewhere in these pieces, one also makes the miserable discovery that the circular and self-consuming nature of each work's inner narrative is expressly designed to frustrate the assertion of identity. *Not I* thus comes into focus as the title of a play; a map of its physical workings (eye looking at mouth, not eye); a description of an obsession of the "she" in its story; *and* a clear professional warning from playwright to performer that nothing is assumable.

The performer is now faced with the dilemma of having to live in public on several levels of selfhood without knowing what those levels are, how to gain access to them, or what they will do to the performer or to one another. This, of course, is also the dilemma faced by the anonymous

onstage speaker, by the "she"/"he" of the fiction, and, through extension
and implication, by every receding level of consciousness, every ghost,
present in the place of performance.

Among the implications of this equation of dilemmas are, I suggest,
the following. Since the search for identity is the core action of tragedy;
since the performer, the anonymous stage being, and the fictional "he"/
"she" are all involved in the search for identity; and since, by the nature
of things and by the narrative shape of these plays, their search is steeped
in suffering, all three partake of the tragic impulse and live in the tragic
world. (This said despite Beckett's obvious distance from several defining
characteristics of the traditional genre.) Second, because the search is the
same for all three, the distinction between the real world (of the performer)
and the world of the fiction is canceled. Reality and imagination become
indistinguishable, with the further implication that the inner world is all.
Finally, and paradoxically, there is the strong indication that the opposite
is also true, that, since selfhood is not achieved at the innermost level, a
failure that radiates outward to the performer, the performer can never
reach an accommodation with her doppelgänger, the mysterious stage being
who lives in her body and speaks through her voice.

Of course, none of this is understood in this way in rehearsal. Much
of it is not understood at all. What *is* sensed by every performer I have
directed in these extraordinary works is the centrality of the issue of
identity—the performer's identity. Who am I? Let us now suppose that
means are found to create the visual and verbal images necessary to
summon Beckett's ghosts. The nightmare begins; the "old terror of night"
lays hold on us again. The performer, at full tilt, in mid-flight, is now
doing the following things, all more or less simultaneously: spinning out
the sonic patterns of tempo, volume, and pitch that most securely walk
the tightrope between subliminal intelligibility and sound-as-image, sound-
as-"buzzing"; opening psychic doors to the narrative's spell so that body
and voice will accurately and organically respond to the play's "charge";
conversely, keeping psychic distance between self and the stranger occu-
pying self; in consequence, successfully sustaining the mask of blank face
and unvarying delivery, except where specified; and, finally, picking up
visual cues—number of steps, curve of body, swing of turn (*Footfalls*),
upward angle of mouth for audience sight line (*Not I*), absolutely motionless
head (*Play*), varying speed and force of hand movement (*Ohio Impromptu*),
rate and distance of head drop (*Rockaby*), rate and distance of head lift

(*Ohio Impromptu*), painful maintenance of unblinking gaze for specified and extended intervals (several plays), and so on.

Skilled performers can do all of these things, despite the very great psychic and physical toll they exact. The central performance issue is not a technical one. Rather, it is structural, having to do with the basic architecture of these plays, and, not surprisingly, it stays focused on the unresolvable dilemma of the performer's identity. Briefly, it is my view that the bedrock purpose of Beckett's final body of work is to expose the nakedness and terror of human existence by exposing a naked and terrified human being on a stage. Since the only human being on the stage is the performer, it is the performer who is the final focus of each work. I think that the stripping of the performer is done like this.

First, Beckett denies the performer a character to impersonate, a fictional identity. The performer is therefore immediately aware at some level that the audience will be looking at and listening to him personally. He reacts with anxiety, fear. Beckett anticipates this and offers him a mask that slightly abstracts him, providing a minimal privacy: his face is not visible, or parts of his body are not visible, or his face becomes a mask, or his voice becomes a mask. The performer feels a bit safer and, though still uneasy, recognizes the trappings of art and takes the bait. Beckett now asks the masked performer to tell a story about another person's life. This story is full of grief but so simple, so typical, and so seemingly ineluctable that performer and audience adopt its emotional field as their own. And yet the performer's mask and the *fact* of the narrative keep the whole thing within the precincts of culture, of aesthetic consumption, of fictional suffering shaped by form and filtered through art. Very soon, however, the story begins to disintegrate. It turns inward and consumes itself, or it accelerates toward the point of flying apart, or it declines toward the point of stasis or death.

In every case the fictional inner being, the subject of the story, threatens to disappear or die. I suspect that the performer senses this looming disaster before the spectator does. The performer now bends every effort to prevent an outcome that would not only signal his professional demise, for he would have nothing to send to the audience, but that would also, in some obscurely sensed fashion, implicate him personally in the nightmare he has been ghosting, by removing the prop of art. As the nightmare advances, therefore, the performer's refusal to relinquish the third-person voice becomes felt as an act of will, necessary to the *performer's* sanity.

Instead of the performer remaining a transparency for "he's" or "she's" nightmare, the nightmare becomes a transparency for the performer's suffering. Once this shift has taken place the content of the interior narrative becomes unimportant; almost anything will do. The audience's focus has now shifted from the "he" or "she" of the story to the actual suffering being onstage in front of it. A consequence of this shift is that both performer and spectator are stripped of fiction's camouflage. The performer is now spiritually and psychologically naked; the spectator is now an enforced voyeur of a human being in extremis. The horror for the performer is the exposure of his nakedness and terror to the spectator. The horror for the spectator is the exposure of his own nakedness and terror to himself.

Freedom

There is the belief among many theater people that Beckett's plays are uninteresting to embark on because the prescriptiveness of his stage directions places unacceptable limits on artists' creativity. It is true that Beckett, particularly in his final body of work, robs us of certain freedoms. But I think it is also true that in exchange he offers us other freedoms, which not only liberate performers and spectators but also, by profoundly recasting the relationship between them, liberate the core energies of theater itself. Therefore, I approach the recent controversy pitting directors' prerogatives against writers' rights less for its intrinsic importance than for the light it can shed on the seemingly inexhaustible possibilities of these marvelous and revolutionary works.

Does a director have the right to ignore Beckett's stage directions? This issue reached an apotheosis of sorts in the recent donnybrook in Boston over *Endgame*. Apparent even at the time of this bitter dispute was the writer's desperate but inevitably futile attempt to claim ownership of a theatrical *event* after the *script* for that event had left his hands. I think that such a claim cannot be sustained and therefore that, in principle, the theater was quite within its rights to stage *Endgame* as it saw fit. A script is not a theatrical event. It is a blueprint for an event. Art is not engineering. Artists are not machines. The animation of the blueprint involves hundreds, thousands, of acts of cocreation by director, designer, performer, each such act being inevitably conditioned by the differing personalities and life histories of the artists involved, by the circumstances of performance, by the pressure of the cultural moment, and so on. To say so much is to dwell in truisms; so, let us leave this level and move from the issue of ownership to the issue of intention.

Are a writer's performance intentions knowable? Can Beckett's own productions of his works be duplicated by other production teams? Was Beckett necessarily the best director of his own plays? I suggest that the answer to each of these questions is no. Even directors with the best will in the world, who study a work (and its surrounding literature), who examine tapes of Beckett's own approaches to it and talk to people who remember what Beckett did to it in reheasal, come out at the end knowing little more about bringing it to life than they did when they read the script initially. This is not to say that this kind of preparation need not be done; it should. It can broaden context, give insight, save rehearsal time, and forestall performance errors (the approach to tempo in *Not I*, for example, crucial to that work's life, is not indicated in the script but is discoverable from the criticism and from the play's production history). Rather, it is only to suggest that the word on the page carries the stamp of failure the moment it leaves the writer's pen, for it is already an imperfect reflection of the maelstrom in the mind that gave it birth; that that maelstrom is irrecoverable, the word its only trace; that those words, if they are to find embodiment, must create fresh turbulence in the minds of the cocreating performers; that that turbulence will be different in every particular, and in every performer, from the original but will partake of its essence; that the embodied stage vision will create new turmoil in the audience; that that turmoil will be different for each spectator; and that it is in that final transaction—single being to single being—that all value resides. The distance between this end and the first mover crosses many generations of intervening activity. It is a great distance, which no amount of "fidelity," "accuracy," or appeal to "original" versions can reduce. It is a distance that is part and parcel of the theatrical process, inherent in the act of theater. Our only defenses against intolerable outcomes—dead, reductive, stupid, self-regarding outcomes—are what they have always been: sensitivity, culture, openness, discernment, and, in the case of Beckett, those prior deposits in our blood that expel pretenders. There are no shortcuts.

That said, it is necessary to add that I have seen no production of *Play* or any work written after it that has been improved by a significant departure from the writer's wishes. The reason for this, in my view, is unique to late Beckett, unique to the nature of these particular works.

While directors and performers have no option but to respond freshly and personally to any script, they encounter in these scripts formal and structural devices that are, as far as I know, entirely new in the history of theater. The central difference, as I see it, is that in theater as we have known it so far, including Beckett's own before *Play*, reality onstage is coextensive with reality offstage, the reality of the world, whereas in late Beckett reality onstage is itself and nothing else, sealed off from the world. Characters do not enter from somewhere and leave to go somewhere else; stage space does not connect in mind's eye with the world's space; stage sight and sound are not experienced as fragments of, referents to, or even symbolic stand-ins for, the sights and sounds of the world. On the contrary, the visual and sonic images that appear in late Beckett seem to me to be the first wholly successful examples in theater of the great modernist project: to make art that, in formal terms, is not about life but, rather, in Flaubert's words, "about nothing but itself." These images—parts of the human body, light, darkness, sound, silence—appear to us as flat, opaque, nonreferential, defiant of interpretation and void of meaning. They are simply and completely *present*, sealed with the audience in the here and now.

If one accepts this view, its most obvious implication is that the stage directions, which solicit the images, *are* the play and that a director or performer who adds to, subtracts from, or alters them in any appreciable way is not tinkering with interpretation but, rather, creating something different, not by Beckett. So, certain prerogatives are undeniably sacrificed. However, far profounder in my view than such a loss of freedom are the new freedoms Beckett offers in exchange, freedoms that flow from the type of interdependence between performer and spectator that he enforces, an interdependence that I think has no parallel in modern theater and that lies not only at the core of these works but at the core of theater itself.

Implicated in an emotional field of suffering, loss, terror, and death—denied release of those feelings, stripped of character, stripped of identity, stripped even of the act of imitation, yet condemned to remain exposed in front of another—the performer lives only through the spectator.

Hallucinatedly fixed on shimmering ghosts, forbidden understanding by self-consuming narratives, cut off from community by darkness or silence, unbalanced by the sub-rosa treachery between sight and sound, prevented from thinking through, with, or about the work, denied any form of message, extractable idea, or separable content, locked to the image in an inescapable embrace, the spectator lives only through the performer.

Performer and spectator experience each other viscerally, sensually, intuitively, immediately, and profoundly intimately. Able to survive only through each other, always alone yet always "tied," performer and spectator finally discover what it means to be human. This experience, like the opening of a furnace door, is the heart of our art form, theater's blazing core. Beckett arrived at it at the end of his life, walked into the flames, and, like alchemists of old, transmuted chaos, grief, and failure into a kind of joy.

A "Fresh Go" for the Skull: Directing *All That Fall,* Samuel Beckett's Play for Radio

Everett C. Frost

I

> I do think we are owed some kind of explanation, Mr. Barrell, if only to
> set our minds at rest.
>
> —*All That Fall*

In the spring of 1985, in spite of my enthusiasm for the undertaking, I had serious doubts that American productions of one or more of Samuel Beckett's radio plays could ever be produced in time for national broadcast as part of the celebrations of Beckett's eightieth birthday that would take place in April 1986. In the absence of a properly budgeted and scheduled place for radio drama in the public radio system (such as is taken for granted in most of the rest of the world) that could absorb a project such as *The Beckett Festival of Radio Plays,* it seemed to me impossible that, in less than a year's time, funding could be secured, actors contracted, a production team assembled, a schedule forecast, distribution secured, and local public radio stations persuaded to broadcast the results—especially since each "next step" depended upon success of the one preceding before it could begin: without funding, no actors, etc. To attempt Beckett's radio plays on too little money, or without adequate facilities or capable performers, or without adequate time to focus conceptually on the plays themselves and their production problems, would, in some respects, be worse than not doing them at all. Therefore, I insisted from the beginning that we would not attempt *All That Fall* or any of Beckett's other radio plays unless we had adequate (not in my vocabulary a synonym for either comfortable or luxurious) resources at our disposal in order to do them properly. Yet without the "hook" provided by the attention Beckett's eight-ieth birthday would get, funding, distribution, and broadcast prospects diminished, and the particular convergence of energies and opportunities (including, as it turned out, the counsel of Samuel Beckett) would probably not ever again be able to align themselves so auspiciously. Therefore, we decided that, despite unlikelihoods, we simply had at least to try. *All That Fall* received its American national broadcast premiere in the United States on Samuel Beckett's eightieth birthday, 13 April 1986—followed three years later by the entire *Beckett Festival of Radio Plays*. But that fortune smiled on the project in this respect does not imply that she did so of her own free will: a lot of helping hands had to conspire to coax her into it.[1]

If the production were to meet April 1986 distribution schedules, it would have to be sent to stations for audition and scheduling by February of that year—which, in practice, meant recorded no later than December of 1985. On such an accelerated and relatively inflexible schedule, much depended not only on fortune smiling, but smiling on our calendars. By March of 1985 Louise Cleveland had assembled and submitted the National Endowment for the Humanities (NEH) grant that would fund most of the production of *All That Fall*. In July, on the strength of unofficial news that partial funding would probably be formally awarded in September, I made arrangements to visit the British Broadcasting Corporation (BBC) Written Archives Center to study the development of the original productions and to meet with Samuel Beckett, who had very kindly offered to discuss the plays with me in preparation for their production.[2]

We were extremely fortunate in our cast: Billie Whitelaw agreed to play Maddy Rooney but had a narrow "window" in her heavily booked schedule during the time we would need her. Fortunately, David Warrilow had about a two-week opening in his schedule that overlapped the period in which Billie Whitelaw could be available. He agreed to play Dan—bringing together for the first time into a single Beckett production the two living actors for whom Beckett had specifically written theatrical works. Alvin Epstein, who had played Lucky in the original Broadway production of *Waiting for Godot* and who had starred in *Endgame* in 1984, agreed to play Mr. Slocum, and Jerome Kilty took a day off from directing Shaw in Hartford to create Christy and Mr. Barrell. Susan Willis, Brad Friedman, George Bartenieff, and ten-year-old Lute Ramblin' (Breuer) completed the cast.

II

You lie in the dark with closed eyes and see the scene.

—Company

In *All That Fall* we encounter Maddy (née Dunne) Rooney (done/ruined),[3] who describes herself as "a hysterical old hag . . . destroyed with sorrows and pining and gentility and churchgoing and fat and rheumatism and childlessness." She labors on foot toward the Boghill railway station to meet her blind husband, Dan, returning from his basement office in the city—a surprise to him on his birthday. Enroute she hears various rural sounds and an old woman listening to Schubert's "Death and the Maiden." She is overtaken by a series of Irish comic characters: Christy, with his dung cart; Mr. Tyler, a prim but lewd-minded retired bill broker, on his bicycle; Connelly's van; Mr. Slocum, her old admirer and the clerk of the racecourse, in his automobile. Mr. Slocum give her a lift to the station, where she is helped out of the automobile by Tommy, a porter with his mind on his racetrack bet. She has a testy conversation with the civil but imperious stationmaster, Mr. Barrell, who leaves her stranded at the bottom of the stairs leading to the railway platform. She intimidates the self-absorbed, emaciated, and religiously obsessed spinster, Miss Fitt, into helping haul her "two hundred pounds of unhealthy fat" up the stairs— a precipice Maddy describes as "worse than the Matterhorn." That the train is an "unheard of" "fifteen minutes late on a thirty minute run" produces an anxious and comic discussion among those waiting on the platform—doing their best to ignore Maddy's rather importunate presence. The Up Mail races through, and, finally, the train from town, with Dan among the passengers, arrives. Dan, assisted by a boy, Jerry, is not entirely pleased to find Maddy waiting for him, but he dismisses Jerry, and they make their laborious way home together, conversing in Beckett's deadpan, comic, and outrageous style. Maddy is concerned to know why the train was so late, but Dan engages in a long "composition" as "a subterfuge to evade answering his wife's question about the delay of his train."[4] They are set upon by the Lynch twins—children who taunt them—and overhear the cries of Mrs. Tully being beaten by her husband, and, as they pass the point at which we first encountered Maddy at the beginning of the play, they hear the "poor old woman all alone in that ruinous old house," still playing the worn out recording of "Death and the Maiden" on her gramophone. The weather, which has been "shrouding, shrouding" all day long, takes a turn for the worse, and it begins to rain. Jerry has been sent after them to give Dan an unidentifiable ball-like object that Mr. Barrell says he left behind. Under Maddy's cross-questioning Jerry spills the news: the train was delayed because a little child fell out of it and under the wheels. The couple continues their way homeward in silence, dissolving into the soundscape of the tempest of wind and rain that concludes the play.

When the biblical phrase "The Lord upholdeth all that fall and raiseth up those that be bowed down," from which the play takes its title, occurs in the drama (as the text from which Sunday's sermon will be drawn) it provokes "*wild laughter*" from Maddy and Dan.[5] "Christianity is a mythology with which I am perfectly familiar, so naturally I use it," Beckett once remarked,[6] and the play is his "gruesome" indictment of the Biblical phrase as it is interpreted by the Christian piety that might be expected from the sermon. As many critics have noticed, the theme is extended by Maddy's discussion of "the sparrows, than many of which we are of more value" and its Biblical resonances,[7] and the play is also a savagely ironic comment on the Biblical admonition to innocence: "a little child shall lead them." In *All That Fall* "it was a little child fell out of the carriage, Ma'am"—leading, presumably, in the direction indicated by Maddy Rooney's response to Mr. Slocum's question:

MR. SLOCUM: Are you going in my direction, Mrs.
                 Rooney? . . .
MRS. ROONEY: I am, Mr. Slocum, we all are.

                                                    (17)

Jerry, another child, has led them to the truth that Dan has taken great pains to avoid. The "tempest of wind and rain" that concludes the play (and about which I'll have more to say), like the storm on Lear's heath, seems the natural analogue to events in the human world (as experienced in the mind of the main character). Unlike Lear howling on the heath, however, the response is silence. Like the immobility of the character at the end of *Act Without Words I* looking at his hands, we do not know whether Maddy and Dan's silence is borne of consternation, despair, defiance, or relief (at being pummeled by the rain and so distracted from the thought of the child under the wheels).

Let these speculations lead where they will (Beckett suspects they lead in the direction of an aspirin bottle,[8] and my turn to reach for it came many times throughout the production and will recur before I've finished the present essay); the play has a plot, characters, and a patina of realism to a degree that is unusual in Beckett's work. As Ruby Cohn has noted, *All That Fall* is composed of a "realistic surface" created out of sound and image that "unfolds in single action replete with repetition," and the plot is balanced: Maddy's "journey from the station inversely repeats her journey towards it" (*Just Play*, 115). Martin Esslin finds "a three-movement structure (Maddy Rooney's anabasis, her wait at the station, her and Dan's katabasis)."[9] The point-for-point structural balance between the journey out and the journey home helps to pace a production of the play and assists with its interpretation. For example, Christy and his hinny-drawn dungcart are linked to Christ riding into Jerusalem on (what, near the end of the play, Maddy supposes to be) a hinny not only thematically but also by their mirroring positions near the beginning and end of the play, respectively.

Although subsequent technical advances in microphones, recording techniques, audiotape, and production mixing have served us well, the demands imposed by the script are no less challenging now than they were when the BBC essayed the premiere production. Martin Esslin, former head of Radio Drama at the BBC, has described the impact of *All That Fall* on the BBC:

> Beckett's script demanded a degree of stylized realism hitherto unheard of in radio drama, and new methods had to be found to extract the sounds needed (both animal and mechanical—footsteps, cars, bicycle wheels, the train, the cart) from the simple naturalism of the hundreds of records in the BBC's effects library. [Desmond] Briscoe [the sound effects designer] (and his Gramophone operator, Norman Baines) had to invent ways and means to remove these sounds from the purely realistic sphere. They did so by treating them electronically: slowing down, speeding up, adding echo, fragmenting them by cutting them into segments, and putting them together in new ways. These experiments, and the discoveries made as they evolved, led directly to the establishment of the BBC's Radiophonic Workshop. Beckett and *All That Fall* thus directly contributed to one of the most important technical advances in the art of radio (and the technique, and indeed technology, of radio in Britain). ("Samuel Beckett," 129)[10]

While some of these problems can be more readily solved now (e.g., high-quality portable tape recorders and a variety of microphones make it possible to gather sound effects tailored to the production, diminishing the reliance on archived records), the major challenges in producing *All That Fall* are conceptual, not technical, and they are as formidable now as they were thirty years ago.

III

> Never thought about radio play technique before, but in the dead of t'other night got a nice gruesome idea full of cartwheels and dragging of feet and puffing and panting which may or may not lead to something.
> —Samuel Beckett, letter to Nancy Cunard

Beckett's admonition about *All That Fall* to his U.S. publisher, Barney Rosset (27 August 1957), has been so often quoted that it hardly needs repetition. Yet it is so singularly integral to the present context that it would be wrong to leave it out:

> *All That Fall* is a specifically radio play, or rather radio text, for voices, not bodies. I have already refused to have it "staged" and I cannot think of it in such terms. . . . It is no more theatre than *End-Game* is radio and to "act" it is to kill it. Even the reduced visual dimension it will receive from the simplest and most static of readings . . . will be destructive of whatever quality it may have and which depends on the whole thing's *coming out of the dark.* . . .
>
> If another *radio* performance could be given in the States, it goes without saying that I'd be very pleased.[11]

Goading everyone involved in the project from the frontispiece of our well-thumbed copies of Zilliacus, the passage was, of course, a great fillip: we made no attempt to restrain ourselves from trying to please Samuel Beckett, late in his life, with the first significant new production of the radio play in English in the thirty years since its BBC premiere and the first substantive American production of it, ever.[12]

Of course it was a source of satisfaction that Samuel Beckett had written *All That Fall* specifically for the radio and that, further, he resisted attempts to adapt it to other media. But, in preparing to direct the play, one of the first reaches for the aspirin bottle came over the conundrum of *why* Samuel Beckett had been insistent that the meaning of the play was so symbiotically tied to the radio that it could not survive separation from it intact. *Why* would any "visual dimension" at all be "destructive of whatever quality it may have," and *why* does that quality "depend on the whole thing's coming out of the dark"?

In such matters the text itself—with its sparse but clear instructions—was, of course, the first and last recourse. It was of some help to listen to the original BBC production, since Beckett had consulted with the director, Donald McWhinnie, more vigorously than it was possible for him to do with me. Another helping hand came from the BBC written archives, which included exchanges of letters between McWhinnie and Beckett about the production strategy for *All That Fall* and the other radio plays. But it will be clear to anybody who hears the BBC and the Beckett Festival productions side by side that my investigations led me to pursue a very different course than McWhinnie had done, and much of this essay will set out the rationale for why that became the case.

For me the terse but precise, and sometimes unconventional, sound effects instructions throughout the play provided a way in, beginning with the enigmatic ones that open it. Struggling with the question of how to do them (there being a number of plausible possibilities) provided a key to answering the questions posed by Beckett's letter to Barney Rosset:

> Rural sounds. Sheep, bird, cow, cock, severally, then together.
> Silence.
> Mrs. Rooney advances along country road towards railroad station.
>
> (*All That Fall*, 12)

Although it is a conventional procedure in radio drama, the instructions would seem deliberately to rule out any attempt to create the general ambience of a rural soundscape—like a stage setting—for Maddy Rooney to walk into, and, as I expected, Beckett firmly ruled out using the opening rural sounds (or any of the other sound effects) to establish a realistic or naturalistic setting. In his book *The Art of Radio* Donald McWhinnie describes the approach he took in the original BBC production:

> It begins with a tiny prelude: "rural sounds"; various animals give voice individually, then together, then, after a silence, the play begins. The purpose of this prelude is not primarily to evoke a visual picture, and if it resolves itself into "farmyard noises" it will in fact be pointless, since it is not directly linked to the action, although echoes of it are heard during the course of the play, in various contexts. It is a stylized form of scene-setting, containing within

itself a pointer to the convention of the play: a mixture of realism and poetry, frustration and farce. It also demands a strict rhythmic composition; a mere miscellany of animal sounds will not achieve the effect. The author specifies four animals; this corresponds exactly to the four-in-a-bar metre of Mrs. Rooney's walk to the station and back, which is the percussive accompaniment to the play and which, in its later stages, becomes charged with emotional significance in itself. But in this case it is impossible to use real animal sounds, since the actual sound of a cow mooing, a cock crowing, a sheep bleating, a dog barking, are complex structures, varying in duration and melodic shape; to put these four sounds in succession would be to create a whole which is only too obviously composed of disparate elements. The way to deal with the problem seemed to be by complete stylization of each sound, that is to say, by having human beings to impersonate the exact sound required. This enabled us to construct an exact rhythmic pattern in which no element was out of place. The same principle was observed in the *ensemble* of animals; each observed strictly the tempo already set, a tempo which gradually slowed down and subsided into inarticulate, choked-off silence. We hoped to achieve the comic overtones, not by any attempt at caricature or grotesqueness in the impersonation, but by the strict stylization of the quartet.[13]

Persuasive as this seemed, my instincts argued against it.[14] Try as I might, I could find no "four-in-a-bar metre of Mrs. Rooney's walk to the station and back" as a structural principle specified by the play (this conclusion would also lead to jettisoning McWhinnie's percussion instruments for footsteps, in favor of the more conventional and unruly box of kitty litter). In the one time that I'd ever actually heard the play (long) before preparing to direct it,[15] the actors impersonating animals seemed to me to draw attention to themselves doing it and, consequently, away from the play; it caused me the, then, unresolved question: Does Beckett mean that we are to understand Maddy Rooney as inhabiting an ironic world in which she imagines humans are reduced to speaking with the tongues of animals? In directing *All That Fall*, McWhinnie had unfortunately been overly restrained by his fondness for the close parallel between radio drama and music as the two sister arts made exclusively out of sound—a parallel that he felt obliged the former to derive its structural principles from the latter.[16] He wanted to achieve a highly stylized version, fundamentally rooted in classical music, as seemed an appropriate response to a serious literary work of distinction by a difficult and intellectually erudite and renowned author.

Ironically, at about this time contemporary music was modifying the very structural principles that interfered with seeing complex composition of disparate elements as a form of music: throughout the 1950s, in Paris, for example, Pierre Schaeffer and other *musique concrète* composers were writing works for radio that included the recorded sounds of animals and the sounds of industrial machinery—an insurrection that dates back to at least the 1920s and 1930s, with Hindemith's inclusion of an airplane propeller in his portion of the Brecht-Weill-Hindemith collaboration on the radio cantata, "The Flight of Lindbergh,"; the propellers and sirens included in the compositions of Edgar Varese; or the noise-as-music experiments of the Italian futurist Luigi Russolo.[17] In any case, the use of humans to impersonate animals failed to please Beckett, and he urged us to get the actual sounds of the animals if we possibly could.[18]

Beckett's play seemed to me to require something rather simple and crude—or, to use his own word, "gruesome"—as appropriate to a play that included a hysterical old woman "weeping her heart out on the highways and byways," a chicken "squashed" on the road right before our ears, and the shocking report of a child, one among all that fall, who "fell, out of the train, ma'am, under the wheels, ma'am." But neither deciding not to use actors to impersonate animals nor replacing them with the farm team could, of itself, answer the question of *why* the "rural sounds" were the way they were at the opening of *All That Fall*.

An answer came from another appearance of animal sounds late in the play. Frustrated in her attempts to extract from Dan what he knows about why the train was "fifteen minutes late! On a thirty minute run!" Maddy Rooney finds consolation in the utterances of the natural world. Weary, defeated, and longing to be comforted and reassured, she hears nature speak with the subdued voice of the evening in a manner that conforms precisely with her mood. It is one of the most beautiful passages in the play:

(*Silence.*)

MRS. ROONEY: All is still. No living soul in sight. There is
                    no one to ask. The world is feeding. The
                    wind—(*Brief Wind*)—scarcely stirs the leaves
                    and the birds—(*Brief Chirp*)—are tired of
                    singing. The cows—(*Brief Moo*)—and sheep—

(*Brief Baa*)—ruminate in silence. The dogs—
(*Brief Bark*)—are hushed and the hens—(*Brief Cackle*)—sprawl torpid in the dust. We are alone. There is no one to ask. (*Silence*)

(32)

The monologue so touches even the flinty Dan that he is prompted to begin the "relation" that will appear to answer her question but, in fact, distracts her so as to avoid doing so. As she has done earlier in the play when she listens "to the cooing of the ringdoves," Maddy derives a comfort denied her by mortals by communing with a natural world whose "way of speaking" "has not changed since Arcady"(*All That Fall*, 13, 34). I shall explore the conceptual implications of her behavior in a moment. For my present purposes it is sufficient to notice that the wind and animals identified "speak" *after,* not before, she invokes them. Yet it would be more plausible if the sound of the animal caused her to include it in her monologue—a response to its utterance, like the ones prompted by the hinny, the ringdove, and, later, the lamb crying for its mother. However it may be with the physical acoustics of the soundscape, the sequence and process is psycho-acoustically accurate. It is the way that, not hearing, but the experience of hearing works—as may be illustrated by the fact that my mention of the sounds that surround you now as you read this page calls them into existence for you—though, of course, they "really" (whatever *that* is) were there all the time and, for all you know, remain there still now that you've stopped attending to them again. (Brief pause for attending to them again.) The passage quoted above makes the intent of the seemingly eccentric use of the sound effects throughout the play clear. In it her mention of the wind or animal precedes—causes—its appearance, almost as if the rural sounds were responding to her *because that is precisely what she experiences them as doing.* But this way of experiencing the sound in the drama can only make sense if we understand ourselves as experiencing the action of the play from within the mind of Maddy Rooney. To experience the action and perceptions of the play as originating entirely and exclusively from within the mind of Maddy Rooney requires that we not be distracted by her exterior, however minimally suggested. (*All That Fall* is, as Enoch Brater might say, "beyond minimalism.")

The enigmatic "rural sounds" that open the play may now be heard as the cacophony of the natural world in the form that it suddenly impinges upon Maddy as she essays her unusual, frightful, and laborious venture

from her sickbed to the railway station to surprise her husband on his
birthday. She hears them in a form appropriate to the vigor of the morning,
with the terror of anticipating the day that yet lies before her. She is, as
Samuel Beckett told Billie Whitelaw, "in a state of abortive explosiveness."[19]
We are *with* her—hearing as she hears—even before her existence as a
character can be identified as such by the audience: difficult on radio but
impossible in any other form in which a visual indication of Maddy's
existence would have either to precede, be simultaneous with, or lag behind
the opening sounds.

Therefore, the rural sounds do not constitute McWhinnie's "tiny
prelude" to introduce the conventions of the play with a "stylized form
of scene setting" but are, themselves, the beginning of the dramatic action
and consist of Maddy Rooney's perception of the world around her at the
opening of the play. Contrary to his observation that the opening rural
sounds are "not directly linked to the action, although echoes of it are
heard during the course of the play in varying contexts" (McWhinnie,
Art of Radio, 133), the way in which animal sounds appear throughout the
drama is consistent with the conclusion that the opening rural sounds are
an integral part of the action and not a prelude to it.

Maddy first becomes known to us by the sounds she hears—even
before she can be identified!—and "even [a] reduced visual dimension . . .
will be destructive of whatever quality it may have. . . . " Experiencing her
in this way "depends," precisely as Beckett had insisted, "on the whole
thing's *coming out of the dark.*"

In the opening scene, as throughout the drama, the animal sounds are
closely connected to Maddy's mood and to her perception of them. Therefore, it was not at all "impossible to use real animal sounds," as McWhinnie
had argued, "since the actual sound of a cow mooing, a cock crowing, a
sheep bleating, a dog barking, are complex structures, varying in duration
and melodic shape; to put these four sounds in succession would be to
create a whole which is only too obviously composed of disparate elements."
It was essential to use them for these very reasons—the more disparate
the better, in keeping with the way the animals would sound in the morning
to a befuddled Maddy Rooney.[20]

When approached as the audible from of the experience of Maddy
Rooney, the way the play is to "sound" makes clear and consistent sense
throughout. "Rural sounds" are called for a second time when Maddy
and Mr. Tyler have nearly been run down by Connelly's van. They emerge

out of the silence that follows Maddy's attempt to catch her breath and gather her wits:

MRS. ROONEY: Let us halt a moment and let this vile dust
                      fall back upon the viler worms. (*Silence. Ru-
                      ral sounds.*)

(15)

The silence is in stark contrast to the roar of the van. The senses— Maddy's senses—have been stunned by the noise and are momentarily incapable of hearing anything else. But the radical dislocation, the sudden fright survived, makes her senses vulnerable to the surrounding soundscape of animals going energetically about their business. Like the van—or, for that matter, the dungcart and the bicycle—they intrude upon her unbidden and are, in consequence, vaguely threatening. From a "realistic" point of view the rural sounds are there all the time. But from an accurate psycho-acoustic point of view, one tunes out the background except when some departure from the norm brings it, unbidden, into our consciousness.

The conventional-minded Mr. Tyler, having escaped with his hide, draws a romantic cliché from the soundscape that annoys Mrs. Rooney more than the vile dust. Attention is diverted from the soundscape and it vanishes.

IV

What's wrong with me, what's wrong with me, never tranquil, seething out of my dirty old pelt, out of my skull, oh to be in atoms, in atoms! (*Frenziedly.*) ATOMS! (*Silence. Cooing. Faintly.*) Jesus! (*Pause*) Jesus!—
All That Fall

If the action of the play is experienced entirely as it "appears" in the mind of Maddy Rooney, then, clearly, I needed to explore that mind and how it worked. Certainly, one key to it is her "way of speaking," which she herself describes (to Christy) as "rather bizarre." It is a matter that is centrally important to the production of the radio play, since the aural nature of the medium affords an opportunity for more concentrated attention to spoken language than any other form of performance art.

Late in the play, as Maddy and Dan are walking home, they hear a lamb bleat (Beckett's instructions call for an "urgent baa"):

MR. ROONEY: You have ceased to care. I speak—and you
                   listen to the wind.
MRS. ROONEY: No, no, I am agog, tell me all, then we
                   shall press on and never pause, never pause,
                   till we come safe to haven. (*Pause.*)
MR. ROONEY: Never pause . . . safe to haven. . . . Do you
                   know, Maddy, sometimes one would think
                   you were struggling with a dead language.
MRS. ROONEY: Yes indeed, Dan, I know full well what you
                   mean, I often have that feeling, it is un-
                   speakably excruciating.
MR. ROONEY: I confess I have it sometimes myself, when I
                   happen to overhear what I'm saying.
MRS. ROONEY: Well, you know, it will be dead in time, just
                   like our poor dear Gaelic, there is that to be
                   said. (*Urgent baa.*)
MR. ROONEY: (*Startled*) Good God!
MRS. ROONEY: Oh the pretty little woolly lamb, crying to
                   suck its mother! Theirs has not changed
                   since Arcady. (*Pause.*)

                                                        (34)

Maddy hears the lamb speaking the language of Arcady, the language
of an unfallen rural paradise closed to all that fall but still inhabited by
"the pretty woolly little lamb," an archetype of unfallen innocence whom
Maddy, suffering from "childlessness," understands to be "crying to suck
its mother"—an utterance from the natural world that twinges her own
pained maternal longing. Strictly speaking, then, the lamb—and one would
have to include the other animal sounds as well—are not sound effects at
all. They are other voices in the text, speaking a language that (unlike
"our own dear Gaelic") survives unchanged from prelapsarian times, and
unintelligible to human ears closed to Arcady by the fall. Maddy (an ironic
earth mother: fat, unhealthy, decrepit, and childless) has glimmers of
understanding it when the animal—or, for that matter, the wind or the
smell of the lovely laburnum—resonates with her mood. And her own
"bizarre" way of speaking (though she claims, incorrectly to fallen ears,
to use "none but the simplest words") is closer to the unfallen world than
that of other people in the play. Unlike the other characters, she tries to
use language for self-expression.[21] Dan indulges in "composition" and

enumeration, Christy does business, Tyler is trapped by supercilious romantic formulas, Slocum is a deadpan cynic, Miss Fitt is consumed by neurotic piety, Mr. Barrell by imperious propriety, and Jerry responds to his elders in catechisms. (Tommy at least manages a bit of scorn and—stifled—laughter, and Mrs. Tully cries in pain.)

Donald Davie argues that Maddy, like Joyce's Molly Bloom, is trapped in a language of romantic formulae that no longer works. Unlike Molly, however, Maddy knows that "the formulae cannot be trusted, even though she uses them." But her feelings are more complex, and she tries not to speak by formula, "though her language continually traps her into it."[22] Dan describes her "never pause . . . safe to haven" as "struggling with a dead language," and she has a penchant for quaint archaic and out-of-the-way words throughout the play: *pismire;* the *ramdam,* which so impresses Mr. Tyler; *hinny,* etc. As David Alpaugh remarks, "Beckett contrasts the timeless language of Arcady with the dying language of Man, which has become formal and inadequate" ("Symbolic Structure," 325).

Maddy's archaisms put her in the same realm as the "poor dear Gaelic" associated with a romantic Ireland that is, as Yeats bitterly complained, "dead and gone." In this play it is murderously ground under like a mother hen under a motor car, a child under a train—the climax of the escalating menace of the forms of travel in the first half of the play: foot, dung cart, bicycle, automobile, and train. The means of conveyance are increasingly mechanized and (therefore?) increasingly unreliable. Maddy's footsteps are "halting." Christy's hinny refuses to budge, and his eyes frighten her. Mr. Tyler's bell also frightens her, and his tire, although he pumped it hard before he set out, goes flat. A passing van terrifies them and nearly runs them down, warning us that these "great roaring machines" can, in fact, kill. Mr. Slocum's car is mercilessly hard for Maddy to negotiate and goes dead until Mr. Slocum "chokes her." It squashes a hen in the road: the roaring machines not only might kill; they do kill. The train is, at it turns out, murderously late. And as Linda Ben-Zvi has indicated, the flaws in mechanized conveyances correspond to the flaws in the artifact of language: "Language also weakens and alters. In Grimm's Law, as Dan points out, sounds move from voiced to voiceless. Words lose their meaning; become archaic; phrases are no longer remembered, or only half-remembered. Languages even die; Gaelic, for example."[23] It is consistent with the themes of the play that, though Maddy communes and empathizes with the natural world—understanding, for example, the mixture of mute defiance and appeal in the "cleg tormented eyes" of Christy's

hinny—she has trouble negotiating the automobile and difficulty in communicating with Mr. Barrell, the stationmaster, who presides over the
Boghill railway station.

Approached from this critical perspective, the play requires an absolute
distinction between the prelapsarian utterances of the animals and the
fallen language of humans. This became, for me, yet another reason why
it seemed essential to use real animal sounds—so that there would be no
possibility of confusing the Arcadian animal language with something
human and fallen. The animals make a wonderful music of their own that
conveys on radio a context that is rural but not real.

Since all the action of the drama makes absolutely consistent sense when
it is all seen to be POV Maddy (from the point of view of Maddy Rooney),
nothing that occurs in *All That Fall* is independent of Maddy Rooney's
awareness of it. If she does not say it, think it, hear it, or overhear it,
neither does the audience. That is to say, whatever she is not aware of
cannot occur in the drama, and when she ceases to be aware of something
it vanishes from the drama. Conversely, things will appear in the drama
the way they do *because* that is the way in which she is aware of them:
sometimes as they might be heard by other people (as with the hinny's
whinny or Mr. Slocum's "stravaging" his gearbox); sometimes in more
exaggerated form (as with the hen squashed by Mr. Slocum's automobile
or, finally, the arrival of the late train at the Boghill station); and sometimes
she "hears" things that are not "there" except in her perception of them:
"Hist! (*Pause.*) Surely to goodness that cannot be the up mail I hear already.
(*Silence . . .*)." And later: "Heavens, there is that up mail again" (12, 14).
In the first instance she is with Christy and nearer the beginning of her
journey. If it *is* (as it isn't) the up mail passing, she can have no hope of
getting to the station on time to meet the down mail. In the second instance
she's aware of herself as a "hysterical old hag" and is not fearing the
arrival of the train so much as mocking herself for hearing things. Later,
talking to Mr. Barrell, she will refer back to this moment, speculating not
about hearing things but, instead, about *not* hearing them:

MRS. ROONEY: Did I understand you to say the twelve thir-
                  ty would soon be upon us?
MR. BARRELL: Those were my words.

MRS. ROONEY: But according to my watch which is more or
                 less right—or was—by the eight o'clock
                 news the time is now coming up to
                 twelve . . . (*Pause as she consults her watch.*) . . .
                 thirty-six. (*Pause.*) And yet upon the other
                 hand the up mail has not yet gone through.
                 (*Pause.*) Or has it sped by unbeknown to
                 me? (*Pause.*) For there was a moment there,
                 I remember now, I was so plunged in sor-
                 row I wouldn't have heard a steam roller go
                 over me.

                                                          (21)

In the deliberately callous absence of any reassurance from Mr. Barrell, she (and consequently we) cannot know whether or not the up mail has gone through until we hear it pass (which helps explain Maddy's rejoicing in its appearance).

But the fact that the audience hears as Maddy hears does not nec- essarily mean that the audience understands as Maddy does or that the audience—outside the drama—shares her perceptions within it. For ex- ample, on the railroad platform, waiting for the train, Maddy thinks she is having trouble being perceived by the other characters on the platform, and she struggles to assert herself in order to gain their attention. This has led some critics to argue that she is, in fact, unperceived by the other characters—that in the absence of some acknowledgment by other speakers (or some other audio device) "the character has no way to continue to establish his or her presence and, in effect, vanishes—literally ceases to exist"; or that "despite Mrs. Rooney's insistence on her presence . . . in actual fact, as long as she is silent she does not and cannot exist"; or that in some other way Beckett is calling attention to the medium of radio; or that since the other characters do not acknowledge her, she may be thinking—or at least talking inaudibly—to herself.[24]

These conclusions seem to me to account inadequately for the dy- namics of the drama. If the audience is tied to Maddy's perceptions but not confined to her understanding of them, then it is possible to see that the other characters are all too aware of her presence and that there is a lively bit of comedy going on that may be understood from the relationship between Maddy and the other characters.

Mr. Barrell and Mr. Tyler have each previously provoked Maddy into insulting them, and they are now, in consequence, taking deliberate pains to ignore her, causing her, in turn, to impose herself on their attention. When she first arrives at the station Maddy forces Mr. Barrell—alone on the platform—into conversation, in expectation that he will be gentlemanly enough to assist her up the stairs without causing her the embarrassment of actually having to admit (by asking) that she can't negotiate "the Matterhorn" by herself. She hints broadly, responding to Mr. Barrell's greeting with a report that she is not well:

MR. BARRELL: . . . Well, Mrs. Rooney, it's nice to see you
                      up and about again. You were laid up there
                      a long time.
MRS. ROONEY: Not long enough, Mr. Barrell. (*Pause.*)
                      Would I were still in bed, Mr. Barrell.
                      (*Pause.*) Would I were lying stretched out in
                      my comfortable bed, Mr. Barrell. . . .

                                                        (20–21)

The pauses are intended to give Mr. Barrell the opportunity to proffer help. In its absence she intensifies her report of her ailments in order to prompt him, until she gets lost in the report and recovers herself with her handkerchief. Her revenge is to insult him:

MRS. ROONEY: You stepped into your father's shoes, I be-
                      lieve, when he took them off.
MR. BARRELL: Poor Pappy! (*Reverent Pause.*) He didn't live
                      long enough to enjoy his ease.
MRS. ROONEY: I remember him clearly. A small ferrety
                      purple-faced widower, deaf as a doornail,
                      very testy and snappy. (*Pause.*) I suppose
                      you'll be retiring soon yourself, Mr. Barrell,
                      and growing your roses. (*Pause.*) Did I un-
                      derstand you to say the twelve thirty would
                      soon be upon us?

                                                        (21)

But her last sentence—a reminder that she has to be got up onto the platform—is greeted, by Mr. Barrell, the man whom she's just insulted, with a terse "Those were my words." Further attempts at conversation fare no better:

MR. BARRELL: (*Testily.*) What is it, Mrs. Rooney, I have my work to do.

(21)

And he leaves her stranded. When they meet again later on the platform he will be at pains to extricate himself from Maddy's presence.

She has also offended Mr. Tyler. When she first encounters him on the road she refuses to let him put his arm on her shoulder in order to steady his bicycle:

MRS. ROONEY: No, Mr. Rooney, Mr. Tyler I mean, I am tired of light old hands on my shoulders and other senseless places.

(14–15)

She resists his prim, though still vaguely suggestive, solicitude—a solicitude that causes her to (again) confuse him with her husband, Dan:

MR. TYLER: Come, Mrs. Rooney, come, the mail has not yet gone up, just take my free arm and we'll be there with time to spare.

MRS. ROONEY: (*Exploding.*) Will you get along with you, Mr. Rooney, Mr. Tyler I mean, will you get along with you now and cease molesting me? What kind of a country is this where a woman can't weep her heart out on the highways and byways without being tormented by retired bill-brokers? (*Mr. Tyler prepares to mount his bicycle.*) Heavens you're not going to ride her flat!

(16–17)

But off he goes.

Thus, it is not surprising that when Maddy and Miss Fitt negotiate the stairs to the platform together, Mr. Barrell and Mr. Tyler greet Miss Fitt but not Mrs. Rooney. When Maddy deliberately intrudes ("Do not imagine, because I am silent, that I am not present and alive, to all that is going on" [27]), they deliberately ignore her. Mr. Tyler now devotes the vaguely lewd solicitousness that had been rebuffed by Maddy to the new object of his attention, Miss Fitt. When Maddy interrupts him he waits politely for her to finish and then goes on as if she hadn't spoken. That he feels compelled to repeat himself from the beginning each time he is interrupted by Maddy ("When you say the last train—") is a clear indication that he is thoroughly aware of Maddy's presence. When speculation turns to an accident as the possible cause of the train's delay, Maddy attempts to draw to herself some of the sympathy that Mr. Tyler is lavishing on Miss Fitt, and the effect is magnificently comic:

MISS FITT:	Not an accident, I trust! (*Pause.*) Do not tell me she has left the track! (*Pause.*) Oh darling mother! With the fresh sole for lunch! (*Loud titter from* TOMMY, *checked as before by* MR. BARRELL.)[25]
MR. BARRELL:	That's enough old guff out of you. Nip up to the box now and see has Mr. Case anything for me. (TOMMY *goes.*)
MRS. ROONEY:	Poor Dan!
MISS FITT:	(*in anguish.*) What terrible thing has happened?
MR. TYLER:	Now now, Miss Fitt, do not—
MRS. ROONEY:	(*with vehement sadness.*) Poor Dan!
MR. TYLER:	Now now, Miss Fitt, do not give way . . . to despair, all will come right . . . in the end. (*Aside to* MR. BARRELL.) What *is* the situation, Mr. Barrell? Not a collision surely?

(26)

Finding the same formula repeated, in which Mr. Tyler begins from the beginning when interrupted by her, Maddy now has her revenge: the "aside to Mr. Barrell" (a confidence among men not meant for the tender ears of women) is overhead by Maddy and broadcast in a way that insures a reaction:

| MRS. ROONEY: | (*Enthusiastically.*) A collision! Oh that would be wonderful! |

MISS FITT: (*Horrified.*) A collision! I knew it!

(27)

In desperation Mr. Tyler suggests that he and Miss Fitt move to another part of the platform where he can be unctuous in peace but (as Maddy's lines indicate) gives up the idea when it becomes clear that Maddy will tag along:

MR. TYLER: Come, Miss Fitt, let us move a little up the
                     platform.
MRS. ROONEY: Yes, let us all do that. (*Pause.*) No? (*Pause.*)
                     You have changed your mind? (*Pause.*) I
                     quite agree, we are better here, in the
                     shadow of the waiting room.

(27)

Maddy succeeds in preventing Mr. Tyler and Miss Fitt from either ignoring her or extricating themselves. Now Mr. Barrell tries to leave, but she buttonholes him also:

MR. BARRELL: Excuse me a moment.
MRS. ROONEY: Before you slink away, Mr. Barrell, please, a
                     statement of some kind, I insist . . :

(27)

And Mr. Tyler is forced to take Mrs. Rooney's part!

MR. TYLER: (*Reasonably.*) I do think we are owed some kind
                     of explanation, Mr. Barrell, if only to set our
                     minds at rest.

(27)

Thus, Maddy, though she has told Miss Fitt to plop her "up against the wall like a roll of tarpaulin," is, as she says, "very much present and alive to all that is going on" and takes an active part in it. Her lines in the scene on the platform are part of the dialogue and not internal monologues. There are many such subtle, comic, and lovely moments as this throughout the play; *All That Fall* admits to an interpretation based on the dramatic interaction of the characters that is rare in the work of Samuel Beckett.

Rooted in Maddy, the drama preserves the classical unities of time and (by a reasonable extension to radio of the principle involved in the term) space. The drama lasts without interruption for as long as it takes Maddy to get from where we encounter her along the road at the beginning of the play to where she and Dan are at the end, at about the same point on the same road (i.e., just past the point at which "Death and the Maiden" emerges from the "ruinous old house") and going in the opposite direction, obliterated by the mental soundscape of the "tempest of wind and rain" pummeled into consciousness from the natural landscape. There is never a scene change in which Maddy Rooney moves suddenly from one location to another in anything other than what radio people call "real time."

V

All that wind and rain![26]

We encounter Maddy on the road as she "advances" toward the railroad station and leave her on the road as she returns, and there are many parallels between her journey toward and her return from the railroad station. The fearful symmetry of the structure of the play noticed by Martin Esslin and others would lead one to suspect that the tempest of wind and rain that concludes the drama deliberately parallels the rural sounds of the beginning. At the end of the play further conversation is pointless: Dan does not need to continue his "relation" to fill up the time and protect Maddy from the news, nor does Maddy need to inquire further. She now knows from Jerry what she has been trying to extract from Dan. The news is particularly gruesome to the woman who has "wept her heart out" for "little Minnie" for forty years and who grieves for the little girl who "had never really been born" whom she heard about in a lecture by "one of those mind doctors." At the beginning of the play the imprint of Maddy's footsteps, hum, thoughts, and talk puts the rural sounds out of conscious hearing. At the end of the play the terrible news and the troubled mind for which the storm is the perfect analogue fills up the void. The fragile footsteps hold out—that is to say, Maddy is aware of them—but even they are subsumed in the mental/natural soundscape of the storm. It was very gratifying that the steadily paced and inexorable vehemence of, in his phrase, "all that wind and rain" at the end of our production was one of the things that seems to have pleased Beckett very much. It is what both text and author clearly wanted, and it is dramatically right as the final "beat" of the drama. The night is dark, and they are far from home, and there is no light to lead kindly any more than there is a Lord to uphold the little child who falls from the train. The last thing we hear is *not* the scene lingering for a fade after Maddy and Dan have left it (a common strategy in radio) but, rather, the storm—the natural world as it atomizes Maddy's mind as a result of this tragic recognition (an oblivion that is, perhaps, as welcome as it is terrible).

Just as Maddy's entrance neither preceded nor followed the rural sounds that began the play but is, itself, the act of hearing the sounds, so now Maddy's existence (and Dan's through her intense and intimate consciousness of him) become absorbed into and dissolve from our scrutiny with the storm she hears. Again this is impossible in any production in which there is a visual dimension. Evidently, the "whole thing depends" not only on "coming out of the dark" but also on returning to it.

VI

Now then, Mrs. Rooney, how shall we do this?

—All That Fall

This discussion of *All That Fall* helped resolve—and then was itself informed by—the practical problems encountered in realizing the production on tape. The play required an approach that pared the audio production and sound effects down to essentials, so that the language and its exquisite revelation of character could emerge. Effects would require precise timing with the dialogues, pauses, and even the breathing rhythms of the actors. Footsteps, for example, sometimes continued when the characters weren't saying anything, but their presence, and even their states of mind, would be conveyed by the way in which the effect was executed. In order to accomplish this the production would have to rely more heavily on the acoustics of recording than on the seductive, but in this instance inappropriate, electronics available for creating radio dramas. The studios and recording strategy were arranged with these particulars in mind. Since the United States does not, like England, have a BBC, we were fortunate to find at RCA in New York affordable studios that would in their acoustics, technical equipment, and engineer, Mike Moran, be fully adequate to the complex and intricate recording problems that we faced. With Charles Potter to

design and execute the in-studio sound effects and David Rapkin as production engineer, we had a production team as skillful as could be found
anywhere.[27]

I divided Maddy Rooney's lines into three categories:

1. Things she said aloud that were, or at least could readily be, overheard by someone else. Dialogue and some of her monologues.
2. Things she said aloud but to herself.
3. Things that were not meant to be said but were a vocalization of an
   interior thought process—words Donald McWhinnie had described
   as "unbroken thought, magically overheard." (*Art of Radio*, 134)

Each of these different forms of utterance required a differnt microphone placement—a different relationship between the actress (Billie Whitelaw), the other characters, and the microphone. For interior monologues
she moved to a distance of four to six inches from a Neumann U-87 (in
cardioid pattern), giving her voice a proximate intimacy from the resulting
boosting of low frequencies and by removing any taint of a surrounding
acoustic space while allowing her to be fully audible although speaking at
the level of a barely vocalized whisper. The other two forms of dialogue
were recorded on Neumann KM 84s (in cardioid pattern) mounted into
an XY stereo pair (fig. 8). When speaking to herself Maddy moved to a
distance of approximately twelve to sixteen inches from the microphones;
in dialogue with other characters or when monologuing alone, out loud,
she ranged from two to six feet from the mikes, as the scene required.
One could "place" (or move) the actors in a stereo field by movement to
the left or right of the center axis of the two microphones and, by moving
closer or further from the mikes, bring them on or move them off. All
this required a good deal of careful coordination of the actors moving in
and out of the microphones and the engineer opening up, shutting down,
and changing the levels of the various mikes as they came into and out
of use.

That the sound effects are best interpreted as being connected with
Maddy's mind, rather than as definitions of location, context, or action
(which functions they also serve, because they serve that function for
Maddy), suggested at one point in our preparations that they might be
produced with one or another of the many forms of electronic alteration
available in a modern sound studio—such as, for example, the addition

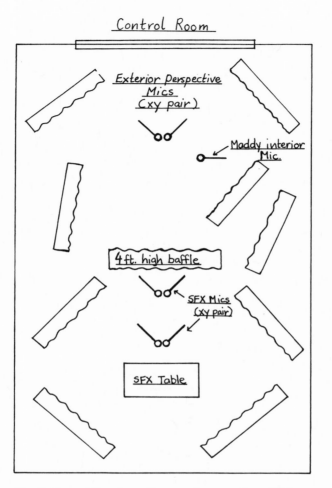

Fig. 8. Everett Frost's studio setup for recording *All That Fall.*

of reverberation (echo), as the BBC production had sometimes done, or digital delay.

After some experimentation with these possibilities I abandoned them for two reasons. First, in the 1980s they have become conventions (even clichés) in radio, television, and film productions of science fiction. As such, they suggested something of the futuristic. The technology tended to call attention to itself, thus working against the crucial evocation of a rural atmosphere. Second, consistency required that all sound effects be handled in the same way. For example, the method used for the approach of the dung

cart would have to correspond to that used for the approach of the bicycle
and also to that used for Connelly's van and Mr. Slocum's automobile—or
to the trains that cross in the middle of the play. The sound effects would
articulate an important theme—that of the increasing mechanization of the
means of travel. In order to do that a consistency of methodology would
have to be accompanied by an increase in intensity. The dung cart is
relatively quiet; it is the silent "cleg tormented eyes" of the hinny that
unnerve. The bicycle is less quiet, though—except for the bell—not formidable. Connelly's van needs to roar by. And Mr. Slocum's automobile
requires an exaggerated realism in order to be consistent with Maddy's
rather frantic state of mind and to achieve its comic, lewd, and menacing
effect.

Finally, there are the trains—a terrifying and exhilarating whirl of
relentless mechanical energy. The railroad station, as Donald McWhinnie
also concluded (*Art of Radio,* 141), must necessarily be overplayed in realistic
fashion. It is not a "real" station but, rather, a sonic hyperbole of one—
for no railroad station sounds like the one created by the BBC team or
by ours:

TOMMY:	(*Excitedly, in the distance.*) She's coming.
	(*Pause. Nearer.*) She's at the level-crossing!
	(*Immediately exaggerated station sounds. Falling signals. Bells. Whistles. Crescendo of train whistle approaching. Sound of train rushing through station.*)
MRS. ROONEY:	(*Above rush of train.*) The up mail! The up mail! (*The up mail recedes, the down train approaches, enters the station, pulls up with great hissing of steam and clashing of couplings. Noise of passengers descending, doors banging,* MR. BARRELL *shouting "Boghill! Boghill!" etc. Piercingly.*)

(27)

Sound effects were either generated in the studio along with the voice
track recordings, "Foleyed"[28] into the voice track in a subsequent recording
session, recorded in the field specifically for *All That Fall* and introduced
in postproduction, or, in a few instances, incorporated in postproduction

from preexisting sound effects libraries. The final sound in the production is often the result of a postproduction mix of several of these elements.

Wherever the script required a precisely timed integration of sound effects and performers, the effects were created along with the voice tracks. For example, the footsteps required careful orchestration with the instructions in the text ("They halt on Mr. Rooney's initiative") and the dialogue and breath rhythms of the performers. The news from Mr. Beckett that Christy's enigmatic line about his hinny, "She's very fresh in herself today," though not accompanied by any sound effects instructions, was in response to a fart produced a prompt raid on the fortunately handy 42d Street novelty shops for a whoopee cusion to comply. (And we put the electronic widgets to work improving its utterance.)

Charles Potter arranged a sound effects desk behind and acoustically isolated from the acting area. The desk was miked with two separate XY stereo pairs—a pair of Neumann KM 84s at a distance of eighteen inches to two feet from the effect and a pair of AKG 451s (cardioid) that varied in distance from four to six feet from the effect. Either of these two pairs could be used alone (to achieve a "near" or "far" distance for the effect), or the two pairs could be blended in combination, depending on the depth of acoustic space ("proximity effect") required. The sound effects area was able to observe the acting area and/or to listen to the performance on headphones (including the sound effects) in exactly the form they were being recorded onto tape. The actors also had headphones available through which they could hear the sound effects (and their voices) as these were being recorded. Both the acting area and the sound effects could be visually sight-cued from the control room or audio-cued through the headphones.

Sometimes for technical reasons and sometimes to prevent the sound effects from inordinately interfering with the concentration of the actors, sound effects were Foleyed in the studios after the actors had departed. Mr. Potter listened to the voice tracks played back through earphones and created the effects in rehearsed synchronization with the already recorded voice track in front of sound effects microphones positioned exactly as they had been in the voice track sessions. This method permitted additional footsteps, the detailed walking on the railroad platform, the welts on Christy's hinny, and most of the sounds that Mr. Tyler would make with his bicycle (such as the bell, the rattle of fenders, the "click" of the pedals going around, etc.).

The rural sounds, wagon effects, and additional bicycle sounds were recorded at Fair Winds farm in Brattleboro, Vermont,[29] in order to control and coordinate the distance of the sounds from the microphones and virtually to eliminate any surrounding farmyard or natural ambience. A predawn drive in Central Park yielded Mr. Slocum's gearbox.

Sounds that we could not acquire for ourselves, such as trains as they might have sounded in Ireland at the beginning of the century, were acquired from archival sources.

In complex scenes several of these methods were used in combination. Mr. Tyler's bell and the rattle of the bicycle, and, later, the sound of his mounting the bicycle, were created in the studio along with the voice tracks. A Foley session augmented the sounds and added a layer of tire on gravel. These were subsequently combined with the sounds of an old bicycle recorded in Vermont: approaching, traveling with, and departing from the microphones (with and without a flat rear tire).

The railroad trains that cross in the center of the play proved ticklish to produce. It is hard for radio to distinguish two similar sounds in close proximity as two separate events—in this case the approach and pass-through of one train followed directly by the arrival of a second. We used two different trains coming from opposite ends of the stereo field. The first train barrels through from left to right. Maddy's voice-over (hollering "The Up Mail!" "The Up Mail!") clearly identifies the train, and further overlays of the crescendo of the sound effects called for in the text—some "looped" during voice tracks, some Foleyed, and most added in production—build the climax. The first train fades to a four-second silence before the arrival of the second train is audible. But it is a very busy moment in the drama, and I have found that some listeners find themselves lost in the confusion, and, consequently, conflate the two trains into one. One solution might be to lengthen the pause between the two trains—at the risk of further dragging out an active scene full of motion that may already be too long.[30]

The Beckett Festival production of *All That Fall* was rehearsed and voice-tracked in a grueling five-day period that began with a day of rehearsal and discussion, first with Billie Whitelaw (Maddy) and then with Ms. Whitelaw and David Warrilow (Dan). The play was divided into and recorded by scenes, like a film, rather than as a continuous performance, like a stage play. Scenes were rehearsed until ready for recording then blocked and rehearsed again in front of the microphones, affording the engineer a run-through for recording levels and for cues in opening up and shutting down microphones. Then the scene was recorded. So that scenes would fit seamlessly together, we generally began recording somewhere in the middle of the preceding scene, and a successful "take" would often continue several lines into the subsequent scene.

One of the great virtues of radio drama recorded on tape is the control it gives over the minute particulars of the performance—an important asset when coping with the exacting instructions for pauses, silences, pacing, and the nuances of delivery. Substantially less expensive than shooting film or videotape, sound recording allows for frequent retakes. In crucial or stubborn places (kept to a minimum to prevent wearing out the actors) there are up to a dozen retakes in our production. With the recording situation controlled with respect to the configuration of the studios, mike placement, and recording levels, these takes can then be edited together or integrated—sometimes word by word or phrase by phrase—in order to capture each nuance and with much more flexibility than visual media. In editing the voice track pauses can be extracted or inserted, lengthened or shortened. Having recorded the voice tracks in early December 1985, and facing the need to send press and audition copies of the production out by February, all this was done under some considerable time constraint and pressure.

The motive throughout was, of course, to make an independent production adequate to the challenge presented by Mr. Beckett's extraordinary radio play. In this essay I have tried to convey something of the conceptual thought and the methodology employed in mounting the production. Having done so, I find myself dissatisfied: the real work did not happen that way. Rather, we learned the play in order to produce it and then found ourselves relearning the play as we faced its practical production problems.

A particular instance may serve as an example. The logistics involved in producing Mr. Slocum's automobile were rather daunting. Once the automobile had been started the scene had to be produced continuously until it arrived at the station, deposited Maddy, and drove off. This involved combining the stravaging gears coordinated with engine rhythms (acceleration/relax; acceleration/relax—cruise) with the dialogue in the departure and having cued up and ready all the effects connected with the squashed hen and the effects to be used when the car arrived at, and departed from, the station. In order to simplify the task I at first elected to produce the car's initial acceleration and departure recorded from an exterior perspective. My thought was to fade this down to silence and then fade up on an interior perspective—on the analogy of a film in which the automobile is "in frame" close up and diminishes into the distance as the fixed-in-place camera follows; then cut to car interior close-up shot. It is a perfectly ordinary and reasonable way to simplify a complicated technical problem, and it was absolutely wrong! The car fading into the distance and the ensuing beat of silence followed by the car from an interior perspective conveyed that we (in a fixed position) heard the car depart from the point at which Maddy boarded it and then joined it further down the road. Arguably, both time and space had elapsed out of our view in the interim of silence. But this is not possible if the drama is to remain in Maddy's consciousness. Maddy's presence cannot depart from the drama for even an instant. It was in this way that I discovered that it was impossible to violate the convention of the unity of time in this production. To have used one highly audible silence in a way that implied a liberty with the unity of time jeopardized every one of the many other silences in the piece by incorrectly indicating that it was within the conventions of the drama that they might be used in that way. We did the scene again, deleting the silence.

In short, what the developing production sounded like "said" what it "meant." The finished production is an interpretation that has partially eluded my attempts to describe it. I hope that it is an interpretation adequate to the work and one that can in some measure make it more readily accessible to its audience. It will take several more such interpretations/productions before we begin to get to the bottom of this wonderful play.

NOTES

1. Many helping hands contributed to the broadcast of *All That Fall*, not the least of which were those belonging to Samuel Beckett and his U.S. representative, Barney Rosset—clearing the way expeditiously with the necessary permissions and providing generous encouragement and useful advice. *All That Fall* was produced under the fiscal agency of Soundscape, Inc., with Louise Cleveland as its executive producer and Martha Fehsenfeld (who had taken the initiative to get the project going) as its first project director. Directed by Everett Frost, the cast included Billie Whitelaw as Maddy Rooney, with David Warrilow as Dan, Alvin Epstein (Mr. Slocum), George Bartenieff (Mr. Tyler), Jerome Kitty (Christy, Mr. Barrell), Susan Willis (Miss Fitt), Melissa Cooper (Female Voice), Lute Ramblin' (Jerry, Lynch twin), and Christine Eddis (Lynch twin). The associate producer was Faith Wilding. *All that Fall* was recorded in the RCA studios in New York in the first week of December 1985. The recording engineer was Mike Moran and the production engineer David Rapkin. Studio sound effects were created by Charles Potter.

The Berlin radio station, RIAS (Rundfunk in Amerikanische Sektor) co produced the play, with Götz Naleppa, the head of the Hörspiel Abteilung (Radio Drama Department) as the administrative liaison. It was distributed in the United States, Canada, and Mexico by American Public Radio (APR) for broadcast on Samuel Beckett's eightieth birthday, 13 April 1986, and was subsequently broadcast on RIAS and on the German-speaking Swiss radio station, ZDF. Major funding was provided by the National Endowment for the Humanities, with additional funds from RIAS and New York University.

The production was advised by a team of humanist scholars that, at various times, included (in addition to Martha Fehsenfeld and Louise Cleveland), Lois More Overbeck (humanist coordinator), Enoch Brater, Thomas Bishop, and Wallace Fowlie. There was considerable help from Beckett's U.S. representative, Barney Rosset, and from Walter Asmus, Antoni Libera, and Linda Ben-Zvi. Dr. Cleveland produced the documentary that now accompanies the play.

The Beckett Festival of Radio Plays, containing productions of all of Beckett's extant plays for radio (*All That Fall, Embers, Words and Music, Cascando,* and *Rough for Radio II*), followed in 1989. Production and funding credits for the entire *Beckett Festival* may be found in my "Fundamental Sounds: Recording Samuel Beckett's Radio Plays," *Theatre Journal* 43, no. 3 (October 1991): 363.

Cassette copies of *All That Fall* and other *Beckett Festival* productions are available from the Pacifica Program Service (PPS), P.O. Box 8092, Universal City, CA 91604. Phone: 800-735-0230.

2. Beckett was very generous in his assistance, discussing the play with me and working with Billie Whitelaw to develop her performance of Maddy. He also genuinely encouraged our efforts to give the radio plays what he liked to refer to as a "fresh go." But one should not infer from this that our production of *All That Fall* or any of the other radio plays have any special authority for that reason or that they were shadow-directed by Beckett. When I offered to arrange the recordings in London or Paris to make it possible for him either to direct or attend the sessions, he considered the opportunity very seriously but declined, remarking that "these are ancient works with which I have lost contact."

The BBC written archives include exchanges of letters between Samuel Beckett and Donald McWhinnie, the director of the original BBC production, about the production strategy for *All That Fall* and other radio plays.

3. Ruby Cohn, *Samuel Beckett: The Comic Gamut* (New Brunswick, N.J.: Rutgers University Press, 1962), 244.

4. Ruby Cohn, *Just Play: Beckett's Theatre* (Princeton, N.J.: Princeton University Press, 1980), 6 (hereafter cited parenthetically in the text).

5. Samuel Beckett, *All That Fall, The Collected Shorter Plays of Samuel Beckett* (New York: Grove Press, 1984), 38. All quotations from Beckett's radio plays are taken from this edition.

6. Quoted in Clas Zilliacus, *Beckett and the Art of Broadcasting* (Abo: Abo Akademi, 1978), 43.

7. Ibid., 41–43. Beryl S. Fletcher et al., *A Student's Guide to the Plays of Samuel Beckett* (London: Faber, 1978), 81.

8. In a letter to Alan Schneider (29 December 1957), Beckett wrote: "My work is a matter of fundamental sounds (no joke intended) made as fully as possible,

and I accept responsibility for nothing else. If people want to have headaches among the overtones, let them. And provide their own aspirin" (quoted in Deirdre Bair, *Samuel Beckett* [New York: 1978], 470).

9. Martin Esslin, "Samuel Beckett and the Art of Broadcasting," *Mediations: Essays on Brecht, Beckett, and the Media* (New York: Grove Press, 1982), 132 (hereafter cited in the text).

10. Also Donald McWhinnie, *The Art of Radio* (London: Faber, 1959), 134–35 (hereafter cited parenthetically in the text); and Desmond Briscoe (sound designer for the BBC production and originator of the BBC's Radiophonic Workshop), in conversations with Everett Frost, August 1985.

11. Quoted as frontispiece to Zilliacus, *Beckett and the Art of Broadcasting.*

12. It meant a great deal to one and all to have received his "congratulations and gratitudes" for the completed production (letter to Everett Frost, 3 March 1986).

13. McWhinnie, *Art of Radio.* Donald McWhinnie died before my efforts to make the pilgrimage to meet him could translate into a schedule. Long before I became involved in the Beckett productions I had admired his distinguished work as a director of radio and television productions. He was an eloquent and polemical advocate of the art of radio, and my argument with one section of it in this essay should not obscure the fact that his astute book remains one of the most insightful ever written about radio drama—and urgently needs to be reprinted and better known.

14. Citing this passage from McWhinnie, Clas Zilliacus remarks, "The solution is a daring one . . . (but) it is by no means the obvious solution" (*Beckett and the Art of Broadcasting,* 69).

15. Many years later, in preparing to direct the plays, I listened to both of the BBC productions and to the French and German versions (and also saw, thanks to Tom Bishop, a videotape of the French television film of the play). I used them, forgive the phrase, to "see" what had counted as solutions to problems I hadn't yet solved (in some cases, hadn't yet identified) and in preparations for meeting with Beckett and examination of the BBC written archives. Then I put them away until after our production was, as they say, "in the can," so as not, even inadvertently, to ape them or to have their "sound" working in my head as a standard or norm for such matters as inflection, oral interpretation, or pacing. This procedure was more or less consistent through the process of directing each of the other plays.

16. See McWhinnie, *Art of Radio,* 39ff.

17. Beckett replied affirmatively when I asked him if he'd heard Schaeffer's work on the radio, but I stopped short of asking him if it had been an influence on *All That Fall.*

18. An examination of the correspondence at the BBC Written Archive Center makes it clear that Beckett was reconfirming to me sentiments that were identical to those he'd expressed at the time of the original BBC broadcast. The center does not permit quotation of materials in its archives without the joint permission of the BBC and the author of the document. Esslin ("Samuel Beckett," 130), Hugh Kenner (*Samuel Beckett: A Critical Study* [Los Angeles: University of California Press,

1968], 171), and Zilliacus (*Beckett and the Art of Broadcasting,* 70) also report Beckett as being unhappy with the rural sounds in the BBC production.

It also bears mentioning that in the mid-1950s getting portable tape equipment into the field, while not impossible, was considerably more difficult than it was in the mid-1980s. Now it is routine to gather sound effects to meet the specific needs of a drama; then one relied upon a small supply of overused sound effects records of unreliable quality. It was reasonable for McWhinnie to try to find a way around them.

19. Interview with Louise Cleveland, December 1985.

20. Whatever else they may be, the rural sounds at the very "top of the show" are also good radio strategy, in the vulgar pop radio sense of the term. The opening few minutes of *any* radio program crave a "hook" to catch the attention of audience members and keep them from tuning out—an "Ah, ah, ah . . . don't touch that dial! Listen to. . . ." (the opening of the Golden era kitsch-com "Blondie"). This necessity is particularly hard on serious drama, which wants time in which to develop its emotional power. *All That Fall* has a notoriously difficult beginning: it will be a minimum of two to three minutes (and that is a very long time on radio) before the audience has been given enough of the drama to be able to figure out what the hell is going on. But the cacophony of animal sounds— "only too obviously composed of disparate elements" (pace McWhinnie, *Art of Radio*)—bursting suddenly into the midst of sophisticated, cultured, proper BBC-3 must have been a delicious attention grabber, even in their anthropomorphic form! This was one of many indications in the play that, though it was a first go, Beckett understood the radio medium very well and from a number of different perspectives and certainly knew how to write for it.

21. David J. Alpaugh, "The Symbolic Structure of Samuel Beckett's *All That Fall,*" *Modern Drama* 9, no. 3 (1966): 325 (hereafter cited parenthetically in the text).

22. Donald Davie, "Kinds of Comedy: *All That Fall,*" *Spectrum* (Winter 1958): 25–31. Reprinted in *Samuel Beckett: The Critical Heritage,* ed. Lawrence Graver and Raymond Federman (London: Routledge and Kegan Paul, 1979), 153.

23. Linda Ben-Zvi, "Samuel Beckett's Media Plays," *Modern Drama* 28, no. 1 (March 1985): 22.

24. It is produced this way in the BBC production. See also Thomas F. Van Laan, "*All That Fall* as a Play for Radio," *Modern Drama* 29, no. 1 (March 1986), 41.

25. Clarifying this audio equivalent of a rolling sight gag (in which Tommy starts to titter and is interrupted by a blow to the stomach) occasioned the only instance in which I asked to make a change in the text and received Beckett's permission to do so. The gag first occurs as Maddy and Miss Fitt become an object of amusement in negotiating the stairs to the railway platform. The lines as given run:

(*Attracted by the noise a group, including* MR. TYLER, MR. BARRELL, *and* TOMMY, *gathers at the top of the steps.*)
MR. BARRELL: What the—
                                   (*Silence.*)

MR. TYLER:	Lovely day for the fixture.
	(*Loud titter from* TOMMY *cut short by* MR. BARRELL *with backhanded blow in the stomach. Appropriate noise from* TOMMY.)
A FEMALE VOICE:	(*Shrill.*) Oh look, Dolly, look!
DOLLY:	What, Mamma?
A FEMALE VOICE:	They are stuck! (*Cackling laugh.*) They are stuck!
MRS. ROONEY:	Now we are the laughing-stock of the twenty-six counties. Or is it thirty-six?
MR. TYLER:	That is a nice way to treat your defenseless subordinates, Mr. Barrell, hitting them without warning in the pit of the stomach.

(24)

Amid the confusion of the entrance of the three characters the sound effect of hitting Tommy's stomach and his reaction get lost: without Mr. Tyler's final line the audience has no way of knowing that Tommy is even there, much less hit. But after the Female Voice, and Mrs. Rooney's reaction to it, it is no longer clear what Mr. Tyler is referring to. The confusion risks spoiling the comedy of the recurrence of this little routine between Tommy and Mr. Barrell throughout the rest of the scene. The solution was to move Mr. Tyler's line to before the Female Voice, so that it comes as a direct and immediate reaction to Mr. Barrell's violence.

There are three other variants that might raise an eyebrow of the minutely attentive:

1. When Tommy is extracting her from Mr. Barrell's automobile, she pleads "Pity!" (20) in some editions but curses "*Merdre!*" in others—including the script of the BBC production. Beckett was concerned that we use "Pity!"

2. In *Collected Shorter Plays* it is unaccountably Miss Fitt (!) who is said to marvel at Mrs. Rooney's use of the word *Ramdam!* (25). (Though Grove gets it right [but *merdre* wrong] in *Krapp's Last Tape and Other Dramatic Pieces by Samuel Beckett* [New York: Evergreen, 1957], 60.) Right, of course, is the pedantic Mr. Tyler: the word would be wasted on the self-absorbed Miss Fitt.

3. "So hinnies whinny," says Maddy to herself when listening to Christy's. But in the BBC production Christy's hinny *brays*. Beckett reconfirmed that "hinnies whinny" with a "light neigh," and that's what it does in our production. It turns out to be important: a hinny is the offspring of a male horse and a female donkey—the opposite of a mule, which brays and is the offspring of a female horse and a male donkey—and is sterile, as a hinny is not. Aspirins anyone?

26. Beckett's reaction to the conclusion of our production of the play.
27. RCA particularly pleased me because the equipment was (at that time)

simple, old-fashioned, and reliable, and the studio production was well supplied with a wide selection of extremely good microphones. Additionally, their studios were built (in an era before plywood and plastic) out of shaped, laminated wood and real fabric for sound deadening. This meant that we could, without difficulty, achieve the considerable deadening of the sound reflected from the walls necessary for creating the illusion of an exterior setting (where sound does not bounce back the way it does in a room)—but also give it a slight "coloration" (as seemed to me appropriate for a sound taking place as much in a disembodied space as in an exterior one). Audiophiles were horrified when, in 1993, despite rigorous protests, these exquisite studios were destroyed and converted into office space.

28. After the Hollywood sound effects man, Jack Foley, who developed the technique for film.

29. With thanks to Jan, Jay, Rebecca, Reuben, and Erica Bailey.

30. The BBC production of *All That Fall* lasts sixty-nine minutes and ten seconds (69:10). At 78:15 ours is, I think, the longest *All That Fall* (in any language) on record. Going back and listening even several years later has not (yet?) tempted me to get back to an edit suite and try to hurry it along.

Directing Beckett "Down Under"

Colin Duckworth

Plays are like people. You have to live with them to understand them fully. The intimate acquaintance afforded by involvement in a performance setting cannot be approximated by even the closest study of the printed text. This view will be shared by many, most, or even all colleagues in departments of drama but by a minority, few, or even none in departments devoted to English literature.

Various kinds of cohabitation are possible, but the descending order of authoritativeness is, in my view, as director, actor, rehearsal observer, or spectator at more than one performance. I have not included reader because, after studying and lecturing on *Waiting for Godot*, *Play*, and *Krapp's Last Tape* for years, it was only after directing them that I felt I had begun to master their detailed complexities.

My first experience of Beckett in performance "down under" was not as director, but as critic. The *New Zealand Herald* asked me to review a production of *Godot* at the Central Theatre, Auckland, in 1973, soon after my arrival there. It was a competent production, but I had to take great exception to director Raymond Hawthorne's whimsical decision to make the Boy appear in white satin, holding a parasol aloft and doing a balancing act along a wall. I pointed out in my review that the director had not thought about the implications of this. In the first place many spectators asked, puzzled, on the way out, "Why did Beckett have that boy prancing about?" So, I jumped up and down, physically and critically, saying, "This was *not* Beckett's idea at all...." Since very few New Zealanders at that time had previously seen the play, the seriousness of this idiosyncrasy was far greater than it would have been in London, Paris, or New York. Second, by making the Boy a fantastic, unreal, dreamlike figure, Hawthorne had operated a closure on the nature of Godot and his entourage (making them unambiguously fantastic and oneiric) that was never Beckett's intention. In a pioneering situation directors have a particular duty to avoid such self-indulgent betrayals of the text.

A couple of years later, overcoming the reluctance I had long felt, I accepted a pressing invitation to direct *Godot* myself at the new Maidment Theatre in Auckland. This reluctance stemmed partly from my reverence for the play and from my feeling I couldn't possibly do it justice and partly from the regrettable fact of life that the cast I regarded as ideal at that time (Peter O'Toole, Nicol Williamson, Jack MacGowran, and Paul Curran) never seemed available to be directed by me—especially Jack MacGowran, rest his soul. Furthermore, I was keen to correct some wrong impressions Aucklanders had about Beckett—about the Boy, and about the widely held belief that *Godot* audiences had to sit stolidly, respectfully, in glum silence as though listening to a Methodist sermon. In the program I put a note saying "If you find something amusing, please feel free to laugh."[1]

The most memorable response to my production came from the critic for the New Zealand Broadcasting Corporation (NZBC) radio, Robert Goodman, who was still stuck in an ideologically committed drama groove of yore. "Beckett," he asserted on behalf of us all, "has nothing to say to us."

Lack of Beckettian sophistication showed itself even in culturally aware Melbourne in 1982 when my productions (for Frozen Rocks at La Mama) of *Play* and of the Australian premieres of *Rockaby* and *Ohio Impromptu* were reviewed. Helen Garner, one of the country's foremost younger authors, wrote in the *National Times* (2 May): "*Theatregoers who, like me, are not familiar with Beckett's work* and are bluffed by the hooha that often accompanies his name, need not approach these three plays nervously. Director Colin Duckworth says in his unusually helpful and unpatronising[2] program notes that the aim of the production is to 'make clear, not to mystify,' and this is what it does." Helen Garner did, to her credit, justify my rejection of Beckett's instruction that the Listener's face should be hidden in his long white hair. This is only one of several examples of Beckett's determination to suppress emotional indicators. My view was that, although the published text stresses the Reader's speech, performance reveals (or should be allowed to reveal) that the mimetic focus is the Listener's face as it shows the emotion created by the realization that this is the last meeting of two people who have become "as one." Garner saw this too, ending her review: "The play of emotion on the extraordinary face of Robin Cuming as the listener, and the gentle service offered to him by the comforter (Alan Madden) are most remarkable. What struck me about this production was a combination of intellectual surefootedness and absolutely solid craft."

Leonard Radic, drama critic of *The Age,* knows Beckett's works well (indeed, he tells me he once wrote a thesis on them). His response, nevertheless, consisted of strong reservations about Beckett's "pursuit of theatrical minimalism" and grudging praise for the productions: "Obviously in tune with Beckett . . . they handle these esoteric exercises with sympathy and skill."[3]

Geoffrey Dutton, a rightly respected doyen among Australian writers, began what turned out to be a very positive review rather ambiguously: "Curiosity, if not devotion, led my footsteps to Carlton. . . ." He continued with the remark of a true litterateur that will raise the eyebrows, if not the ire, of dramatic Becketteers: "They [the three plays] are not theatrical in the sense of being tailored for the stage, *indeed the two recent sketches could be given as readings without losing much of their impact.*"[4] I defy any reading to reproduce the shock of that first knock on the table by the Listener, which always dispelled any torpor lingering in the audience after *Rockaby.*

For *Rockaby* the procedure adopted in rehearsal focused on establishing minute differences of pitch, volume, intensity, pace, and intonation, in order to render the variations in context for the oft-repeated leitmotifs. Moira Claux, whose characterful face gave the recital of life's solitude an added poignancy, was understandably at sea to begin with. She was greatly helped, I think, by my providing her with two kinds of commentary:

—a reconstitution of the subtext, which enabled her to flesh out the merely hinted-at semantic message, and
—an analysis of the successive themes that appear in counterpoint to repeated leitmotifs, broadening in each of the four sections of the text.

In performance the accumulation of repeated thoughts was subordinated to the key phrases, which were rendered with either slower emphasis or faster urgency, depending on the rhythms and cadences that developed in rehearsal once this separation of functions had been clarified. The text was thus imbued with momentum and a sort of dramatic development that was enhanced by her varying the movements of the rocking chair in the normal, natural way. Once again we supplied the emotional indicator suppressed by Beckett, who demands that the rocker be "controlled mechanically without assistance."

It must be said that audiences responded to the stark fare offered them with fierce and appreciative concentration, even when a drunk stormed into the small avant-garde theater during *Rockaby*, shouting "I wanna be in theatre!" and had to be forcibly ejected down the steps by me, director and unlicensed bouncer.

Paul Monaghan ended his review of the productions in the *Melbourne Times* with words that I shall record here because they show that my approach to the director's task is not completely wasted: "Beckett's form stretches the director as well as the actors, in that he must maintain the play's accessibility for the audience. With the direction of Colin Duckworth, the very human content of these three plays by Samuel Beckett was enhanced (as the playwright obviously intended) rather than distorted, by their difficult form."[5]

Just before these productions I had been invited to participate in a distance-learning course for Deakin University on Beckett: twenty-four hours of lectures and discussions on audiotapes, with excerpts and readings, a book of course material,[6] and a television production of *Krapp's Last Tape*. Funding was available to employ an actor of my choice—Robin Cuming. Although he was a highly experienced professional, he had never acted Beckett before. Neither had he done a solo drama performance, which is testing not only onstage but also in rehearsal, since the actor-director relationship assumes extreme concentration (as Billie Whitelaw notably discovered when doing *Not I* with Beckett). But these disadvantages were outweighed by his sensitivity—and he did bear an uncanny resemblance to Pat Magee. He was to play the Man in *Play* and, as noted by Helen Garner, Listener in *Ohio Impromptu* soon after.

Halfway through the first rehearsal of *Krapp's Last Tape* Robin agreed that we should tape-record our sessions and that I could use them if I felt they threw any light on problems of interpreting the play. As a result, this production is extraordinarily well documented, and I shall therefore devote most of the rest of this essay to it, in the hope that the comments may forewarn aspiring directors and actors of *Krapp* about the intensity of the experience they are in for. Out of the sixty-odd hours of rehearsal about five hours of solid discussion emerged, amounting to eighty pages of transcription. I have narrowed these down to a number of points, some very practical but nevertheless crucial, others concerned with characterization, visualization, intonation, and other aspects of mimesis. One striking quality of the exchanges is, in fact, the coexistence and interaction of apparently very trivial points of detail and probings into not only Krapp's experience but also that of the two protagonists of the creative act, Robin Cuming and myself.

A number of basic factors involving interpretation (in both senses) came up very early in rehearsals. Here is a summary of them:

1. Beckett's own creative process in production of *Krapp:* To what extent should it affect our own work?
2. What is the tune of "Now the Day Is Over"?
3. Fixing K69's (Krapp at 69) reactions to what he has taped.
4. Fixing the character of K39 (Krapp at 39) in our minds, so that the voice sounds right.
5. K39's awareness of the seeds of failure—imagining his physical alterness to this and his mind's refusal to accept it.
6. The importance of the thirty-ninth year.
7. The slow erosion of time. Beckett's essay on Proust. Geological cuts across time.
8. Where to concentrate first—on K39 or K69?
9. Comparisons with another production we had just seen. Its failure to establish age contrasts.
10. The need to stand and use diaphragm breathing, chest voice, for K39, like a singer.
11. The perfection and irony of the line "crest of the wave."
12. Need to be clear about K39's attitude toward himself and K69's attitude toward himself and K39.
13. K39's lack of awareness of his pomposity; K69's sharp alertness to this.
14. The quality of the "Ah, wells."
15. Why did Beckett choose those three particular birthdays?
16. Is K69 an advance on K39 or a deterioration?
17. Beckett and the search for wisdom.
18. Beckett's religious views and their application to *Krapp*.
19. Krapp's vision as part of Beckett's own worldview.
20. The effect of Beckett's having provided so much production detail. Does this detract from the universality of the play?
21. Acting and staging as a form of exploration.
22. Beckett's stress (as director) on exact intonation.
23. Beckett's plays are mostly old men's plays but increasing applicable to younger people.
24. The vital force is K69, and this depends on the vitality of K39,

against which K69 has to react. The more difference, the greater
the unity in performance.

25. Pronunciation of *spool*. Sensuality.
26. Mastering the suggestion of Irishness in voice.
27. The "emotional stuff" easier to cope with than the "reasony stuff."
28. The actor's problems of working with just one other person.
29. Relationship between director and actor.
30. Mercurial quality of Krapp's character difficult to "block."
31. Facial mime.
32. Beckett's own relationships with people as a guide to understanding Krapps' statements about life.
33. What light is thrown on K69 by Beckett's own situation in 1958?
34. Details about the initial business: bananas, drawers, keys, corks, etc. Elaboration of a precise pantomime.
35. Watched video of *Eh Joe*. Actor's reactions. Motivation behind Joe's self-centeredness: self-preservation rather than self-pity.
36. Musical phrasing of certain sentences. Rendering ambiguous bombast and self-doubt.
37. More work on the accent. Listen to Dave Allen.
38. The rhythm of "intellectually . . . at the crest of the wave—or thereabouts."

That takes us to halfway through the second rehearsal. The most
interesting single event from then on was when I set Robin down in front
of a videocamera and got him to listen to the voice of K39. It was when
he saw the replay that he really began to make progress with his facial
acting, realizing the importance of fixing every reaction K69 registered
with as much precision as with the voice. The same for the hands. The
details of makeup, especially hand makeup, since we intended to make
much of Krapp's hands on the table and on the tape recorder. Then the
set, the type of boxes, where they should be, how to cope with ripping off
the tape of K69 and replacing K39's on the machine. How to deal with
peeling the bananas (some have very tough skins. Answer: nick them
across the top and cut them downward slightly—but not an obvious cut,
as in Rick Cluchey's performance).

For the video recording we had problems with the lighting, but this
is always a problem with this play. The only source of "real" light is the
single lamp over the table, which is inadequate as stage lighting. But other
light sources throw shadows and change the areas of light and dark, which

are such important parts of the play's visual architecture. We finally settled for having *no* light coming from the lamp over the desk. The reflected light gave the impression it was lit. But the shade did have genuine dust on it.

It is surprising to me now that Beckett did not write *Krapp's Last Tape* specifically for television. It was only after several rehearsals that the similiarities (both in dramatic effect and in challenges for the actor) with *Eh Joe* became marked. In the theater the spectator's attention is deflected constantly to parts of the mimetic area other than the circle of light within which Krapp acts out the final episode in his life. Furthermore, the distance separating protagonist and spectator diminishes the intensity of the Joe-like role played by Krapp in his reactions to the disembodied voice. One could say that this is also true for *Play* and *Ohio Impromptu,* but the extent to which *Krapp* is primarily a facial ballet is far greater. I soon felt that this was going to be an enrichment of the dramatic text by virtue of the minute attention to features afforded by the camera.

As the above summary of points indicates, one of the first problems we had to come to terms with in rehearsal was how to interpret the reality of someone we never meet: K39. What did he sound like? What were his attitudes? How was he different from the Krapp we see onstage: K69? Each of the three layers of personality presented violently rejects the former one. Why? To understand that I suggested we ought to take into account the crucial importance for many men of that age, thirty-nine. A watershed.

Robin and I mention his first taping of K39's voice. In all we made six versions. The second we used for rehearsals. We thought the fourth was going to be *it.* But by then every syllable was in our heads like music, and we had to be sure it sounded right all through, since that voice is all we have to go on for an understanding of the central Krapp: the one whom K29 became, the one out of whom K69 developed.

> COLIN DUCKWORTH: What would you like to do today? Look at the words other than the taped bits? That is, the remaining text? Or go through your reactions to what we've taped? Or what?
>
> ROBIN CUMING: I think we should see if we agree on reactions, because you were listening to it while it was taped, and, of course, it's a different experience for me. . . . Basically, I felt that at the beginning, when I was

wondering where the hell I was at anyway, it is too obviously uptight, which was a remark you made. But in fact he's got to be, on the surface at least, more at ease with himself and doesn't know how uptight he is. Would you agree that though he is strung up he is uptight in himself, that he has that particular middle-aged quality, or moving into middle age, that is fantastically competitive, anxious to make something of himself, and consequently fucks up his life?

CD: He has. I don't know whether it's consequently, but he clearly has.

RC: It's as a consequence of other things?

CD: There's a kind of pushiness about him at this age, which certainly you've got to let through.

RC: The pompous quality of his assurance comes from his need for that self-assurance?

CD: Right. Because, in fact, I think that he's already conscious of the seeds of failure.

RC: Or even that his body is already alert to the fact that the seeds of failure are there, but he won't allow his consciousness to accept it.

CD: Yes. I was just thinking that it's a crucial year, this thirty-nine, before the magical forty, more for women than for men usually. But I remember a colleague of mine in London was in tears on his fortieth birthday. We were having a private chat in the Senior Common Room, the tears fell rolling out of his eyes and he said, "Here I am at forty, and when I think of all the things I'd intended to do by this time. . . . All the books I haven't written, all the mistresses I haven't had." And he was a really successful academic, a very good scholar, but he was shattered. So, there may be something of that in Krapp, the realization that he is just coming up to the turning point, and that this vision is the last thing he's got. At last, he's had it, and it has to be good to make something of it.

RC: I'd agree with you there entirely. It's what's so desperate about it.

CD: I think that's what accounts for the tightness.

RC: Yes. I know so many people who've gone through the same thing, myself included, bang on cue, in my late thirties, three years of pretty extraordinary depression. A fantastic change-of-gear time, when you realize not so much that you have or haven't done things you were going to do, as that things are important in a different way. You're a different sort of person from what you thought you were. So, you get on with it if you're lucky. Krapp hasn't been. I sometimes wonder what the tape would be like on his sixty-eighth birthday. I wonder what the degrees are between them.

(I had asked Robin to read James Knowlson's article "Krapp's Last Tape: The Evolution of a Play, 1958–75.")[7]

RC: This article puts the whole thing in very black-and-white terms, and it appears that Beckett thinks in much more black-and-white terms than I had believed. I'm at the stage of feeling that Beckett is far from being beyond criticism in wanting some kind of synthesis between the dark and the light. And what he calls these at times seems to me to be meaningless. It seems to be purely academic, you know, just making a statement of "Oh, all right, so now we synthesize them, so isn't that an important thought?" In fact, he hasn't described what this involves. The play doesn't seem to answer anything at all. Does it approve of the old man?

CD: I think so, because he is so much more self-aware.

RC: That's just about it.

CD: And self-depreciating. Beckett himself is very aware of this slow erosion of time. His essay on Proust has some marvelous things to say about this slow irreversibility of the hours and the days. "There is no escape from yesterday because yesterday has deformed us." In *Krapp* he takes a couple of cuts across the geological equivalent of, say, 500,000 years. You wouldn't see the differences in values formed from one day to the next, but at that distance in time he can show the self-destructions that have taken place. In *Happy Days* he's more conscious of the slowness of the erosion process.

RC: It's funny, because it's so much at odds with the directions in which I've been thinking in recent times. Not necessarily in disagreement, but it takes a lot of getting into. Which is good.

We then went over the K39 tape in detail. Robin remarked that he had been wondering—well, he hadn't even known where to begin to wonder—how to rehearse it and have a workout with me, concentrating on being the thirty-nine-year-old and forgetting about the person (K69) listening to the tape. He had been to Bruce Keller's performance of *Krapp* at La Mama, Melbourne, the previous week. "One of the things I found really distressing," Robin said, "was that there was no contrast between the two of them at all." I replied that he must have lost it: the difference was there some weeks before at the first performance, but the director, Jean-Pierre Mignon, probably needed to go and look at it again.

RC: This is where I come back to your remark about the pomposity. It just isn't there, in my performance, nor in his either. It's funny, you know, I've been acting a lot of old people recently, and one of the things that I find about them is that in a way they're much younger than middle-aged people. That's part of their beauty. So, the middle-aged person often has an "I've heard-it-all-before" quality. An older person is desperately near the end of his time, and he's going to bloody pick at stuff, like kids do to survive.

We agreed to forget about the older Krapp for a while, to concentrate on the voice of K39: a richer, fuller, healthier, chest voice. Standing up, I suggested, like a singer, so as to use the diaphragm better. Walking up and down, microphone in hand, as K39 may well have done. We came to "crest of the wave."

RC: Being at the crest of a wave means that not only have you reached it, but it's going to go down.

CD: Right. Absolutely right. There should be a hesitation there. We've got to think what else he could say: "top of the tree," "peak of his powers," or "heights of something or other," indicating no dynamism that's going to continue beyond that point.

RC: In terms of surfing the crest of the wave carries you home to the beach. "Sailing along on the crest of a wave"—it's a very Beckett thought; it's very musical.

CD: True. (*Humming the song.*) But there's the same irony as in *Happy Days.* "Happy days are here again." Like hell they are, for Winnie.

RC: So, the second thought might come on the "Or thereabouts"?

CD: Yes. A dying fall there. We've got to be clear about K39's attitude toward himself, K69's attitude toward himself and toward K39. I reckon we'll get it about 26 November (we were due to record on twenty-seventh).

RC: Yes, right with you. So, what we're saying about K39 today is, OK, he may be headed for the wave going down, he may be uptight, all these things, but it's the degree of consciousness of this uptightness. I feel he's very unaware, indeed, of the degree he's at odds. It's only when he gets into remembering that he gets lost in things, maybe when he's talking about being with the girl in the punt. There is a reason for his "Ah, wells." Then he gets carried away, saying, "Well, you know, I really must be the terrific thirty-nine-year old." Then he's not remotely aware of his pomposity, and this sharpens the alterness of K69 to it, because of the contrast between the two.

CD: If we look at the three stages and try to work out why Beckett opted for those particular occasions, and the details he chooses, it seems to me that the first one, K29, shows intellectual potentiality and aspirations plus weak affectivity, replaced by an emotionally mature K39 who rejects love in the belief that it weakens his intellectual powers. Then K69, the trough of the wave when all the potentialities have disappeared. What's he left with? Fanny. So he's able to look at them both in a detached and ironical way, with a self-knowledge he'd never had before.

From Robin's uneasiness about the way Krapp juxtaposes "intellectually" and "spiritually" we moved into a long discussion of Beckett's attitudes to religion, especially Christianity. Robin needed to know what the structure was behind the facade of the text we were exploring. "He seems to me," he concluded, "to be a person who has decided what he's looking for and then found he couldn't find it, and consequently has been bitterly disappointed. But Krapp, at the end, seems to be saying with some wisdom that you can't decide what you're looking for. I'm still wondering what I'm even thinking about it, I mean . . . "

CD: We can't know what we're looking for until we've found it, because we wouldn't recognize it. As with Godot, even if he came, they wouldn't know him, because they've never seen him.

RC: I can understand that disappointment going very deep, but I think one of the feelings I had on Sunday night [at the performance of *Krapp* at La Mama] was that the disappointment I was being obliged to go through by partaking of that evening was kind of out of date. An indulgence on the part of the performers and the people who put it forward. It's not an indulgence for Beckett, because that's what he's going through, and so it's absolutely legitimate. It's really quite difficult to compromise.

CD: After all, it is something he expressed and got out of his system, what, a quarter of a century ago. So, in that sense, obviously, it's out of date, except that it's something we can always recreate . . .

RC: In my view the whole business of doing a play is this two-way exploration. There are terrible odds. It's difficult to get back into the mind of even Sam Shepard [Robin had just been playing Dodge in *Buried Child,* at the Playbox Theatre]. I don't agree with the production we did, but it's productive; this exploration has had to be made. It comes out with its own life as well as Sam Shepard's.

CD: I think that's true in Beckett's case as well. That is,
        every production is so different; there are still an enor-
        mous number of creative choices to be made. But not
        ones that work against the very clear intentions that he
        had at the time of writing. He had in his head what
        he wants, and this is quite clear, not only from the
        point of view of the words but of the music as well. I
        think it's sheer chance he hasn't actually put the thing
        down on a kind of musical score and told us exactly
        how to say it. He's done that in his own productions,
        of course. He works very musically, in that the voice
        has to be used like a musical instrument.

RC: Well. That's interesting. . . . I find one of the worries is
        this: I believe the play was written as presenting some
        problem that many people could identify with at the
        time of writing. But I just wonder whether there's a
        change happening. You can find yourself sitting in
        front of a play witnessing a person going through
        those things and not necessarily identifying with them
        at all. Like going to see *The Deep Blue Sea*. It can
        cheapen it terribly. I feel it's something we're going to
        have to watch, anyway, if we don't want to end up
        with a whole lot of young people watching a tape of
        some poor old bugger that they pity but don't begin to
        identify with.

CD: It's quite clear that we've all got to come to that point,
        eventually. I suppose most of Beckett's plays are old
        men's plays, about people who've tried everything,
        who've found nothing that really works, and who are
        then thrust back onto themselves because there are
        none of the daily distractions that normally prevent it.
        But it's not going to take till sixty-nine, or even sixty-
        five, for very many people to be in that situation,
        when people are getting thrust out, redundant, and so
        on, at twenty-five, thirty. They're pushed into them-
        selves; they've got nothing to do; they don't know how
        to spend the time. They reminisce, chat in the pub . . .

RC: I can remember feeling at about thirteen and twenty—
        my God, how old I am. Younger people may indeed

identify much more strongly with this than a person our age.

More line rehearsals, intonation, pace, timing. . . . The song: "Now the day is over . . ."

RC: He probably wouldn't be able to sing it in tune, anyway.

CD: No excuses!

RC: Oh, no, I sing opera, I can sing it in tune for you, but he says "quavering." My God, every bloody thing I come across in this play is more difficult than I ever dreamt it was going to be. It's so unrelaxing working on it, somehow—I don't know why.

CD: You could do it all on your own, that's why!

RC: I think it is—yes, that's it.

CD: No help from anybody, nothing to react against, no-body to give you anything. No, it doesn't stay high, just quavering, so don't make it too high. . . . You're beginning to establish a kind of rapport with the tape recorder.

RC: Yes, I felt it so strongly.

CD: That's very good.

RC: I tell you what's happening, actually. I find that I'm working through the reasony stuff into the much more emotional stuff, and all of the reasony stuff is lousy at the moment. The emotional stuff is much easier in a way, much more immediate stuff to do, and it's beau-tifully written. In both cases they are sort of parallel, aren't they? . . . Thank you for making me read that. I was trying to escape a bit; it's so embarrassing work-ing with one other person.

CD: You'll get used to it.

RC: Yes, I shall. We don't know one another from a bar of soap, and it takes a while.

CD: Yes, quite, thrust into it like this.

RC: You're very brave. But please insist on. I mean, I think a lot of directors don't realize how much an ac-tor insists on putting the director in an authoritative situation. I mean, a lot of directors insist on being in an authoritative position and, I think, suffer by it. But I certainly found as a director that no one has to accept this position you're put in by the actor of being Dad a bit and saying, "Now come on, we're going to do this."

CD: Well, my aim will be to see, on the basis of what I gradually get to know about the way you do things, to see how to get around to your doing it the way that I feel is the ideal way, and there'll be compromise all the way along the line between the two. You'll only go the way that you can do it and the way it's natural for you to do it, for your character.

RC: I want to go the way that it is to be done, which involves moving around from my position a lot. I mean, what I have to do is go from my position. Yes. But I wouldn't say that what we have to reach is a compromise—unless you're using *compromise* as a creative term—that, in fact, there is a perfect compromise, you know, in other words . . .

CD: I prefer *collaboration*. Working from within the actor, using his strengths and qualities, not imposing something perhaps alien from the outside through some sort of ego trip. No doubt, there will come a time when there will be certain intonations, certain pauses, a certain force, and so on that I want you to put into particular words. And I shall make those very, very clear. But there will be aspects of that I won't want to impose on you because it won't be right for you. And that's where you have got to make those creative transfers.

RC: But you're not saying, are you, I hope, that you have a very specific idea of what you want and that it is an idea no actor would, in fact, be able to do exactly?

CD: No. I'm mentally creating my ideal performance for this production on the basis of what I've seen you doing four or five times. This is not an idealization of somebody else doing it that I want to impose on you. It's you doing it.

RC: Well, I thought I should ask that question, because I didn't think it was but I thought I'd better ask. That's great, because I think we can get to something. But I am sort of appalled by this part in a way I haven't been with any other part that I have ever done, ever. It augurs well. I had it a bit too easy with Dodge and all the other parts I've done this year. They've been parts that I could see the logic of before I did them, and I could see a rough blocking of characterization for them before I did them and handle it off the cuff and then work at it. But this one [Krapp], there's not one thing in it that I can seize. I find the intellectual side of it extraordinary, trying to work out what my beliefs are and what his beliefs are and what his commentators' beliefs are. Perhaps they will all meet. It's nice to be working on those little bits of him. The tape is so aware of his presence when you're reading the play that you're not aware of how much of it is tape. I mean, what he actually comes out with.

CD: Or alternatively, how much of it is mimed.

RC: Well, yes, this silent presence.

CD: The constant reaction to what's going on there, facial mime. . . .

RC: This intellectual/spiritual thing is something I don't know that can be worked out, because I don't know if the difference between the two matters to Beckett. I think he thinks that the spiritual just doesn't exist. In certain ways I'd say he has retired into vagueness about certain issues. He's just saying that certain things haven't come up to scratch, and so you're only left with a sort of husk.

CD: Something like that would be true.

RC: It seems to me to be an unreasonable, unreasoning statement. It lacks the reason Beckett seems to be talking in terms of.

CD: I think it's evidence of some kind of strangely inhibited and stunted emotional view within him, which has always been there, except with particular people. Very close and intimate friendships with individuals, both

men and women. But they are very strangely the opposite of expansive. Closed in. I think he's got a horror of self-revelation, of being quoted out of context.
It's happened so often to him, you know. He's very
cagey about anybody he doesn't know well. But once
he trusts you he's a tremendous friend, but always on
the defensive. I think the years of nonrecognition took
their toll, when he was full of so much self-doubt, self-
torment. It's not knowing if he was capable of doing
anything worthwhile.

RC: Or if what he was doing mattered.

CD: Yes, exactly. He couldn't be sure if it was a flash in
the pan with *Godot*. He was just beginning to realize,
probably, that he could make something of himself as
a playwright, still without understanding why, or being
sure it would last. Then there was the disappointment
of *Endgame,* of not being able to get it on in French in
Paris; it had its French premiere in London. So, there
was still tremendous doubt about the whole thing.

RC: That's interesting. It seems to me to make *Krapp* much
more of a personal document. It just lines up, doesn't
it? In all sorts of ways. . . .
"The grain, now what I wonder do I mean by that? I
mean . . . I suppose I mean those things worth having
when all the dust has—when all *my* dust has settled. I
close my eyes and try and imagine them."

CD: Try stressing *"grain"* the first time. Second time, a silent "Ha! Got it! I *mean*." Third time, stress *"suppose."* Self-doubting.

RC: I see. I was using *mean* in two different ways.

CD: Yes. It's very ambiguous, that.

RC: Pedantic, really. Really up himself.

CD: But he undercuts it straightaway. All he can do is ap-
proximate. Self-consciously intellectualizing.

RC: "When all my dust has settled." It's a fantastic description of death. ". . . try and imagine them."

CD: I think the implication there is that there aren't any.
Try as he may, he can't find anything that was really
worth having. Try to give it the feeling that you've

tried to imagine them, but you can't. It *should* then go
on to enumerate some of these things that are worth
having, and we've got to underscore the fact that you
don't say what they are because you couldn't find
them.

The transcript of our discussions then develops into what could, I suppose,
constitute a critical commentary on the creation of a performance text,
almost line by line. But for it to make a lot of sense—what with the
importance given over to intonation, pauses, expressions, and so on—one
would need to be watching the videotape at the same time. Perhaps we'll
market the two together one of these days! How's that for modish academic
entrepreneurial initiative? *Ah, well.*

The deadline for this essay precludes comment on the finished production of the Australian premiere of Beckett's *Rough for Theatre I.*[8] After
fifteen hours of rehearsals we have reached the stage of complete blocking,
and fine tuning of musicality, intonation, and physical-vocal contrast between the two characters is under way. A turning point was the acquisition
of the wheelchair last week, a very heavy chromium-plated affair. I dis-
lodged a disc from its rightful position between two vertebrae while lifting
it into my car in the hospital car park. The wheelchair has been most
useful. Beckett would have appreciated the irony. Don't you, Sam?

NOTES

1. Audience surveys, identical to the ones published in *Angels of Darkness*
(North Sydney: Allen and Unwin, 1972, 116–43), were undertaken for the Central
and Maidment Theatre productions and for the San Quentin Drama Workshop
production in Melbourne in 1984. The statistical results have been completed, and
I am finally applying myself to transcribing spectators' comments for (I hope)
publication in the near future. In-depth discussions with Rick Cluchey, Bud Thorpe,
and Larry Held, about the San Quentin production, were published in my essay,
"Beckett's New *Godot*," in *Beckett's Later Fiction and Drama: Texts for Company,* ed.
James Acheson and Kateryna Arthur (London: Macmillan, 1987), 175–92.
2. I hope she didn't mean unusual for me!
3. *The Age* (Melbourne), 27 April 1982.
4. The italics symbolize *my* raised eyebrows.
5. 28 April 1982.
6. *Alienation in Literature: Samuel Beckett* (with Douglas Kirsner) (Geelong,
Australia: Deakin University Press, 1982), 153.

7. *Journal of Beckett Studies* (Winter 1976): 50–65.

8. By the Frozen Rocks Company. Performances scheduled at the Theatre Royal, Castlemaine, as part of the 1992 State Festival, in early November, then at La Mama, Melbourne, 11–15 November. Double bill, with my translation of Jean Tardieu's *The Enquiry Office*.

Waiting for Godot as Political Theater

Ilan Ronen

Samuel Beckett's *Waiting for Godot* shocked the world of theater in 1953 and revolutionized concepts in the theory of drama. Beckett wrote an abstract existential allegory whose protagonists wait for Godot, who will never arrive, waiting that has come to symbolize the search for meaning. Over the years all those who staged the play competed to see who could come up with the most abstract and profound interpretation. And they all set the action in No-time and in No-place.

In the production I directed at the Haifa Municipal Theatre in November 1984 we placed the tramps in the Here and Now. We tried to disassociate the play from the textbook *isms*, in the belief that this would add another dimension to the play's boundless potential. I wanted to make the audience identify emotionally with the characters and become involved with their fate. All the previous Israeli productions of *Waiting for Godot* had provided their audiences with a primarily aesthetic and intellectual experience, with a stress on the play's stylized elements.

The Arabic Stage at the Haifa Municipal Theatre

The idea of staging *Waiting for Godot* with this new approach evolved as a result of a conversation between me, Omry Nitzan, then the artistic director of the Haifa Municipal Theatre, and Noam Semel, the theater's general manager. These two had set up the Arabic stage with the idea of mounting plays in Arabic for Arab audiences in Haifa. The first play performed in this setting was *The Island* by Athol Fugard, featuring two excellent Arab actors—Yussef Abu-Varda, who had played leading roles in the Hebrew theater with great success, and Muhram Khoury, who was famous for the title role he played in the television series "Michael Safrai and His Sons," about a Jewish family in the Syrian city of Aleppo in the 1940s. For this role, as well as for a long list of brilliant performances in the Israeli theater, Khoury was awarded the prestigious Israel Prize. The new acting qualities of these two actors, performing in their mother tongue, were already evident in *The Island,* and the production was greatly acclaimed.

When I met with them they both expressed their desire to act in a play that would enable them to demonstrate their ability to do stylized body work in a realistic setting. Beckett's *Waiting for Godot* seemed to me the most appropriate vehicle for these two actors, who complement each other in their contrasting personality traits. Yussef Abu-Varda, whom I chose to cast as Vladimir, has a fine rhetorical talent, a strong stage presence, and a very expressive, intense political involvement. In contrast, Muhram Khoury, whom I cast as Estragon, is an actor with the rare comic sense of a sad clown. He is very intuitive, human, and warm, moderate in his political stance, very down-to-earth.

I decided in my production to transform Beckett's two tramps into two Palestinian laborers waiting for a Godot to deliver them from their misery. I had no doubt that by portraying Vladimir and Estragon in the Israeli political reality of the period I would only deepen the audience's identification with the characters.

The Political Reality of Israel in 1984

The decision to ascribe a political meaning to *Waiting for Godot* had a special significance against the background of the Israeli scene at that time. Nearly all the construction workers in Israel were Palestinians from the West Bank or Gaza. Each day, in the early morning hours, they left their homes, traveling in convoys to the cities of Israel. There they sat and waited for contractors and foremen to hire them. This created an absurd situation, in which the country, including the Jewish settlements in the occupied territories, was being built almost exclusively by Palestinians under the rule of Israeli occupation.

A few years later, when the Intifada, the popular uprising in the territories, erupted, on more than one occasion all the construction in Israel drew to a halt when the Palestinian workers, under orders by the local leadership, failed to turn up to work. In 1984 the situation of the Palestinians was at its lowest ebb, two years after the Palestinian leadership had suffered a staggering blow in the Lebanese war and was exiled to distant countries such as Libya and Tunisia.

The Israeli occupation of the territories was already in its seventeenth year, and there was no sign of any impending change. The Israeli government showed itself to be helpless as the draw between the right- and left-wing blocs in the Knesset stymied any initiative for change in the political situation. All sides seemed to be waiting for a Godot to arrive and extricate them from the deadlock in which they found themselves. On the economic scene, in which both peoples depended on each other and needed each other, there was also enormous tension in face of the Palestinians' frustration and bitterness under the seemingly endless occupation.

Four years later, when the Intifada began, the local Palestinian leadership seemed to shake off its feeling of impotency and began to lead its people in a popular uprising, with women and children in its forefront. This would later lead to the diplomatic moves and dialogue with the Israeli government, beginning in September 1991.

Within the Israeli society developments have also been gaining momentum in recent years. The leftist movements, led by the "Peace Now" movement, have been making the Israeli public aware of the process of demoralization, the loss of direction and moral values, that arises mainly from the long-drawn-out rule over more than a million and a half Palestinians in the territories. These voices reverberated throughout the Israeli public, culminating in the recent political reversal in June 1992, when the majority of Israelis supported the left-wing parties, led by the Labor party. And now for the first time a serious dialogue for peace is being conducted with the Palestinians.

Eight years earlier, when relations between the Palestinians and Israelis were at their lowest point, in November 1984, the play *Waiting for Godot* was mounted with a local political slant, immediately arousing virulent reactions from the right-wing camp. One of the criticisms leveled against us was that we had marred an important work by a renowned playwright and turned it into a propaganda tool for the Palestine Liberation Organization (PLO) and the leftist camp. A furious public debate ensued. It even reached the Knesset benches, and several right-wing Knesset members demanded that the Haifa Municipal Theatre take the play off the stage. Most of the production's severest critics never even saw it, but only read about it in the press and rushed to vilify it. Those who did see the play and were favorably impressed by it noted that it was not simply a

Fig. 9. Doron Tavory, Ilan Toren, Youssef Abu-Varda, and Muhram Khoury in Ilan Ronen's Hebrew/Arabic bilingual production of *Waiting for Godot* at the Haifa Municipal Theater, 1984. Photo credit: Moral Drepler.

flat, pasteboard piece of political theater but, rather, that the political interpretation underscored Beckett's existential message.

A Bilingual Performance

The man chosen to translate the play was the Arabic author and journalist Anton Shammas, the author of several articles on the identity of the Israeli Arab that had aroused a heated controversy among Israeli writers. The bilingual translation was part of our conception of bringing together the Israeli and the Palestinian on the same stage, confronting each other also through the medium of the two languages, both of which are so emotionally charged and arouse countless associations. We decided that Shammas would translate the scenes between Estragon and Vladimir into Arabic, while the scenes with Pozzo and Lucky would be partially in Hebrew and partially in Arabic. In translating the dialogue between Vladimir and Estragon, the translator tried to create certain disparities between them. Gogo would represent the Arab villager speaking a more common language, while Didi was a city dweller. The difference lay not only in the words but in the way they pronounced them. The third Arabic-speaking character in the play was Lucky—an elderly man, of the old generation, his speech in literary Arabic, in contrast to the younger men, who spoke vernacular Arabic (there are significant differences between spoken and literary Arabic). The fourth character is the messenger, whom Beckett calls simply Boy. We chose to portray him as a young boy from a refugee camp who spoke very simple Arabic.

Pozzo represented the Israeli and naturally spoke Hebrew, except for a few curses and orders to Lucky in Arabic. (Israelis generally do not know Arabic other than some curses or orders, some of which have found their way into Hebrew slang.) Thus, Gogo and Didi speak Hebrew to Pozzo and Arabic to each other.

From the very first reading we already sensed something compelling about the Arabic-Hebrew dialogue between Beckett's characters. The first performances were put on before an audience of Arab students from Haifa, who responded vigorously to every word uttered, as if Beckett had written the play in this version especially for them. When the play was performed before a Hebrew-speaking audience, it was interesting to follow the facial expressions of the spectators and at the end of the play to hear the associations and reactions Beckett's dialogue in Arabic had awakened in them. Israeli audiences generally reacted with a sense of confusion and uneasiness at hearing Arabic and experiencing the feelings that language arouses.

The Stage Setting, Costumes, and Props

Since for Beckett every prop onstage has a special significance, we were very careful in selecting the elements that made up the setting. Instead of the tree under which the two tramps wait, we chose to place an iron scaffolding emerging from a concrete pole, with concrete construction blocks scattered around it. Charlie Leon's stage design looked like a building site. The stage apron was designed like a ship's prow jutting into the audience, thus creating an intimate contact between the actors and the spectators surrounding them.

Vladimir and Estragon wore workmen's clothing. One wore a woolen hat and an old army coat, while the other wore a sweater and a cloth hat with its brim turned up (somewhat reminiscent of Arlecchino). Pozzo was dressed in an elegant beige suit and wore a hat that was a cross between a pith helmet and a "tembel hat" (which for years has symbolized the native-born Israeli, the "sabra"). Pozzo held a whip according to Beckett's stage directions, and we added an attaché case, held for him by Lucky, of course. White-haired Lucky, his body frail and bent over, wore a white cap, the typical headgear of devout Muslims. There was a dog collar around his neck that was connected by a long tape measure to his master's belt. On his back Lucky carried a land surveyor's tripod and rolled-up maps. In the second act the collar around his neck became a metal collar of the kind usually worn by seeing-eye dogs. Pozzo wore dark sunglasses.

The Actors' Work Inspired by the Political Interpretation

Two Jewish actors joined the production. Ilan Toren, a veteran actor, had played Lucky in an earlier version of *Waiting for Godot* produced by the Habima National Theatre. In our production we cast him as Pozzo. His big build and his typically Israeli manner of speech made him eminently suited for the part as we conceived it. At first an Arab actor was slated to play Lucky. Since he was busy doing another play, this didn't work out. I was then approached by Doron Tabori, a Jewish actor considered to be the star of the Haifa Municipal Theatre (who had made his name mainly in plays by the Israeli playwright Yehoshua Sobol, such as *Ghetto* and *A Jewish Soul,* in which he played leading roles). Doron told me he'd like to join the cast of *Waiting for Godot* as Lucky. The challenge confronting him was Lucky's long monologue as well as the need to portray him in a way that would convey a political message of identification with the suffering of the Palestinians. All of the critics praised Tabori's delivery of Lucky's moving speech, which was one of the peak moments of the play. Doron learned Lucky's monologue in literary Arabic so well that even Arab spectators were convinced that they were watching an Arab actor.

All four actors had already worked together on previous occasions, so they had a very creative relationship. The fifth actor was an Arab child from Haifa, who played the Boy. The actors were conscious of the fact that the political interpretation I had chosen for the play presented many obstacles, but they began rehearsals with tremendous enthusiasm. The special texture of Arabic and Jewish actors working together was an added value to the play. Without our having changed one word of Beckett's, the play lent itself beautifully to the political treatment, as if it were intrinsic to it.

Some lines in the play took on a completely new meaning, due to the topical treatment. For example, when he says, "On our hands and knees," Didi-Abu Varda raises his arms and crosses them behind his head as if he were in a police lineup. When Gogo-Khoury asks, "We've lost our rights?" Didi replies, "We got rid of them." When Gogo-Khoury hands Didi the famous carrot he does a stylized pantomime of a waiter carrying a tray loaded with coffee cups (in 1984 most of the waiters in Israel were Arabs), and when Didi-Abu Varda imitates Lucky he ends his mime with a typically Eastern obscene gesture, which adds an amusing sting to the entire sequence. As soon as Pozzo-Toren makes his appearance, he shouts, "So you were waiting for him? . . . Here? On my land?" When Pozzo tries to understand the two miserable fellows (". . . I might just as well have been in his shoes and he in mine. . . . To each one his due"), he sounds like a parlor liberal brandishing with self-satisfaction his smug acceptance of the fate that has made him the stronger one. When he says, "It is true the population has increased," to our ears it sounds as if he is alluding to a very specific "population."

Several of Beckett's stage directions seemed to have been written especially for our interpretation of the play. In the second act Pozzo-the-Israeli is blind, dragged along behind Lucky, and when Lucky falls he brings Pozzo down with him. The suggestion here seems to be that the two people are dependent on each other, for better or for worse. And indeed, later in this scene Gogo and Didi also fail in an attempt to help the other two, until there is a heap of helpless wretched creatures onstage, as Pozzo's cries of "Help!" in Hebrew blend with the cries of the others in Arabic. Pozzo finally succeeds in getting up, with the help of the two construction workers, Didi and Gogo, who support him throughout the scene and help him find his way again.

An additional dimension is added to the characterization of the two. Vladimir becomes the political leader crying out against the wrongs inflicted on Lucky by Pozzo ("Why doesn't he put down his bags? It's a scandal! To treat a man . . . like that"). Here he is the leader of a rebellion pointing an accusing finger at the occupier-ruler. Pozzo reacts with violence, cracking his whip and shouting: "A moment ago you were calling me sir. . . . Now you're asking me questions?" We based our characterizations of the two on the physical pain they suffer. Gogo has aches in his legs, while Didi suffers from pain in his urinary tract. Thus, Didi–Abu Varda makes his most vehement political demonstration after going out to urinate and coming back onstage writhing in pain. He kicks the stool belonging to the Israeli ruler and knocks down the suitcases the submissive Lucky has been holding onto for dear life. But as soon as his pain subsides, he rushes to put everything back in place.

In our production Lucky began his monologue as a low mumble while standing on a concrete block in the center of the stage and obeying Pozzo's commands. Pozzo sits with his back to the audience at the front edge of the stage, with the two construction workers sitting on the ground on either side of him, as they all watch Lucky's performance. But at a certain stage we decided something was wrong, and the low mumble of the ever-submissive Lucky turned into a terrible cry of pain and anger. The image I suggested to the actor was that of a "dormant" volcano that becomes "active" with the words spewing forth like boiling lava, getting all mixed up, and making a tremendous din like rocks tumbling down from the mountain peak.

Didi and Gogo, panic-stricken, try to shut Lucky's mouth with their hats. Pozzo hides under the folding chair. Finally, he throws the chair at Lucky and yells to the other two to remove Lucky's hat. The moment his hat is no longer on his head Lucky falls into a dead faint from exhaustion. In our version Pozzo goes wild, brutally kicking Lucky in the shin and yelling in Arabic, "Get up, you pig!" while Gogo, the Arab construction worker, begs him to leave his fellow Arab alone, whimpering in Hebrew, "You'll kill him." This was one of the main scenes that aroused the ire of some right-wing circles, who were unprepared to accept the fact that Beckett had written the scene just that way.

The Acting Style

The acting was very physical while remaining realistic, somewhat like a TV documentary filmed in the territories. We were careful not to overdo the actors' movements by making them too stylized, but we did give the characters physical attributes. Khoury based his portrayal of Gogo on the classical character of Arlecchino—very earthy and full of mischief. Much of the time he sits cross-legged, Bedouin-fashion, like Arab construction workers sitting on the pavement. Didi, on the other hand, stands upright, frequently stretching his body upward with brusqe, nervous movements. He often grimaces and crosses his legs, due to the pains in his urinary tract. Every time he laughs an attack of pain makes him double over. We laid a particular stress on body movements because we knew Israeli audiences would not understand every word in Arabic, and the actors' movements were often an illustration of the spoken text. Both of these characters expressed their feelings through body language, embracing each other every time they met, holding their noses because of Didi's bad breath or Gogo's smelly feet, exchanging blows to console each other. One of the most moving scenes was one in which Gogo-Khoury lay sleeping in the arms of Didi–Abu Varda, who was lamenting the length of time that elapses between birth and death. In the scene in which Godot's messenger, the Boy-refugee, appears, Didi embraces Gogo with his right hand and with his left makes a *V* for victory sign, saying to the boy, "Tell him [Godot] you saw us." This is one of the few moments in which we gave political emphasis to the action of the characters. And here, too, we had quite a few arguments before we finally came to a decision.

Underscoring the Comic Elements

"This may be the only time I have ever seen a production of *Waiting for Godot* that really exploits the play's vast comic potential," were the words of the critic Boaz Evron (*Yedioth Aharonot,* 16 January 1985).

In all previous productions of this play in Israel, in my view, there was a tendency to stage *Godot* with too much seriousness and gravity. I think Beckett wrote a comic allegory, with many painful and heartrending moments, within a very funny theatrical framework.

I mentioned before that in our characterizations we were inspired by the commedia dell'arte. Silent films, expecially those with Charlie Chaplin and Laurel and Hardy, were another influence. In all the difficult moments, when the two Arab workers try to commit suicide, we stressed the comic elements Beckett chose to insert at these very moments. At first they weigh each to see which one is heavier and might break the bough of the tree (which in our stage design is a scaffold) when he hangs himself, leaving the other without a bough on which to commit suicide. They exchange places in front of the scaffold, each one evading the opportunity to be the first to take his own life. Their movements here are reminiscent of the Marx Brothers' slapstick. At the end of one of the saddest moments in the play Gogo removes the rope holding up his pants, places it around his neck, and tries to tie the other end to the scaffold, while the audience is convulsed by laughter as his pants fall down and he stands there in his underwear. At the beginning of the second act there is a blatantly comic scene, when they try on the boots. We tried to wrest the greatest comic effect from this scene. Each time, the confused Gogo extends the wrong foot to Didi, who is trying to get the boot on his foot. Didi showers blows on Gogo until he realizes his error and quickly lifts his right foot, but by accident it hits Didi in the groin. Writhing in pain, he hits Gogo again, and the whole sequence of blows is repeated. The blind Pozzo's repeated attempts to get up only to fall again also aroused peals of laughter from the audience, as the two Arab workers gave him their hands to try to pull him up, resulting in a human chain that keeps coming apart, reminding the spectators of images from their childhood.

In the juggling exchange of hats that occurs after Pozzo's first exit, Didi and Gogo amuse themselves with Lucky's hat and their own two hats, moving them from one head to another as if playing a game of basketball. They also imitate with nearly caricaturist exaggeration the original owner of the hat they happen to be wearing at the moment.

These are only a few examples of comic moments that blended fantastically with the emotional and political experience we attempted to transmit to our audience.

Summary

An inherent value of a great work is that it adapts itself to contemporary reality without losing an iota of its power. Our interpretation of *Godot* was beset with many obstacles. In their attempt to overcome these hurdles the creators had many arguments among themselves. We tried to avoid tampering with Beckett's text by imposing our conception on it. In our production we only omitted those parts of the text that relate directly to the Christian tradition. These did not fit our interpretation and were also too far removed from the world of the Israeli spectator.

We were delighted that the audiences and the critics did not view the production as merely a one-dimensional political allegory but, instead, recognized that it added a new facet to the play's universal existential statement.

The review of the play in the *HaAretz* newspaper stated:

Due to the metaphoric nature of *Waiting for Godot,* it can be produced in various ways without changing its structure or action. When the characters are placed in the Here and Now they become more real. It also adds a dimension of truth to their suffering and an additional dimension to the play . . . the play is a relevant political statement thanks mainly to the actors' superb performances in Hebrew and Arabic. The ring of the Arabic language spoken by the actors takes on a special political hue, and the actors' presence on the stage expresses a great deal of the painful significance of the play due to their powerful acting, which is pure "Beckett," over and above the political significance. (M. Handelsaltz, *HaAretz,* 12 December 1984)

I have no doubt that were it not for the actors' amazing identification with the characters in the present conception and their superb level of acting, the play would not have been such a success. Thanks to them, the idea became an unmediated tangible experience for audiences in Israel.

Emptying the Theater: On Directing the Plays of Samuel Beckett

Gerry McCarthy

Beckett has variously deplored the excesses of modern direction, worked supportively with certain directors of his plays, and implied a personal understanding of directing that would ensure failure. In a 1956 letter to Alan Schneider he explains how, with a London production of *Waiting for Godot* being mooted, he told the producers, "If they did it my way, they would empty the theatre."[1] Any strain between directors and Beckett is the result of a feeling that they must "do it his way." Even in the early days, and with the sympathetic Schneider, the correspondence shows the dramatist dissenting: "I don't in my ignorance agree with the round and feel that 'Godot' needs a very closed box. . . ."[2]

Of what did Beckett feel he was ignorant, and, therefore, what might the director alone know? The evidence is that he was, in fact, unwilling to give ground and that he was confident in the primacy of the writer's knowledge. Beckett preferred *Endgame* to *Waiting for Godot* because of the greater exigency of the physical disposition of the piece, and the tightening of the playwright's requirements has continued ever since. Beckett's writing now appears to squeeze "directing" (as mise-en-scène) out of the system, while the actor turns ever more to the director to solve a series of daunting practical problems. The question is no longer what does the director want of the actor but, rather, given the demands of the text, what does the playwright require? More important still is the actor's question: How is this work to be performed? Rarely now is the director an experienced actor, and still more rarely, as with a Roger Blin, are they one and the same person. Directors come up with a set of demands, based on personal conceptions and insights, which actors satisfy. It is certainly the case in the British theater that many actors believe that directors have neither interest nor competence in the means whereby the actor delivers the goods.[3]

Beckett implicitly refuses the director's "vision," or interpretation, of the play and reveals its essential naïveté. I would describe the difficulty (for the present) as a pictorialism, in which the "image" the director creates is best likened to the subjects of figurative art. Linked to this is the conception of the directorial statement. Such a statement is posited on the superior knowledge of the director as expert reader of the play, capable of relocating it within cultural and historical fields that are unknown to those who lack knowledge. The impulse toward a cultural relocation of the play is strengthened by the director's experience in the organization of the physical and human resources of the playhouse—in particular, stage management—and by the considerable dependence of contemporary direction on the talents of the scene designer. Thus, the director of Shakespeare imposes his or her authority by imagining a new location that will stress modern relevance. The consequence is that the audience becomes increasingly aware of what the director knows about the play, since this is clear in the theatrical presentation but rather less of its value in performance. In none of this does the actor figure.

The field and style of knowledge of the contemporary director is now a crucial question. His interpretative function is seen as paramount, and productions are seen as the work of almost an independent *auteur*. The director makes something of the play, and it is expected that he should innovate. This explains the predilection of directors for the classical repertoire: works that have strong dramatic value but whose relationship to theatrical presentation is weakened with the passage of time and the passing of the medium for which they were originally created. Beckett is less accommodating, sharing with the director a common knowledge of the contemporary dramatic medium and expressing a requirement that is, to a theater professional, unambiguous, although occasionally strange.

It is tempting to ascribe some of the tensions between writing and direction to the influence of the modern university. The contemporary director inhabits a world of interpretation, that is to say, private knowledge. From journalistic criticism, in itself highly influential, to scholarly monographs, writers explain the represented world of the play: what is to be imitated by the players. I would argue that this interpretation is the product of badly digested Aristotle and, in particular, the notion of mimesis. The styles of representation that follow this approach are predominantly theatrical rather than dramatic and are grounded in what I would term a mimetic fallacy.

The ancient idea of imitation is to do with the relationship of forms, not the exactness of reproduction. Simply stated, the imitative value of drama is not a question of the appearances of life but, rather, the experience of life.[4] It is in the nature of the medium to reveal what it is like to live. When Aristotle refers to the process of mimesis he describes a response to the performance that is grounded in the recognition of the forms of life within the forms of drama. Drama is the imitation of action in the medium of rhythm, language, and melody, and the manner of imitation is by acting (rather than narration). The actor's art requires a knowledge of language and its relationship to thought. I understand the argument to be that thought is manifest in and controls language and that it is the actor's job to integrate the two.

> Knowledge of this concerns the performer's art, and those trained in the scientific side of style [Does Aristotle mean what we would call linguistics?]: for instance, the distinction between command and entreaty, exposition and threat, question and answer and so forth.[5]

This is a slender but useful discussion of the actor's "manner" of using the "medium" of rhythm, language, and melody. I think we would see the whole process integrated into "action."

The performer who "knows how" the play is performable employs the medium of action, and the director who "knows that" the play is "like" a certain world is trapped in a form of narration.[6] The director discounts the mere playing in which understandings remain unstated in favor of a theatricalization of events: images that show (reify) particular concepts or "objects" the director knows that the play can be deemed to represent. Beckett, however, addresses the actor directly and inhibits the gratuitous theatricalization of the play-text. His compositions are conceived for performance on a stage of his devising, not to be staged in a scene of the director's imagining. My contention will be that this revitalizes the director by a process of induction into the true nature of the medium in which he or she works. Beckett communicates "knowledge how" rather than "knowledge that," and he does so through his absolute and genial insistence on the experience of dramatic play acutely defined within its theatrical parameters.

Beckett's directness derives from the absolute consistency of his drama with his use of the dramatic medium. His philosophical position is well-known and casts doubt on everything except the need to articulate the experience of life. The famous *Three Dialogues* deliver the most powerful statement of the Beckettian aesthetic, applied here, *mutatis mutandis,* to the discussion of painting.

> B. [SAMUEL BECKETT]. . . . what we have to consider in the case of Italian painters is not that they surveyed the world with the eyes of building contractors, a mere means like any other, but that they never stirred from the field of the possible, however much they may have enlarged it. The only thing disturbed by the revolutionaries Matisse and Tal Coat is a certain order on the plane of the feasible.
>
> D. [GEORGES DUTHUIT] What other plane can there be for the maker?
>
> B. Logically none. Yet I speak of an art turning from it in disgust, weary of its puny exploits, weary of pretending to be able, of being able, of doing a little better the same old thing, of going a little further along a dreary road.
>
> D. And preferring what?
>
> B. The expression that there is nothing to express, nothing with which to express, nothing from which to express, no power to express, no desire to express, together with the obligation to express.
>
> D. But that is a violently personal and extreme point of view. . . .[7]

On the logical plane art sets out to render objects within the surveyable landscape, but on the personal plane such defined tasks do not interest Beckett nor, he suspects, the painters he admires. The *Three Dialogues* are an important statement of the function of art in giving expression to indeterminate conditions of life, in which the "object" is somehow absent and unseizable.

The relevance of this to prevailing styles in direction is not hard to find. The very presence of the director in the modern production ensemble relies heavily on the acceptance of an art object that it is the director's prerogative to "know" and even, in extreme cases, to determine. If there

is no determinate "object" but only the need to express, then the director
cannot know where he or she is going, for the play does not, to take the
misinterpretaion of Aristotle, "imitate" a given reality. It does, however,
teach "how" to adopt particular physical forms.

The history of Beckett production is marked by occasional crises, even
scandals, in which Beckett, or his publisher acting for him, has objected
to the way in which his plays have been mishandled by directors. There
are also those occasions in which texts, particularly prose texts, are adapted
for the stage. Beckett has usually given his consent for this to happen,
and, of course, the consequences are less scandalous and may even be
felicitous, since one is dealing not with a play but with an obvious theatrical
presentation of writings that were conceived in another medium. The
problems that arise are easily stated, since they come from the endemic
directorial obsession with location and interpretation. When *Endgame* is
"placed" inside a skull with the windows for eyes, or on a subway or
wherever, the theatrical forms are accordingly altered to insist on a personal
vision being translated to the stage. This is the clearest example of the
power of a misplaced mimesis or possibly what Beckett would style looking
at the world like a building contractor. Beckett's "violently personal view"
of his indeterminate art confronts an equally violently personal insistence
that certain determined objects of the director's contemplation will be
represented on the stage.

Even when actor and director collaborate on a technical level one sees
the temptation to collude in perpetuating the interpretative fiction that
explains the impact but not the performance of a role. So it is that actors
ask directors "Who is this character?" and can expect a detailed reply,
above all where the influence of Stanislavski has been transmitted by his
U.S. followers. The question derives from the mimetic fallacy—that the
character can be seen as a part of a determinate object, putatively knowable
and open to discursive examination. In every play the character is an
illusion: the result of a process of mind whereby the role is received and
understood by the spectator. The character is also an illusion to the player,
who experiences a conscious rhythm of thought and behavior that alters
the perception of the world, without unfixing the player's identity. The
role is never the description of a person. It is a determination of a performance that mobilizes in the actor a certain range of experience and
that delivers an impression of personality, not described but presently
manifest in behavior.

In all of Beckett, and increasingly clearly in the later plays, the actor lacks stable indicators of character, of mood, of emotional register, and information from which these may be inferred. Not only is it impossible to detach from the plays an account of the personality types of the characters, but they have an ill-determined history against which any life experience may be hypothesized. Neither mood nor affect can be predetermined for the performance. The actor asks: Who is the character? What has happened before? How does he or she feel?—and there is no answer.[8] Sadly for the performer it is affect that is taken to confirm the life of the performance as well as assumed to indicate its quality. Actors search for indicators of depth and expression in the delivery of the text as the guarantee of psychological truth. Beckett's text disappoints such an expectation.

The text with its explicit requirements and restrictions demands a revolution in thinking and playing. The blocking of habitual methods can be extremely painful, as the example of Hildegard Schmahl rehearsing *Footfalls* with Beckett reveals.[9] Working with younger actors has brought me the notable benefit of a greater curiosity about the process and also a more immediate physical response from younger reflexes. Nevertheless, in the current theatrical culture, in which the life of characters governs much expression, Beckett's text appears problematic, particularly in the late plays, seeming to demand an inexpressive performance, a soulless automaton for an actor, and characters understandable as almost extinct and scarcely human creations, arousing little interest or sympathy.

When viewed from the rehearsal room, however, the "life" of the character is of no *direct* use in preparing the performance. The actual forms of life experience do not afford a global picture, still less an analysis, of one's persona. For these to be hypothetically available to the actor implies a clinically determinate account of an individual. This is to be used, *somehow*, to create an illusion of personality arising from human life being lived before us with all its mystery, complexity, and existential bafflement. If one starts with the completed account, understood, of the character, one presumes an acting performance that gives a report *on another*. I fear that this is what gives acting a familiar past-tense quality, which in turn needs to be animated by recourse to the spurious life of generalized emotions, generalized since there is nothing truly personal and spontaneous from which emotion may arise.

The difficulties of characterization in Beckett point both actor and director toward a performance played in real time, rather than the indication of a story arising in imaginative impressions. Crucially, the director must aid the actor in the discovery of the physical forms of acting. Beckett's texts create quite unusual demands in terms of the delivery of the text and the management of the emotional flow in the actor. Rather like Stravinsky's evolving preference for the astringency of winds and his movement away from the emotional quality of the string-based orchestra, Beckett looks for a lapidary, exact use of speech in the actor. Lucky's speech in *Waiting for Godot* is a prime example of the problem of delivery in rapid tempo, of a complex flow of interrupted and obscure propositions. This is triggered by the instruction "Think, pig!" (not feel), and yet the forms of coherent thought are not easily discernible. It is the first and clearest example of the creative impossibilities with which Beckett torments his actors. Since there is no completion possible to the task, there is only the effort of thought, and only the dismembered forms of thought are available to the actor as he or she strains toward the impossible objective of completing a necessary task. It is, after all, built into the role that the thinking goes on against the increasing resistance of the other actors onstage, and in an increasingly manic and disordered fashion.

In *Endgame* another characteristic problem makes its appearance in the Beckett oeuvre, with the instruction to the actor playing Clov to speak the pivotal speeches at the opening and close of the play ("Over ... etc." "They said to me ...") with "fixed gaze, tonelessly." This is felt by the performer initially as a sort of amputation, as the most expressive instrument becomes somehow "merely" functional. The actor inevitably raises the questions What does this mean? How is it possible to lose all emotion? and, particularly, Is there not a danger of the style becoming dangerously affected? The difficulty is compounded by the sensitive actor insisting on the poignancy of the precise moments in which he must apparently resist an emotional reading of the lines. At the same time the actor playing Hamm comments on his exaggeration of affect in the burlesque passages of his role. (The spontaneous emotion of the actor is subverted by the amplification created in Hamm's declamation and obvious theatricality.) What is Beckett doing with this area of intimate acting experience, in which vocal quality is the way the actor experiences the emotional truth of the performance? This rejoins similar problems in *Play*, in which the requirement for "toneless" delivery and rapid tempo throughout heap together the difficulties of the roles of Lucky and Clov.

For the director to approach and understand these problems requires an alliance with, rather than a dominance over, the actor, as they unite in as near to common knowledge of a problem as is possible. What this strange delivery conveys can hardly be determined before it is experienced.

The director must then address directly the significance of the delivery of the word: as the physical forms of speech are developed, they complete the integration of the intentional mind and the energetic body pursuing objectives in the world. The physical life of the speech as part of expressive action is the key to Beckett's particular *via negativa*. In different ways all the plays require the actor to "constrain" the verbal performance within limits that are unfamiliar and that reflect the physical and spatial restrictions on performance that are so evident in Beckett. Pitch and speed are subjected to unfamiliar and unwanted choice and control. Where previously the actor "thought" about emotional states, and the voice and delivery of the text inflected as a function of that state (or at least of the actor's reflections upon that state), he must now control what was instinctive and initially resist the wash of feeling that originates in the imagination and then invades voice and expression.

Without intonation speech loses affective power, but it does not lose its basic structure. The restriction of vocal color reveals how prevalent it is in the usual preparation of a role, to the neglect of linguistic structure and the associated physical forms of action. The intuitive pursuit of character and emotion is commonly based on rather hasty constructions of what the action of the play is at any particular point, but that basis is undeclared. The consequence is that the crucial aspect of drama, the scheme of actions, is arrived at instinctively, as part of a right *feeling* of the dramatic moment, rather than a right *doing*. Beckett's insistence on the articulation of drama through the primacy of action throws one back to a peculiarly intense search for the structure of speech. This begins with detailed linguistic analysis. In Lucky's speech the fragments must be isolated and the arrangement of the "argument" roughly perceived, for it is never specifically articulated. Similarly, the text in *Play*, although punctuated, *must* be broken down into semantic units and groups. If these units and groups are not clear, then the rhythm will not emerge, and the text cannot be *learned* except with agonizing difficulty. There are a variety of different notations used by Beckett for his text, some of which, like *That Time*, leave the actor to make fundamental decisions about structure, and most of which alert performers to the problem of physical form. Basic exercises on the stress pattern of the text (whispered text, interrogation and substitution exercises) made it clear that Beckett's style offers a much greater authenticity to an actor prepared to undertake the arduous problem of working out the actual stress patterns that ground the text in bodily experience.

Fundamentally, Beckett allows the actor to organize an energy flow, rather than a flow of emotions. Since the first is active and the second reactive, this places him much more securely within the performative act. Whatever the "meaning" or the "feeling," *he can do it*. If the actor and director can preserve their creative alliance in the pursuit of the textual rhythm, then the Beckett play suddenly becomes extraordinarily negotiable. The two can determine with some degree of exactitude what the form of the text must be. Since neither is haunted by the ghosts of "characters" speaking in "their" voices, the director encounters the text in the actor's physicalization, initially body to body, then as the sense of integration that is the "knowledge" of drama. The actor may be threatened by the physical forms and sheer athleticism of the task; he or she may need reassurance and shrewd, capable support. But this encounter, shaped as it is by the physical forms of text-generated acting, creates a shared experience in which *both* "know how": how it is and how it will be as it evolves. As the actor tries to work out textual structure, he becomes aware of the resonance of his action in the director and so builds the organic link that allows an external agent the access to an internally generated performance. The actor "knows how," and the director "knows how the actor knows." He also "knows how" the actor gets lost and stops, marooned in his ignorance. This can produce the malaise when the actor "just says the text" and experiences the formlessness of the result. Without the director there is nothing upon which to print the defective form of the acting. It feels wrong, but why? Under these circumstances the mismatch between actor and director carries the clue to the revised, and rectified, performance. As the actor runs the text, the director is shaped by its physical structures and rhythm. This naturally generates a sense of wholeness and a progression in time. At the point of acting breakdown, not only does the director *directly* know the confusion of the actor but also, given the overall sense generated, he is in the better position to convey the shadow experience of the integrated performance that he apprehends at the point of breakdown.

What I describe here will, I hope, be recognized as the process of empathy. When Francis Fergusson describes the "histrionic sensibility" he identifies the way in which "we do actually in some sense perceive the shifting life of the psyche directly, before all predication."[10] The audience "knows how" the actor thinks, *directly*, not by a process of extrapolation nor by some sympathetic process of deduction but, instead, as direct knowledge. Fergusson describes, with an unusual and brilliant under-standing of Aristotle's meaning, what drama is, as communication and as

art. The integrated act is known by the spectator by the operation of
isomorphism between human bodies: the sharing of physical rhythm. For
the director the result is a new agenda and a new approach to rehearsal. He
must realize practically what rehearsal is teaching him: that the playing of
drama begins with physical forms integrating mind and body in the actor
and that this playing is directly apprehended through the physical receptiv-
ity of an audience. This empathic bond is the condition both for successful
work with the actor and for any realization of the director's conventional
task: the mediation of the play to the audience. This requires the director
to conceive the play as action whose result is predictable but never
determinate.

The actor's work on text and physical form yields an inbuilt gestalt—
a rhythm, a way of playing—and out of the rhythm a doing, an action.
At this point the text begins to generate a context, in a sort of figure-
ground relationship. As the director becomes directly aware of the essential
actions, he is in a position to "ghost" the performance in rehearsal, with
some confidence that his observations are based on sound knowledge of
how the action is actually being played (rather than virtually received).
As the actions of the play generate their own context, so the realization
of the inherent dramatic structure in the role declares itself. This exists
very much in the "tacit dimension" Michael Polanyi has described, in
which the actor or agent is aware of the matrix of physical features that
constitute an act but, in Polanyi's phraseology, "attends to" an objective.[11]
Faced with critical inquiry, the actor cannot "tell" his knowledge nor
explain his meaning, but both inhere in the performance. The *practice* of
making dramatic performances can be interrogated in this way but not
the tacit meanings that lie in the structures of human action. These can
be interrogated only in dramatic terms, and, indeed, this has its place
within the Beckett play. The question of understanding can be pursued
only within the organic conditions of the performance itself; otherwise, we
ask the actor to speculate. One of the key dramatic structures in Beckett
is the futile inquiry about the likelihood of meaning:

HAMM: Clov!
CLOV: (*Impatiently.*) What is it?
HAMM: We're not beginning to ... to ... mean something?
CLOV: Mean something! You and I, mean something!
           (*Brief laugh.*) Ah, that's a good one![12]

The indeterminacy of drama requires confidence in the actor that performance will ultimately integrate mind and body and that there will emerge a certain "sense of significance" inhering in the performance. The director must understand that this significance cannot be imposed (at which point it becomes an indication), nor can it be sought out by any other means than acting. Beckett's plays ask the actor to perform first and seek significance second, as a dancer or musician would approach a choreography or a score. Once this happens the actor experiences levels of performance structure that are simply lost in the elliptical methods more commonly used. Playing determined actions, he encounters a detailed environment that is the performance context of his "doings." This constitutes the familiar array of restrictions that surounds the Beckett character: dismembered, aphasic, physically restrained, plunged into darkness, and so on. There are not visual representations of characters but, rather, actual restrictions placed on the actor. Beckett uses the forms of life and thought as they can be composed with the actor's body and mental experience. No "imitation" here of a Clov who is lame. The actor must restrict his movement and then execute the moves allotted. The etiology of Clov's orthopedic condition is neither here nor there nor, again, is the precise condition of Hamm's sight. To an actor immobilized in a chair, which is wheeled laboriously through the stage space, and playing behind black [sic] glasses, the question does not arise. He plays with eyes shut and asserts that Clov will one day be blind "like me." The question that is asked, amazingly, "Is Hamm *really* blind?" belongs to some other medium. For the actor to play the entire performance never using his sight, but visualizing through his narratives and through his interrogation of Clov, brings a sighted actor as near to a representation of blindness as we can expect. The question of sight or blindness is never examined in dramatic terms. It is, therefore, not a valid question. Beckett gives the actors problems of performance, not of interpretation.

The richness of these two roles is directly related to the resistances built into the environment. Clov must come and go; Hamm is surrounded by "infinite emptiness." In *Play, Happy Days, Rockaby, Footfalls,* and *A Piece of Monologue* the actor is constrained by the theatrical exigencies of space, lighting, set, and costume. In *Ohio Impromptu* the performance is subject to constraint even in its progression, being governed by the listener's knocking, which stops the reading. There is much in the acting that can be seen to impel the actor toward the limits on performance, making the resulting tensions less a matter of creative imagination than of real time and space negotiated onstage.

Critical, in my view, are *Play* and *Not I,* in which the composition involves a narrative that is delivered under constant pressure, both of time and, brilliantly conceived, of reception. In either instance there is a formulation of the actual pressure that every actor feels, in which ultimately every aspect of the performance is subject to acceptance by the audience. Both plays introduce via the actor the criticism of the narrative as it is being delivered. This reflects equally the tentative nature of the rehearsal as it is carried forward into performance. The spotlight that actually provokes and cuts the narrative in *Play* has the physical effect of disrupting or disappointing the player. This contrasts with the conventional idea of drama, in which the unrestrained expression of personal feeling and experience is thought to be dramatic when it is, in fact, lyrical. Here the account is scarcely begun, but the performance is interrupted, either by the spot leaving the face, in *Play,* or by the "inner voice" arresting the flow, in *Not I:* "coming up to sixty when . . . seventy? . . . good God! . . . coming up to seventy. . . ."[13] This leads to a structure of action, resistance, and reaction within the performer, whereby he experiences the space and time of the theater as charged with significance. It is axiomatic now that this is directly felt by the audience by the operation of empathy, and this invests the time and space of performance with its fundamental capacity to act as a medium of symbolic performance.

Again let me remark that no possible idea can intervene to suggest that the actor imitates. Whichever Beckett role one considers, an examination of the physical, temporal, and mental constraints reveals ways in which the actor encounters and experiences his actions played out in the medium of the lived environment of raw space and time. The austerity of the procedure produces an absolute truth of experience. This is the feeling of life, augmented and pinned down so acutely as to assume that value of a determined artistic symbol. If "meaning" is thought unclear because we imitate no given observation or particular occasion taken from mundane life, this is of no importance. Such meanings establish superficial resemblances that leave the existential fundamentals as obscure as ever. In this respect Pinter is quite right when he asks whether the character that can deliver a lucid account of a life is not surely a frightening and inhuman construct, being endowed by the writer with the capacity to explain the meanings and conditions of the individual existence, which no human possesses.[14] The actual condition of life is to search for meaning; plays in which meanings are easily explained and demonstrated, above all by directors, ought to alarm us. Viewed from this standpoint, interpretations that emerge clearly from a theater production are the desiccated remains of ideas about life and a betrayal of the play as a symbolic act in which we can all recognize its nature and the forms of living.

Within the overall scheme of the play this system of action and reaction generates a feedback in the actor that characterizes the action in a truly expressive manner. The forward movement of the action is felt as a sort of intentional vector, despite the famously abortive nature of the Beckett action. The actor senses the vital need to advance against the welter of resistance and the sense of inadequacy that is the condition of every action, and here one encounters the real beauty of Beckett's drama and the human depth of his aesthetic. "The expression that there is nothing to express . . ." becomes a reality. Yet in this Beckett adheres to the fundamental nature of drama: every actor knows that the basic datum of acting is the action played with intention and objective, despite the knowledge that it is without direct consequence. Beckett apprehends the essentially indeterminate nature of the art of the actor and seizes on it as the medium that is perhaps truest to his aesthetic and to his sentiment of life. The evidence of the oeuvre is that Beckett progressively retreats from action played as an efficient cause to action played, as purely as possible, without determined consequence: "what? . . . not that? . . . nothing to do with that? . . . all right . . . nothing she could tell? . . . try something else. . . ."[15] *Not I* shows action being maintained under circumstances in which it can never be completed. The play articulates a system of failure in which the actress goes on trying, according to Beckett's text, not knowing what to try.

The problematic role structure in *Not I* is paralleled elsewhere in Beckett. Repetition, in particular, is a well-known characteristic of his writing. It is also risky for the performer. What good is it to have analyzed and rehearsed a text if you lose your way in certain formulations and word groups? Recall is hazardous, since the plays are written partly in terms of "routines" that do not place themselves easily in a time sequence. Frequently, as in *Not I,* the text is delivered by a single actor, and so the collaborative mnemonic effect is lost. A narrative mode can help the performer by establishing a sequence that has variety and interest—for example, Nagg's joke or Hamm's story—but Beckett's narratives become progressively emptied of striking detail and more abstract. The narrative of *Not I* is notable, in its own terms, for little:

nothing of any note till coming up to sixty . . .[16]

a few steps then stop . . . stare into space . . . then on . . . a few more . . . stop and stare again . . . so on . . . drifting around . . . day after day . . . or that time she cried . . . the one time she could remember . . . since she was a baby . . . must have cried as a baby . . . perhaps not . . . not essential to life. . . .[17]

Professionalism demands that the text be learned and easily recovered. In fact, Beckett skirts the precipice of disaster uncomfortably close. Billie Whitelaw has announced that she will not perform *Not I* again, such is the strain of performance. In my work at Birmingham, given the house tradition that there is never a prompt, the problem of recall becomes ever more urgent. Beckett runs the actor close to the point of breakdown, instinctively, I think, so that the conditions in which the performance is experienced are absolutely acute. The need to build a secure performance reveals the problem as part of the play. We all know the deadening effect of the memorized text churned out in the routine production. Such a thing is almost impossible in Beckett, for the reliance on anything but a securely prepared and lived performance courts disaster. Text that has been prepared privately, working from the book and ahead of rehearsal, remains essentially that, a recollection of the pages. Many actors will confess to being able to identify paragraphs in their mind's eye as they inhabit the world of the play.

The sharing of attention with the invisible book is impossible in Beckett, for he governs the attention with extreme care: "All part of the same . . . keep an eye on that too . . . corner of the eye. . . ."[18] The mind simply cannot preserve confidently the memory of a reading to which it will return. (This is one reason why I find it next to impossible to contemplate a performance of *Not I* that uses a prompt as anything other than the ultimate safety net. The account of Jessica Tandy's understudy using a teleprompt is as appalling as the idea of anyone understudying this particular role.) The negotiation of memory in performance is a crucial instance of the human experience of time. Any performance that sits comfortably in the present—effectively "remembering" or "recalling" past decisions, readings, and moves—becomes little more than a reflection of something that, to take Edward de Bono's phrase, has "not unhappened" but happened before.[19] This is a reason for the emotionalism of such performance. It is essentially lyrical: emotion recollected in something like tranquility, to borrow from Wordsworth, or at least in security. Beckett's performance structures are clearly organized to disturb that tranquility, and the dangers that one sets out to overcome transmute themselves when

seen from another angle. Beckett drives the actor into the position in which
memory experience is properly located in narrative, while action inhabits
an uneasy present full of the characteristic adjustments and interrogations
that keep the mind constantly refocusing:

> just as the odd time . . . in her life . . . when clearly intended to be hav-
> ing pleasure . . . she was in fact . . . having none . . . not the slightest . . .
> in which case of course . . . that notion of punishment [. . .] which had
> first occurred to her . . . brought up as she had been to believe . . . with
> the other waifs . . . in a merciful . . . (*Brief laugh.*) . . . God . . . (*Good
> laugh.*) . . . first occurred to her . . . then dismissed . . . as foolish . . . was
> perhaps not so foolish . . . after all. . . .[20]

Beckett's disruptions ensure that the actor's attention is constantly
dislocated and refocuses in the present, in the way that any dramatic
writing must primarily engage the actor in negotiating the passage of
events in real time. The predominant mode of drama is consequently
dialogue, in which the crux of action and interaction produces a series of
jolts to the actor's attention and engages the prepared action as part of
the dynamic process of dramatic play. The automatic recall of lines permits
the progressive buildup of attention on present change and future objectives. In the extreme case of *Not I* the structure of cue and action is denied
the actor. She must instead cue her own actions by the incorporation of
an internal interrogation of the story she tells and an acceptance of inbuilt
critical moments in which she "relays" an objection:

> something she had to— . . . what? . . . who? . . . no! . . . she! . . . (*Pause
> and movement* 3.) . . . something she had to— . . . what? . . . the buzz-
> ing? . . . yes . . . all the time the buzzing. . . .[21]

So, the memorizing of this text involves the identification of different levels
of action unsustained by the participation of a second actor (auditor is
silent). Rehearsal of these difficulties reveals how the inbuilt blocks return
the attention repeatedly into the vital, dangerous area of the present. The
actor experiences the physical interruption "something she had to— . . ."
as a bodily sensation in which the energy flow is suddenly bound, for this
is what she has trained her muscles to do. She does not decide to insert
this block: it arises as part of a physical flow and is also tacitly known to
be part of the symbolic action of the play. The question, which is advanced

by critics, of the external resistance being "part of the fiction" seems to me irrelevant, or at least insufficiently specific to the processes of performance to admit of a sensible answer. The actor is called on to go through a process of confabulation with the apparent object of telling "how it was." The rehearsed blocks and the outside inquiry they represent is not "invented" by the actor, nor does she imitate a person who is interrupted. She is interrupted. She responds, and another block interrupts her response.

This process is comparable to the effects in *Play* in which narrative is subject to a combined internal rhythmic interruption and the cuing of the outside light. The combination is particularly difficult and imposes a horrific responsibility on the operator of the traveling spot, which provokes the continuation of the three narratives. If there is any serious hesitation in this, the fourth performance, the three actors are left physically heaving with effort and unable to play. From a simple professional point of view Beckett's invention takes up an important aspect of acting and elevates it to the status of a dramatic metaphor. For every actor the spontaneous and sensitive response to cues is part of a creative technique: action deriving from the dramatic context prevailing at the time and the forms of action earlier played. Beckett isolates the phenomenon, and one sees the cue as an evident event in the delivery of a text that aspires to recollect the past. The effect is to throw the actor into the present and onto a crux in which he cannot ever know that the text is such and such but, instead, must know how it goes at a given point through the operation of the bodily forms of speech.

Such effects demonstrate the integrity of Beckett's conception and invite the director to assume some of his traditional functions. The professional way to know a text is to do it, and, as the doings proceed, the structural implications emerge. The director must identify the physical and mental struggles of the artistic personality engaging in the ritual examination of itself. Like the musical director in performance, the theater director in rehearsal must integrate himself with the performers, the so-called interpretation emerging as the form of the playing. In the concert hall results are achieved organically at the point of playing by the empathic participation of the conductor. The musical soloist both responds to the execution of demanding musical passages by adopting physical forms and also discovers the significance of such physical experience. Moreover, in an intriguing way the musician is "characterized" by these various efforts. In all this the conductor empathically accompanies. If one can dissociate the dramatic director from the fictions in his head, the comparison becomes clear. He shapes dramatic form by attending to its necessary disposition *in performance* and by aiding in the realization of what is innate in the actor's work.

The resistance of the Beckett "character" to being treated as a naive imitation of an imagined person is strong evidence of what we, in fact, expect of the performer: that the human self is questioned through a process of action. The fiction is no more than the creative hypothesis, the equivalent of the sonneteer's "Shall I compare thee to a Summer's day?" It is certainly not a magical world to be transferred to the stage. The implications for the performer are rigorous. Terrifying aspects of stage performance are no longer to be glossed over: the invasive sense of personal exposure; the embarrassment of physical and spatial life; the sense of time passing and the demand for action; the threat of meaninglessness and breakdown. These are the stuff that make the structures of experience and the structures of Beckett's quintessentially existentialist drama. All drama carries the threat of performance, but more often than not the loose fictive world of the play coaches the actor's responses and preserves the sense of integration without which the performance cannot proceed. Beckett writes plays that make states of disintegration performable and then calls on the actor to play out the disintegrating self in the full apprehension of a personal collapse.

The role, then, becomes the occasion of the purest expression of a human dilemma, as the hunt for explanations draws the mind into a consciousness of the ultimate folly of the enterprise and of the temporary nature of the structures that hold the inquiry together and avert disaster. Following my actors I have witnessed the real process of acting, which starts and ends with the actor's self. It involves the careful synthesis of the role out of the actions of the drama and the realization that these are played as an artistic process that cannot immediately reintegrate the actor as "another," a character. As rehearsal proceeds, the disintegrative effect of the role has to be accepted and the conditions for its reintegration built up from within. Gradually, the inner coherence of the role establishes itself. It is the director's job to know how this happens, because the performer develops a fragmentary experience of the life of the role. The completion of this effect gives the coherence of a process of symbolic composition, a symbolic reintegration of the personality. This is entirely different from the creation of a spurious emotion that gives the impression of a change.

The sense of the individuality of the performer is extremely powerful, and it is, I think, the reason why occasionally Beckett's acting style is likened to that of Brecht and discussed as a species of alienation. I am never too happy about this, but I understand why the comparison should be made. The reason is to be sought in the inability of many actors and most critics and directors to get away from characterization as a sort of fantastic transubstantiation out of the real self. The true mode of acting in any style requires the exposure of the self to the experience of the actions of the self and a confrontation with the embedded knowledge that results. Beckett's unerring artistic sense not only seizes upon the fundamentals of drama but focuses performance itself as the source of a dramatic inquisition into the forms of life.

NOTES

1. Samuel Beckett, *Disjecta: Miscellaneous Writings and a Dramatic Fragment,* ed. Ruby Cohn (London: John Calder, 1983), 106.

2. Ibid., 107.

3. The recent Gulbenkian report on direction in the British theater makes this matter abundantly clear.

4. It is worth observing that the great classical theaters are not scenic but environmental and make a virtue of the fact.

5. *Aristotle on the Art of Fiction,* ed. L. J. Potts (Cambridge: Cambridge University Press, 1953), 44.

6. I am greatly indebted to Gilbert Ryle's *The Concept of Mind* (London: Hutchinson, 1949), for the discussion of "knowing how" and "knowing that" (see chap. 2).

7. Samuel Beckett, "Three Dialogues with Georges Duthuit," in Cohn, *Disjecta,* 139.

8. For examples, see Jonathan Kalb, *Beckett in Performance* (Cambridge: Cambridge University Press, 1989), 29 and passim.

9. Ibid., 65.

10. Francis Fergusson, *The Idea of a Theatre* (New York: Doubleday, n.d.), 255.

11. Michael Polanyi, *The Tacit Dimension* (London: Routledge and Kegan Paul, 1967).

12. Samuel Beckett, *Endgame* (London: Faber, 1958), 26–27.

13. Samuel Beckett, *Not I, Collected Shorter Plays* (London: Faber, 1984), 216.

14. Harold Pinter, "Writing for the Theatre," in *Plays,* vol. 1 (London: Methuen, 1976), 11.

15. Beckett, *Not I,* 222.

16. Ibid., 216.

17. Ibid., 220.

18. Ibid., 221.

19. Edward de Bono, *The Mechanism of Mind* (London: Penguin, 1971), 41.

20. Beckett, *Not I,* 217.

21. Ibid., 221.

Beckett in Repertory

Eve Adamson

In 1971 I founded a theater in New York, the Jean Cocteau Repertory, a resident company of actors committed to performing works of world theater in rotating repertory—that is, one play one night and another the next, one for the matinee performance, and another on the evening of the same day. As far as I am concerned, repertory is the only way to work in the theater. Productions stay fresh because performance energy is focused in several different directions at once, never settling and jelling in one place. In repertory a production continues to grow throughout its run, enriched by the next production that opens to run along with it, deepened by the third that is in rehearsal. Working in repertory, you live simultaneously in the worlds of Sophocles and Molière, Corneille and Chekhov, Shakespeare and Beckett.

Are Shakespeare and Beckett strange bedfellows? Not at all. From its inception my theater was dedicated to the premise that a classic work of theater, old or new, must—especially in this time of sophisticated film and television techniques—demand to live only on a stage. Its setting can be a blasted heath, Elsinore, Faust's study, or a country road with a tree, but each of these places is only a metaphor. A true classic takes place in an empty and sacred space, be it a ring of stones or a high-tech auditorium, in which life summons art, which in turn brings new experience and awareness of life.

Just as painting was liberated by the still camera, theater was liberated by the motion picture camera. We tend to forget this in America, as we continue to fill our stages with painted bookcases, astroturf, and case histories.

Lear, Juliet, Othello, Macbeth. These are not case histories but embodiments of their time, which is also our time. No matter when they first came to life on a page, they hold our thoughts and passions, doubts and yearnings. They endure because they are large enough and generous enough to assume and assimilate currents of contemporary thought and passing fancies and fashions. Hamlet can embody political intrigue, existential ennui, angry-young-manism, or Freudian kinks and still survive with grace. He is universal and timeless. Shakespeare's world, whatever trappings we adorn it with, remains ours.

And so it is with Beckett. Gogo, Didi, Hamm, and Clov may have arrived onstage centuries later, but they possess the souls of Hamlet or Lear, and they have the same ability to speak directly and timelessly to us.

Most twentieth-century play writing, which can be traced back to Ibsen, concerns itself with theses and motivations. Just like the movie of the week. This or that ethical stance is right or wrong. This or that social issue demands our attention or action. This character behaves the way he does because of his childhood; that one, because of his economic background.

These considerations are irrelevant in Shakespeare and Beckett. Leontes is jealous. We accept this as a given and get on with the action of *The Winter's Tale*. We can waste a good deal of rehearsal time probing the causes of his jealousy, but we'll be spining our wheels because Shakespeare doesn't give us any clues. His characters, like Beckett's, tell us all we need to know by their words and actions. When we look for theses and create needless motivations, we confuse the audience and obscure the play.

Repertory actors who have played a great deal in the pre-Ibsen classics know this. So do vaudevillians. That is why these kinds of performers have been the most successful interpreters of Beckett. They don't confuse or complicate things by demanding and creating definitive answers about Clov's childhood or Lucky's servitude. They just trust the playwright and get on with it.

Trust is a vital element in art. Trust of the process to which you commit yourself. It is especially important in theater, a collaborative art form—and not always easy. As a director, I consider it my responsibility to establish an atmosphere of trust. Not blind faith, but trust born of experience and discernment. First of all, I myself must be trustworthy: committed to open communication, to experiment, to having my ideas challenged and tested—able to stand firm and, when necessary, absorb flak. Then I must carefully choose the artists with whom I am to collaborate and, having chosen them, must trust their instincts, their risks, and their commitment. This is the collective journey into the unknown that creates art in theater. While keeping your critical faculties constantly alert, you must relinquish control of the course.

Since U.S. theater is a network of adversarial relationships, it is almost impossible to create this atmosphere except in resident repertory. But when you are lucky enough to work in repertory with a totally trustworthy playwright, the job becomes easy. Shakespeare is like the ocean. You can kick and thrash about, but he is eternally buoyant. If you realize this, you cannot sink. Beckett, on the other hand, is like a pomegranate or a beehive—an enclosed and delineated microcosm bearing many tiny chambers of infinite sweetness and richness. He knows, and tells us, exactly how he wants us to inhabit each chamber, each given theatrical moment: when to speak, when to pause, when to move, and how many steps to take. Each of his plays is a carefully crafted dramatic poem. It is not a matter, as in Shakespeare, of creating an interpretive structure but, instead, of filling and bringing life to the fuguelike structure he has already so precisely shaped. Once you have experienced this you know it works. Hence, the trust.

I have directed over seventy productions, most of them classics, including some twenty-odd by Shakespeare and five by Beckett: *Waiting for Godot, Endgame* in two different productions, and *Act Without Words II* in two different productions. As a director I approach each play differently. Some require lots of reading and text analysis. Some benefit from extensive improvisation. In many I give the actors tremendous freedom to find the physicality of their characters and their spatial interrelationships before setting stage movement. In others I block movement immediately so that we may find our freedom within a structure. But however I may approach a play, it is always a process, a journey.

Each time I direct a well-known play from another century, I pretend that it is a brand-new script from an unknown playwright. I must find that in it which speaks to us today, that which demands to be seen and heard in the time and place in which its audience, actors, and I are living. The generational issues in *King Lear,* for instance, are as real and painful to us today as they were when the play was written. So is the all-too-human tendency to relinquish power with one hand while attempting to hold onto it with the other. If I have experienced or witnessed these forces at play in a specific political arena, say, and believe my audience has too, then I will focus the production in that direction, letting it influence choice of costuming, music, lighting, and, to a lesser extent, scenery. (With

Shakespeare and Beckett scenery must remain minimal so as not to hamper the movement of the play.)

Beckett, however, is quintessentially of our century. No such search for relevance is necessary with his plays because each moment, each image, each line, pulses with contemporary currents of meaning, thought, and feeling. Conceptual productions of Beckett fail, I believe, because attempts to clarify or focus his theater only serve to muddy it. He has done our dramaturgical and directorial homework for us. Our job is to illuminate what he has already given us. This is not to say that he robs us of creative freedom. Rather, he challenges us to find this freedom within his already delineated form. But how, as a director, do I find the practical means to meet this challenge? How do I guide my actors into Beckett's world?

I began my rehearsal periods for *Godot* and the two *Endgames* by reading the plays aloud with the actors again and again. With many plays at this initial stage of rehearsal I will bypass stage directions and indicated pauses and actions, but with Beckett we read them aloud as part of the process because they are every bit as carefully chosen and as important as the words themselves.

Some plays demand a lot of reading in the early rehearsals; others don't. Sometimes you read and discuss. With plays of the Ibsen genre I'll constantly stop the readings to ask an actor why he just said something and whether he means it. You make interpretive decisions at this stage, although they are always open to change as the play grows in rehearsal. We'll read Shakespeare again and again for understanding and psychic enrichment—to assimilate layers of meaning and resonances. Some of Shakespeare's contemporaries—Ben Jonson, for example—require multiple readings in order to make sense of the language and to plot line readings that will make the meaning clear to an audience.

But Beckett's lines are pristine and exact. His words are clear. His motivations are given. His characters live moment to moment. Hunger, physical pain, psychic anguish and its release into humor or distraction are all there in the lines and actions he has given us. We read him again and again in order to feel his music, to inhale and ingest it until it is a part of us.

Beginning to read a Beckett play aloud is like sight-reading Bach. When you follow the notes to and through the phrases and observe the rests without predetermining or interpreting anything, you find yourself in a musical universe that has declared its own rules. The less you do, the more you simply read the language, the more you will allow Beckett's

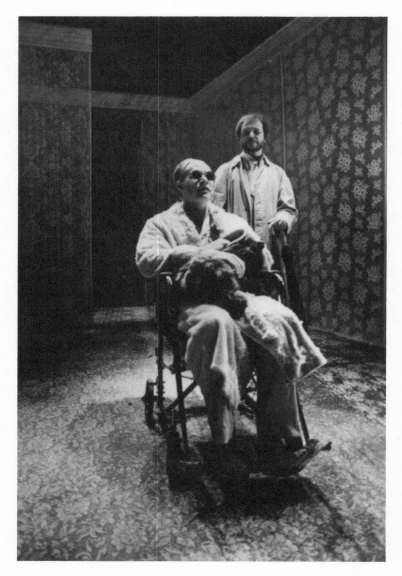

Fig. 10. Mark Waterman as Hamm, Harris Berlinski as Clov, in the Jean Cocteau Repertory *Endgame,* directed by Eve Adamson, 1992. Photo credit: Shirley Curtin/Jonathan Slaff Associates.

resonances and nuances to flow through you to the audience. This is particularly true for the long sections of short lines interspersed with pauses. The longer speeches are more difficult because they present more opportunity for choice, for interpretive reading. But just when you begin to get carried away with one of them, Beckett stops you with a silence.

Actors find Beckett's lines easy to commit to memory. This is invariably a test of good play writing: it finds its way into the subconscious easily. You don't have to work at it. Both in *Godot* and in my two productions of *Endgame* the lines became so intrinsic that Gogo/Didi and Hamm/Clov would often unconsciously trade speeches in rehearsal. One must guard against becoming too comfortable!

Another danger inherent in the rightness and ease of the language is a tendency in the playing to let it snowball, running away with whole sections of the action, like a record spinning out of control with Keystone Cops choreography. This happened more often in *Godot* than in *Endgame*—perhaps Didi and Gogo are more in accord, more of a cooperative unit than Hamm and Clov. Or maybe it is because they are allowed more freedom of stage movement. Then, too, *Endgame*'s dialogue, more peppered with pauses than *Godot*'s, affords more natural stops.

Once the actors have a visceral sense of the language, it is time to put the play on its feet. I approach the challenge of stage movement differently with each project, even if it is a production of a play that I have directed before. *Endgame* is a case in point. The play allows very little innovation of movement. Nagg and Nell are confined to dustbins. (In my second production they occupied two halves of a dumpster, each with its own lid.) Beckett tells us when he wants them to appear, withdraw, suck a biscuit, or attempt unsuccessfully to kiss each other.

Hamm, too, is confined—to his wheelchair. He can move through space only when assisted by Clov. By himself his mobility is limited to head and arms. Opaque glasses mask his eyes, thereby significantly limiting his facial expressions. (My second Hamm, Mark Waterman, was spurred by this limitation to an ingenious and memorable bit of characterization. He blacked out all but a few of his teeth and devised a veritable vocabulary of gapes, yawns, silent laughs, and open-mouthed masks of agony.) Beckett again is specific in his directions: Hamm wipes his glasses, lifts his hat, takes an object from Clov, throws it away. In both productions I chose to limit his arm movements even further, paralyzing his upper arms. In order to remove his hat he had either to lower his head or slowly to nudge the

right arm up with the fingers of the left, while the left elbow rested on
the chair arm.

Constraint and enclosure are central images in *Endgame*. Even Clov,
the one spatially mobile character, is confined in his movements by the
walls of the room, the will of Hamm, and the pain in his legs. Beckett
specifies the directions in which he moves and sometimes even the number
of steps he takes. Clov's steps should be audible, for they are every bit as
much a part of the music of the play as are the words and pauses.

I was much more aware of this in my second production. In working
on the opening pantomime I beat out a rhythm for Harris Berlinsky, who
played Clov, until he developed his own internal metronome for steps,
ladder business, window openings, and the unveilings of Nagg, Nell, and
Hamm. The single staccato "Hah!"'s as he looked out each window were
a part of the scoring. This pantomime served as the first musical movement
of the play. The second movement began with his first uttered word:
Finished. The Clov of my first production, James S. Payne, had played
Gogo in *Waiting for Godot,* which had run in the repertory for two years.
While this enabled him to come to Beckett more easily than the other
actors in that *Endgame,* it also posed initial difficulties in containing and
streamlining Clov's physicality. Once we began to work on Clov's movement, however, these difficulties were easily surmounted.

Much more physical freedom is allowed, even invited, in *Waiting for Godot.* While Didi and Gogo do suffer from their respective bodily complaints,
these in no significant way inhibit their movements. Beckett gives detailed
instructions for each character's physical relationship with objects—Didi's
with his hat, Gogo's with his boots, Pozzo's with his paraphernalia,
Lucky's with his baggage—but, except for indicating an attitude or a
direction, he leaves choreography and quality of movement to director and
actors.

We were challenged in *Godot* to find movement that was organic and
specific to each actor and the character he played and at the same time
stylistically consistent among the four. It also had to evoke the world of
the play, a world in which, at the ultimate moment of spiritual anguish,
one's pants fall down. I thought of Bruegel and burlesque, church and
circus, and the films of Keaton and Fellini. I pulled together a motley of
baggy rehearsal clothing (including, of course, hats), had the actors apply
whiteface and exaggerated clown expressions, and found recordings of the
film scores of Nino Rota, Fellini's composer. To the joyful and melancholy
music of *8½* we danced the play, mimed it, clowned it. The wonderfully

liberating effects of mask and music freed the actors to explore a physical reality that never would have come to them under a more traditional rehearsal regime. Nor would they have applied these modes and ideas to other plays in the repertory (although they also would have been most appropriate for Shakespeare's clowns).

Finally, when words and movement became second nature to the actors, although separately, we put them together. At first we kept the whiteface and the Rota music then gradually let go of it until we inhabited Beckett's world naturally, without external aids. We had found its truth and its theatricality.

Act without Words II, while fraught with technical challenges, presents few difficulties for the actor and director attuned to Beckett. He has given us a detailed blueprint for a pantomime. My function both times was more critical than idea generating—sitting outside the action, trying to see it through the audience's eyes, keeping it clear, crisp, and inevitable.

I directed *Waiting for Godot* in 1973—almost twenty years ago. It was early in the life of the Jean Cocteau Repertory. We were still a small, struggling theater company, without the subscription audience we would later acquire. Although we performed in rotating repertory, we had not yet grown to the point where we had to commit to a schedule a year in advance. My artistic choices were spontaneous and unrestrained. I chose *Godot* merely because I loved it. I had four actors I believed in—Coral S. Potter, James S. Payne, Carmen Finestra, and John Mitchell—and I felt that it would be good for them, along with the Shakespeare, Fielding, Anouilh, and Ibsen they had been performing in repertory, to work on Beckett. Our set was a large tree limb I had found on the street. I hung it from fishing line so that it seemed suspended in midair in an otherwise empty space, drilled four holes in it, and placed leaves in these holes during the interval. I didn't anticipate much audience interest in this labor of love and inititally scheduled six performances. *Godot* garnered us our first recognition from the *New York Times* and remained in repertory, playing to full houses, for over two years.

My first production of *Endgame* was during the middle years of the Cocteau. We had gained an audience, visibility, and funding. We had become a small but important part of the New York theater scene. Our repertory was still adventurous, but now, when making decisions, I had also to consider box office projection, subscribers, funding sources, a board, and the responsibility of a larger resident acting company. *Endgame,* in a more expensive physical production than *Godot,* but one that was equally minimalist, seemed a bleaker play, less joyful, less life affirming. But I knew that the time had come to revisit Beckett, just as, in order to remain centered as a director, I must periodically reenter the world of Shakespeare. I was gratified when audiences of all shapes, sizes, and orientations responded viscerally to the play.

Three years ago I resigned as artistic director of the Jean Cocteau Repertory. The company was stable. It was artistically solid. It had survived the economic perils of the 1980s, which had caused the demise of so many New York theaters. Robert Hupp, who had worked with me for five years, was now ready to assume artistic leadership. I had had my fill of boards, fundraising, promotion, and administration. I wanted the freedom of the early years, the years of *Godot,* when choices were clear and risk was exhilarating.

I continue to direct plays, at the Cocteau and elsewhere. Last year I directed *Endgame* again. Shakespeare has always been with me, but it had been a long time since I had worked on Beckett. I wondered how it would feel. Then I remembered that, as when Gogo tried to hang himself and his pants fell down, laughter liberates tears and that from bare trees— miraculously (after an interval)—spring leaves.

On Directing Beckett: In and Out of Ireland

Robert McNamara

On the staging of the plays of Samuel Beckett there are two schools of thought. The first is that one ought to remain relentlessly and tenaciously beholden to the earlier productions of Beckett's own staging of his work, at the Schiller Theater or elsewhere, or to those directed by the playwright's closest collaborators and disciples, Walter Asmus, Pierre Chabert, and Rick Cluchey. There have, in fact, been video productions of most of those productions, acknowledged by the playwright as being as close as possible to his final visions of his plays. And that is fine, for these "final" productions by Beckett in association with his collaborators serve both as a blueprint, a mold, and, ultimately, as a guide to the staging of his plays.

There is also another way to explore the staging of Beckett's texts, however, both the plays and the prose that can be adapted for the theater, for the theater is a constantly changing and fluid process whereby a play has not one life but many. And that will be the thrust of this essay. I will attempt to describe from the director's point of view just exactly what that process of collaboration between Beckett's work and a stage director is. And I shall address my own work and research on Beckett's major productions—as well as the lesser-known stagings of his prose pieces, from the novels and poems to other literary fragments—in an effort to clarify my position with regard to the staging of this work.

I first began directing plays by Samuel Beckett in 1977 in Dublin, Ireland, while I was a student at Trinity College. It was my early interest in the writings of James Joyce that set me on a path to Beckett's theater. In June of that year I directed Joyce's only extant play, *Exiles,* a play set in turn-of-the-century Dublin, in repertory with Beckett's *Krapp's Last Tape*—a tour de force for one actor and voices. The challenge presented here was quite simply how to make two such diverse plays unite and work together effectively in the same space. Joyce's play required an elaborately furnished set placed firmly and squarely in the time period of 1909 Edwardian Dublin—replete with plush, overstuffed sofas, potted plants, and ornate portraits—while *Krapp's Last Tape* demanded isolation, solitude, and, finally, darkness.

When it came time to perform *Krapp's Last Tape* all of the furniture was stripped away so that not one piece of the household remained. The stage was made completely bare. The maroon curtains were pulled out from their sashes to mask any infiltration of light from the windows. To the image of Krapp (Irish actor Don Foley), isolated among the spools of tape, I felt compelled to add clusters of rather large, oversized tea chests straight from a Dublin cafe. Inside these large wooden chests bins of tape were inserted to give Krapp's den a cluttered and claustrophobic atmosphere. And Krapp was seated at his table, head on his hands, as the audience entered the theater.[1] Otherwise, Beckett's stage directions were fully honored—unlike in the 1975 production of *Waiting for Godot* at the Abbey Theatre in Dublin, in which directorial conceit allowed for an abandoned automobile to be part of the decor. In this writer's opinion this was a deliberate sabotaging of Beckett's play, as nothing much else is needed at the base of the tree, where all man's hope and despair is contained.

This production was followed by a double-bill matinee performance of *Play* and the rarely seen and rarely performed "dramaticule" *Breath,* once again at Trinity College Dublin Players Theatre in July 1977. The approach to the first piece, *Play,* was direct and simple.[2] Peter Crisp, Caryn Hurwitz, and Kate Thompson (Man, Woman 1 [W1], and Woman 2 [W2], respectively) were instructed to play the text as if it were half–Grand Guignol and the other half as though it were the acidly funny stuff of a Feydeau farce—in Dante's inferno. In working with Irish and English actors I was able to instill a very South County Dublin flair into the proceedings. Man (Peter Crisp) wore the required round spectacles and played the tortured husband and lover with a lucid academic forthrightness. W1 (Caryn Hurwitz) was dark, complementing the blondness of W2 (Kate Thompson). The lighting was the enemy. Due to the confines of the space, I was forced to place the lightboard operator in the back rows of the theater, where he played the levers as though they were a piano's keys. Usually, the audience was faintly perplexed and then amused when the play ended. And then, as per Beckett's instructions, it *repeated* itself entirely. After this, of course, this journey into a tripartite hell, a pastiche sadly gone astray, almost anything would appear to be comic. Such, generally, was the case with *Breath*.

There was a brief interval when the houselights would come up and a perplexed series of mutterings would again arise from the audience. Then the lights would once more dim, and *Breath* would commence. This production lasted all of thirty-five seconds, sparking these comments from the critics: "This is drama reduced to its absolute minimum. Beckett, that great innovator, can condense no further. A joke? But Beckett doesn't trifle; you are expected to take him seriously. However many in the large audience could not refrain from laughter as the 35 seconds ended."[3] And: "'Breath'— a short signal from Beckett that he still exists?—is a cutaway shot in a tenement film; a heap of rubbish, the cry of a newborn child, the last breath of an old man or woman, the cry of a newborn child, darkness again. Stage One manages this neatly. Theater reduced to the irreducible."[4]

Needless to say, these early Dublin Stage One productions of the Beckett plays were a learning and growth process for me as a director. At the time (the mid- and late 1970s) there was not a great deal of Beckett's work being staged in Dublin. There would be the occasional Irish Student Drama Festival, in which one would be permitted to see a student-acted version of *Krapp's Last Tape* or *Act Without Words II*. In 1977 the Schiller Theater from Berlin came to the Abbey Theatre and performed *Warten auf Godot* in German under Beckett's direction. This production provided an opportunity for me to apprise myself of Beckett's vision in terms of his own stagings. I still view this as one of the key stagings of this play by any director.

In 1978 I produced a one-man show based on Beckett's early prose and plays. This farrago evening was compiled by Irish director Jim Sheridan and was directed by Séan Tracy at the Dublin Focus Theatre for Stage One. The play's many characters were all portrayed by Peter Caffrey. And in many ways I consider *Waiting for Beckett* to be as successful as any of the earlier one-man Beckett shows, such as Jackie MacGowran's *From Beginning to End* and, more recently, Barry McGovern's *I'll Go On*. *Waiting for Beckett* featured excerpts from Beckett's 1938 novel *Murphy*, the radio play *Embers*, a puppet show of Hamm and Clov from *Endgame*, snippets from *Malone Dies*, as well as many other delights for the aficionado of Beckett's earlier and more obscure works.

As Man, Peter Caffrey appeared naked with his back to the audience. After he had fallen out of a rocking chair, and while he was spread-eagle out on the floor, a goad would appear from behind a screen, house right, and poke the indolent and slothful hero to get him to attempt a day's work. This, of course, was a gloss from *Act Without Words II*. Gradually, Man would clothe himself in whatever cast-off garments were available to him: a pair of baggy black trousers, a stiff white shirtfront replete with ready-made bow tie, a short and very much abused tailcoat. And, finally, the pièces de résistance: a straw boater crowned with what Beckett declared the only hatwear fit for a true Anglo-Irish gentleman—the block hat, or bowler. One of the chief strengths of this evening was that *Waiting for Beckett* drew heavily upon less-utilized Beckett resources such as *Murphy, Watt,* and *Embers*. It was also, to the best of my knowledge, one of the first of the fusion evenings that successfully presented both Beckett's prose and plays as a unity. This run was extended several times, and the production was subsequently revived to tour North America.

Stage One mounted another Beckett reprise in Dublin in 1978. Again it was a double bill, *Endgame* and *Not I,* also performed at the Focus Theatre. This production presented another set of challenges, as *Not I* requires a nonrealistic setting, and *Endgame,* with its *fin du monde* atmosphere, calls out for at least a semblance of realistic details and decor. This problem was partially solved by setting Hamm's last refuge, stage left, as a combination urban factory and the last bunker of all bunkers: a large pile of miscellaneous debris, including a partially collapsed pillar. This served as Clov's entranceway to his kitchen as well. Directly upstage and to the center, and behind Hamm's chair, was an eight-foot-tall metal door, sealed and padlocked. This could be taken either for a meat locker door or for the "larder," or cupboard, with which Hamm alternately threatens and cajoles Clov.

This sturdy, tall metal door also provided the position from which *Not I* was performed. During a blackout the door was opened slightly; blacks were then placed in front of the actress playing Mouth (Olwen Fouéré), and she was literally strapped into a wooden frame. Her head was inserted into a kind of grip, or vise, from which she could not move. Her mouth was set directly against an aperture onto which a pinpoint lighting instrument had been painstakingly set. Mouth's lips were not daubed with red lipstick but, rather, a far more eerie and chilling effect was created by using black lipstick. The role of the Auditor, "in loose black djeballa, with hood, fully faintly lit,"[5] was dispensed with, thereby focusing the audience's attention exclusively on Mouth. In this production Fouéré played Mouth with a pronounced Galway accent, once more creating an otherworld effect of Irishness such as can be heard in Sian Phillips's voice in *Eh Joe.*

Fouéré's blackened lips, suggestive of more than a shriek or a ghostly howl from beyond the grave, gave this version of *Not I* a special missle-like impetus from its initial choruslike mutterings (which can be seen as an ironic parody by Beckett of what an actor hears from the "other side" of the curtain before a performance) to her succinct and sharp pauses before each scream or howl. There was a lyrically maddening quality to her whole range that, together with her Galway speech pattern, made this unforgettably haunting and Irish.

The Druid Theatre in Galway and other venues throughout Ireland were the sites of the final Stage One Beckett productions. *Happy Days* featured Claire Mullan as Winnie and Terence Orr as Willie. It had originated in Dublin and thence had a second life touring Cork, Galway, and the west of Ireland. What made this version remarkable, and thereby memorable, was the direction that made Winnie into a true South County Dublin Anglo-Irishwoman, a real denizen of Killiney Bay and environs. And in that sense Winnie was a deadly accurate portrayal of what Beckett had in mind when he created the play in 1961. Winnie is of a particular class, alternately with and without the pretensions she may once have espoused.

From 1980 to 1984 I had a long hiatus from directing Beckett, although I always had the intention in the back of my mind to sometime stage *Waiting for Godot* or *Endgame* in the United States. After leaving Ireland, I had decided to avoid directing Irish plays, including Beckett, so as not to be typed as an Irish director by critics here. When first offered a choice between directing Sean O'Casey's *The Plough and the Stars* and Peter Shaffer's *Equus,* therefore, I chose the latter.

In 1984 I turned to what I consider a unique project. It was a fusion evening linking the most remarkable poet of our century with the playwright I consider to be the century's most important. Included in *Yeats after Life* were the plays *The Cat and the Moon, Purgatory,* and *Words upon the Window-Pane.* Situated between *The Cat and the Moon* and *Purgatory* was a fragment from Beckett's 1949 *Textes pour rien* (Texts for Nothing), #10. Framing Beckett's *Texts* with the Yeats plays stressed their common background, wandering bums "searching for a life."

That W. B. Yeats, with his refined and miniature dreams, was a precursor to another Irishman with the same proclivity for brief plays, or dramaticules, I have no doubt.[6] That the young Beckett also read Yeats voluminously and even saw his plays upon the stage of the Old Abbey Theatre I also believe.[7] *The Cat and the Moon* seems to be a none-too-distant ancestor to both of the pseudocouples we later enjoy in *Waiting for Godot,* with Vladimir and Estragon as direct corollaries to the Lame Beggar and the Blind Beggar in Yeats's play. The beggars even more closely resemble Hamm and Clov in *Endgame,* however, with their identical sets of problems and goals. As Beckett says, *"Nec tecum, ne sine te,"*[8] which is echoed by Yeats's beggars: "Forty years we've been knocking about the roads together."

Yeats's play *Purgatory,* in which a father and a bastard son are condemned to wander the bleak barren roads in search of hope and renewal, resembles much of Beckett's dramaturgy and writing. In Yeats's play, however, the Old Man is continuously damned to witness his own procreation, his mother's death, and then the murder of his father, with his son to be the next victim. In staging *Purgatory,* I had the son spit blood when the father stabs him with the same knife that killed his own father. After the Old Man completes a victory jig he collapses, and the son comes back to life on the line: "How quickly it returns-beat-beat-!"[9] Is the son a haunting, never vanishing specter that has come to life again? Or one that never quite ceased to be in the first place? In any case, the Old Man and the Boy, like so many of Beckett's creations, are condemned for all eternity to haunt deserted byways and derelict ruins. This is familiar to readers of Beckett, from Belacqua in *More Pricks Than Kicks* to *Godot* and, finally, to the more minimalist dramas of the 1970s and 1980s, such as *Footfalls, Rockaby,* and even *Ohio Impromptu,* with its Joycean elegy.

What was unusual about the adaptation of *Texts for Nothing #10* was that, in its use of music, it broke the so-called rules for adapting Beckett's prose works for the stage. There is already an innate musicality in much of Beckett's writing. So, why bother, one may ask, to alter what is already unified and preexistent? The idea was to provide continuity between the Beckett and Yeats pieces. The musicians underscored *Cat* and *Purgatory* and also succeeded in creating a common bond for the wandering vagrants as heroes in both Yeats and Beckett.

The instruments used in *Texts* were a string bass, a violin, and, at times, a *bodhran.*[10] Man, or tramp (Kryztov Lindquist), entered in a flurry of agitation pursued by a piercing, white-hot beam of light. He carried two bags à la Lucky in *Godot.* His apparel consisted of a top hat replete with cord, tied tightly around his head, a full-length and much battered greatcoat, and fingerless gloves. Eighteenth-century breeches and shoes, either from a French nobleman's wardrobe or that of a lackey, completed Man's sartorial getup. He would cross the stage in a vain attempt to avoid the searching, penetrating light. And finally, in a fit, he would collapse onto the center of the stage. Head raised, he intoned against the driving force of the music: "Give up, but it's all given up, it's nothing new, I'm nothing new."[11] What followed was almost a jazz ballet, as Man constantly struggled to arise from the mysterious set of difficulties and metaphysical pitfalls that ever so vigorously assaulted him.

The continual source of tension in this adaptation of *Texts* is that of the music driving Man ever onward to arrive at an impossible and ambiguous destination. The music pushes. Man moves like a projectile (much as if in response to Pozzo's jerking of Lucky's rope or Hamm's repeatedly ironic and brutal hammerings in *Endgame*). But the Man keeps falling. He attempts to progress: "This is most reassuring, after such a fright and emboldens me to go on, once again. But there is not silence." On this line a pastiche of Shostakovich is played by the musicians and then a series of atonal chords for: "No, there is utterance, somewhere someone is uttering. Inanities agreed. . . . " Man rises and attempts to complete a circle— the circumference of the light—and, as he rises, the music drives him on frenetically until once more he collapses, deliberately, on: "So home to roost it comes among my other assets. . . . "[12]

Man drops his two bags (one a Pan Am flight bag and the other an American Air Force V-4 case) and executes a backward pratfall. "Home yet again and no trickery involved. . . . " The music here bombards Man with musical clichés and references, as he desperately crawls backward in a vain effort to elude the light and music. At the precise moment of "to utter, for my own good, what I must utter, for my future good, well-known ditty . . . ," the musicians play a brief snatch from Franz Lehar's "The Merry Widow," which is punctuated by a brief burst of joyless laughter from Man. The passage about souls and the "unborn" is underscored by staccato passages from the string bass and sharp pings from the violin. Man rises on "charitable suckers" and searches forlornly until the line "I may not be accused of having faltered," whereupon the inevitable occurs, and he collapses. He comments from the prone position, as do Didi and Gogo, "This is awful, awful, at least there's that to be thankful for."[13]

Constantly, Man, with the music, creates a pattern of interrupted movement, of arrested action, which always brings him back to earth, always flat on his back. Man in *Texts* is a not-so-distant cousin of Lucky's, a precursor of the novelistic antiheroes, like Molloy, crawling through the mud, and of the voices urging us to go on in *The Unnamable* and *How It Is*. Man, in *Texts for Nothing #10,* echoes Clov's final speeches in *Endgame:* "I open the door of the cell and go. I am so bowed I only see my feet, if I open my eyes, and between my legs a little trail of black dust. I say to myself that the earth is extinguished though I never saw it lit. . . . When I fall I'll weep for happiness."[14]

Ultimately, there is a prefiguring of Lucky in Man as he escapes from the pages of Beckett's prose and enters into a more theatrical world. One may argue that the integrity of the piece has been drastically altered by placing *Texts* onstage, but I do not agree. In these miniature prose fragments one explores the same dramatic sensibility inherent in much of Beckett's late writing. The school of thought that says "don't" is in error. Beckett's prose works can stand and have stood the test of theatrical adaptation.

The Narrator (Man) in *Texts* finally comes to a halt. Could this be it? Could this be the place? Let us find out. In the tradition of Beckett characters he begins with an attempt at sleep—". . . I'll go to sleep, so that I may say, hear myself say, a little later, I've slept, he's slept . . ."— which is accompanied by an ironic lullaby. This seeming approach of sleep is nothing less than an illusion. The light has narrowed around Man's throat like a noose: "He'll have done nothing, nothing but go on, giving up, that's it, I'll have gone on giving up, having had nothing, not being there."[15] There is a twelve-second pause after Man announces his intention to "erase" himself. He bows his head. Very slowly he raises it again, and, on a count of twelve beats, he grins slyly at the audience and sharply states: "Not being there." This is punctuated by a harsh exhaling of breath—as forceful as a "vagitus" in reverse—as he tries to escape the complexities of the world. There is a snap blackout followed by the crushing jazz rhythms of the string basis, as Man vanishes into the darkness of the stage.

As far as adapting Beckett's prose for the stage is concerned, one might ask, "Why?" to which I might reply, "Why not?" for the prose pieces, such as *Premier Amour* (First Love) and *Texts for Nothing #10,* appear to cry out for dramatization. It is appropriate and within the spirit of the Beckett canon to bring them onto the stage. It is more a question of execution than one of aesthetics. Normally, within the world of Beckett's fiction the narrators are solitaries who meander and perhaps eventually find their way to a hovel, a crossroads, or an empty house, as in *Malone Dies, Molloy,* and *Watt.* In the cold, grayish world of *Texts for Nothing #10* the Narrator's voice is cool and assured, even as he tosses and turns at random, a prisoner to his colossal doubts and isolation. Yet these voices are physicalized within the perimeters of Beckett's own specifications: Vladimir and Estragon, Hamm and Clov, and even the clochards Mercier and Camier set up parallel patterns of behavior that can fit into a newly "renovated" Beckett character.

I have been directing *Texts for Nothing #10* for over seven years, first in Washington, D.C., in *Yeats after Life,* and later on in a double bill with *The Winter Man* by Niall Montgomery,[16] with Synge's *In the Shadow of the Glen,* in *Beckett at Eighty-three, The Beckett Festival* (at the Scena Theatre in April 1990), and, most recently, in *Beckett Shorts,* pieces staged for the 1992 New European Play Festival. It continues to change and evolve. Recently, I also worked on *Premier Amour* on the same bill as *Texts.* The approach was perhaps similar to that used in dealing with *Krapp's Last Tape.* A table; a pool of light; a man clad in black, white, and gray, who ever so reluctantly opens a book—a child's worn school copybook—and begins to narrate for us some of the key events in his life. To his surprise he says, "I associate, rightly or wrongly, my marriage with the death of my father, in time." We are swept along by the Narrator as he informs us, with caustic humor, of the details of, and series of deprivations in, the comedy of his life: "Personally I have no bones to pick with graveyards, I take the air there willingly . . . when take the air I must."[17]

It is a laconic, controlled, and almost irritatingly rational piece of writing. By putting it onstage, one gains access to a key to the logic that permeates so many of Beckett's short prose fragments. These are prose pieces that oftentimes seem like dress rehearsals for the larger monologues of Lucky and Pozzo in *Godot* or those of Hamm and Clov in *Endgame* or even the later miniature dramas such as *Footfalls, Rockaby,* and especially *A Piece of Monologue.* Yet contrasted with these later dramas is the great mine of verbal humor found in the short prose writings that can be physicalized onstage. There is a wealth of early Beckett stories and novels suitable for theatrical adaptation. Works such as *Premier Amour, Mercier and Camier, Texts for Nothing,* and the longer companion pieces such as *The Expelled, The Calmative,* and *The End* all lend themselves to a skilled adaptor's hand. It would be timely to see these early works by Beckett adapted with a biographical throughline analogous to what Sir John Gielgud did with his acclaimed *Seven Ages of Man.*

The early Beckett pieces could be adapted so that the arc of the writer's life and fiction might be yoked together and then jointly assessed. This adaptation could rely on more minimalist prose pieces such as *Company,* *Worstward Ho,* and the late *Stirrings Still.* The 1930s novel, *Murphy,* and the Dublin stories in *More Pricks than Kicks* could then be used as a framing device to make of the evening a realistic appraisal of a young writer's origins and points of departure. For far too long the field of the Beckett one-man show has been the fertile terrain of the trilogy—*Molloy, Malone Dies,* and *The Unnamable*—in the brilliant turns by the late Irish actor Jack MacGowran in *End of Day* or *From Beginning to End* (which I chanced to see in Dublin in 1972 at the Gaiety Theatre).[18] More recently, Barry McGovern has managed a triumphant assay at these daunting works with his critically hailed one-man show *I'll Go On.* There are other areas for exploration in the earlier prose works, however, such as *From an Abandoned Work,* which would be especially valuable in the context of this new concept.

In 1987 I was faced with my next major challenge in directing Beckett, and that was to be my version of his magnificent play *Endgame.* Again, as director or producer of Beckett's stage plays, as opposed to director or adaptor of the prose, one is faced with some difficult choices. Is one to imitate fairly catholically what has already been done, including those landmark productions that the playwright himself has orchestrated? As always, when posed with this dilemma I feel that it is best to first research and then arrive at an accurate reading and assessment of the play in one's own terms. When the work is a masterpiece (and *Endgame* is Beckett's own preferred work) one is faced with a true test of one's ability to interpret. I had seen many Beckett productions since Dublin, including the 1984 revival of *Endgame* in New York directed by Alvin Epstein. Earlier, in 1980, at the Abbey Theatre's Peacock Theatre in Dublin, I had seen a double bill of *Endgame* and *Krapp's Last Tape* with the San Quentin Drama Work-shop, directed by Beckett. How had my own vision of the play grown since I had last directed *Endgame* back in Dublin?

First, though now back in the United States, I felt more comfortable exploring Beckett's Irish roots—especially with regard to the major works. The clarity of the relationship between Nagg and Nell completed and echoed the relation (one hesitates to call it a relationship) between Hamm the Father and Clov the Factotum. Both couples share and ritually enact each "day" of their lives in the interdependence revealed in plays by Yeats, Synge, and O'Casey. Also, from my time spent in Dublin I was accustomed to seeing and hearing Irish actors perform Beckett, and, with their diction and sharp patois, I was able to see the expertness with which they delineate the light from the dark, the comic from the merely awful, the clarity from the midst of absurdity.

Then there is the fundamental question of humor in Beckett's writing. Audiences and critics alike ask themselves, "Is this really meant to be funny?" The answer most decidedly is yes. Too often the humor is relegated to the ash heap. Or worse still, only intermittently perceived and understood. For me, as a director, Nagg and Nell are the scions of the world of Oscar Wilde, with his witty parlor talk in *The Importance of Being Earnest* with its seeming non sequiturs and wit for wit's sake. And Vladimir and Estragon, in any of their lengthy banterings, bear an almost uncanny resemblance to scenes in George Bernard Shaw's *Heartbreak House,* in which Ellie and Mrs. Hushabye chat away idly and blithely while Mangan is in a trance. This is an uncanny doppelgänger for the scene in *Godot* in which Estragon and Vladimir debate what to do with the supine Pozzo. The humor in Nagg and Nell's dialogue is heavily South County Dublin— Killiney, Greystones, Foxrock, what have you. But it could also just as easily be the same witty brilliant speech of Beckett's other colleague playwrights from Dublin, Shaw and Wilde, with their own predilection for jokes and non sequiturs. The Scena Theatre *Endgame* was thus imbued with a rather lively Irish sense of the grotesque and the humorous. Joined with precise physical movement, this can become a disorienting and deadly effective choice in the staging of Beckett's plays.

The other technical choice that I made with our actors was one whose rationale, again, usually remains unknown to the critics and the public alike, and that concerns the question of pacing. This *Endgame* was played fast. Seventy-five minutes was the goal. One particular performance brought the run in at seventy minutes, which is, I believe (in accordance with Michael Haerdter's rehearsal notes),[19] very close to Beckett's intentions. It is generally thought that the "silences," or "pauses," must be long. This means that they weigh rather heavily on the rhythm and pace of the production. Too often, I would assert, this has created a false sense of inaction during the pauses. In any case, as Beckett states, they are not all the same length, and a good stage director will inform you that the pauses all mean different things and signify a completely different dynamic within the play's overall concept. Normally, I would gradate pauses from three to five and, finally, to categories of ten seconds.

Before rehearsals of *Endgame* can properly begin one must also deal with the question of whether this is the "last" day of the excruciating routine between Hamm and Clov. (Otherwise, the actors themselves will raise this issue.) After exhaustive research (we rehearsed this Scena production of *Endgame* for three months, which is most unusual in the American theater), rehearsals, arguments with actors and many conversations with designers, I came to the conclusion that it didn't matter. Being *too* literal with Beckett's texts is a sure way to boredom and an onstage death. Also Beckett intends everything in *Endgame* (as in *Waiting for Godot*) to have not just one but several layers of meaning. And to assign merely one reading to a given situation seems to make vulgar concessions to an audience capable of more than that assumption.

Later productions of Beckett's work that I have supervised include a stage adaptation of *Rough for Radio #2*, *The Beckett Festival*, *Havel/Beckett*,[20] and, most recently, *Beckett Shorts*. This last production featured *Texts for Nothing #10* and a large excerpt from *Premier Amour* and closed with a reading of Beckett's last known poem, "What Is the Word." The evening was well balanced between the shorter plays (*Ohio Impromptu*, *Eh Joe*, and *Catastrophe*) and the prose pieces.

What conclusions were garnered from the staging of these lesser-known prose fragments? Apart from the perception of an innate dramatic quality in Beckett's work it became evident that the concept of a one-man narration works effectively when juxtaposed to the shorter playlets. I would also argue that, as Beckett entered into his later career as a dramatist, there was almost a lessening of the differences between what constitutes his prose and his plays. The authorial voices of *Footfalls*, *Not I*, and *Rockaby* are more than similar to the narrative voices of *Stirrings Still*, the earlier *Texts for Nothing*, and *Premier Amour*. I would also put forth that the limited use of music to underscore some of Beckett's prose adapted for the stage is a valid choice. It is not a case of committing the heresy that some Beckett scholars and critics might consider it to be but, rather, a legitimate means of exploring a new frontier of Beckett's writing.

Finally, as I have attempted to demonstrate here, there is a need for more theatrical exploration of the novels and earlier prose of the Beckett oeuvre. There is room for another genre of one- (or even two-) man show based on Beckett's nontheater writings. One might argue for "a portrait of the artist" both as a young man and as a mature artist and, ultimately, as one gazing objectively at the prospect of one's own end. In theory this piece might commence with *Company* then move on to *More Pricks than Kicks*, enter into the world of *Murphy*, take a brief sojourn with *Premier Amour* and *Texts*, and then glide cursorily toward *Embers* and onto *Worstward*

Fig. 11. Kryztov Lindquist and Helen Patton (*rear*) in *Catastrophe,* directed by Robert McNamara, Scena Theatre, Washington, D.C., 1989. Photo credit: Jeffrey Crespi.

Ho and *All Strange Away.* The concluding piece on the bill, obviously, might be *Stirrings Still,* with its tribute to A. D., Dr. Arthur Darley, Beckett's friend.

This area of Beckett prose adaptation is a relatively uncharted one, as the director and literary adaptor must make wide and sweeping choices in the realm of text, staging, and overall interpretation. In the future, whatever form adaptations of Beckett's prose may take, they must conform to the voices of his vision. No matter how spare, they must remain as precise and elegant as his prose.

NOTES

1. In his review in the *Evening Herald* (Dublin, 23 June 1977) John Finegan wrote: "When first seen on entering the theatre Krapp is asleep at the table, his head resting on his arms. When Foley raises his magnificent head it is like Neptune rising from the sea."

2. See Finegan's review: "Their speech is in fragments, as they relive the

past in toneless voices, three lost souls who go on repeating themselves exactly in deliberately banal dialogue until the end of time" (Ibid.).

3. Ibid.

4. Kane Archer, *Irish Times* (Dublin), 23 July 1977.

5. *Not I, The Collected Shorter Plays of Samuel Beckett* (New York: Grove Press, 1984), 216.

6. See James W. Flannery, *W. B. Yeats and the Idea of a Theatre* (New Haven, Conn.: Yale University Press, 1976), 101–27. See also Katherine Worth, *The Irish Drama of Europe from Yeats to Beckett* (London: Athlone Press, 1978), 2, 253–60.

7. See Murphy's last will and testament in Beckett's *Murphy* (New York: Grove Press, 1957), 269:

> With regard to the disposal of these my body, mind, and soul, I desire that they be burnt and placed in a paper bag and brought to the Abbey Theatre, Lr. Abbey Street, Dublin, and without pause into what the great and good Lord Chesterfield calls the necessary house, where their happiest hours have been spent, on the right as one goes down into the pit, and I desire that the chain be pulled upon them, if possible during the performance of the piece, the whole to be executed without ceremony or show of grief.

See also Worth, *Irish Drama of Europe,* 241–42, 252–54.

8. Letter from Beckett to Alan Schneider, 29 December 1957, in *Village Voice Reader,* 185, cited in Dougald McMillan and Martha Fehsenfeld, *Beckett in the Theatre* (London: John Calder, 1988), 163.

9. W. B. Yeats, *Purgatory, The Collected Plays of W. B. Yeats* (London: Macmillan, 1934), 689.

10. The *bodhran* is a traditional Irish instrument.

11. Samuel Beckett, *Texts for Nothing* (London: Calder and Boyers, Ltd., 1954), 50.

12. Ibid., 50, 51.

13. Ibid., 52, 51.

14. Samuel Beckett, *Endgame* (New York: Grove Press, 1958), 81.

15. Beckett, *Texts for Nothing,* 52.

16. Niall Montgomery was a friend of Beckett's whose father was the first Irish film censor and reputed to be the wittiest man in the Dublin of his day.

17. Samuel Beckett, *First Love, The Expelled and Other Novellas* (London: Penguin Books, 1980), 9.

18. The reader is referred to Virginia Cooke, *Beckett on File* (London: Methuen, 1985), 66–67.

19. See McMillan and Fehsenfeld, *Beckett in the Theatre* (212, 230), with regard to Michael Haerdter's rehearsal diary from the 1967 Schiller Theater *Endspiel* production directed by Beckett.

20. *Havel/Beckett* was a Scena Theatre production staged in Washington, D.C., in February and March 1991. It consisted of a virtual dialogue between Samuel Beckett and Václav Havel, with *Audience, Catastrophe,* and the U.S. premiere of *Mistake.* The chief character, Ferdinand, in *Audience,* Protagonist in *Catastrophe,* and

Xiboy in *Mistake* were portrayed by actor Christopher Henley, thus linking the playlets. *Mistake* was written by Havel upon his release from prison in Czechoslovakia as a response to Beckett's *Catastrophe*. It was first performed in 1983 in Stockholm.

Appendixes

Letters from Samuel Beckett to Roger Blin

```
19/12/50                    6 Rue des Favorites

Mon cher Blin
    J'ai une idée pour le décor. Il faudrait qu'on se voie.
Pourriez-vous passez chez nous un jour de cette semaine?
Vous me trouverez toujours au début de l'après-midi, jusqu'à
trois heures. Ou bien donnez-moi rendez-vous dehors, si ça
vous arrange mieux.
                    Amitiés
```

19/12/50   6 Rue des Favorites

My dear Blin

I have an idea for the set. We must get together. Could you pass by our house one day this week? You will always find me in the early afternoon, until three o'clock. Or else give me a time to meet elsewhere, if that suits you better.

    Best regards,

    Sam Beckett

The translation of these letters is mine. In all three I have remained as close to the French as possible.

Ussy 9/1/53

Mon cher Roger

Bravo à tous. Je suis si content de votre succès à tous.

Ne m'en veuillez pas de m'être barre, je n'en pouvais plus.

Il y a une chose qui me chiffonne, c'est le froc d'Estragon.
J'ai naturellement demande à Suzanne s'il tombe bien. Elle me ait
qu'il le retient à mi-chemin. Il ne le faut absolument pas, c'est
on ne peut plus hors de situation. Il n'a vraiment pas la tête à
ça à ce moment-là, il ne se rend même pas compte qu'il est tombe.
Quant aux rires qui pourraient saluer la chute complète, au grand
dam de ce touchant tableau final, il n'y a absolument rien à y
objecter, ils seraient du même ordre que les précedents. L'esprit
de la pièce, dans la mesure où elle en a, c'est que rien n'est plus
grotesque que le tragique, et il faut l'exprimer jusqu'à la fin, et
surtout à la fin. J'ai un tas d'autres raisons pour vouloir que ce
jeu de scène ne soit pas escamote, mais je vous en fais grace. Soyez
seulement assez gentil de le rétablir comme c'est indique dans le
texte, et comme nous l'avions toujours prévu au cours des répé-
titions, et que le pantalon tombe complètement, autour des chevilles
Ca doit vous sembler stupide, mais pour moi c'est capital. Et je
vous croyais tous les deux d'accord avec moi là-dessus, quand je
vous ai vus samedi dernier après l'incident de la couturière, et que
j'emportais votre assurance que cette scène serait jouée comme je
la vois.

Bonne continuation et une amicale poignée de main à tous.

Ussy 9/1/53

My dear Roger

Bravo to all. I am so happy about everyone's success.[1]

Don't be angry with me pulling out, I couldn't take it anymore.

There is one thing that disturbs me, that's Estragon's frock. I naturally asked Suzanne if it falls well. She tells me that he stops it halfway. He absolutely must not, nothing could be more wrong. He's really too preoccupied at that moment, he doesn't even realize it has fallen. As for the laughs that its falling all the way might provoke, to the great detriment of this touching final tableau, there is absolutely nothing to object to there, they would be on the same order as the preceding ones. The spirit of the play, to the extent that is has one, is that nothing is more grotesque than the tragic, and it must be expressed up to the end, and above all at the end. I have many other reasons for not wanting to skip this stage business, but I'll spare you them. Just be kind enough to restore it as indicated in the text,[2] and as we had agreed upon in rehearsal, and have the trousers fall completely around his ankles. This must seem stupid to you, but for me it is essential. And I believed that you both agreed with me on this, when I saw you last Saturday after the dress rehearsal incident, and that I had your assurance that this scene would be played as I see it.

Keep up the good work and a friendly handshake to all.

Sam

Ussy
3. 4. 68

cher Roger
je te recommande vivement
les simplifications suivantes :

1. Pas de sang sur le mouchoir
de Hamm

2. Simplifier début de Clov. Il
va avec l'escabeau à la fenêtre mer,
monte, tire le rideau, regarde, rit,
redescend, va tout droit (sans oublier
l'escabeau) à l'autre fenêtre, même
jeu, va tout droit (sans prendre l'escabeau)
aux poubelles, etc.

3. P. 45. après "Ça redevient gai" Clov
monte sur l'escabeau et tout de suite "Voyons
voir", c'est à dire couper gag de la lunette
braquée sur la salle.

3. P. 103
Hamm : Encore des complications ! (Clov ne descend
pas.) Pourvu que ça ne rebondisse pas !
Clov : On dirait un môme.
Hamm : (sarcastique.) Un môme !
Clov : Je vais y aller.
Etc.

4. P. 107. Couper chanson. Ça donne :
Hamm Quelques mots ... de ton cœur.
Clov On m'a dit etc.

Couper : Articule !
    "   Assez ! (p. 108)

Bon travail.
affectueusement
Sam

Ussy 3/4/68

Dear Roger

   I strongly recommend to you the following simplifications:[3]

1. No blood on Hamm's handkerchief

2. Simplify Clov's beginning. He goes with the ladder to the sea window, gets up on it, draws back the curtain, looks out of window, laughs, gets down, goes straight (without forgetting the ladder) to the other window, same thing, goes straight (without taking the ladder) to the ash bins, etc.

3. p. 45.[4] After "things are livening up" Clov gets up on the ladder and immediately "Let's see," this is to say cut gag of the telescope turned on the auditorium.

3. [*sic*] p. 103

   Hamm: More complications! (*Clov doesn't get down.*) Not an underplot,
      I trust.

   Clov: Looks like a small boy!

   Hamm: (*sarcastic*) A small boy!

   Clov: I'll go and see.
      Etc.

4. p. 107. Cut song. That gives:

   Hamm A few words . . . from your heart.

   Clov: They said to me etc.

   cut   Articulate!

   "   Enough! (p. 108)

   Work well.
   Affectionately
   Sam

NOTES

   1. The world premiere of *Waiting for Godot* took place on 5 January 1953 at the Théâtre de Babylone. Under Roger Blin's direction the cast was as follows: Lucien Raimbourg (Estragon), Pierre Latour (Vladimir), Jean Martin (Lucky), Roger Blin (Pozzo). This production was staged by Blin on several other occasions in Paris.

   2. Beckett's stage direction, near the end of the play, reads: "(*Estragon loosens the cord that holds up his trousers which, much too big for him, fall about his ankles. They look at the cord.*)"

   3. *Fin de partie* was first performed, under the direction of Roger Blin, in

1957, at the Royal Court Theatre in London. The French premiere was 27 April 1968 at the Studio des Champs Elysées in Paris. This production was again mounted in 1968 at the Théâtre Chaptal 347. *Fin de partie* is dedicated to Roger Blin.

4. Page references are to the French edition of *Fin de partie,* published by Les Editions de Minuit in 1957.

Appendix 2

Interview with Roger Blin by Joan Stevens

Actor, director ROGER BLIN (1907–84) was the first to direct the work of Samuel Beckett and that of a number of other contemporary playwrights as well. Blin staged the world premieres of *En attendant Godot* (5 January 1953, Théâtre de Babylone, Paris) and *Fin de partie* (3 April 1957, Royal Court Theatre, London). He also directed *La dernière bande* and *Oh les beaux jours*.

This previously unpublished interview with Joan Stevens took place in Paris on 2 March 1975. In its original form it included sections on Antonin Artaud and Jean Genet. It was translated by Joan Stevens.

JOAN STEVENS: Was it Beckett who came to see you?

ROGER BLIN: No, I'd heard his name. A poem of his had appeared in a small literary magazine called *Soute* before the war. The name was well-known. It had made its mark right away. I don't know how exactly, but that's how it was. I had possibly heard of him on the radio, through Max Pol-Fouchet—there was a program after the war, an international program with translations of foreign poems. So, I must be talking about an old poem of Beckett's. And then Tristan Tzara had talked to me about Beckett because he knew him, and he had read *Godot,* which he'd written in 1947–48, I think. And at that time, in 1948, I was a director, a poor director of a theater that subsequently went bankrupt. Then someone brought me the play. I think it was Beckett's wife, Suzanne Beckett. And that's what happened. I started reading it. There was quite a lot of it, but I read it, anyway. And I was bowled over, without knowing where it was going to lead or how important this text might be.

JS: Did you have any idea at first what the play meant?

RB: Absolutely not. I just thought: I must stage it. That was all. It was essential to stage it.

JS: Without any idea of the meaning?

RB: Without any clear idea. Only an idea of the structure of the play, the humor. And so I approached my colleagues. I had no money; my colleagues had a bit. There was no female role; nothing happened—so they wanted nothing to do with it. I went to everyone I knew in Paris. I had a few copies of the play typed, and I went around to all the theaters in Paris, not the biggest ones, of course—the little ones where I knew the directors. And everyone laughed in my face.

JS: Why?

RB: Because they didn't like the play at all. It was beyond them. They just weren't interested. Just the same, on the advice of a friend, Jean-Marie Serreau, who had just started the little Théâtre de Babylone at the time, I took the play to what was called the "Commission de l'Aide à la Première Pièce" [Council for Aid to New Plays], which was an official organization dealing with the literary arts and not yet an official cultural ministry. I waited a while before casting it, and then one day, by chance, I met one of the people on the jury, Georges Neveux, a playwright himself whom I knew slightly, and I said to him, "You wouldn't have a play that I left with you for a grant for a first play, *Waiting for Godot?*" He said, "I might, in amongst a pile of plays waiting to be read. Look, I'll read it." And the next day I got a note, a telegram or a letter, saying: "I'll take this on. I am absolutely for it. I think it's very beautiful. I'll do what I can." And I got a sort of grant, about 3,000 new francs or thereabouts. It was 500,000 francs at the time. No, it was a bit more, about 5,000 new francs. And I took this to Serreau, but he was in no hurry to stage it or to allow me to stage it, and I had already been to other theaters. I had nearly arranged something with the Théâtre de Poche, but the director at the time, who was not the same as the one there now, said, "We could do without the tree, there's no room for the tree, and the child, do we have to have him?"

JS: Didn't Beckett come himself?

RB: No, I didn't know him until a year later, a year after writing to him to say how much I liked his play and that I would do everything I could to put it on. So, we met one day at his place. He had been aware of my efforts to find a theater. [Jérôme] Lindon helped me, too. And we finally managed it, after two years of work, with various actors playing the parts because, as there were no plans to stage it, the actors, who were very excited about it for a time, were put off. In the end there were a few who hung on; most of them hung on. Finally, we managed to stage it on 3 January 1953.

JS: Was the direction all your own idea? Did Beckett contribute?

RB: Beckett knew nothing about people of the theater. I think he had already taken the play to colleagues, who had not been at all interested. It happened that I had directed *The Ghost Sonata* by Strindberg. Beckett had seen the play, and he came back to see it again. So, it was after that that he sent me the play. I strongly suspect that he was interested in me because, first, without wishing to boast, he might have thought I wouldn't let him down, that my way of working was appropriate, and, second, that it would be quite unsuccessful.

JS: And he didn't care about that?

RB: That's right. These were the two things he liked, I think, and only about eleven to twenty people per night were coming to see *The Ghost Sonata.*

JS: Had you directed many plays before?

RB: Many? No, not many. I had played in a number as an actor. With [Charles] Dullin. I had played in *Richard III.* I had been in a few films, too. But I had hardly directed at all. I was already old, but I hadn't directed anything. I was waiting until I was a bit more secure financially, and I was lazy and didn't have any money.

JS: Was it your decision to play Pozzo?

RB: No. I had a friend who worked on the radio, playing parts in plays that hadn't yet been staged, interesting plays that might or might not be staged but from which he broadcast substantial segments. I talked to him about *Godot,* and we broadcast a segment from *Godot.* On that occasion I played Lucky. I think [Lucien] Raimbourg played Vladimir, and Pozzo was played by someone else. I can't remember who took the other parts.

JS: And were you not working on anything else all this time?

RB: Oh yes, all the time. But I was working in radio. You know what this profession is like. You earn a bit of money here and there, not much. Anyway, I put it on. There was no scenery. I drew a tree, which the stage manager put up. He looked after the sets, a paper tree on a trellis, a miserable-looking thing. I didn't have a platform, just a little thing in the distance, at the back. It was a theater with a width of 3.5 to 4 meters and a depth of 4 meters, so we couldn't go crazy.

My first problem was how to light the sky independently of what was going on onstage, so that there would be no shadow thrown by the actors on the wall, onto the sky. And then I needed to have a moon passing behind. So, we did what we could in this little theater, and the critics came, and the play was reasonably well understood. We had a few days' uncertainty, and then after about ten days it was a great success.

JS: Not everywhere.

RB: It was in Paris. That's how it works in Paris, by word of mouth.

JS: You said you didn't understand the play when you first read it. How did you approach the direction then?

RB: I didn't understand it when I first read it, but after two years I was able to understand it.

JS: Did you discuss it with Beckett?

RB: I talked to him about the costumes, about their significance. He said, "I've no idea about the costumes." I know he had no idea about their physical appearance.

JS: Apart from the bowler hats.

RB: Apart from the bowler hats. He said, "I'm sure they wear bowler hats."

JS: Why was that, do you think? Because of Laurel and Hardy?

RB: Yes, and Chaplin, too. And it signified dignity. Also, it was common in Ireland. If you look at photos taken thirty years ago, even in Ireland, people wore bowler hats on Sundays. They still do, I'm sure.

JS: And you played Pozzo?

RB: The way it worked out, I played Pozzo, because I had asked a friend, who was fat and bald, but in the end he was scared off by the play. He didn't understand it. He saw Pozzo as a kind of traitor, a wicked character, treacherous. He was right, but there's more to it. Pozzo is the saddest of them all. Definitely. I didn't ask Beckett about the symbolic significance.

JS: Why is he the saddest? Because he doesn't live in the real world?

RB: I think he's the oldest.

JS: He's the one who has lost the most?

RB: He has only vocal power. He has no real power.

JS: And since words are meaningless and he has vocal power, that makes things worse?

RB: Yes. That is—what attracted me to the play, and why I still like it so much—is its human quality and the humor in the writing. Every word has a hidden meaning under its banal exterior, without poetic metaphors, ametaphoric, and just the rhythm of those short, sharp, banal sentences alone makes a symphony. There is a musical quality, which is very important and which he caught in French. A phrase can be set off by periods, and you have a complete sentence that you can punctuate with commas when you say it. But if you set it off with periods, the meaning is twice as strong. And these periods and the parts of this sentence cancel each other out. Or they reinforce each other or increase the meaning. That's what I liked.

As for the symbolism of the play, what it means, I recognized the sort of biblical framework at once. From the beginning Beckett gave me a free hand. He didn't talk about "Godot" or "God." On the contrary, he said he didn't know what *God* meant. Maybe he meant *Godillots,* which means "old shoes." He said, "Estragon's old shoes, maybe that's what it is." But I knew that adding the *ot* in French, as in Godot, is often a way of showing contempt, of ridiculing at least.

JS: Why did he deny it, then?

RB: Because that's how he talks, and that's the kind of relationship we had.

JS: And then after that came *Endgame,* which he dedicated to you. Do you think he was influenced by your direction of *Godot?*

RB: Yes, I think so. Not as far as the writing was concerned, of course, but I did have *Godot* in my possession, and I was the first person to show an interest, to fight to stage it, and to try to stage it in a way that gave it its true meaning, its essential meaning, its most important meaning. The rest emerged after, within the very structure of the thing. If you try to start from the symbolism, to tell intuitive actors like [Lucien] Raimbourg or [Pierre] Latour [Estragon and Vladimir] what to do. . . . I didn't want to shoot them a line, to burden them with the deep significance of the play all the time, which may have puzzled Beckett when he came to the rehearsals, because, in my opinion, when you're directing you should enjoy it, without losing the importance of what you are trying to do. When you're working I think you should be relaxed with the people you're directing.

Beckett knew nothing about the theater. His play is a wonderful piece of theater, but all his instructions, silences, pauses, and so on—he said these were more for the reader. You can't just determine the length of a pause. One silence has to be relative to others. The pauses, the silences, relate to each other. You can't say in advance how long they should be—that one is half a second, that one eight seconds, seven and a half seconds. The director has to determine the pace of the play from the rhythm and, from this pace, incorporate the silences to make them as meaningful as possible or sometimes ignore them or sometimes move them a bit. But I always trust the writer implicitly, as far as I can, until I find, it can happen, that he has a personal vision that lacks dramatic force. What I mean by "personal vision" is a sudden abstract element, or a geometric element, that is repetitive, something like that.

When you like something you feel it instinctively. Being an actor myself, I could feel it in relation to other people. So, that's how I played Pozzo. Pozzo was physically quite different from me. His voice was different from mine, but, just the same, I saw him as a kind of lord. For his costume I looked at some English sketches I'd seen of "gentleman farmers." That's how I dressed him. The problem of Lucky's costume was different. I talked to Beckett, who didn't know. Then he said maybe he could be more like a railway porter. So, I trusted him, because I was mad about this play. I dreamt about it. I trust intuitions in dreams to some degree. In my dream one night I saw the four people. Lucky was a sort of old memory of some kind, or maybe there was some surrealistic influence. Or maybe to show the peculiarity of the play, I dressed him in a sort of Old French coat, red, with stripes, a knitted sailor cardigan too, and very short black trousers, big shoes, and long hair, as Sam wanted. The play was put on like this in several countries, although it was an entirely personal concept.

JS: Did you choose the costume you describe to show his isolation?

RB: He was an old valet, an old servant. But more important, it's the peculiarity of this miserable being who was rich once, as if he were in the service of an old lord of the manor. I dressed Vladimir, who loves to talk, as a teacher, with a broken, stiff collar, a bit of string for a black tie, and then a starched pink shirtfront underneath, which kept riding up, and without anything underneath. He was just wearing underwear underneath. This shirtfront was tied with a string, which you could see when he lifted it. He had a morning coat and creased black trousers. On the other hand, I dressed Estragon, who is very withdrawn, in a pink scarf. I don't know why I felt the need to dress the two of them in pink like that, with that feeling of ambiguity. . . . So, that's what we did.

JS: Some critics say that Hamm is a continuation of Pozzo; this is their own idea. But I wonder, since he dedicated *Endgame* to you, whether the character of Hamm was influenced by your interpretation of Pozzo.

RB: I couldn't really say. After *Godot, Molloy, Malone Dies,* and then *The Unnamable* were published. After that Sam told me: "I seem to be completely stuck now as far as the novel is concerned. I can't go beyond

The Unnamable. All my characters have come to nothing. I'm at rock bottom. So, maybe I could find something new to say in the theater, something different."

JS: But he wrote *The Lost Ones* after that.

RB: Yes, but we didn't know that at the time. The progression was not as clear as that. But that's how it was. His characters have become increasingly immobile, stuck until they are just a mouth, an object, but a thinking object. He said to me, "I'll do something else." But I didn't know what. What's more, others knew before I did. He said to me: "Yes, *Godot* was alright, but it was a frantic western. I want to do something less active, with people who are less mobile, because all this movement. . . . " So, he brought me *Endgame.* I have no idea whether it was out of loyalty, friendship, or "gratitude." I didn't question it, because, if anyone should have been grateful, it was me, for he had dedicated the play to me and asked me to play in it with Jean Martin, who had played Lucky, as Clov. This was in 1957.

So, once again I started looking for a theater because, in spite of the success of *Godot,* I couldn't find one in Paris. I went to see old Hébertot. He said, "Yes, it's good, but do you have any financial backing?" And others had the same reaction. Then we tried the Théâtre de l'Oeuvre (the Theater Workshop), but it went under. So, we rehearsed anyway, and then George Devine invited us to take part in a French fortnight at the Royal Court, which was partly gastronomic, partly cultural, and so we presented *Endgame* in April 1957, its world premiere in French at the Royal Court.

JS: Have you read *Not I?*

RB: Yes, I've read and seen it. It's on now. Beckett has staged it. At the moment he's in Berlin putting on *Godot.*

JS: And is he directing it?

RB: Yes, he's directing it, with *Krapp's Last Tape.* I saw it in London, too. I went with Madeleine Renaud, who wanted to play in all Beckett's works after *Happy Days.* I thought it was very, very good, and Billie Whitelaw was really excellent. I directed *Happy Days* in 1963. But it wasn't a French premiere. That was in Venice.

JS: Do you have a favorite play?

RB: I don't know. I can't say.

JS: Personally, I find *Happy Days* much more frightening [than *Krapp* or *Godot*].

RB: Yes, it is much more frightening. But I like all his plays. I've physically played in *Endgame* about four hundred times. What's more, it was different every time, over eleven years, because it opened in 1957 at the Court. And Beckett was in the audience. This time he was much more interested in the staging than for *Godot*. We didn't seriously disagree, but he wouldn't accept—well, I mean that that there are some things in an actor's gut that you can't ask him to ignore. For instance, to go from laughter to anger—there is, after all, a fraction of a second where the two feelings merge. Beckett saw his text in musical terms, with absolutely strict divisions. When the word *Clov* was repeated, or when some things, some words were repeated, they had to be said in exactly the same way, like the same note in music played by the same instrument, paying no attention to where this sentence might come in the plot, in the context.

I think he's changed his ideas a bit over the last eleven years. I know that when we did it again he did admit that there was a sense of tragedy there. Because he didn't want tragedy. From the moment Clov said, "Finished, it's finished, nearly finished, it must be nearly finished," everything that came after had a certain agitation, but everything was closed. There was no suspense, whether or not Clov left was unimportant.

JS: For Beckett?

RB: Yes. So, I said, "But the audience will walk out after quarter of an hour." He said, "I don't care." "But," I said, "there is tragedy there. It's in the words. It's between the lines. It's in the text. There is even that part where the end is still in doubt." So, finally, I think, when it was staged later he was able to accept certain things.

JS: I read somewhere that for *Godot* you were given a fairly free hand, but after that he was much more insistent about specific stage directions.

RB: Yes, but he was right, and I was very pleased he was there. Though he did make us start *Endgame* much too loudly by shouting "Clov." Each "Clov" was shouted out, several times. As a result, it was too much. Consequently, after three or four days I felt we shouldn't overdo it, that the main interest of a play is to reach an extraordinary intensity, that this intensity must not reach its high point at the start. You have to trap the audience for this intensity to work. That's the danger when there is a kind of internal force. If you bring it out too much at the start, you risk saturation and boredom.

JS: So after *Endgame* there was *Happy Days?*

RB: Yes, I had this play in my hands, and, of course, I said to myself: "Who can play her? I don't know." There were various possibilities. Because the description of the character is very clear—"About fifty, well preserved"—you need someone quite well built, with large breasts, and a rather ridiculous face. I thought: "That's fair enough, but that will make them laugh for five minutes. I need a great actress," thinking of this or that actress, but not of Madeleine. Finally, I took it to Madeleine Renaud, because I knew she was an amazing actress. (She's a friend.) And furthermore, it's so complex. There is such a range. And then there's all that general chattering in the first part, coming from a birdbrain. For an actress who has played Feydeau it could work. She has played Molière. She has played classical and modern plays. But that kind of charm she deploys and courage, too—it's almost a kind of homage to Madeleine Renaud's personal courage, especially as I was asking so much more of her over and above her great talent.

We worked with Sam in 1963, in June or July. And then after that I continued to work on it, and we presented the play in Venice, in a very, very difficult theater, the Ridotto, which is not at all nice. Then we presented it again at the Odéon, changing the theater a bit by bringing Madeleine's scenery, her ground, her mound, downstage and blocking off the last and next-to-last balconies with canvas for acoustic reasons. It worked very well, and she has such perfect diction that you could hear every word.

And so I worked with Matias, who produced something really good, because if you want to give the impression of all that weight—the sky, the heat—it would be a mistake to have a blue sky. We thought about it. He decided on a completely orange sky, which gets lighter, violently so, at its highest point, and which fades, bit by bit, until it becomes a kind of grayish pink around the actress and her mound. And the ground is a mixture of oranges and browns, too. That makes the audience—should it be tempted to look elsewhere, to look up at the sky—upset by this orange, and it forces it to look back again at this point, at this little head, which had so much force that it might as well have been three meters high. Each member of the audience was forced to sort of zoom in on her.

js: Was it the same sky in both acts?

rb: Yes, of course, because there is no change. Madeleine would like to have played it without an intermission, but Beckett insisted on the intermission.

js: Then you did *Krapp's Last Tape?*

rb: That was before, between the two—about 1959 or 1960. It was when the TNF [French National Theatre] had the little Théâtre Récamier. We presented it with a [Robert] Pinget play that Jean Martin had directed, called *Lettre morte.* And I asked a friend to play Krapp.

JS: Because you didn't want to do it?

RB: Yes, I was tired, and I had played Pozzo for three hundred performances, Hamm for almost as many, and I became a bit frightened of all Beckett's old men who had befallen me. I asked a friend—[R.-J.] Chauffard, who died last year, a great guy, and who was, of course, quite young—to do it. He gave a very in-depth performance. I don't think Beckett liked him much. But I used him because Beckett had seen him in another play. He had said nice things about him. But I think Beckett was a bit annoyed with me because I didn't take the part. It's probably the play that moves me least. Maybe it's the sentimental side of the play that I don't like. Though it's a very beautiful, wonderful play. But if there are degrees of admiration, it's perhaps the one I like the least.

JS: And *Embers,* which came after—did you direct that?

RB: No, I played in it on the radio. It was written for radio. Between you and me, that's a subject that has always been a bit painful for me. Beckett absolutely didn't want me to try to do *Embers* for the theater because, when you listen, you don't know if Ada exists or not, whether she only exists in the imagination of the character Henry. But I thought I could find a way of doing it onstage. But then again there are lots of descriptions, and I know you shouldn't describe something you see in the theater. It's one or the other. But I think you could get around that by using some kind of apparition in all the scenes with the old people, abstract colors, certain movements in the background, things that would not have been descriptive. I think it could be done.

JS: For example, when the sea gives orders—how would you have done that? by sound?

RB: By sound. I think I would have had a kind of pebble beach. Cork pebbles, or something light, but all the pebbles mounted on a pivot. And at a particular moment, as Ada comes in, the pebbles would have turned, would have shown a dark underside, like a kind of shadow that spreads out and lays down beside the man. And of course, you would also hear a voice, which wouldn't be quite "off," but neither would it be. . . . I think you can avoid too much artistic precision, the metallic recording. I did it on the radio with Delphine Seyrig, who played Ada. Alain Trutas directed. And then *Cascando,* too, with Jean Martin.

JS: I found that very difficult.

RB: Yes, it is very difficult. I played one of the voices, the voice of the Opener.

JS: How did you interpret the voice of the Opener? Is it the author or the life of the writer in general?

RB: There is always the underlying problem of the writer. Pozzo thinks he's a poet and talks about the twilight. Hamm, in his dialogue, is a caricature of the naturalist author, who doesn't neglect a single detail, who talks about the weather, the sun, the kind of sun, and what effect it has.

JS: Do you agree that you have to respect the author?

RB: When he merits it. You can put on an old text or a text of a minor author that can lead to something good. But when the author has something inside him, and when the text is beautiful, you do what he wants, but not in a passive way. Sometimes you have to help him, I mean go a bit deeper . . .

As for the symbolism in the plays, you mustn't show it. When I got hold of *Godot* I said to myself: "Oh, I see, I see, great! It's a circus. We'll have a bench in red velvet and a mattress and a kind of metal cross beam. And then we'll unroll a canvas with the word *sky* written on it; and then the actors Estragon and Vladimir will come on carrying the tree in a box; and then they'll come on in robes, rubbing powder on their feet in a corner so as not to slip on the waxed floor; then they'll take off their robes and throw them into the wings, and the action will start."

Well, I thought about that for three days. And then I said, "No, it's impossible." If you start in a clown mode, a circus mode, in the second part there are things that clowns couldn't say. But the circus element is there. That's why Estragon and Vladimir have red and white blotches in their makeup. Lucky too, me too. But 90 percent of the directors of *Godot* have fallen into that trap. I retracted it later. I said: "No, nothing. A tree, a little tree." And I have friends who used a tree when they staged it in Geneva. They cut down a real little tree, and they stuck it onstage. That's the least realistic presentation I've seen. It's not really important in the end. But yes, it is at the start. In Poland they did a whole thing using folk imagery—loads of meaningless things—and they all said to me, "But it's a circus." No, no, at least not for me.

In the first place, with Beckett everything is more or less gray, and then, had he wanted it to take place in a circus, he would have written: "The action takes place in a circus. Vladimir and Estragon . . . go round in the ring. There is a stand with a tree in it, and so on." He would have written it.

JS: But they did go around the stage in the production that you did of *Godot*.

RB: No, there wasn't room at the Babylone. Later, when I staged it at the Hébertot, I had a platform; that is, the road didn't end at the back, but it sloped. And then there was the tree but so that everyone could see it. And a slope at the back so that when Pozzo left he was able to do a complete circle. That was the only concession I made to the circus afterward. There are the early retorts, of course, which are clown retorts: "I'm going." Quick retorts like that. But you have to feel the circus, not show it. It's implied.

JS: I have noticed the significance of dreams in Beckett—in *Godot,* for example.

RB: That's not explicit. Estragon stops at once when Vladimir says, "Don't tell me, don't tell me."

JS: But why? Because it's disturbing, but why?

RB: There is always an extraordinary reticence in Beckett. "Don't tell me your dreams." I think it's something like that, inasmuch as dreams can reveal so many things.

JS: About the person recounting them?

RB: You also have the Beckett characters: there's not a single adult. They are all immature. You have to remember that when you're acting. And I started from there. I didn't start from the symbols, which I could understand. I didn't explain it at all to the actors. They discovered it for themselves in the final rehearsals. I tried to lead them to an understanding of it once they had a basis for understanding on a primary level, on a material level, on the level of the life force of the play, the words, the ideas. But I didn't want to knock them out by saying, "Watch out, this is a masterpiece."

JS: Have you read what Billie Whitelaw said about *Not I?* She said she didn't understand, that Beckett didn't explain at rehearsals. But he told her it was perfect, and she compared the dialogue with her child's illness, meningitis. And that's how she succeeded in interpreting it. Beckett did not give her his ideas.

RB: No. He has far fewer than one would think, or he wants them hidden. Perhaps it's intellectual vultures like you who have to find all the meanings. Because there have been interpretations. A lady once said—an English woman, I think—that *Godot* was very simple: Vladimir and Estragon represent England and France, who are always arguing but who can't actually do without each other, who have to live together. And Pozzo is Soviet Russia with Czechoslovakia on a lead, or maybe Poland or another satellite country, and Godot represents hope, the United States. It's SHAEF [Supreme Headquarters Allied Expeditionary Forces]. It was simple, absolutely simple.

JS: You have thought of writing yourself, have you not?

RB: Yes, I started some entirely insolent sketches. But no, I draw. That's enough. I did intend to write. But I'm lazy, and then there's my spine, my heart. . . . You can't do everything. I don't know what I would have written. Lyrical things, I think. But I don't have the talent.

There is another thing about *Godot* that is relevant to my work. I started by making the characters move, by making them live the thing. I started from their sickness, their physical peculiarities. Estragon's feet hurt and keep him from sleeping. He's always tired; he drops off; he's not there; he's not listening; and suddenly, he has inspired, intuitive thoughts: "Are you sure it wasn't him? . . . Godot." Suddenly, he wakes up.

And Vladimir, who has trouble with his prostate, who wants to pee all the time, moves around a lot. He can't stand still. Pozzo is fat, with a swollen heart. His heart is too big, he's breathless, and he's dragged around by his stomach.

Lucky represents a kind of wicked senility. He is the most evil. He's a kind of scapegoat, who's taking revenge, who listens and who also goes to sleep from time to time. From the first rehearsal Jean Martin—whom I used because he's an extraordinary actor and a friend and who is at least 1.92 meters high—started to play the role shaking. He managed it, though he trembled for forty minutes. He managed to clench his legs and his feet and to tremble naturally. It affected him when he played other parts later. I didn't ask him to do that. And I hadn't seen it like that. But when I saw him do it, and he did it so well, for me he gave the play its truly cruel dimension, which it might not have had without that. Yes, it is cruel, but Lucky's trembling counterbalances the possible sentimentality of the other actors.

JS: Toward Lucky?

RB: No, not toward Lucky, but in relation to the audience, to the balance of the play. In Holland I had very good actors, but, when I happened by chance to go back to Holland to see the play when it was in another town, the actor who was playing Vladimir played him as if he were being crucified. He cried and did a number of things I wouldn't have asked him to do. It was histrionic acting. And that's why I asked the actors in France, because they were clowns too, to be careful not to be overly sentimental. That's exactly what Beckett wanted, for them not to burst into tears. Because there are two acts, but there could just as easily be three; there could just as easily be four. So, you must not play the second act as though it's the end of the play. It's not the end of the play.

JS: You said that for you Lucky is the most evil.

RB: I mean he's the character who is lucid at times and who is in a state of total servitude. But he unburdens himself in the end. He finally manages to unburden himself through words, in a speech that is in no way without meaning, a speech that has a very, very real but broken meaning. You can follow the whole speech in relation to hygiene, in relation to a number of things. Lucky's speech is actually very clear. But it's broken up, like a puzzle.

JS: Since you said he was the most evil . . .

RB: No, not the most evil. That's a ridiculous word because it doesn't mean anything. But there is a buildup of hatred, which you have to anticipate throughout the play.

JS: I don't understand the shaking.

RB: It's just a physical shaking. There is a guy carrying suitcases, and Martin did a number of things with his tongue, with his gasping. It was very impressive. Everyday there were some people who couldn't take it, who left. So, I was very pleased. It was a victory.

APPENDIX 3

"On *Play* and Other Plays": Lecture by Alan Schneider

So, following *A Texas Trilogy*'s somewhat less than triumphant tour of New York, I'm back in Washington once more—this time with a Beckett trio.[1] And, as always, since Sam won't come over here (he doesn't like the way we treat writers, I guess), I've just gone to Berlin to talk with him, see his own staged versions of the plays in question, and try to clear up a few of the normal mysteries involved in their stage production.

What can I tell you? That these three very small and quite special pieces are going to be easy to "understand"? (They are and are not.) That actually, as with all of Beckett, from that once baffling and now practically all-too-clear foursome in *Godot* to that mystically enigmatic and eventually lucid *Not I* you watched Jessica Tandy mouthing at the Kreeger a couple of seasons back, they should be experienced and felt, rather than figured out or explained in orderly, rational, nonpoetic terms. (They should.) That with all of Beckett, as with so many contemporary artists, content comes from the form itself, that in Beckett meaning depends on the sounds and images that are evoked. That it is precisely from within his ambiguities and overtones that his dramatic tension arises. (It does.) All of which has, of course, been said over and over again before.

In the twenty years or so in which I have had the good fortune to begin work on a new Beckett script, the process has always involved a spirit of adventure and exaltation—as well as trepidation. But, always, the adventure has led to a series of deepening discoveries—not only of the plays themselves but of their performers and of my own innermost depths. To me, Sam Beckett has always been and remains now a true poet of the

This 1976 talk is held in the Alan Schneider Papers (MSS 103), Mandeville Department of Special Collections, University of California–San Diego.

theater, his creative imagination totally attuned to the essential nature and constantly shifting limits of dramatic expression. With each new work, he has propelled those limits farther than any other playwright of our time; yet he remains aloof from the struggles and pain of the marketplace, personally vulnerable, gentle, unsure of his own achievement.

These three short plays, each less than half an hour in length, the latter two being presented at the Arena Stage for the first time in the American theater, represent a kind of theatrical chamber music. In each of them, and in very different ways, sounds and silences, cadences and rhythm, are selected, arranged, balanced, and counterpointed, as are the plots and counterplots, characters and dialogue, of more conventional playwrights. Together the three concern themselves with the obsessive influence of the past; of our constant, unsuccessful, yet all-too-human need to deny the void surrounding human existence. Each one suggests a kind of metaphor, at once unique and universal, speaking to us all in a small but insistently clear voice of our mystical mortality and facing that mortality with courage—and, occasionally, even humor.

These are not easy plays to come to, or to face. But then *Godot,* twenty years back, was not exactly easy to take—more than half of its original American audiences at Miami Beach walked out (and lived to rue the day or night, because *Godot* has survived that experience to become a world classic in its own time). Nor was *Endgame*—although it is now considered a modern *Lear.* Nor *Happy Days* nor *Krapp's Last Tape,* dramatic monologues without peers in all of world drama. *Not I* when first presented at the Lincoln Center had almost the same percentage of walkouts as the original *Godot*; many of those who left came back to admire and be moved. And *Play,* where for the first and only time in my career I actually betrayed the author's stated intention (to have it played through twice at top speed),[2] because my producers felt that New York audiences were too "sophisticated" or jaded, has survived to prove all over the world that both those producers and those first audiences were wrong.

Each of these three plays seems to strip the stage bare, even as each one drives unerringly to absorb the spectator's senses and mind. As in Tiffany's windows, the process of selection is unerringly ultimate. In *Play,* ashened faces are frozen in their funeral urns and are doomed for always to repeat and repeat their banal stories of a love triangle no longer real. In *That Time,* someone is visited by and tormented by constantly changing visions of his past floating up to him from his uncertain past; but this time the image is not that of a decrepit old man crouched beside an equally ancient tape recorder but simply that of a human head floating somewhere in space—as well as time. (The process of greater and greater selection never stops.) And, finally, in *Footfalls,* one ghostly figure and a distant voice come together in a ghost story about the nature of reality. Is she really there, or has she ever been there? Is the mother listening, or is the daughter imagining everything? Who is imagining whom? Beckett seems to be asking. And to me the joy, as always, is not so much in answering that question beyond a reasonable doubt but in sharing in the eloquence of the question itself. After all, as everyone knows by now, it doesn't matter who or what Godot is—if Beckett had known, he would have told us immediately—what matters is that we are all waiting.

For me, each new Beckett play, through its compassionate view of humanity, through the intensity and scope of its vision, through its musicality and poetic intensity, enlarges and enriches the whole of theater, the whole of life. Even Buster Keaton, not exactly an avant-garde enthusiast, seemed to sense that when, in the middle of a Beckett film I once directed in which he had not one line of dialogue, he burst out with "Now, I'm getting this Shakespearian stuff." Buster knew what he was talking about. For these three plays, two new and one not so old, silence and inscrutability and whatever else they may offer up to audiences willing enough and patient enough to accept them on some basis, are classic in their structure as well as eternal in their truths about our all-too-human nature. I feel immensely grateful to the theatrical fates that have led me and the Arena Stage to offer them up to you. And, I'm hoping against hope that no one will want to take them up to New York.

NOTES

1. The Beckett trio that Schneider speaks about is *Play, Footfalls,* and *That Time.* The trio opened on 3 December 1976 at the Arena Stage in Washington, D.C., and again on 14 December 1977 at the Manhattan Theatre Club in New York. It played in 1983 as well at New York's American Place Theatre.

2. In his autobiography, *Entrances* (1986; reprint, New York: Limelight Editions, 1987), Schneider writes:

According to Sam's exact instructions, *Play* was to be played through twice without interruption and at a very fast pace, each time taking no longer than nine minutes. The idea was that whatever references the audience didn't get the first time—most of them—would be absorbed the second time around.

> My producers, all three of them, objected strongly to Sam's idea. That was all right for less sophisticated audiences. . . . I tried to explain that Sam had something very specific in mind when he demanded that repetition. It was not just a matter of additional information; it was a tonal matter, a question of rhythm, of establishing a circular pattern. (341–42)

When Schneider's producers threatened to make the change themselves or cancel *Play* if the director did not get Beckett's permission for the lines to be said only once, much more slowly, he was forced to write the playwright with the request. Permission was reluctantly granted, but Schneider ultimately regretted his "betrayal" of Beckett.

Contributors

Eve Adamson was the founder of Jean Cocteau Repertory in New York City and its artistic director from 1971 through 1989. As a theater artist, she has been the guest of the governments of Bulgaria, Georgia (formerly Soviet Georgia), Hungary, India, Latvia, Poland, and Russia. She has directed over seventy productions, among them Beckett's *Waiting for Godot, Endgame,* and *Act without Words II.*

Gildas Bourdet was director of the Théâtre National de la Région du Nord from 1974 to 1991. He is currently a free-lance director of theater and opera and a writer for television and cinema.

Colin Duckworth—novelist, translator, actor, and director—is an emeritus professor at Melbourne University. He has worked in radio, television, and film as well as on numerous stage productions.

Everett Frost is both director and producer of Voices International and a professor in the Department of Television and Film at New York University. He directed the American national premiere productions of Beckett's radio plays, which were distributed in 1989 by National Public Radio as "The Beckett Festival of Radio Plays."

Gerry McCarthy works in the School of Performance Studies at the University of Birmingham, England, where he was director of drama from 1987 to 1992. He has worked extensively with young actors on the problems of acting Beckett. This has included productions of *Endgame, Krapp's Last Tape, Play, Not I,* and *Happy Days.* He directed *Not I* a second time for the first International Beckett Symposium at Stirling, Scotland, in 1986.

Robert McNamara was founder and artistic director for the Dublin Stage One Theatre Company in Dublin, Ireland, where he directed numerous Beckett productions. He also directed "Yeats after Life" at the Source Theatre and, in his current position as artistic director of SCENA Theatre in Washington, D.C., *Endgame* and *Beckett at 83: An Evening of Samuel Beckett's One Act Plays* (1989).

Xerxes Mehta is the founder and artistic director of the Maryland Stage Company. He has directed eight of Beckett's plays. His Tribute to Samuel Beckett included *Not I, Ohio Impromptu,* and *Rockaby.* Xerxes Mehta teaches theater at the University of Maryland in Baltimore.

Carey Perloff, formerly artistic director of CSC Repertory in New York, is currently serving in that capacity at the Actors Conservatory Theatre in San Francisco. She has also directed at a number of other theaters in this country and in England. In addition to Beckett's *Happy Days,* she has directed plays by Wilder, Pound, Pinter, O'Casey, and Brecht, among others.

Ilan Ronen was the artistic director of the Jerusalem Khan Theatre (1975–82) and the Cameri Theatre in Tel-Aviv (1984–92), where he directed his political interpretation of *Waiting for Godot* in Arabic and Hebrew. He has also directed the works of a number of international playwrights and was invited in 1990 to direct his version of *The Bourgeois Gentleman* for the Maly Theatre in Moscow.

Robert Scanlan is the literary director of the American Repertory Theatre in Cambridge, Massachusetts, and lecturer on dramatic arts at Harvard University, where he heads the Dramaturgy Program at the Institute for Advanced Theatre Training. He has directed in the People's Republic of China and in Eastern Europe. Scanlan has directed (or supervised the production of) all but two of Beckett's plays, and he writes frequently about the staging of Beckett's work.

DIRECTING BECKETT features Lois Oppenheim's interviews with prominent international directors of Samuel Beckett's work and collects essays by them. Many of these directors worked closely with Beckett, some assisting him with his own productions or acting under his direction before directing his work themselves. The contributors—including JoAnne Akalaitis, Edward Albee, Herbert Blau, Joseph Chaikin, and Carey Perloff—have achieved great renown in the theater. Oppenheim's interviews and the directors' essays offer insight into what it means to direct for the theater—and particularly what it means to direct the work of perhaps the greatest playwright of the twentieth century. The book's highlights include photographs from the productions; an unpublished lecture by the late Alan Schneider, Beckett's most accomplished American director; and a previously unpublished interview with the late Roger Blin, the first director of Beckett's work.

The book offers rich insights into many Beckett productions, the complexities of the director's role, and the meaning of directorial integrity and fidelity to the playwright's vision, an issue of particular relevance to a playwright whose exactitude, with respect to stage directions, is well documented. The book also recounts Beckett's reactions to productions of his work, reveals the circumstances surrounding the most controversial stagings of his work, and elucidates the kind of relationship Beckett had with those dedicated to his theater. It will appeal to a wide range of theater scholars, students, and devotees.

LOIS OPPENHEIM is Associate Professor of French at Montclair State University.